The American Scheme:
The Cold Blooded Naked Truth

Arnold *"Fass Cass"* Hannon

ORDER BOOK @
WWW.AMERICANSCHEMEBOOK.COM

To Gwen, enjoy the journey

SECOND EDITION

Copyright 2009

The American Scheme: The Cold Blooded Naked Truth
Arnold "Fass Cass" Hannon

ISBN-978-1-60725-3297

Certificate of Registration - TX-1-577-622
Effective September 13th, 2007

Arnold Hannon
americanscheme@comcast.net
P.O. Box 442596 | Detroit, Michigan 48224

Dedications

I'm dedicating my autobiography to my deceased mother, Bennie Mae Hannon / Moore, and her parents, who are my deceased grandparents, James and Ora Hannon, for doing all the heavy lifting to keep our family intact. I thank my aunt, Helen Hannon, for steering me in the right direction regarding historical family facts. I give a big shout-out to all of my family members whose own lives were an intricate part of my life. I thank my dear wife, Terry Coleman-Hannon for being the wonderful person that she is. She has been my sounding board and inspiration to stay focused. I love her more with each sunrise.

Lastly, (with tongue planted firmly in cheek.) I dedicate this book to the five putrid souls who interrupted my fourteen-year-old future mother's morning trek to Garfield Junior High School, in Detroit Michigan, in the spring of 1948. You've made it almost impossible for my mother to look at me without conjuring up the pain and humiliation y'all thrust upon her. You have ravaged her soul forever. We survived your dasterly acts, we came to grips with it all nearing the end of my mother's life in June of 2001. We embraced each other with a long over-due hug laced with love. Y'all lost. We won!

Arnold Hannon

Foreword

Now that I'm approaching my golden years, I've discovered that some seniors spend a great deal of their waning years reminiscing about their lives, and all that was or could have been. I've come to understand that life can be compared to a paradigm shift. "A bridge from one point to another point." A steady progression toward something else. Life never reveals its true destination. One can plot one's course in life and something else may sway you off course, pulling you in directions totally oblivious to you.

At times you may find yourself in rough, threatening waters without a boat or paddle to get you up stream. On the other side of the equation, life may bless you with a powerful yacht to navigate the treacherous oceans of life.

No matter the destination, like the old adage states, it's the journey that's remembered. I remember my journey every step of the way. I've been up the river, down the river and in the river; but, the river of life has not consumed me thus far, like the many young and old lives cast overboard into life's vast seas, to succumb to life's mighty girth, before they had their day to show the world their worth.

This is our story, we're in this boat together, no one travels though life alone, even if by some remote possibility one finds himself, or herself locked away in solitary confinement in some man's jail. Someone must turn the key.

I've rubbed shoulders with many individuals along the way; but, never with the man who planted the seed of life in my mother, the man responsible for 23 of my 46 chromosomes, thus responsible for half of my existence. I will have to close my eyes on this big blue planet some day, without that connection with the other half of my DNA makeup. That's OK. I made it without his love, his help, or his hand to help me up. I picked myself up and kept stepping. Writing my memoirs was easy compared to giving it a title. My life's journey was already written. I lived it, it was the title that I agonized over.

What's in a name? If you're writing a book, it can be a daunting endeavor. I wrestled day and night to come up with the appropriate title for my autobiography. My poor wife ears got a good work out. I would call her at work, wake her up in the middle of the night to get her opinion on my latest idea for a title. Day after day, night after night, week after week, month after month ideas came and went with the speed of thought. I've changed the title of my memoirs more than Imelda Marco changed shoes. Here's a sampling of some of the gems I've discarded. I started with the working title, "Reminiscing," which gave way to "Nostalia," which surrendered to "Native Detroiter." No, readers may think I'm of Indian heritage. Then I came up with the short-lived, "Destination to Die Old." When I ran that one by my wife, she gave it two big thumbs down, so "Destination" died young. Most of the titles that I came up with, had the life span of a fruit fly: two days tops. Then there were these beauties, "Something For The Record." No. How about "Immorality Becomes the Norm." Say what? Two thumbs down again! Scribing my memoirs had its bumps in the road; but, nothing compared to the anxiety of coming up with a title. It was a journey into the abyss. I would have to dive in and pull out the right title. "The Past Is Always Present" was one I strongly considered. I opted out and chose it for the Chapter One title. "Getting played by the game of life," was a title I strongly considered.

I needed something short and precise. "Honey, how's this, Identity Crisis?" She responded, if I named the book that it would be a real crisis. So, "Identity Crisis" was laid to rest in the title cemetery. It went on in that vein for nearly a year and a half into my writings. "Dead Men Don't Write Books" was a strong candidate, and so was, "No Sweet Lullaby's For Me." "Trip Down Memory Lane" took a trip down memory drain. I also considered, "With Every Fiber Of My Being," "Deception," and "Glory Days." Then I remembered Denzel Washingtons, Civil War movie, "Glory " and that was the end of that. "Last Man Standing." Nope. I liked, "Nowhere To Be A Square" and "Dead Men Don't Write Books." I also strongly considered, "Introspections." Well readers, my search for a title came to a halt eighteen months into my writings. Without fanfare and much blood, sweat, and fears, I present to you. "The American Scheme: The Cold Blooded Naked Truth." Enjoy the journey.

Prologue

When quizzed by a reporter, on how he would like historians to remember him, Ex-President Richard Millhouse Nixon, quipped. "I know they will get my history right, I'm going to write it myself." I'm no big fan of Nixon; nevertheless, he got my attention. His words reverberated through my thoughts as if he were delivering me a personal edict to take a look at my own existence, from my own perspective. After all, who would be more astute about one's life journey than the individual living it? Just like President Nixon, I'm taking my life, with pen in hand and delivering it from a first person perspective: the good, the bad and the scandalous ...It's all here. It's my journey from my pen.

My autobiography is permanent evidence of my existence; prayerfully, "Long after I am no more." A phase that Stevie Wonder, wrote and sang in one of his hits. It is my personal testament to my ancestors, so that the readers and my family members who come after me can fathom the notion that there is an inextricable link between one's ancestors and one's future. We are linked throughout the ages by chains of DNA, and strands of chromosomes forming an unbroken link between past and future.

At times the link may seem broken, but our own lives are testaments that the strands are indeed intact. That earlier quote from President Nixon, was and still is a motivating force behind my inklings to pen my own life's journey. I'll get it out there before it fades into oblivion.

According to Webster's Dictionary, the term "Inspiration" means to "Breathe life into...to stimulate energy, ideals or reverence." Some are inspired by their parent's diligence to have a better life, others are inspired by personal challenges, such as the desire to become the first to achieve greater heights in one's family structure. For example, many aspire to become the first to earn a college degree in one's family. Many are inspired through their religion. Webster goes further; "Inspirational creativity or action can be as wide-ranging as there are individuals in the world."

My main inspiration to pen my memoirs was born out of a dream I had one night in 2004. In my dream I was conversing with God. I asked God, "What is my purpose? You carried me through thick and thin for over half a century, I've been a witness to the demise of countless friends, family members and foes alike; many whose attributes out-shined my own, yet you've taken them away before, or in their prime and spared me. I'm perplexed dear Lord, what is my purpose?" God smiled, looked at me wryly, then lucidly proclaimed with his booming voice. "You're going to write the story, Dummy...now go out there and write a best seller." God, nodded in my direction as if he were granting me permission to write my story. In that instant a moment of pure clarity came over me. Suddenly I understood ...everyone has a story. Here's mine.

My autobiograpy's intent is not to glamorize a certain genre or lifestyle. I only attempted to depict the realities of my life's journey; however significant or insignificant, these depictions are based on reality. God knows, if armed with enlightenment, that I would have chosen another route. As with life and everything it entails, you have to play the hand that you are dealt. My life's journey is a proclamation that even in uncharted dangerous waters, one can find his or her way back to shore. Upon learning that I was writing my autobiography, one of my friends asked me why was I writing a book? I replied. "Because dead men don't write books. It is either now or never." Hold onto your hats, Ladies and Gents." I present to you "The American Scheme: The Cold Blooded, Naked Truth."

Table of Contents

PART ONE

I often wonder what the original name of my ancestors was before they were enslaved in America. This mystery will probably go unsolved in my lifetime. Like the old folk Adage states, "Too much water under the bridge." At times carrying a European name, I feel like I am living a lie: regardless, it is the only name I know. My true surname is buried deep in the annals of history and I don't know how to get there.

Arnold Hannon: Son of God

Chapter 1

THE PAST IS ALWAYS PRESENT

It's April 14th, the sky is bluer than blue outside, family legend has it that on that glorious sunny Easter Sunday, in 1933, Ora Hannon, the wife of James Hannon, mother of 3-year old Ida Bell Hannon, had went into labor inside the maternity ward at Woman's Hospital in Detroit, Michigan.

Ora Hannon, was moments away from giving birth to her and Jame's second child. My future mother, Bennie Mae Hannon, is about to enter this world.

She will become the second of three daughters born to that happy union. Seven years later in 1940, Ida Bell, and Bennie Mae's sister, Helen Hannon, will complete this trio of girls. In 1933 the country was at war with Germany. Those were lean times, not only for Detroiters; but, throughout the nation and the world. America was in the throes of a Great Depression. Locally Detroit, was a segregated bastion of discrimination, growth, greed, crooked politicians, bully cops, corrupted unions, and King Kong, ruled at the box office.

All is not lost, my mother is pushing her way into the fray. She will be introduced into a society that had much disdain for the Black race. As James, waited nervously for his new arrival, I often wonder, did he ponder all the obstacles such as racism, sexism and the lack of educational opportunities that lay ahead for his new born.

My grandfather, James Hannon, was a son of the south, born in Russellville, Kentucky in Lincoln County in 1898. My grandmother, Ora West, was born in Houston County, Tennessee around 1895. Legend has it that James, and Ora, met somewhere down south. James followed Ora to Detroit, in the early 1920's. They had their struggles along-the-way when they arrived in Detroit. Once they settled in, James, eventually found work as a laborer at the long defunct Packard Motor Car Company, located on East Grand Boulevard, and Concord. Several decades later, in the mid-1960's, I too worked in that same complex. At the time of my employment, it was a warehouse for small manufacturers and wholesale distributors. I worked there for a wholesale distributor called Super Toys. I was a energetic teenager at the time.

Around, 1992, I was perusing the Burton Historical Archives, located inside the main branch of the Detroit Public Library, I discovered records of my grandparent's address in Detroit in 1937. They resided at 4420 Beaubien, near Forest Street. My grandmother died in 1946, two years before I was born. What little I do know about her life is from family stories and faded photographs. Those sources affirm that she was a great homemaker and an even greater cook, who prepared enormous meals for her family and friends. My mother would inherit my grandmother's culinary skills. I've never met any of my grandparents family members, other than my mother's two sisters and their family's. My family's history begins for me with my grandparents on my mother's side. Most of my life I assumed that my surname, Hannon, was of German origin; but, I discovered during my research that Hannon, is of Scottish, origin. That led me to speculate about how my grandfather, a Black man, inherited a Scottish surname. Slavery had to be the culprit. My grandfather's father, was probably the property of a Scottish, family of Hannons, and he inherited that White family's surname. That was the rule of the day during those turbulent times.

I often wonder what was the original name of my ancestors before they were enslaved in America. This mystery will probably go unsolved in my lifetime. Like the old folk adage states, "Too much water under the bridge." At times carrying a European name, I feel like I'm living a lie; regardless, it is the only name I know. My true surname is buried deep in the annals of history and I don't know how to get there.

Another interesting facet of my heredity is that Bennie's, mother's mother was a full-blooded Cherokee Indian, which would make her my great-great- grandmother. That adds another layer of mystery to my true identity. I can always visit great-great-grandma' through the one old photograph my mother inherited after her own mother's death. Only the strong survive. My ancestors were mighty survivors. I can only imagine the toil and grit they had to endure in the span of their lifetimes.

My mother was only thirteen when her mother died of diabetes in June of 1946. It was time for Ida Bell, and Bennie Mae to grow up, they had a grief stricken father and a baby sister to care for. There were plenty of chores, cooking, cleaning, and other matters to attend to. Both girls were in school, which added to their plight and their education suffered. They did the best they could considering their circumstances. Ida, still in her early teens became pregnant with her first child, and James first grandchild Louise. Louise, was born out-of-wedlock. A year or so later, Ida gave birth to her second child, Sybil. Sybil's father, Leon Davis, fresh home from the Korean war married Ida Bell. They settled in a quaint tree-lined community on the westside of Detroit. They went on to produce my younger cousins, Yvonne (Evie), Leon Junior, and Melvin. Bennie and Helen remained at home with James. In the early spring of 1948, nearing her 15th birthday, Bennie Mae, took a short-cut to Garfield Junior High School, in Detroit, Michigan; On that day, eighth-grader Bennie Mae's young life was altered forever...Fast forward nine months to December 15, 1948. 15-year-old, Bennie Mae Hannon, had went into labor with her first child, and Jame's first male grandchild was making his way into their hearts.

December 15, 1948. I, Arnold Hannon, began my trek through time. I was born out-of-wedlock inside the maternity ward of Herman Kiefer Hospital, in the City of Detroit. Welcome to the planet, Arnold. My mother's plan was to give me up for adoption, granddad was having none of that... my mother told me that when she saw me for the first time, she couldn't part with the curly-haired, big brown-eyed bundle of innocence cuddled in her arms. I was welcomed into the Hannon family.

My earliest conscious recollections were at about two years old. I remember big images whizzing by me as I sat in the middle of a busy street. I now know those whizzing images were automobiles. I must have crawled out into the street. I can't imagine someone placing me in harm's way. I was completely oblivious to my surroundings, sitting there in my dirty diaper watching the cars go by.

I have visions of a young Black man gathering me up and whisking me away. He was with a group of young people who carried me to a basement, cleaned me up, then put fresh clothes on me. I can close my eyes and almost smell the dank, musty, stale air of that basement. Over in a corner I can visualize the sink they bathed me in. Those images are forever etched into my mind's eye, as if it happened last week. Looking back, the only way for me to explain it is that God had sent me guardian angels. I'm forever grateful for God's blessings. As I matured, I became mentally better equipped to evaluate my early life's interactions with others in my social and economic settings.

Some events occurring in my early youth are more vivid than others. I clearly remember my mother skating in the street with some of her friends. My two brothers played nearby as my mother frolicked with her friends on that hot summer's night somewhere around 1953. I remember both my brothers had begun walking at that time. They too were born out-of-wedlock. My mother gave birth to us at Herman Kiefer Hospital in her teens. Times were tough. I didn't realize that as a child. I thought that everyone had holes in their shoes.

My brother Eugene, had a twin sister named Rudene. Rudene died of kidney failure about two months after she was born. I don't remember her, but, I'm sure I loved her. For as long as I can remember, Slim, my youngest brother had a mean streak. He was born in 1952. He was always mad at something or someone, that someone usually was me. Eugene was the second eldest and quite the opposite of Slim. He was mild-mannered and generally a good-natured kid. Eugene was rarely without his trademark smile.

From the time me and Slim could walk, we fought over any and everything; usually, he was the aggressor. I tried to hold back, because that's what older brothers do.

I don't know if it was due to economics or an oversight; We never had any baby pictures taken of us, and that bothers me. Our first photos were taken when we were 8, 9 and 11 years old. The three of us were posing in front of the window in our third floor apartment on Bethune Street. We were decked out in our Christmas duds brandishing Christmas gifts. That was one of my favorite moments of prosperity. I now own that precious piece of our young lives.

I don't know if the term "Baby Boomers" applied to Black people back then; but, me and my brothers were born during the baby-boom explosion.

When most babies speak their first words, it's usually "mama." My mother told us our first word was "Beanie," a slight variation of Bennie, her birth name. I probably picked it up from others addressing her by her first name. I was the oldest. There was no one else around to call her mama; therefore, my calling her "Beanie" was learned behavior. When my brothers heard me calling her Beanie they followed suit. Beanie never taught us differently. It never occurred to the three of us that any disrespect was intended. We respected our mother immensely, as long as Beanie was all right with that, it was good enough for us.

It was about 1954, when, me, my cousins and my brother, Eugene, were playing in our apartment, located in the newly-built Brewster Projects high rise. A pot belly stove sat in the middle of the room. The stove was piping hot. I strayed a little too close to the hot stove. I was accidently pushed or fell against the hot stove, burning me on the stomach. I remember howling out in pain. I still bear the scars from that accident, that I had in my adolescence decades ago.

By the time I had turned five years old, Beanie had rented an upper flat on Cherry Street, located near Tiger Stadium, two blocks east of Trumbull Avenue. At the time I-96 was a work in progress. I can remember spying on construction workers (busy building the freeway), from our second floor window over-looking the massive project. My grandfather lived with us at that time. He often walked me to the corner store. Reminiscing, it seems that I can still feel my little hand nestled in his big hand as we strolled along the sidewalk. During that time in our young lives, Beanie was barely making ends meet.

For a hot minute Eugene's father, Willie Ghouston, would show up now and then bearing gifts, always for them. It was cruel and unusual punishment for a five year old to see Willie, hugging and kissing Eugene and Slim, while never acknowledging my presence. I sat in a corner soaking it all in as he showered them with love and hugs. His visits always left me feeling dejected and confused. I often fantasized about how much more fulfilling my life may have been if I had received love and affection from my own father. Eugene and Slim were criers, I never cried, even while getting some major ass whoopings. Well, most of the time I never cried. At times, Beanie, would beat me harder and longer to induce tears; sometimes it worked, most of the time it didn't. My brothers would cry before Beanie, got the belt out. I'm not the touchy, feel-type. I'm not always comfortable greeting people with hugs, at times it could be an awkward situation for me. I suppose it has much to do with my psychological conditioning.

These conditions are defense mechanisms developed over time, unconscious mechanisms developed to combat rejections. What may appear as aloaftness in my personality and demeanor are actually defense mechanisms at work, warding off predators, who are there to rob me of my emotional stability. I had my grandfather for only seven years of my life. Other than him, I've never experienced the guidance or bonding, between father and son; therefore, it is difficult for me to relate too father figures without negative emotions bubbling from deep within my sub-consciousness. As hard as I try to understand the father-son dynamic, I can't reinvent the wheel. It saddens me at times. Somehow I've managed to survive its impact.

That little fiasco between, Willie Ghoulston, Slim and Eugene didn't last long. Willie just up and disappeared, just like that, (quick as a snap) he was gone. With him went the hugs, the kisses, and worst of all, the love for my brothers. I would advise fathers who lead separate lives from their children to show a little love for your child's siblings as well. This could help eliminate envy and jealousy among brothers and sisters with different fathers.

In 1955 we had a tiny black and white television set. At six years old I was a big fan of the TV program "The Adventures of Superman." I was mesmerized by the caped crusader flying across our tiny black-and-white TV screen. I wanted to be Superman. I yearned to fly. Once after watching my favorite program, I was so pumped that I actually got one of Beanie's sheets, tied it around my neck, then I proceeded to jump out of our second floor window. I attempted to fly like Superman, needless to say gravity took hold and I hit the ground with a thud. Luckily the only thing bruised was my ego. After that, I never tried to fly again. Early June, 1956, James Hannon, clutching his chest came crashing to the floor at my young feet. Frozen like a statue, I stared as he dug at the flame burning deep in his chest, writhing on the floor in pain, while foaming at the mouth. I was too stunned to speak as I tried to comprehend the unfolding tragedy. Beanie, rushed in and brushed me aside. I saw my mother as I had never saw her before or since. She sprung into action with the swiftness of a cat, pleading for James to hold on. With panic in her voice. She screamed, "James, James, please don't die on us. Please, God help him?" Her pleas stung my young ears. Jame's lifeless, glaring eyes made her sob and cry. She was crying for someone she loved dearly and may possibly never see him alive again.

It was a rude awakening for me and my youthful sensibilities, emotions so foreign to me, that I crumpled at my mother's feet and began sobbing in unison with her. What seemed like hours was in actuality only a few minutes. Wailing loudly, Beanie, bolted out the door to get help. The last time I saw my grandfather, he was lying in a casket inside a small funeral home, surrounded by family and friends. We bid, James Hannon, farewell on that hot day in June. I couldn't find the words then to express my love for him, so I'm expressing them now: Thank you for loving and accepting me, caring and saving me from the state. I keep your picture on my mantle to remind me of who I belong to.

Soon after James died, Beanie met her future husband, William Moore, better known as "Wig." Later in their relationship, he answered to "Wine head Willie." I liked Wig better. Wig was a short, bald-headed dark-skinned man. He hailed from Nashville, Tennessee. Wig had five brothers and one sister, Katherine, the oldest and the most stable of the brood. She and her husband, Woodrow, settled in Detroit, in the mid-1940's. Her other siblings followed suit: Odell, Eddie, Robert Lee (better known as "Whistling Bob"), and their older brother, Ben. They came to Detroit on their own initiatives to escape the poverty and racism in Tennessee. The year Wig was born (1925) was one of the bloodiest against blacks in modern American History. Lynchings, beatings and other hateful acts were prevalent throughout the old south. As mentioned, Wigs sister and brothers left Nashville on their own accord. Wig left for other reasons.

The story goes that, Wig, while working as a 20-year-old Bellhop at a Nashville hotel, was accused of eye-balling a White woman. That was taboo in the south during that stretch of history in America. A White man, asked Wig what was he looking at? Wig had to think fast on his feet. He blurted. "I'm a sissy and I don't like girls." Thinking he was in the clear, Wig went home to his mother's house after work. Later on that night, Wig and his family had visitors, the local chapter of the KKK came calling. A voice in the night bellowed. "Get that nigger son of yours out of Nashville by sundown tomorrow, or we gon' barbeque his black ass." With that, the clan sped off leaving behind a very frightened family. Wig's mother was a seasoned southerner and knew that this was no idle threat. That same night they scurried Wig off to Memphis, and put him on a bus headed to Detroit. Once in Detroit, he joined his other family members who were already in Detroit.

Beanie, was a 22 year old cute fat woman when she met Wig. After a brief courtship he married a woman with three young boys, just like that we had a stepfather. Wig's last two brothers, Eddie and Odell, found their way to Detroit. They didn't stay long before they made it back to Tennessee.

The brothers were called the "Mo'" boys, I now know how Moore became "Mo." The Black community has a peculiar way of putting our own spin on certain words. For instance, "show," becomes "sho," "you" becomes "y'all," and "them" becomes "dem"...get the picture. So "Moore" becomes "Mo." This by no means is an indictment on Black Culture. Black southerners brought their own culture and dialect north with them. The northen cities have a more diverse population because of this.

Wig and his brothers were a tough bunch. They drank hard, played hard, and fought hard. Sometimes they fought each other, like many Black men from that era, especially men fresh from the south. For many of those men, money was always tight.

Things were happening fast during those perilous times. My grandfather had died and Beanie got married. Soon after she and Wig's marriage, we had a new address, 405 East Bethune Street, smack dab in the heart of the northend of Detroit, in 1956. I was 7 years old when we moved into a three-story, red brick apartment building, with two family's on each floor. A caretaker named, Smitty, lived in the basement apartment with his wife and cat. I don't remember Smitty's wife's name, but, I do remember their cat's name was Micky. That building was not the Taj Mahal, by no stretch of the imagination. It was a run-down, rat and roach-infested dwelling, with a dilapidated balcony on each floor. The hallway was dark and dank, and it stank from all the odors emitting from poorly ventilated apartments. Inside the apartments were five small rooms, including the bathroom and kitchen, It wasn't much, but it was home and we were thankful. We knew others who were doing worst.

The landlord was a Jewish fellow named, Mr. Brimmer. We only saw him when he came around to collect rent. I still remember: $18.50 a week. Our new home was located on the corner of Bethune and Brush. Across the street on the northwest side of the street sat a huge church. The Gospel Temple. We watched from our third floor bedroom window: a steady stream of parishioners, dressed to impress in their Sunday best, attending Sunday service. Looking back I remember that our neighborhood had a small-town quality. Most neighbors were friendly and cordial toward each other, regardless of one's economic status.

James Tate, was on the high end of the economic food chain. He was a prosperous, Black businessman. He owned the apartment building across the street from our building on the southeast corner of Bethune and Brush. The building was a well-constructed, beige brick, with about ten small apartments. In front of the building was a walk-down basement store inappropriately called, Tate's Market. It was hardly a market, it was more liken to a funky little store. It was cramped and reeked of spoiled lunch meat. There was a handwritten sign out front proclaiming, "Tate's Market," in big, bold crooked letters. As I think back on it: a few potatoes, onions, old cheese, and spoiled lunch meat, does not make it a market. James Tate must have known what he was doing. He was the only square in our immediate area driving a new convertible Caddy every year. He also wore the latest styles in clothes. Mr. Tate was a Black man whose family was deeply rooted in the community. There was Papa Tate, and Mama Tate, the craggy old ninety something year old, patriarch and matriarch of the Tate family. There were several sisters who wielded just as much clout in the neighborhood as their brother James.

The other stores in the community included the Three Brothers Grocery Store, located across the street from Tate's Market. The three short Jewish brothers were Tate's main competition, due to their close proximity. The Three Brothers store had a little more variety than Tate's and their lunch meat didn't smell up their premises. They kept fresh spinach stored in a basket near the front door. Popeye was one of my favorite cartoons and spinach made him strong. On my way out of the Three Brother's Store, I would sneak a pinch of spinach and eat it raw, just like Popeye. Once outside I would make a muscle to see if the spinach made me strong, like "Popeye, the Sailor Man." Down the block on Bethune and Beaubien Street, sat Septini's Market.

Septini's was more market-like than Tate's and, or, the Three Brothers. It was owned by Italians. On the other side of the street on Beaubien sat a night club known as the Cotton Club. Next door to the Cotton Club was Seto's, owned and operated by the only Chinese-American family in the area. Seto's was a small dark and smelly store. It made Tate's smell like a rose garden by comparison. Seto's lunch meat, like Tate's, was horrific. Somehow they managed to eke out a living. Black people must have eaten a lot of bad lunch meat back in the day. For twenty-five cent a pound, you could buy a lot of lunch meat. Seto, his wife and three children lived upstairs above their store. The family was never seen after dark. Seto's children were: Lindsey, the oldest son, and the athletic type, JoJo, the next oldest son, was quiet as a mouse, Amy was the youngest and most studious of the siblings, she always had her books with her. All three were intelligent students. They worked and played in harmony with Blacks in our community.

There were other types of businesses, such as, Jake's Shoe Shine Parlor, where all the old-timers hung out and played checkers upstairs. They played a card game called "Coon Cane" in the basement for money. Jake's was located on the same side of the street as Septini's. Jake was a happy, jovial, little fellow. His claim to fame was that he could shine a pair of shoes like nobody else. He danced a little jig while he spit-shined his customers shoes. Jake's was also a place where adults could play their street numbers, ran by one of the local hucksters, Robert Earl the number man. Nestled between Jake's and Septini's Market was Mr. Popular's Ice Cream Parlor, like Jake's, it was owned by a Black man. Mr. Popular's was the best and cleanest business on Beaubien and Bethune. It was called a confectionary, with well-stocked products from cold remedies to ladies hosiery, and his hot ham-and-cheese sandwiches were deliciously made. Mr. Popular's sold giant scoops of ice cream cones that came in many flavors. There was a long counter with stools for patrons to sit and enjoy their snacks. The juke box was the main attraction; well-stocked with the latest hits of the day. One could buy an ice cream cone or a hot sandwich, put a dime in the juke box and hear the Temptation's, "Dream Come True," or Jackie Wilson's "Say You Will." My all-time favorite was "There Goes My Baby," by The Drifters. Every time I ventured into Mr. Popular's, and had a dime to spare, I'd play "There Goes My Baby;" even though I was too young to have a girlfriend.

I attended Palmer Elementary School, a few blocks south from where my family resided. All the children would hit Mr. Brent's, a small candy store around the corner from Palmer Elementary School. Mr. Brent, had the best candy. If we didn't have money to pay for our treats, we just swiped them. With a store full of noisy children, it was hard for old man, Brent, to keep up with them all.

Our community was an economically diverse community. We had doctors, teachers, businessmen, and other Black professionals, though few in numbers. They were sprinkled throughout our communities, co-existing with the hustler types, pimps, prostitutes and wanna'-be pimps. Some were actually factory workers, masquerading as pimps. During that period in our city's history, Detroit, was still a segregated city with most Blacks, contained mainly in an area east of Woodward; the main artery that separated east and west. Pushed from "Black Bottom," due to the construction of I-75, Blacks migrated across the eastside and the northend. The majority of the inhabitants in our neck of the woods were poor Black citizens, doing the best they could with what they had.

With our new ghetto dwelling came our extended family's, tenants who shared our plight and blight. On the first floor lived, Billy Gillum, and his alcoholic dim-witted wife, Betty Gillum, and their three daughters, who shared the same bedroom. All the apartments had the same floor plan with only two bedrooms. If there were multiple children they had to sleep in the same bedroom, or one could sleep on the living room couch, which was a scary proposition with all the critters running around at night. Billy Gillum, had a filthy mouth. We could hear him cussing day and night. When some of his low-down friends were over visiting, the profanity intensified. It was as if they were trying to out-curse each other. The walls were thin and the hallway had an echo that bounced off the grimy walls. The ears of the tenants in the building were held hostage to the Gillum's and their guest's filthy barrage about whose wife had the biggest ass, or some other sexual garbage. The women visiting the Gillum's would openly discuss the size of their mate's penis, with the Gillum's daughters there to take in every nasty little tidbit. I was eight years old when I was hearing that crap.

There was an elderly woman who lived across the hall from the Gillum's. Her name escapes me, but, she usually could be seen peering out of her front room window wearing an old tattered house coat. She lived alone and no one ever came to visit her, other than the tenants in our building. Their children did minor chores or ran errands for her: like, going to the store for her or that kind of thing. Living next door to the Gillum's, she got the brunt of the foul talk coming out of the Gillum's apartment.

On the second floor, in the apartment directly above the Gillum's, lived a single mother and her three young children: Two girls and a boy, who were the same age as me and my brothers. They were well-mannered and studious, rarely mixing with other kids, education was their main focus. Their bad-ass cousins lived across the hall from them. They were relatives; but, they were complete opposites in their behavior. The bad cousins consisted of two boys and two girls. It had to be cramped in their small apartment with a mother and four hard-headed kids competing for two bedrooms. My family lived on the third floor. Across the hall from us resided Theodore and his drunk, whorish wife, LuLu, who talked to him like he was a dog. They had a fourteen-year-old weirdo son, who was sneaky and always up to no good. There were poor people in my neighborhood and there were po' people. Every resident in our building was po,' all trying to make it to the promised land.

I spent countless hours gazing out of our third floor bedroom window at the traffic cascading down Brush Street, in the evening. I saw all the White commuters pass under our window, driving home from their downtown jobs. Neither the Lodge or I-75 expressways had not been completed during the mid-to-late fifties. Brush was a one-way street, going north. Commuters had to take John R, one block west of Brush Street, to get to their downtown jobs in the morning.

As night fall approached things got interesting. At dusk, out came the neighborhood drunks and rowdys. At the first sign of darkness, the hookers, pimps, and tricks came out. The police shadowed them all. Most of the hookers were Black and the majority of the tricks were White. Since it was going down in a Black community, the police turned a blind eye to the activities below our third floor window. At dawn, like clock work the commuters would appear and the night lifers would disappear. One, afternoon, I was checking out the scene below There was a fender-bender directly below my lofty perch on the third floor. I had a bird's eye view of the unfolding drama below. A car struck another car then all hell broke loose. The Dude whose car was hit, jumped out of his damaged vehicle, then proceeded to attack the driver of the car that hit his car. With straight razor in hand, he was relentless in his pursuit of the victim. He slashed and cut that poor fellow several times. Each time the perpetrator's blade slashed his victim's flesh, his face would burst open exposing deep pink wounds. That poor fella's face was shredded on both sides. It was a horrible sight not only for a child, but, also for grown-ups. When the dude was finished with his assault on the victim, he jumped in his ride and hit the gas with the whining sounds of police sirens in hot pursuit. I don't know if he was caught; but, he deserved to be locked away for what he did to that unfortunate man. I often wondered whatever happened to the victim. Did he survive, or did he die from the assault?

Legend has it that the Big Four would crack a Black man's head with the quickness. On that day, I didn't care, because they saved my ass from a Black man.

The Big Four

Chapter 2

ON THE PROWL WITH THE BIG FOUR

Beanie, soon discovered that Wig, had a drinking problem, he had began drinking more and more as their marriage progressed. I now believe that Wig, also had a Napoleonic complex. Being a short man made him aggressive. When, Wig, was drinking he could be a mean little son-of-a-bitch. He better be glad we were children or we would have kicked his natural ass. Wig didn't always bring home the bacon either. I think it had much to do with his drinking.

Wig's best buddy at the time was a man shorter than him. His name was W.L.. He and Wig were drinking buddies and on occasions, Mr. W.L. would tap dance for our family... man could he hoof! Anyone in ear shot could hear his lightning fast steps. The tenants living in the apartment below ours would joke. "Y'all up there killing roaches again?"

Beanie didn't work at the time, but she was a very creative cook. Beanie could take the meagerist of government issued staples and make generous meals for us. She used staples such as: government cheese, pork and gravy, and powdered eggs. We called those government issued products, "commodities." At one stretch that was all we had to get us through most days. I can testify that we never went hungry. Beanie shared our small resources with strangers. For example, one evening in about, 1954, when I was six years old, we were residing on Cherry Street at the time, and we had few resources. There was a knock at our door. When, Beanie opened the door a gaunt-looking White man was standing there with his hat in his hand. With pleading eyes he humbly said. "Mam, I haven't eaten in days, can you please help me?" Beanie, looked the stranger over and said. "Wait there." She shut the door and disappeared into the kitchen. When she reappeared she was carrying a bowl of butter beans, with a hamhock in the beans and a generous slice of cornbread on the side. She gave it to the stranger then closed the door. Later, after the man had left, Beanie, gathered up the empty bowl with it's naked ham hock bone. That brought a smile to her face. Yep, Beanie Mae, had a big heart for people going through trying times. Far as I know, Beanie, never received any child support from our fathers. She survived in those early years of our lives on Aid for Dependent Children, (ADC) when we were younger. When she married, Wig, our financial burdens were somewhat eased.

Eugene, was such a scrawny little kid. Wig started calling him Runt. Runt, would eventually grow to be 6' 3," but, still he acknowledged his identity as Runt, even as a grown man. The moral of this is: be careful what you call your children, they may out-grow their nickname and be stuck with it for life. As a young child, Runt would pee in the bed, making our room reek with the smell of piss every morning. That sent Wig into a rage. After Wig checked our bed he would line us up in our underwear, then he'd beat the shit out of us with a belt or an ironing cord. We dreaded the morning Sun. The beatings went on for a long time. Poor, Runt, he just couldn't help it.

I learned early in life that if I wanted some money, I had to work for it. First, I worked as a paper boy delivering newspapers on a regular route. I was about eight years old when I got that gig. I had about one hundred customers on a route that started east on Melrose Street, then snaked its way around to East Grand Boulevard, then west to Woodward Avenue. I worked that route five days a week after school and before noon on Saturdays and Sundays. It was tedious work for a skinny eight year old. It was my first taste of making an honest buck. One sunny Saturday afternoon (Saturday was collection day on the routes), I was delivering newspapers and collecting money in a boarding room house on East Grand Boulevard, It was a two-story building. I was on the second floor doing my business. When I was finished and about to make my descent down the stairs, I noticed a teenager hanging around the front entrance in the hallway on the main floor. He was about seventeen and rugged-looking. He made me nervous, because I had never seen him before. I had to pass him to exit the building. Before I hustled down the stairs, I stepped back and hid my money in my shoe, then I hurried down the stairs. Just as I was about to grab the door knob he stepped in front of me and grabbed my arm. He made up some "cock-a-maney" story about me robbing his little brother. That was hog-wash. I was too scared to talk and I was shaking like Don Knots. He pulled out a butcher knife and demanded that I empty my pockets. I did as

I was told. When he saw my empty pockets, he ordered me out of my shoes. There he discovered the hidden collection money. The encounter shook me up. I was nervous as hell. He grabbed the loot and bolted out the door in one direction. I was right behind him running in the opposite direction, headed towards the paper station. You think Jesse Owens was fast? On that day Jesse, had nothing on me. I was dragging my wagon with newspapers flying everywhere. Out of breath, I spilled into the paper station. "He. He robbed me, he had a knife and took my money," I blurted out. The station manager calmed me down. I explained to him what had happened. He told me to take some time off. The offer was tempting: but, I declined, because I needed the money.

I was back on the job the next day, with a keen eye, I quickly got back into the groove of being a paperboy. Then about three weeks after getting stuck-up, I was getting ready to make my turn onto East Grand Boulevard. My young 20/20 vision spied him two blocks away, headed in my direction. It was something about the way he walked that alerted my senses. As I got closer, I honed in on his features. It was him. He didn't see me; but, I had seen him walking menacingly down the Boulevard toward me, looking over his shoulder as he sulked down the sidewalk. I dropped everything this time...the wagon, newspapers and all. I fired up the jets and hauled ass once again back to the paper station. Again, I ran into the station out of breath with panic in my voice. "He's back. He's back. The guy that robbed me... he's coming back to rob me." Once again the station manager had to calm me down. In a nervous tone he asked. "What? Where? Who?" The manager looked at me wide-eyed as if he suddenly understood what I was trying to convey to him. "Oh shit, you mean the guy that robbed you?" I eagerly replied. "Yeah," shaking my head up and down vigorously. He grabbed the phone and called the Detroit Police Department.

There must have been a police cruiser in the area... they were there "Lickity split." The long black Chrysler sedan, with "Detroit Police" in bold gold letters, creeped up to the front door of the paper station. I could see the outline of four huge men as the sedan rolled to a stop. Three of the figures unfurled their tall frames as they exited the sedan. Three big, tall, White cops strolled along the sidewalk into the paper station, where I waited anxiously on their arrival. All three wore sport coats that looked too small for their huge frames. Two of the cops wore straw hats and the cop without a hat, had a crew cut and was chewing on an unlit cigar. None of them were smiling. One of the hats pointed at me and asked the manager. "Is that the kid?" The manager shook his head up and down. "Yeah, that's him." With that, they quickly hustled me out of the paper station past a curious crowd that had gathered out front. A big, burly, uniformed officer was driving. I sat in the back seat between the two straw hats. They were in full police mode cruising down East Grand Boulevard... predators stalking a predator, as we eased across the Boulevard, I felt empowered sitting between my new friends. Up to that point in my life, I had never rode in a car that big and fancy. I spotted the robber on the south side of the street. He pretended that he didn't see the black sedan. We were riding west, approaching Woodward Avenue. One of the hats pointed for the driver to pull into the center lane. It was-a-well-choreographed exercise as the driver eased into the center lane, slowing down just enough for the two hats to slide out of the vehicle with the precision of fleet-footed dancers. They quickened their pace toward the suspect. On cue, the driver whipped the car around through the alley behind the culprit. When he saw the two hats coming his way, the culprit ran toward the alley. There he was met by the cigar and uniform with there snub-nosed pistols drawn. The suspect stopped dead in his tracks when he saw me get out of the vehicle. He knew what time it was. To get the suspect's attention, one of the hats cupped his hand and smacked dude in the mouth so hard that it made me whence. Then he threw him against their vehicle with a little mustard on it. Searching him, they pulled out the butcher knife he had robbed me with earlier, then hand-cuffed him. I watched as he took my place in the back seat between the two hats. Before they drove away, the cigar sitting in the front passenger seat winked at me and proclaimed. "Stay out of trouble kid." With that, they sped away in a cloud of victory.

As I finished up my route, I couldn't believe the nerve of that dude, that fool came back to rob me again. When I checked back into the paper station, the Italian newspaper station manager asked me. "How did it go?" I explained to him what had transpired. He asked me if I knew who the cops were? I said. "Naw." He explained in a mellow cavalier tone. "That was The Big Four." Then he barked out their names. The tall slim cop in one of the hats was "Rotation Slim," and the other hat was a cop called "Mustache." The cigar-chomping cop was called "Chew Tobacco" and their driver's name was "Burly." Legend has it that The Big Four would crack a Black man's head with the quickness. On that day, I didn't care, because they had saved my ass from a Black man. A few weeks later, I got a summons to appear in court. Beanie took me downtown to Recorders Court, where I would have to testify against the fool that had robbed me. The judge assigned to the arraignment was Judge Alvin Davenport, the first Black judge to sit on the bench in Detroit's Recorders Court. Little did I know then that forty-seven years later, twenty-odd-years after his death; my wife and I are sole owners and residents of the condo that, Judge Davenport, owned during the years he served on the bench in Recorders Court. As an added bonus, I inherited his world-class rose garden. Our condo was the last property we viewed, it was the perfect match. We didn't know it at the time of purchase that the judge was its original owner. We learned about that little tidbit from the little old lady we purchased our new home from, Mrs. Mary Jane Hock. I shared with my wife and Mrs. Hock, about the time I had to testify before, Judge Davenport, way back in 1957, boy what a co-incidence.

A few years into Wig and Beanie's marriage, Wig was drinking heavily. Wig and his drinking buddies drink of choice, was a cheap-ass wine called Silver Satin. Wig, could often be seen staggering up and down Oakland Avenue. I guess that's how he became to be known as, "Wine head Willie." He was drunk, day after day, week after week, month after month. As I grew, I often wondered what demons drove Wig to self-destruct. Wig's life was spiraling out of control, so was ours. Beanie, was fed-up and at the end of her rope. My mother grappled mightily about Wig's drinking, as she proclaimed. "Tattered, torn, used and abused," we all felt the sting of Wig's alcoholism; things had to change. Beanie had to find a solution to this dilemma. As I eluded to earlier we had varmints in our apartment. They came out at night, soon as the lights were out. Saturday night was horror night. Beanie and Wig, went out on Saturday night from time to time. We were left at home to watch our tiny black-and-white TV set. Our favorite show was "Shock Theater," one of the scariest shows on TV. The TV show's tag line was, "Lock your doors, close your windows, get ready for shock." That was followed by a blood-curdling scream, then a skull floated across the screen. The program featured scary movies, such as "Dracula," starring Bella Lugosi and Boris Karloff starred as "Frankenstein." The series also featured "The Wolfman" and "The Mummy," both starring Lon Chaney Jr., another favorite was "The Creeper." We viewed it all on a tiny black-and-white TV that exuded a gothic-glow, illuminating the darkened apartment. We would huddle together on the couch in the dark absorbing all the gory details. Our fear was heightened by the noise that the rats were making in the kitchen. When, Beanie and Wig came home they were greeted by three scared little Negroes. We were always glad to see them walking through the door.

Once we got settled in our new digs on Bethune, we started classes at our new school, Palmer Elementry, which had an all-black student body, with the exception of three Chinese students: Lindsey, JoJo and their younger sister, Amy, their parents owned the smelly little store, Seto's. The majority of the teachers were white and all the administrators were white. The White Principal, had a passion for patting the smaller male students on their butts. I wish I could travel back in time to kick his ass. I never saw any blacks above the position of teacher. We had a short, little runt for a gym teacher, named Mr. Skanasky, who was of Polish descent. He was responsible for melting out punishments to Black students. Skanasky acted as the school's enforcer. If a teacher had a problem with a student, they would send them to see Mr. Skanasky. He wielded a big wooden paddle with holes drilled in it. Once inside of Mr. Skanasky's office the students lined up and watched him whack other students until it was their turn. When it was your turn, you had to bend over and get smacked across the butt by that grinning munchkin, who seemed to be enjoying himself in some kind of perverted way. To add insult to injury, you had to bellow, "Thank you Mr. Skanasky," in a non threatening tone. Some of the bigger boys would fight back. For instance on one occasion, Skanesky, had the usual suspects lined up. Before, Skanasky, could unleash his wrath, they turned on him. About four of the hard-heads jumped him and beat the crap out of him. That pretty much stopped that practice. Damn, what White people got away with back then is amazing. Thank God, for Martin Luther King Jr..

Wig and Runt shared a birth date: December 14th, as usual, I celebrated mine on December 15th. Runt and I usually celebrated our birthdays together. Some years we had to choose between our birthday or Christmas, to receive our gifts. Our birthdays were so close to Christmas, that it was purely economical. For some years, Beanie, just couldn't afford both birthday and Christmas presents. One year stands out in particular. It was the Christmas of 1960, my 12th birthday. That year we decided we wanted our presents at Christmas time. On Christmas day we all got up early and rushed to the Christmas tree. There it sat, a shiny new black-and-chrome "Schwinn Phathom" bike. It was all mine. The only other times in my life, that I've been as excited about something material, was when I purchased my first new Caddy in 1971... when me and my wife Terry purchased our home, and when I walked across the stage at my graduation from the University of Detroit, and was handed my Bachelors of Arts degree, in 1990. On that cold snowy Christmas morning back in 1960, the weather didn't faze me. I got dressed and took my new bike out for a spin. I was one happy camper riding up and down Bethune Street, with a wintry wind at my back. I couldn't wait until Spring. After my little romp on my new bike, it was time to put it away for the winter. I was warned: no riding untill Spring. It was pure torture to see it parked in the corner every morning. Spring couldn't come fast enough! Life wasn't always that sweet. It was times like that, that made it all worth while.

As I stated before, Beanie, never received any child support from any of our fathers; as was the case for the majority of my fellow constituents running amok on the northend. We provided our own child support, it was called WORK. It was either hustle, get a job, steal, or go without. In some extreme cases there was another choice... starve to death. I liked to dress well, and I liked the independence that money allotted me. When I wasn't delivering the Detroit Times, I was hawking the Michigan Chronicle, and Jet magazine's. I also held down a job at the local movie theatre, cleaning up the previous night's trash made by movie patrons. I got up at 5 a.m. in the morning, that was even earlier than when Wig got up. A posse of my buddies would meet at my apartment building before the crack of dawn, then we headed off to the Center Theater, several blocks away on Woodward and the Grand Boulevard. We made fifty cents an hour and free admission to see movies. When we were finished cleaning the movie house, we hustled home to get ready for school.

Wigs brother, Whistling Bob, was a tall, muscular, brown skinned man with black curly hair and keen features. Like many southern men, Bob, sported a mouth full of gold teeth. He had a slow, laid-back swagger when he strolled our block early in the morning, whistling one of his signature tunes. Everyone in ear shot would be reminded that Whistling Bob, was on the block. Whistling Bob, lived on the dole. He was a street-fighter, good with his fist and the trusty slim Jim knife he carried. Bob wasn't the type to play with. He never pulled his knife for show. If he had to pull it, some fool was gonna get cut. I've seen Bob, slice and dice some of the hardest so-called tough guys on the northend. The majority of men who migrated to Detroit, from the south were looking for opportunities in the automobile plants, then to get married, have kids and settle down. Not so with, Whistling Bob, and those of his ilk: hard living, hard drinking, and hard loving was their creed. Bob wasn't a pimp in the traditional sense. He would lay up on a woman until she got tried of him. Bob dressed well and sported a big Fedora hat, that made him look even taller than his 6'1" frame. The ladies loved Bob, even though he was no good for them financially. Basically, he was a "rolling-stone who marched to the beat of his own drummer." At times he'd pull out his harmonica and strike up a tune to the delight of those within ear shot. The man was funny as hell and he bellowed a rambunctious laugh. Bob, had a unique talent to whistle a tune as clean and clear as any man-made instrument. He would always give the same rendition of unsolicited advice. "Don't get used to going to the penitentiary. Don't mess your life up going in and out of jail." That was always the extent of his unsolicited advice. Many heard, but few listened. Bob, had served prison bits from the south to the north, and in small towns along the way. Therefore, he knew what he was talking about. Bob was older than Wig. I don't know the brothers pecking-order according to age...other than, Bob was older than Wig. Wig had six brothers, a potpourri of brotherhood. Some were tall, some short, some dark skinned, and some were brown skinned. Although, Bob, wasn't my blood uncle, he felt like family. I suppose it was because he was always hovering around the perimeters of our daily lives. His step-son, Robert Slaugter, was much older than me and he possessed criminal tendencies. When my family lived on Cherry Street, Robert hung around our house with Bob. Robert was Bob's girlfriend Kate's son. During one of their visits, the ice cream man was making his way down Cherry Street, in his musical treat truck. I wanted some ice cream in the worst way, so I asked, Robert, to buy me some ice cream. He pointed at Beanie's purse and whispered to me that all I had to do was too get some money out of Beanie's purse and we both could buy some ice cream. I was five years old with limited knowledge and quite naive about the tricks being played by the much older teen. When, Beanie, wasn't looking I lifted five dollars from her purse, then gave it to Robert, who bought us some ice cream and kept the change. It wasn't long before Beanie, discovered the missing loot, and with me sucking on that ice cream it didn't help my cause any. I became the prime suspect. Beanie was livid. I knew that look: it reassured me that she wasn't playing and that I was in big trouble. She calmly asked me where did I get the ice cream. I just blurted out that, Robert, made me do it. By that time Robert was long gone. I braced myself for the fireworks to follow. She screamed. "You're lying. Get your ass in the house right now." The tone and content of her voice reminded me that I had made a big "boo boo." For the first time before a whoopin,' I felt like crying, because I knew I was guilty. Hoping to help my dilemma, I spat out the truth. Then, Beanie, demanded the change from the five dollars. I sheepishly answered that, Robert, had kept the change. Beanie ordered me out of my clothes and promptly lit into my ass with an extension cord. That was one of the few times I shed tears. I just wanted it to stop. Beanie was steaming. She gave me one of the worst beatings I had ever had up to that point in my young life...one that I will never forget.

Robert, didn't take Bob's advice about not going to prison. He was in and out of the pokey on minor bits, until he caught a major case and was locked up in Jackson prison doing some major time. He went on to spend fifteen years behind those mighty walls. When he was cut loose in the early 1970's, he had a hard time adjusting. He couldn't relate to women. I would see him hanging out with Sissies. He earned a living selling popsicles and ice cream from a push cart. Just observing Robert, I could tell he had lost much of his old-self behind Jackson Prison's mighty walls.

On a hot summer's night around 1976, Robert was making his way down Second Avenue near Hazelwood, when two plain-clothes cops in an unmarked police vehicle rolled up on him. The story was carried in the only African-American newspaper in the city, the Michican Chronicle. The two White cops started hassling Robert, as they cruised along side of him. They ordered, Robert, to stop so that they could question him. Mr. Slaughter, was not in the mood. He stopped, he turned, he fired, bang! He shot the cop on the passenger side, who had ordered him to stop right in the face at point blank range, bang! It happened that damn fast. The cop who was driving, hit the gas and took off in one direction, with Robert, running in another direction. Within minutes the area was flooded with cops coming from all directions. Most of them were white, because that's the way it was back then. There was an over-whelming majority White police force. They cornered Robert, a few blocks away. He was hiding behind an apartment building, where they proceeded to beat him to death. The Michigan Chronicle, ran his before-the-incident and his after-the-incident photos. I couldn't recognize him from the after the incident photo, they had beat him to a bloody pulp. The militants in the community were outraged and so was I. Protesters, including myself, picketed police headquarters with picket signs proclaiming, "The Pigs Slaughtered, Robert Slaughter." And that's the truth, Ruth.

I learned later in life, that the bare-footed runner had been shot to death, as was the case with a young Chessy Lay, after he returned home from a tour in Vietnam. Both of them could have been contenders. When someone speaks to me of today's competitors being the fastest this, or fastest that, I always interject (tongue in cheek), "The fastest man alive is dead."

Fleet-footed sprinters

Chapter 3

THE FASTEST MAN ALIVE IS DEAD

We were growing faster than a teenager's feet by the time we reached eleven, twelve, and thirteen. Although I was the oldest, now I was the shortest and it would remain that way. Ronald, was now called, Slim. He was the youngest and tallest, he would eventually grow to be 6' 8." The only person to call him Ronald, was Beanie, and she was the only family member to call Runt, by his birth name, Eugene. I was always called by my given name, Arnold, by my family members and most of my friends; except for a few years in my early twenties. I was known in some circles as "Fass Cass."

Slim, was a cantankerous individual, with a mean disposition, a violent temperament and he was ignorant as hell. He was not the friendly type. He was also the best athlete with a lean, slim body. At one point in our young lives, Slim, was the fastest kid in our elementary and junior high schools. We played hardball on a summer recreation league team. Slim, was the pitcher and I was the catcher. He had an awesome fast ball. The kid could bring the smoke. Other than that we hardly ever got along. I never understood the level of disdain he had for me, and others as well. Anti-social wouldn't begin to describe his personality. When it came down to your ass or his ass, it would be your ass every time. For example, there was an ice cream factory not far from where we lived on Bethune. We hadn't quite reached our teen years when that incident occurred. On a hot Summer night, a bunch of bored kids decided we wanted some ice cream. We sneaked down to the ice cream factory to hit the trucks. When I say hit the trucks, I'm referring to ice cream trucks, the custom built freezer trucks that were used to distribute the products. The factory made fudgebars, popsicles and other assorted ice cream treats. The refrigerated trucks were loaded the night before deliveries. The local juveniles knew about their little secret.

The plan was to pull the bottom of the fence up and then crawl under it, then proceed to break into the trucks freezers to steal some ice cream. Then we would steal away into the night. Everything went smooth, that is, until Slim, the last one to crawl out from under the fence got his size twelve foot caught under the fence and we couldn't pull it free. As we struggled to free his foot, two shining, bright headlights were fast approaching in our direction. The closer they got, the louder Slim screamed. We recognized the red light on top of the car...it was the police. We took off and left Slim, to fend for himself. We could hear him hollering hysterically as we fled down a dark alley. As the cops approached, Slim, was frozen with fear like "a deer caught in their headlights." We could hear him screaming a block away. I made it home sweaty and nervous. I crawled into bed hoping to avoid the impending mess we had gotten ourselves into. A couple of hours later, I heard Beanie shouting. "Arnold, get up right now." It was her tone that made me worry. I jumped up, fearing the worst. Gingerly, I eased into the living room where I spied Slim, with two White cops explaining to Beanie, what went down at the ice cream factory. Beanie was hot, we were in big trouble. I visualized, Beanie, tearing my ass to pieces. Slim, the big bad-ass had snitched on everybody. He wasn't about to take the ass whoopin' by himself. That night, Beanie and Wig took turns on our ass.

Runt was the total opposite of Slim. He was more of a follower. Runt also was the quiet one...quiet and friendly. As the second oldest, he was also the best cook between the three of us. He was neat and meticulous to a fault. Wig started calling Eugene, Runt, when we were young children. Wig was short and I'm sure he was called Runt at some point in his life. Eugene was the shortest at the time; therefore, the name fit his stature. But, Runt soon out-grew his nickname. Runt would eventually grow to be 6' 3," nonetheless, he still answered to Runt. There are days when I feel responsible for some of the turmoil in his life. Growing up he was an impressionable kid. Runt followed my and Slim's lead. We followed the lead of bad role models who we came into contact with in the streets during our teenage years. Our role models were pimps and other underworld types. Like many young men, then and now, we idolized the wrong people in our community. We could only see the glitz and glamour. I never, ever considered the destructive aspects of life in the fast lane. I was attracted to the swagger and notoriety of the street lifestyles. While we were learning from the streets, Runt was learning from us. I don't have one bad thing to write about Runt. I just pray that my younger brother is doing well. It has been years since I've heard from him. I miss him. He has my number. My wish is that he will use it. I regret that I couldn't do more to help Runt, through his plight in life. Peace, and may God be his guide. I miss the Runt I used to know.

We were choir boys compared to some of the ruffians in our new neighborhood. Jimmy Evans was the prototype for juvenile delinquency. Growing up on the northend in the fifties and sixties, street gangs ruled the playgrounds, the corners and schools. There co-existed the Shakers and the Baby Shakers, the Chilli Macs, the Casinos, and other gangs based throughout the northend. Before we moved to the northend, the only gang I had encountered was a Mexican motorcycle gang when we lived near downtown on Cherry Street. To encounter the many gangs in our new neighborhood was a cultural shock. The gangs mainly fought over turf and other stupid shit like that. Their weapons of choice were either knives, brass knuckles, or fists. It was rare for someone to pull out a gun.

Jimmy Evans, all of 13 years old was the leader of a band of thugs called the Casinos. The Casinos were not a fun-loving bunch... smiling was a sign of weakness to them. I tried not to even look at them, because I didn't want to bring attention to myself. Jimmy, the ring leader had a foul disposition and was to be avoided at all cost. Most of us had to pass the gang on our way to school. They hung out on the corner of Oakland and Clay: Nine and ten deep like hyenas in the jungle surveying their prey. If one got close enough they would pat you down for your lunch money, and slap you upside the head, that kind of shit. If you resisted you got your ass whipped. They were a motley crew and they didn't play with you. They were made up of, rejects and dropouts: Rejected by their parents, (those who had parents) dismissed by the school system, scorned by the mainstream, and loathed by their enemies and victims. Despite all of their flaws, they were a well-organized bunch. They stood out in their all-black attire: black cotton jackets with Casinos written in big gold letters on the back, a pair of black slacks and black high-top Chuck Taylor, All Star gym shoes. To top it all off, most of them wore their hair in a process, tied down with black doo rags as they jousted playfully with each other with their knives, while waiting to catch some unfortunate kid slippin,' so that they could pounce on him. I still remember some of their names. There was the short, blue-black leader, Jimmy Evans and his second in command, Ralph. Their henchmen consisted of Donny Young, Wilbert, Tyrone Russell, Jelly, and Fish. There were a few others whose names escape me. Jimmy was a jealous fool and his little minions followed his lead. Jimmy called the shots. If you had a girl that Jimmy deemed too pretty for you, you got stabbed if you came around him with her. If you dressed better than him, you got stabbed. If you looked at him wrong, you got stabbed. Get the point?

Jimmy and his older brother, Gene, lived with their aunt on Melrose Street, around the corner from where Jimmy, and his gang hungout on Clay and Oakland. Their aunt was one of my customers on my paper route. They lived in a small cramped flat. Their flat was so small that when Jimmy and Gene had there rollaway bed out, you had to turn sideways to walk through their dwelling to reach the kitchen. There were just two small rooms for Jimmy, Gene and their aunt. I was always curious about where Jimmy's and Gene's mother was. There were some things you dare not bring up to Jimmy. I don't know how he would have responded to such an inquiry. I felt that the absence of his mother contributed to Jimmy's anti-social behavior, his violent temperament and his blatant disdain for others, including the members of his own gang. In Jimmy's own vernacular. "They get out of line, I stab they black Ass." Needless to say, I never asked Jimmy about that mother thang.

On a few occasions both brothers would be up shooting the breeze or eating breakfast when I came by to collect for the papers. On one such occasion, Jimmy started talking with me like we were old chums. As long as none of his boys were around, at times he'll let his guard down. As I was about to leave, Jimmy turned to me with that, "Cat ate the Canary grin," and said. "See you. I'll be robbin' yo' ass later." A nervous laugh slithered out of my throat, I couldn't tell if he was playing or not.

I had forgotten all about Jimmy's remarks about robbing me. When Monday rolled around it was business as usual, so I thought. I took my usual route to school. As always, there were the Casinos, shaking down their prey. They owned the corner of Oakland and Clay. When you became the focus of their attention it was bad news. On this particular day it was bad news for me, right on cue, the gang's eyes zeroed in on me. They were not friendly stares either. My instincts and senses were heightened as I picked up my stride. I nervously eyed the gang. Jimmy motioned for me to come over to them. I kept right on steppin'. I felt threatened. Then I heard his scurrilous command. "Come here, mahfucka." I fired up the jets and hauled ass towards the school. Jim and the boys were in hot pursuit, they chased me all the way to the edge of the playground. Fatigue was setting in. I felt my time was up. I was just a few feet from the front entrance of the school, they were just a reach away from snagging their prey. I dropped quickly to the ground, the gang's momentum sent them tumbling over me.

I jumped up and hopped over their prone bodies squirming on the ground. I then made my way into the school and then down the hallway, where I disappeared into my classroom... whew, close call. After that I didn't deliver papers to Jimmy's aunt for a while. As a matter of fact, I tried avoiding the Casinos at all cost for the time being.

I had just about forgotten about our last encounter month's earlier. I still kept my distance, operating on the fringes, ducking and dodging.

On a hot summer afternoon I was in one of the stores near my apartment building. I had my back turned toward the entrance when someone tapped me on the shoulder. I turned around with nowhere to run. There stood my worst nightmare: Jimmy Evans, cleaning his finger nails with his slim-jim knife, looking at me sheepishly. Wilburt and Ralph were at his side. They were in full-battle-gear. All I could think was. "Oh shit, this is how I'm going to die." What I heard come out of Jimmy's mouth, almost threw me for a loop." Nice move mahfucka," he said, with a wry smirk etched across his face. Then he began to laugh in unison with Ralph and Wilburt. With that, they waltzed toward the entrance. Before Jimmy stepped out of the store, he turned to me and said. "Yo,' quick-ass thinking saved yo' ass." They then went on about their business, and I started delivering papers to his aunt again. Soon after my little encounter with Jimmy and the boy's, I'm chosen as one of twenty recipients to win paper boy of the year. I won in my district. On hand to present us with our awards was none other than the seven-foot tall Eastern High School phenol and then Detroit Pistons rookie basketball center, Reggie Harden, man was he big. We dinned on a delicious spaghetti dinner, with meatballs, and it all went down at the then famous, Roma Hall on Gratiot near Chene Street. This was big time stuff for me.

From time to time I attempted to quiz, Beanie, regarding my biological father's identity. My inquiries brought her great consternation whenever the subject was revisited. Her reactions left me perplexed. What was the big mystery surrounding my conception? Maybe, Beanie, thought I would grow up to be an idiot, unconcerned with my inherited DNA. She made me feel like an ass for asking, therefore, for the time being, I left it alone.

I was a pretty decent student from the first through the ninth grades. I loved to run and jump over fences. I was an active kid. I played baseball in summer, football in the fall, and basketball in the winter. Those were the days. We played most of our games on the playground at Palmer Elementary School, on gravel, no grass for us. When it came to football, it was tackle, no helmets, no pads, no grass, and the iron mesh fence was out of bounds. You had to be tough to play with us. While the younger guys played on the playground, the older guys played high school ball, and, or ran track. Some of the football players and track team members, would often race each other in the street in front of our playground.

Chessy Lay was a tall muscular teen, who just happened to be the fastest dude on Northern High School's football and track team. I got a kick out of watching Chessy beat anyone who dared to race him. Fast as Chessy was, I reminisce back to when I was about five years old, when we lived on Cherry Street. I was a witness to what may have been the fastest man I have ever seen up close and personal. I can't recall his name. What I do remember is a short, stocky dark-skinned young man. I remember him with his pants legs rolled up, with no shirt on, and he was bare-footed. I remember the excited faces of those gathered to watch man vs machine. In one lane in the street, you had the bare footed dude. In the other lane, you had a guy on a motorcycle gunning the motor raring to go. Someone in the mix had a starter pistol. There was an air of anticipation as the racers steadied themselves, waiting for the big bang of the starter pistol. Ready, get set. Bang! The bare-footed runner took off " like a bat shot out of hell." He crossed the finish line just as the motorcycle was about to hit full throttle. It was a short race. The fleet-footed runner beat the motorcycle by about two yards to win the race. I learned later in my life that the bare-footed runner had been shot to death, as was the case with a young Chessy Lay, after he returned home from a tour of duty in Vietnam. Both of them could have been major Olympic contenders. When someone speaks to me of today's competitors being the fastest this, or fastest that, I always interject. (tongue in cheek) "The fastest man alive is dead."

At age nine I was a bony little guy, a prime target for bullies. I learned to think fast on my feet. I was more of a loner than a follower. I daydreamed a lot, mainly about the future. I envisioned a world of flying cars and super highways, darting the landscape, leading up to an iridescent city in the sky. My imagination was way ahead of reality.

I got real excited when I got new clothes. Beanie didn't have the money to buy new clothes for us. At times, it didn't matter. I managed to dress well between my low-paying jobs, the lay-a-way and my new hustle, which I'm not proud of. But, If I'm gonna tell it, I'm gonna tell the naked truth. I learned how to boost clothes. I learned the trade from one of my childhood friends, Steve Walker. Steve was a little older than me. In the ghetto one did what one had to do to get by. When you're young and poor, with lax supervision, the rules of engagement are different. Survival of the fittest is the mantra. At one stretch in my youth, I dressed so well that I had older dudes borrowing my duds. I never borrowed other's clothes. I was into my own style. Steve Walker, was the older brother of one of my best childhood friends, Anthony Walker. Anthony was better known as Antman, because of his short stature. Steve's the culprit who introduced me to boosting clothes. Boosting is a ghetto term for stealing. Our target was Demry's Department Store, located on Woodward and Milwaukee. Being small in stature, I was perfect for Steve's little caper.

The plan was to tag along behind an adult, like I was shopping with them. That maneuver was designed to fool the store detectives. Demry's was an upscale little department store, a smaller version of Hudson's. That was our little secret on how we spent our Saturday afternoons stealing clothes out of Demry's. Steve would pilfer one of their shopping bags, then sneak around Demry's stuffing it with clothes. He then would place the bag of items near a dressing room. Then he would leave the store. That was decades before buzzer tags and elaborate security systems. I would strike when an adult passed by the stuffed bag. I swooped the bag up and walked out of the store on the heels of the adult. We worked that little scam that entire summer. We never got busted, we just got bored with it. We were two sharp cookies that summer of 1958.

In my neighborhood on the northend, children were always fighting. From time to time, I was involved in my share of scuffles. One of the most unusual fights that I was involved in occurred on the traffic side of our apartment building, on Brush Street. I was about twelve years old at the time of the fight. I was approached by two neighborhood bullies: Tiger and his side kick, Country. My back was leaning against a street sign post; the metal post holding the no parking sign. The two boys were feeling frisky. Tiger and Country didn't go to a traditional public school, they went to Moore for Boys. Moore was an all boys school for juvenile delinquents. They didn't prepare students for college at Moore, Moore prepared students for the penitentiary. The school was located in one of the toughest neighborhoods on the northend, Camaron and Hague. My fellow northenders can testify to that. Bullies are always looking for victims. Country, flexing his muscles was going to show off on me to impress Tiger. It was a case of little thug, trying to impress big thug by goading me into a fight. I didn't want to fight Country. I knew that once the fight started, that Tiger was going to help Country. There was some name-calling back and forth between me and Country. I said something that struck a nerve. Then, Country, lowered his head and charged blindly at me. I slid to the side like a Matador, and Country's head hit the pole. Bam! On impact his head rattled the pole. Country, crumpled like a deflated doll in a puddle of his own blood. Tiger helped a dazed Country to his feet. Country, swore that I had hit him in the head with a pipe. He knew what had happened; he was just too embarrassed to admit that he had knocked his own ass out.

I used to hate fighting. Most of the time I stood my ground. I was never the aggressor.

I'm not sure; but, there seemed to be something about me that attracted bullies. I was small in stature, wiry, and hard-to grab. I tried boxing at Considine Recreation Center, not far from where I lived. I wasn't disciplined enough to sustain boxing. In my old neighborhood, when challenged, you fought... win or lose. If you didn't fight you were labeled a punk, the bottom of the macho food chain. Fighting with my brother Slim, everyday growing up prepared me for the bullies. With Slim, if you didn't fight back, he'd just beat the shit out of you. Did I already mention that me and Slim never got alone? There are forces at work with roots buried deep in our psyche. It is the same phenomenon that drives the dog to hate the cat.

Don't get me wrong, everyone on the northend wasn't a thug or a low life, by no means. There were decent law abiding, God-fearing folks who cut their grass, nurtured their children and set standards in our community. Examples were the Taylors down the street from us, or the Jordans across the street. Both had two biological parents in their households. That is just a small example of the kind of folks who were the glue that held our community together.

My family didn't attend church much, even though the Gospel Temple Baptist Church stood across the street from where we lived. Frankly speaking, as a child I thought we were too poor to attend church. This is how I rationalized things I didn't understand during my youth.

In 1959 land was at a minimum in the black community. Most black's were squeezed together in cramped segregated neighborhoods. We had a diverse class of black's living side-by-side. The factory worker lived next door to the doctor. The plumber lived across the street. The welfare and ADC recipients were right there in the mix. That social grouping was repeated ten-fold throughout our communities. The neighborhoods were one big potpourri of blood, sweat, and struggle. I remember one particularly hard-working family man in our community. Mr. Brown had nine children. He worked in the foundry at one of the auto factories. He also did odd-jobs on the side, they were handy man type jobs. To make sure his family could make ends meet, everyone over ten had to have what Mr. Brown called. "Some kind of piece of job."

There were domestics, waiters, and bus-boys sprinkled in the mix of our community as well. I worked as a bus-boy going into my early teens. I can't recall how I got the gig at the Recess Club, which was located on the eleventh floor of the Fisher Building, on the Boulevard and Second Avenue. If you were white, rich and prominent, then if you could pass the blue blood test and could afford the astronomical membership fees, that was the place for you. All the fancy Chef's were white. The fine linen was white, the Matradee's were white. The only thing black was the waiters and bus-boys. If I were an illegal alien, I would be singing praises of "Welcome to America. I was already a young American, the only thing I was singing was, "Is this all there is?" On my new job, I got a chance to clean up behind some of the biggest movers and shakers in Michigan. When I looked around the Recess Club, all I saw were old Black men, who had spent a lifetime serving and grinning for White folks. At some point, I began to ponder my own future. I worked the lunch and dinner crowd. I soon discovered that rich people are different. Some of their dinner tabs were more than I made in a month. That's no exaggeration. I worked for an old waiter named Mitch. Every waiter had a bus-boy assigned to them to clear the tables in their area. I had an opportunity to sample some of the best cuisine in the world: Jumbo shrimp, lobster, steaks and much more. No, they didn't allow the help to partake of those luscious delicacies, but, with a quick spin-and-grab, one could eat like a King.

Some parents die and leave their offspring unsolvable challenges regarding their DNA makeup. It's like trying to solve a no beginning, no ending paradox about one's own existence. It can be a daunting endeavor, tracing one's roots, when there's no trail to follow.

Arnold Hannon

Chapter 4

NO TRAIL TO FOLLOW

One of the more prominent notable subjects to call the northend home was Smokey Robinson of the "Miracles." Mr. Robinson, grew up on Belmont Street. Belmont, was located south of Highland Park, and west of Hamtramck, two small cities bordering Detroit. I occasionally visited Belmont Street, to hang out with my play Cousin, Jimmy "Blue" Robinson and his mother, Evelyn. They were not related to me, as was the case with Smokey and Jimmy. They just shared the same last name. Smokey, is an alumni of Northern High School, also. By the time that I entered Northern in 1964, Smokey was long gone. However, I did rub elbows in the halls of Northern with Smokey's nieces and nephews, who were among the best-dressed students at Northern. They and other slicksters would strut their wears like peacocks amongst the crows in the hallways of Northern High, in the mid-1960's.

Melvin Franklin, one of the original members of the Temptations, didn't exactly reside on the northend. Melvin, also was older than me. Melvin was about Smokey's age. They were young men, at the time that I was a teenager in high school. Melvin's sister who was affectionately called, Tootsie, was a friend of mine at Northern. On occasion, I visited, Tootsie, at her mother's house located on the westside on Clairmont Street, across the street from Herman Kiefer Hospital. I never had an opportunity to meet Smokey or Melvin; but, I got to meet and know some members of their family's. Therefore, I'm taking it upon myself to anoint, Melvin Frankin, as an honorary northender. Tootsie's real name was Geradine Franklin. I lost touch with her after I dropped out of high school.

From time to time, I got glimpses of Tootsie, riding out with one of the westside fly guys in his brand new shiny, black 1967 convertible Deville, with its opulent black-and-white Leopard-print-top dropped, exposing the exotic (for the times), black Leopard-print interior, that made suckers feel inferior. On a warm summer's evening, Tootsie's hair was flowing in the air, she was looking suave and debonair, leaning with a gangstress lean. The pair looked like black, Hollywood movie stars on that warm summer night. I stood alone on the sidewalk watching them cruise by me like a first-run movie made in the streets. Riding out in that classy Cadillac convertible, seemingly without a care, with their hair flowing in the warm night air. The object of Tootsie's affection was a smooth fair skinned young player, who was known by his street name, Pigeon. Pigeon, had more game and finesse than your average nineteen year old. I witnessed playa's driving some slick-ass rides during that era, parading up and down Woodward Avenue in the spring of 1967. There were many slick rides out cruising; but, only one new Cadillac sporting a custom-Leopard-print convertible top, featuring matching Leopard-print interior. That made suckers once again feel inferior. Pigeon, had his own signature flavor when it came to stylin' and profilin.' Pigeon, knew how to get his hook-up on too, from head to toe. A year later the black Deville, was upgraded for a new 1968, lavender El Capaliro Eldorado, with a decked-out pearl white leather top, with white leather interior. That was some vicious game back in 1968, for a 20-year-old player. His hair stayed whipped and his bankroll stayed flipped. Pretty boy, had Macaroni runnin' all thru his veins. Too bad it was all short-lived. He caught a case for being a little to slick. The young man did a good bit. Five years later he was cut loose. When paroled he attracted the jealousy crowd. Pigeon, was stabbed to death in Paul William's after-hour Joint, the Celebrity Club on Purtian and Prairie, on the northwest side in the late seventies. You had to be a cowardly merchant of evil to hurt Pigeon like that, he was slick, but, he had a good heart and he wouldn't hurt a fly. Pigeon shined in his prime. Too bad he got played by "The game of life." Pigeon didn't live to see thirty years old.

Me and some of my young buddies hung out in front of Phelps Lounge, on Oakland near Owens on the northend. We were there to catch a glimpse of the headline acts, such as Jackie Wilson, Ike and Tina Turner, Chuck Jackson and other black entertainers of that ilk who were entering Phelps Lounge. I was just a green-ass kid hanging out front checking out the scene. John Lee Hooker, the famous blues man played the Apex Lounge on Oakland and Clay. Hooker lived near the Apex Lounge. Judge Samual Gardner, at one point in his illustrious career in the 1980's, was the Chief Judge of Detroit's Recorders Court. Judge Gardner, was also an alumni of

Northern High School. All of the original members of the Four Tops, singing group lived on the northend before their fame. There was a Welterweight boxer, by the name of Hedgamon Lewis. In the beginning of his sterling career, Hedgamon trained at the Considine Center on the northend. Later he went on to become the "Welterweight Champion of the World" in the mid-seventies. For a hot minute, I tried my hand at boxing during that moment in time. At times, I trained with Hedgemon. Hedgemon, was a serious fighter and all business when it came to boxing. Cornius Brooks, was a different kind of friend. Cornius, was more intellectual than my usual crop of friends who were considered as my mellows. Corny, (That's what I called him.) was an aspiring musician who also sang. The real reason that I hung out with Corny, was that he had an older brother who was in a singing group. They used to rehearse in their family's small cramped apartment. I can remember them singing, "Blue Moon." Boy, could they sing. The quartet consisted of four male teens. I don't remember the name of their group; but, they were real good. Corny's family didn't live in the area very long.

Like a lot of northenders, some family's started moving up to higher ground. In most cases others were pushed down to public housing. The Brewster Projects, Jefferies Projects and other low-rent districts. Hanging out I mainly stuck with a core group of friends who lived in my vicinity.

I started Palmer Elementary School, in the 2nd grade. Palmer was a small red-brick school house of lower expectation. Regardless, it was a fun place. I couldn't wait to get there in the morning. Even though the school was small, it looked and felt huge to a second grader. One of the first kids to befriend me (as mentioned before) was Anthony Walker, AKA, Antman and his older brother, Steve. Ant and Steve were very good athletes and lived with their grandmother. When their grandmother died they were just about on their own. Before we reached our teens, Steve and Ant were out there trying to survive. On some cold nights they would wait up in our apartment until their uncle Ray came to pick them up late at night. I learned a valuable lesson watching Steve and Ant go through their trials and tribulations at such a young age. The lesson I learned was: no matter how poor you are, or how low your life may appear, there's always someone in a deeper hole. In high school, Steve was the star quarterback on Northern's football team, even though he was a short man who stood around 5' 6," he had a body like Adonis. I like writing about the people who touched my life in some profound way. After all, I couldn't tell my story without interjecting bits of their stories. After high school, Steve went on to serve his country in Vietnam. He survived Vietnam's carnage; but, he couldn't survive the war at home. The drugs, the thugs, the guns, the racism and blight proved to be a toxic blend for a young man coming home from a war. The drugs led Steve to robbery, the robbery led him to murder, and the murder led him to prison. He served 13 years inside of Jackson Prison. When paroled he finished college and settled down. Unfortunately, on this August day in 2007, I'm reading Steve's obituary. Given to me by another childhood friend, Wanda Crisp. Steve died in 2006, this was the first I had heard of his death. Farewell my friend may God, bless you. Steve joins his younger brother and my childhood friend, Antman. Antman, self-destructed in the late 1970's, may his soul also rest in peace.

I hated bullies and my neighborhood was full of bullies. Bullies are actually cowards who pick on smaller kids. Like the bully, Elijah Colly, AKA, Bootie Bop. He was generally referred to as Bop. That's a strange name. I don't know the origin of his nickname; but, it fit him to a "T." I suppose it had much to do with his Jones for fighting. I remember Bop arguing with another neighborhood bully on the steps of my apartment building. The older bully was Eddie Will. Eddie, was a nonchalant bully. You fuck with Eddie, Eddie, fuck you up, plain and simple. The confrontation turned violent. Eddie, stepped up to Bop in a threatening manner and Bop, ran off toward his family's shack. I'm calling it a shack, because that's what it was. A two-room shack shared by him, his three brothers, his mother and her boy friend. Don't ask me. I don't know where they all slept. Maybe their shack transformed into a metamorphosis at night and got bigger. Anyway, a few moments later, Bop, returned. He was carrying a paper bag and eating potato chips out of it. He casually walked up to an unsuspecting Eddie. Bop, extended his hand as if he wanted to make peace. Eddie, extended his own hand as an olive branch. In a flash, the paper bag came crashing down on top of Eddie's head. The bag had a hammer concealed inside of it. Bop, took off running like a frightened, Rat. Eddie, laid sprawled out on our steps, bleeding profusely from his head wound. I lost track of Eddie Will over time. Bop eventually found his way to Jackson Prison for armed robbery. He had to feed his Heroin habit. Prison was good for Bop. When he was paroled, Bop earned his bachelor's degree and a masters degree from U Of M's Dearborn Campus. Eventually, he went on to work as a drug counselor. Bop, turned his life all the way around. He remained good friends with Beanie and Slim, until cancer and diabetes laid him to rest in 2002.

Charlie Coleman, AKA, Junie Boy and his younger brother, Ninny, along with their cousin, Edmond Monroe, AKA, Blood, were all destined to die young. They were teenage drug dealers, who lived an unsupervised-"Helter-Skelter" existence, where anything and everything goes. I don't remember them attending school. They lived around the corner from me on Custer Street, next door to Bop. Success came quickly for them in the 1970's slinging that "tragic magic," better known as "mixed jive," a diluted form of Heroin. They drove black Cadillacs and sported fancy duds. In the end both brothers (Junie and Ninny) were shot dead. Neither of them made it to their 25th birthday. Blood didn't fare much better. He went on to do a lengthy stretch in prison. Once released he found his way back into the drug trade. His fate sealed, he too was murdered on the mean streets of Detroit. Their mentor and role model, Tom (Teribble Tom) Morgan, has been in a California Prison, for more than 25 years doing natural life for murder. Rumer has it that Tom died in prison.

About three months into my new school, Palmer Elementary, on a cold snowy morning, me and other children were playing on the playground before the school bell rang to start morning classes. Suddenly, I spotted my target, the new kid in the thin blue-jean jacket with his hands tucked in his pockets trying to keep them warm. He was just like me once, fresh and didn't know anyone. So I packed a snowball tight and hurled it at the new kid's head. Blam! it found its mark. The new kid was not in a playful mood. All of seven years old, he whipped out a knife and chased me into the school. Fortunately for me I ran into a teacher. The teacher asked me if there was a problem? I could have busted the new kid and gotten him in trouble for pulling the knife out. I felt partly to blame. After all, I did smack him in the head with a snowball. "Ain't nothing happening" was my reply to the teacher. The new kid was impressed. I didn't snitch on him. We offered each other apologies and walked to class together. I introduced my new friend, to my old friends. "My name is Malon Mckinny. Everybody calls me Mack." I found out later that Mack, came from a large family. Mack's mother, Tina, gave birth to seven boys and one girl. When I first met Mack, I didn't know what to make of him. Here was this dirt-poor kid, poorer than me with a lot of siblings. From the oldest to the youngest, there was Joe, who was one strange cookie. Joe was about 15 or 16 when the Mckinnys moved on Bethune. Joe would leave the neighborhood and disappear for weeks and months at a time, and I never heard Joe speak a word, ever. To this day I don't know what his voice sounds like. I learned from Mack, that when Joe disappeared, he was most likely in jail. Somewhere down the line, Joe, just up and vanished for good, he probably was in jail.

Julius, was the next oldest and the most well-adjusted sibling in that family. He was one of two brothers in their family whose father was involved in their lives. The Mckinnys, all had different fathers. Julius, who everyone called Boot and his family lived down the street from me on Bethune. I could look down the street and see Boot's father pick him up every week like clock work. In our neighborhood that was a rarity. Being in Boot's siblings position myself with my own brothers, I'm sure the attention that Boot, received from his father made his siblings jealous, as was the case with me watching my own brothers bask in the attention showered on them by their father. Boot, was the square in the family. He will be destined to bury most of his family members.

The next eldest was Arthur Mckinny, everyone affectionately called him Jerry, or Jerry Ross, the ladies boss with the hot sauce. Don't let the soft name fool you. Jerry, was one of the toughest little fellows you ever gon' scrap with. Like his brother Mack, he too wore a thin blue jean jacket to school in the dead of winter. Jerry was the smartest and the best looking of the brood. He looked soft; but, was tough as nails. Due to his frail stature he was a prime target for bullies in our neighborhood. Many a bully would find out that he was not to be fucked with. Jerry didn't play when it came to fighting. I can recall one fight he had on a cold blustery winter's day. I was making my usual trek home from school, up ahead a fight had broken out. When a fight broke out all the students would form a circle around the combatants to instigate and egg the combatants on. I couldn't see who the combatants were from my vantage point. As I walked closer, I could see one of the neighborhood bullies, Johnny Collins, a tall sixth-grader with buck-teeth getting man-handled by a little frail 4th grader who had to jump up to hit, Johnny, in the mouth. Jerry, was pounding the bully relentlessly. This small, cold, frail kid who was the hunted, has now become the hunter. Johnny was stunned. "Ain't no fun when the rabbit's got the gun." Johnny had a panicked, pained expression etched across his bloody face, like a Elephant, trying to flee a Mouse. Poor fella' tried to get away, but, Jerry, had him collared as he blooded Johnnie's nose and mouth some more. Johnny, managed to break lose and hauled ass down the street with fear in his heart and embarrassment in his eyes. Jerry, was cheered like a hero. From that moment on all the bullies got the message that Jerry Ross was nothing to be fucked with.

As we got older, Jerry was the life of the party, and the good looking young girls all clamored for his attention, which made the fellows jealous, including me. Jerry, was a complex individual who seemed to struggle between good and evil acts. I'm of the notion that if evil permeates one's environment, evil will attract those individuals who are most vulnerable to evil's lure, poor folks and others living on the fringes of our society. There are powerful forces and influences at work here, that infiltrates the psyche of some young poor boys and girls. Black, white, yellow and brown individuals who gravitate toward evil's power. I characterized Jerry, as being a wolf in sheep's clothing, soft on the outside, ferocious on the inside.

When I was about twenty-two years old, I had an apartment on Hazelwood, between Second and Third Street, on the lower westside. One of Jerry's girl friends lived down the street. One must keep in mind that this was the early 1970's and there was a fashion-fad sweeping the nation: men carrying saddle-bag type purses. Mack, and I were leaving my apartment one afternoon when we spotted Jerry, leaving his girl's apartment down the street. We hustled down there to kick it with him. He was carrying one of those purses. Jerry, pulled out a thick wad of cash from the purse, then said. "Y'all better get some of this shit." His brother, Mack, who was fresh home from the pen, at the sight of the cash in Jerry's hand, joked. "Somebody gon' snatch yo' purse." Jerry, laughing, replied. "Yeah, and they gon' snatch this" as he slid a .45 caliber pistol out of the saddle-bag type purse. Mack, Jerry and I had a good chuckle over that line. It's strange how some people can have a profound impact on individuals long after they've passed away. For me, Jerry, was one of those individuals. It pains me to imagine what that smart, intelligent, brave brother could have been if he had had more positive strokes in his adolescence. The inner city's are full of neglected kids; males and females. They are no good to the human race if they die young.

Jerry, pulled off something that even, Steve Walker, couldn't do, and Steve was tough, tough. Jerry, whipped Bop's ass and chased him off the bean house porch. Jerry, had a bag full of beans (Barbiturates) on him. Just as a police cruiser pulled up, Bop ran up to the edge of the porch and stabbed Jerry in the leg. Bop, was to embarrassed not to retaliate from the ass-whoopin' Jerry put on him. The two cops drew their weapons and arrested Bop on the spot.

Malon, the fourth youngest brother was my age (as alluded to earlier) and everyone called him Mack. He was the conflicted brother who possessed genius like artistic talents. Mack and I became confidants. Mack, would reveal to me some of the darkest moments of his young life. Mack, confided in me about a frightening experience he had. When he was about three years old, rats attacked him in his bed. He would always start the story; but, he could never finish it. Mack, would always break out in a cold sweat, as if he were re-living a nightmare. My personal observation on that is, that some individuals are so traumatized by certain events in their development, that they can never escape its impact. We need more concerned, competent child psychologists working in concert with at-risk mothers, who are struggling with child-rearing. Most poor young mothers are trying to cope with a myriad of social issues stacked on top of other problems. Society must find solutions to curb learning abnormalities in targeted-individuals while in their adolescence. Society would benefit greatly by producing happy well-adjusted individuals. We're raising our children as if we're expecting them to fail. Malon Mckinny, and those of us reared such as him and shared a similar plight, we are prime examples of that ("fail") phenomenon. At times, Mack, would vent his displeasure regarding the lack of information regarding his biological father's identity. I shared my concerns regarding my own father's identity. We both had a burning desire to understand and to be a part of our family's heritage. Mack confided that he would often try to pull snippets of information from his mother about his father; but, to no avail. I confided in Mack about my own concerns as well. I had similar concerns surrounding my own lack of information regarding my own conception. The venting session with Mack, prompted me once again to confront, Beanie, about my dear old dad. Some parents die and leave their children unsolvable challenges regarding their DNA makeup. It's like trying to solve a no beginning, no ending paradox about one's own existence. It can be a daunting endeavor tracing one's roots, when there's no trail to follow.

Mack, was a talented artist with a God given gift. Even as a young boy Mack could create remarkable works of art. He created in pencil, charcoal, water colors, as well as oils. He also had the ability to sculpt an ordinary clothes hanger into an elaborate piece of art. For example, we were sitting on his mothers front porch one evening, Mack, was twisting and bending a clothes hanger. When he was finished he held in his hand a perfectly sculpted rocking horse. The intensity in his eyes while creating the horse was a study in concentration. I was really in awe of Mack's talents.

Mr. Hubbard, had golden blonde hair and was of German descent. He spoke English in a German accent. Mack and I learned later that Mr. Hubbard, was an art collector, who leaned toward the old masters: Van Gogh, Monet, Gaughan, Micheal Angelo, and other old-world artists. Mack and I had the same homeroom and the same classes. We shared an art class as well. Mack would draw beautiful landscapes, and detailed portraits of some of our teachers and students; while the rest of the class was scribbling out mediocre pieces. Not Mack, he meticulously and methodically created masterpieces, compared to his classmates. We were just your average 10-year-old Negroes. Our social studies class started right after art class. Mack brought some of his art to Mr. Hubbard's class one day for safe keeping. A curious Mr. Hubbard got a glance at some of Mack's art laying on his desk. It was by chance that he was passing by Mack's desk. Mr. Hubbard began rifling through the stack of drawings. Mr. Hubbard was impressed. He quizzed Mack about who drew the pictures. Mack replied. "I did." With that, we gained a new friend. I was befriended because I was Mack's buddy. Mr. Hubbard, this German teacher with our mothers blessings showed us a Detroit, that we would otherwise never have known existed. Detroit is a big city. Being young, poor and black our world was mainly limited to our neighborhood. Mr. Hubbard took us on field trips after school. He would pick us up at home and load us into his trusty Volkswagen. We visited Tiger Stadium to watch the Detroit Tigers play in summer and the Detroit Lions play in winter. I once caught a chin strap thrown into the stands by Lucien Reburg, Reburg a rarity at the time was a 300 pound rookie tackle for the Lions. Mr. Reburg only played a couple of seasons before succumbing to Leukemia. I remember reading about his death in the Detroit Times, on my paper route.

There were visits to the Detroit Zoo, and the Main Public Library. After we left the library we headed across the street to the Detroit Institute of Arts. (DIA) As the three of us strolled the storied galleries of the DIA, Mr. Hubbard critiqued the art and artist as we passed their creations. The art history lessons were eye-openers. They had a profound effect on my growing intellect. Those lessons will remain with me "until the day that I am no more."

We discovered the mastery of the artists, Vincent Van Gogh, Pablo Picasso, Caghal, Chezan, Monet and many more of the great masterpieces, from throughout the ages. There was much to absorb with our virgin vision and mentalities as we strolled along the treasured galleries of that place called the DIA. There was one piece of art that struck a cord with Mack. It was one of Van Gogh's self-portraits. The one featuring Van Gogh, wearing a bright, yellow straw hat with his bandaged ear; In a battle with depression Van Gogh cut off his ear. The raised brush strokes, Van Gogh's piercing blue eyes and the vivid colors must have been awe-inspiring to Mack. The next day when Mack showed up for classes he presented Mr.

Hubbard, with his crude version of Van Gogh's painting with all the details down to the straw hat and bandaged ear. In Mack's version there was a slight twist, Mack had painted Mr. Hubbard's face in the painting instead of Van Gogh's. When Mack, presented the painting to Mr. Hubbard, he just stared at it shaking his head in disbelief. At that moment in time, Mack, had created admirers for life in Mr. Hubbard, and me. I'm now fifty-six-years old as of this writing, Mack and Mr. Hubbard, are no longer residing on planet earth. They went on to meet their maker. I would like to add that Mr. Hubbard, gave me new vision on how to view the world and all its wonders. He was the closest thing to a caring father, that I, or Mack, would come to know. Today, many of the artists named in this writing; some of their works have adorned my walls throughout my adult life. Though only prints, they are all important to me because of all the fond memories they evoke. Thank you, Mr. Hubbard, for your knowledge, insight and diligence.

Interacting with Mr. Hubbard, made me even more curious about my biological father. Again, I conjured up the nerve to inquire about my dear old dad. Soon as I got Fa...out of my mouth. Beanie cut me off. She knew what was coming and chose not to deal with it. Something bad must have happened between the two people responsible for my being. I try to rationalize and move on; but, it keeps seeping back into my consciousness. In my mind only an idiot would disregard his or her own heritage. Humans inherit forty six chromosomes, 23 from their mother and 23 from their father. I just can't ignore my DNA makeup. Unfortunately, this is how many a parent, (or parents) are raising their children; as if they are going to grow into idiots, oblivious to their own lineage. I would urge parents in similar predicaments to deal with the truth early in their child's development: the good, the bad, and the scandalous. Get it out early so you and your children can move forward in your relationship.

As we grew older, Mack became more and more violent, mainly stabbings and robberies. Mack was too light to fight and too thin to win. But, baby-boy was deadly with a weapon in his hand. He wouldn't hesitate to use one either. From time to time I would run into Mack. One night I was standing outside of Tate's Market, kickin' it with Mack and a few of my neighborhood chums. We were about 15 years old at the time, just horse playing on a warm summer's night. A stranger parked his car on the side of Tate's building and got out of his car to enter Tate's Market. Mack caught everyone off guard. Mack casually walked up to the stranger and stabbed him in the collar bone area. Blood shot out of the man's wound like a spigot. Mack looked wide-eyed at the blade on his knife and proclaimed,

"Damn, it didn't break." With that, everybody scattered in different directions. I was stunned at his actions. I think when Mack stabbed that poor fellow, perhaps in his twisted mind he was stabbing his father. That's just my take on that. I didn't hang with Mack much after that incident. At seventeen, Mack committed an armed robbery. The year was 1966 and Malon Mckinny, all of 17 years old, was on his way to the Wayne County Jail to await his trial. I'm referring to the old concrete-and-steel jail, which is still in operation today, located on Monroe in downtown Detroit. The new county jail was a few decades away from being built. The jail featured no modern conveniences of todays jails, this was the real deal. After being locked up for several months, Mack's family managed to bail him out of jail until his trial. Unfortunately, Mack's life was in his hands and he fumbled the ball. He committed another armed robbery while out on bail. This time there will be no bail. He was out on bail for only a few weeks before he was headed back to jail. After six months in the county jail it was time for Mack to pay the piper. Mack opted out for a trial and plea bargained with the court. Both sentences ran concurrent. In other words he would do both sentences as one. Mack received seven and a half to fifteen years in the Michigan penal system. In prison, he would learn to be even more deadly.

Now comes Wizard. He was the strange son, even more strange than his older brother, Joe. Wizard was a sullen figure who sulked around our neighborhood in search of trouble. His eyes conveyed a tale of neglect. One could surmise that Wizard had been through some serious shit. He was Zombie-like roaming through our neighborhood in search of something to steal. Wizard's a difficult subject. From time to time I would revisit my old stumping grounds on the northend. Often I would see Wizard, roaming the same streets some forty-odd years later. The only difference now he gets around with the aid of crutches.

Their sister was more tragic than them all. Out of respect for her family, even though most of them are dead. I'll just leave her be.

They had another brother who was orphaned off at a young age. The youngest son, Harry, also knew his father. Harry maintained and seemed to have defeated the demons that claimed most of his family member's lives.

There you have 'em the Mckinnys, one big (at some point in time) happy, dysfunctional family, warts and all. Led by the two fisted Matriarch of the clan Tina Mckinny, their mother was tougher than them all put together.

"Fried, dyed, whipped to the side," was one of the favorable quotes expressed after one's hair was freshly laid. One of the local true Macaroni's Jimmy Diamond, put his own spin on his hair style. When complimented on his hair, Diamond would exclaim in his slick pimp-tone. "That's why I got two barbers: one to lay 'em down, and one to lift 'em up." That was Jimmy Diamond's signature tag when complimented on his freshly whipped doo, followed by his familiar cackle.

Pimpin' Jimmy Diamond

Chapter 5

FRIED, DYED, WHIPPED TO THE SIDE

My family struggled through the gloom and doom days of yesteryear, then forged ahead to the glory days of tomorrow. On a warm beautiful summer evening on Cherry Street, children played in that mixed neighborhood of poor African-Americans and Mexican citizens. My brother, Slim, and a neighborhood little Mexican girl (both were no older than six years old at the time), were playing in the front yard. Their play turned into anger, their anger turned into shoving, and their shoving turned into hitting, and the hitting led to Slim getting stabbed in the back by the little Mexican girl, wielding a broken umbrella spoke clutched in her hand. Slim, even at the tender age of six, he was always getting into scraps with other kids. This particular spat almost led to Slims demise. Slim was bleeding profusely from the deep gash in his back. He started crying at the top of his lungs. We were scared to death at the sight of all his blood gushing from the wound. Beanie rushed him to a hospital. He had lost a lot of blood. The Doctor that attended to him told Beanie that another inch and a main artery would have been ruptured. He, then would have bled to death, Slim survived to live another day.

A violent incident involving myself also occurred on Cherry Street. Several months before Slim's stabbing, I was sitting in the hull of the burnt-out-shell of an old car decaying in a vacant field near our house. I was sitting in the car pretending to drive. I was in my own little world. I wasn't paying attention to the gathering horde of boys and girls, until it was too late to act. They had me surrounded and began throwing hands full of gravel at me from all directions. I couldn't escape their barrage, they were pounding me from all sides, with the stinging gravel assaulting my body and face. I was in trouble. I had no one there to help me. I threw my hands up trying to ward off their assault. They were laughing and having a good time at my suffering. Somehow, I found the strength to pull myself out of that torture chamber. I thought I was going to die, it was that bad. Decades later it still smolders in my consciousness. That was one of my first lessons on ghetto living, always be aware of your surroundings. The older I got the more adventurous I became. At age fourteen me and some of my mellow's rode the Woodward bus downtown. We referred to those trips as the other world, where White people ruled, and downtown was wall-to-wall with White people. Window shopping downtown is where I discovered hip fashion and the secrets of where all the sharp dudes in my neighborhood shopped. I now know where they got their sharp-fresh pieces from: at stores like Kosin's, which was the ultimate place in hip men's fashions. Harry and Ben Kosin, were the owners of Kosin's Men's Wear. The Jewish brothers dressed like black players. If Harry and Ben were not Jews, some would have declared them entertainers or pimps. I guess it was part of their marketing ploy. Kosin's was where most of the pimps and other underworld-money-men shopped. I would hang outside of the store drooling over the fabulous window display, imagining myself stepping out in Kosin's finery. Around the corner on Washington Boulevard, sat Whitehouse and Hardy's, a ritzy, upscale store that intimidated me with its glitz. I dared not to venture inside that glitzy abode. One block south on Washington Boulevard, sat Scholnick's Fine Menswear, whose display-window rivaled Kosin's for the slick dude dollar. One block further south on Washington Boulevard sat, Citron's. The virgin wool Hi-Lo shirts and Alpaca sweaters were Citron's main attractions. North on Washington Boulevard, across from Grand Circus Park, on Adams was Ben B. Burkes, home of the Old Masters Stetson Shoes. If one had any game or style, they bought their Gypsy Splits, Gators, Lizards and a wide range of other Stetson shoes from Ben B. Burke's collection. Stetson's was to my generation what Air Jordans are to today's youth. East, over on Randolph, you had Serman's Menswear, Todd's Menswear and Cancellation Shoes. Around the corner was Hot Sams Menswear. All the stores mentioned were owned and operated by Jews. In the middle of all that, stood the giants, Hudson's and Crowley's Department stores, whose owners were pure Anglo-Saxon Whites. Hudson's was number one in volume and Crowley's was a distant second. Yeah, downtown was booming: restaurants, five-and-ten-cent stores, along with an array of jewelry stores and other retail outlets like Mary Jane's, United Shirts, Jacobson's and Sanders Ice Cream Parlor. Movie theaters like the Fox on Woodward were the creme-de-le-creme along with the United Artist on Adams, and the Palms on Woodward, (A stones throw from the Fox) the Madison, the Fine Arts, and the Grand Circus, were all downtown jewels that littered the landscape of a very busy downtown Detroit. I didn't realize it then, but, looking back on it. The sad thing about downtown Detroit, was that Black people didn't own any of the Jewel's back in the good old days.

Back home things had gone from bad to worst between Beanie and Wig. During this period of our lives, our next door neighbor, Lula, and her family had moved out. A new family moved in. The Salmons hailed from Mississippi. They were a dirt-poor hard working family, like many poor blacks who migrated north from the south. Poor and illiterate, Mr. John, couldn't read or write. I don't know if that applied to his other family members. Despite his short comings, Mr. John managed to land a job at a local auto plant, Dodge Main. Mr. John, A tall muscular man who smelled of Nozema face cream, was destined to become my mother's knight in shiny armor. Mr. John's wife worked as a maid at Lee Plaza Hotel on the Boulevard. Across the street from Northwestern High School. Mr. John had two sons, both were named John: John Henry and John Jr.. John Jr. was my age, John Henry, was older than us by at least ten years. Since we were neighbors and John Jr. was my age. I took it upon myself to show him the ropes.

Fannie Jones, was a girl in my class at Palmer, she had a crush on me. One day after school she asked me to walk her home. I jumped at the opportunity and employed John Jr. to join me because I would be going into a hostile environment. I felt the need for backup. When we approached the building Fannie lived in, four young dudes were sitting on her front porch. They gave me and John a hard stare-down. I asked her who were they. She replied, that one of them was her boyfriend. "No shit," was my response. With that, the quartet was off the porch and headed in our direction. I told John to follow my lead. I took off running like I had stole something. Jr. was on my tail. We made it back to Bethune, where familiar faces waited to take up our slack. The quartet realized they were now, themselves in hostile territory and quickly hauled ass back to Smith Street. John was slow and country. He didn't know the ins and outs of big city living. He'll learn or get his ass kicked. Mr. John worked days and was home in the evening. His wife worked evenings. Wig was off somewhere drinking most evenings when he got off work at midnight. To reach our apartment you had to walk up three flights of stairs. From the entrance, I could look up and see Beanie and Mr. John talking in the dark hallway on occasion. By the time that I had reached the top of the stairs, he had ducked back into his apartment. At the time they were having their little rendezvous in the hallway. I thought nothing about what was transpiring between Beanie and Mr. John.

I graduated from Palmer Elementary in 1960, I was headed to Sherrard Jr. High. I was officially a teenager. I had made it to the seventh grade. Sherrard was located in a tough neighborhood on Euclid and Camaron. The students were older, bigger and better dressed. Sherrard was a big, sturdy, brick building with a huge playfield. Students from all of the local elementary schools on the northend found their way to Sherrard, once they graduated from the various elementary schools in the area. Most students landed in Sherrard or Hutchinson Jr. High School on the westside, in the Philadaphia-Woodrow Wilson area. The classrooms and gym at Sherrard were much bigger than Palmers. Sherrard also had a swimming pool. Life was looking pretty good. Sherrard also had intramural basketball teams, made up of the student body. Academics were structured. To top it all off we had recreation three nights a week. My brothers and I could get out of our cramped apartment and go swimming or play organized basketball in the winter. We had some great mentors and coaches, older high school students who gave of their time and energy without retribution or pay; just plain old self-gratification was their reward. The only person to get paid for his service's was Mr. Sheppard who happened to be a white referee in an all-black school league. Damn, how in the hell did the darker persuasion stand for that. I was just a kid and often wondered about that. I now realize it was the times we were living in.

Blue Massey, was an All-City high school athlete who excelled in four sports: football, basketball, baseball and track. Yeah, I said, Massey, was All-City in four sports. That was in the early 1960's. Somehow the powers that be let Massey slip through their lily white fingers. Massey gave us lessons in sports and in life. Life lessons were taught not so much in what he said; but, how he carried himself. Massey, was a quiet, dignified poor young man; whom, I never saw smoke or drink. Another one of his unique characteristics was that he never used foul language in our presence. Blue Massey in my book was not only an All-City athlete; but, an all-world citizen of these United States of America. Bill Buntin was one of "the tallest trees in the forest," both physically and spiritually, cut from the same fabric of life as Blue Massey. Bill Buntin honed his athletic skills on the play fields of the northend. Then he went on to lead Northern High School to basketball championships in the late fifties. Buntin was recruited by the University of Michigan, where he teamed up with another future All-American basketball player, Cassie Russell, to lead the Wolverines to a championship during the 1964-1965 season. Mr. Buntin, was a great basketball player and an even greater humanitarian. I can recall one hot summer's day in the late fifties, Mr. Buntin was putting our little league baseball team through some drills, when Jimmy Evans and his gang came on the playground looking for trouble. Jimmy started hassling our third-baseman about some old-beef the gang had with him. Mr. Buntin stepped in and ordered Jimmy and his gang off the playground; while he stood in front of the threatened kid. Buntin, later walked the kid home to ensure his safety. I never understood why Blue Massey never became a pro' athlete. Buntin, on the other hand was too tall, too talented and too smart to be over-looked by college recruiters. Buntin was a ferocious re-bounder. His rebounds, even today have stood the test of time. He's the second all-time re-bounder for U of M, with a 13.1 average per game, and ranks fourth in career scoring, with a 21.8 points per game average. The team's annual most valuable players award is named after Buntin. Buntin died from a heart attack in 1968 at age twenty-six.

Two of his brothers also died from the same genetic defect. The Pistons drafted Buntin in 1965. He also signed a contract with the Detroit Lions. Due to his untimely illness, he never played for the Lions. If God had blessed me with a big brother, Bill Buntin and Blue Massey would have been the perfect template. I Just finished reading a story in the Detroit Free Press that Buntin's Jersey, No. 22, will be retired at U of M's basketball opener for the 2005-2006 season, it's long over due.

The year was 1962, I was nearing my 14th birthday. I was primping in the mirror trying to decide which side of my head that the new stingy-brimmed hat looked the best on. Hey, that was a big deal to a 14-year-old, who's never possessed a hat that sharp before. My libido was awakening and sweet young damsels are dancing in my head. In our small apartment, with one bathroom to serve five people, one hardly had a chance to primp in the mirror before being interrupted by someone wanting to use the bathroom. Girls were not the only thing I'd discovered. I too had discovered Konk, the hair straightener (when applied right), could transform the ordinary-looking guy, into an extraordinary-looking guy. Most of the older fellows wore a doo, or its technical term, a process. In my neighborhood the place to go get your hair processed was Joe's Barbershop, located on Oakland near Clay Street. Warren and Dickie, were wave masters of processed hair. Preachers, pimps, gang-bangers, gamblers, and plain old working folks, even high school students got their hair laid at Joe's Barbershop. There were many hair styles to choose from: the quo vadis, slicked-down to the front, or with finger waves, or one could go with a straight back with finger waves pumped up in the front. The slant-back-was combed slanted to the side with finger waves. We even had a hair style named after a president "The JFK," was named after President Kennedy. There was also a hair style named after the actor, Tony Curtis." Fried, dyed, whipped to the side," was one of the more favorable quotes expressed after one's hair was freshly whipped. One of the local true pimps, Jimmy Diamond, put his own spin on his hair style. When complimented on his hair, Diamond would exclaim in his slick pimp-tone. "That's why I got two barbers: one to lay 'em down, and one to lift 'em up." That was Jimmy Diamond's signature tag when complimented on his freshly-whipped doo, followed by his familiar cackle.

My first process was an experiment done in our bathroom on Bethune. I can't recall how I got my hands on the konk. I opened up the jar of konk then I proceeded to give myself a doo. I fucked my whole head up, I burned my scalp and pulled out patches of my hair. I was a mess. Steve Walker came to my rescue and lent me the money ($4.50) to let the pros at Joe's, fix up what I had screwed up. At 14, I was ripe for new experiences. My first visit to Joe's Barbershop was an adventure into strange new terrain for me. Entering the barbershop, the first thing to hit you was the aroma: konk, Wildroot Cream Oil, hair conditioner, and an assortment of hair sprays drifted throughout the barbershop, like a fine mist on a foggy morning. The scents pulled me in with the swirl of sweet aromatic aromas assaulting my senses. My ears perked up as I tried to decipher the colorful language being spewed out by the restless patrons, waiting for their turn in their favorite barber's chair. Then my eyes focused on the stylish customers with their freshly-coifed hair and impeccable attire, decked out in Hi-Lo shirts, (the cool fashionable shirts of that era) with either iridescent or silk and wool slack's. Lizards and Alligator shoes reigned supreme inside of Joe's Barbershop, while the barbers were busy plying their trade. Joe's was a cool place to a young-blood like me getting his first professional doo. When it was my turn, Warren waved me over to his chair, sat me down, then he draped me with his barber's apron, then he proceeded to run his fingers through my hair. Chewing on his unlit cigar, Warren proclaimed in his southern drawl. "Yo hair kinda dry, you got to keep oil in it." Then he belted out. "Hey man, what you done to your hair?" I explained that I tried to do my own hair. Shaking his head, he said. "Gon' give you a touch-up for now and a good conditioner. I'll bring it back to life." First he trimmed the edges, then he shaped and tapered the back with his barber clippers. He began to straighten the edges with konk until my head started tingling. Warren blurted. "Is it getting warm to you?" I said. "Yeah." With that, he laid my head back into a sink, then he started washing the chemicals out of my hair. After he finished rinsing my hair, he poured some cold liquid conditioner over my hair. Then he massaged the conditioner into my hair, then he rinsed it out, pulled the chair back to an upright position, then he began to work his magic. He asked me how did I want it styled? I told him a quo vadis with waves. With that, he let his fingers go to work combing and pulling my hair into place. When he had it slicked down all the way around, he began to press finger waves into the top of my head with his fingers and a comb. When Warren was finished waving me, he tied two white tissue strips around his handy work, tapped me on the shoulders to get up, then led me to a dryer and placed my head under the dryer. All of that was done with music from the Juke box swirling throughout the shop. It was Christmas time and every other song being played by the patrons was Nat King Cole's, "The Little Boy Santa Claus Forgot" or Nat's, "The Christmas Song" which put the customers in a mellow mood with its melodic sound. Yeah, Christmas time in Joe's was a good place to escape and enjoy the good camaraderie of other's who were there with the same goal as you: to look good for the holidays. As Warren was putting the finishing touches on my doo, in walked none other than the great, Little Stevie Wonder, holding the arm of his brother, Calvin. They were out of breath, as if they had run to the barbershop. I found out, through their conversation with the owner Joe, they were there inquiring about Stevie's father, Scar, who was living on the northend. Someone played one of Stevie's records on the junk box. If memory serves me right, they played "Finger Tips" and the barbershop started rocking with happy patrons. I'll never forget that day. Stevie and Calvin left before Warren had finished setting my hair. When Warren finished laying my last set of waves. He handed me a mirror to admire his handy work, I was looking real cool, which made me smile. I stepped out of the barber's chair and paid him. I didn't walk out of the barbershop. I glided across the floor with my head held high and slid on out of the door.

During the spring of 1963 at 15 years old, I began to venture away from my neighborhood, into uncharted territories. During one of my ventures, I discovered 12th Street. 12th Street was like no other street in Detroit, I had ever come across in my young life. 12th was a lively thriving section of Detroit on the lower westside, about a mile and half west from where I lived on Bethune. The heart of 12th Street, began at West Grand

Boulevard and ended at Clairmont. One could travel on 12th Street from downtown, due north, on out to Oakman Boulevard, where it ended, a six-mile stretch. The main hub where all the action took place was between West Grand Boulevard and Clairmont. 12th Street had all the trappings and fresh traps for pimps. Jews owned the pawn shops, deli's and most of the grocery stores. One could pawn anything from a pair of shoes to a suit of clothes. Brothers owned and operated the barbershops that were lined up and down the strip. That's when I discovered that Joe's wasn't the only barbershop that specialized in processing hair. The sisters owned their fair share of beauty shops. Whites owned a sprinkling of restaurants, a few confectioneries and drug stores. The Italians controlled most of the illegal activities; such as gambling, loan-sharking and in some cases, whorehouses...not the pros themselves, but, the houses of ill repute, where the pros plied their trade. The Black pimps controlled the prostitutes, who worked the streets and houses on 12th. I've got to tell you that when it comes to looking good, pimps and pros were some of the most narcissistic people on the planet. There were clothing stores and shoe stores, most were owned by Jews and whites. The brothers operated the bars and night clubs that provided top-notch black entertainment. All persuasions patronized their night clubs; such as the Chit Chat Lounge and Chesterfields Show Bar. Those were prime gathering spots for dapper men and steamy women, who played the night away. Don't read me wrong, I was too young and green to venture off into most clubs on 12th Street, but, I had big eyes, and big ears. I always listened to elders who recollected about the good old days on 12th street. As usual, the pimps and pros were the stars of 12th street, which was always packed with lively bodies. There were loads of places to get yo' groove on while bumping on 12th Street.

The barbershops were bountiful such as the Flamingo, owned and operated by a pretty, light-skinned pimp, named Benny Mullen's. The Flamingo served entertainers, pimps and other flamboyant characters who were hustling around 12th Street. The Flamingo offered hair and manicure services. Bennie Mullen's knew anybody and everybody in the game. Mr. Mullen's game was so tight that he knocked off the Motown star, Mary Wells, in her prime and made her his lovely wife. Down the strip sat the House of Process, which was equally busy with hip young players driving their ice-cream-color Cadillacs, with their matching colorful hook-ups, strutting their stuff along the avenue. It was nothing to see members of the Temptations, Four Tops, and Smoky Robinson and the Miracles getting their hair whipped, alongside of pimps like Pretty Rick, Diamond Jim Riley, Arthur

Baby, T-man, Allen Underworld, Verdell, Gerald McReynolds and the super-star entertainer, Jackie Wilson were frequent patrons of 12th Street bar-bershops. The first time I traveled to New york was in 1972. New York reminded me of 12th Street, but, on a much grander scale. New York pros were black, white and every hue in between. Most belonged to the Black pimps who were Manhattan-cruising in their super-fly drop tops looking slicker than goose shit...and that's the truth, Ruth. For most of my teen years, I was drawned back to this glitzy world called 12th street. (the baby New York.)

Elvis Presley, knew how to shake 'em down; but, Arthur Baby brought it to town. The Baby couldn't be touched when it came to that thing called dancing. On cue Arthur, broke out in dance doing the jerk. This was Arthur Baby's night. He didn't need a dance partner he brought the house down going solo. After the Baby's finale, a cluster of dazzled damsels rushed him with handkerchiefs drawned to wipe his sweaty brow.

Arthur Baby: circa 1965

Chapter 6

ARTHUR BABY'S GRAND ENTRANCE

1962 was the year that I encountered my first washed-up pimp whose game didn't keep pace with his future. He failed to diversify his game. His name was Pimp Willie. Willie resided around the corner from me on Smith Street. Pimp Willie, by the time he had meandered his broken spirit into my presence was a washed-up-ex-pimp. Willie was what was commonly referred to in the Black community as a Kool-aid pimp, the bottom of the pimp food chain. I guess Willie was about forty years old at that time. To a twelve-year-old kid that was old.

Our front steps were treated as a rest stop for the neighborhood stragglers, a place to sit and shoot the breeze with other stragglers. Pimp Willie, was one of those stragglers. Willie's doo was way past due. It was straight on the top, and nappy and mated underneath, and to add insult to injury, it was dry as hell and turning red. Willie was wearing clothes from his glory days. They were filthy and wrinkled. He looked like he had slept on someone's floor. On top of all of that he was drunk, reeking with the smell of cheap wine. What was sadder than all that shit put together. He still answered to the name Pimp Willie.

Sherrard Jr. High had some tough customers for students. One of those customers was a kid named, Al Dye. Dye, lived on the northend, across the street from my play cousin, Jimmy Blue, Dye was my age and in the same class as me. One day two burly White cops walked into our eighth-grade class one bright sunny afternoon and snatched Al out of his seat, then they dragged him out of the classroom. Al was destined to spend a lot of time locked up. I don't remember Al returning back to school, and I didn't see him again for quite sometime after his arrest in our classroom. Years later in our mid-teens he was incarcerated for a long stretch on a major bit. One could make the case that Mr. Dye grew up in the penitentiary. Many years later in the early eighties, I picked up a newspaper and read about a young man and a Highland Park police officer named Nixon, engaged in a shootout on Chandler and Woodward.

Officer Nixon, pulled Dye over, who was a motorist. Luckily, officer Nixon was wearing his bullet proof vest. As Officer Nixon exited his patrol car he was met by a hail of bullets from Dye's 357 magnum. Three rounds slammed into Nixon's chest area. Al Dye, fresh out the pen, is at it again. Dye had vowed he wasn't going back to prison. On that day he was on his way to meet his maker. Officer Nixon, returned fire with his own 357 magnum, pumping out a volley of hot-lead, striking Mr. Dye down. Time's up, Mr. Dye. You ain't going back to prison. May God be with you.

It's graduation day. I was ready to roll into high school. We didn't have a formal graduation or ceremony from Sherrard Jr. High. We just received our final report cards, then our class was assembled together and marched over to our new school, Northern High. Northern, was located half a mile north of Sherrard. Upon arrival we were given an orientation and a tour of the new school that we would be attending in the fall. My first day at Northern, I was greeted with "What's up freshy?" "Whats up freshy?" was all I heard everywhere I turned. The hazing lasted for about a month, then it was over. No more freshy. I came to understand that all incoming freshmen were initiated in this manner. That was our transitional period, from Jr. high to high school. All freshman were fair game. You had to just shut up and take it.

Mr. John and Beanie, were meeting in the top hallway a lot lately. It had gotten to the point where they didn't care if we saw them or not. No more ducking into his apartment when we came up the stairs. I don't think that was the case with his own kids. Little did we know at that time, that Mr. John and Beanie were planning her escape. Wig's life was on the brink of collapse; he hardly ever came home. His brother, Whistling Bob, was locked up. Curry had moved to St. Louis, Missouri, where he opened a liquor store. Word filtered down from St. Louis, that Curry had become quite successful. Curry's wife, Tollie Mae, had passed away and Curry had gotten married again. That was in the early 1970's. I haven't heard anything else about him since then.

High school was a learning curve, there were so many fine girls and sharp dressed fellows. Don't get me wrong, there were a lot of squares too, including me compared to the older seasoned students. When I was away from school, I was often asked by others which high school did I attend? I would of course, answer, Northern. Most inquirer's would develop a look of disdain etched across their face and express. "Northern, they don't turn out nothing but pimps and whores." I was alway's puzzled by other's remarks about my school. I knew plenty of people who had attended Northern, or, who had graduated from Northern, and they were neither pimps or whores. I just shrugged it off as school envy. Once I got acclimated to my new school, I must admit there were some cool dudes sporting expensive duds in the flyest styles strutting the halls between classes, steppin' hard in their fancy footwear. Stetsons over there, Nunn-Bush over here, Johnson and Murphys coming at me. Gypsy spilts, Lizards, Gators, fancy footwear to compliment the mohair suits, suede-front sweaters and beautifully designed Alpaca sweaters. Watching this fashion parade made me feel like a vagabond. I had to step my game up. I recognized the styles from my window shopping days downtown. The best dressed students resided in the Brewster Projects. Everyday was a fashion parade in the hallways of Northern High School. I soon discovered that Image was everything, if you wanted to attract the girls. Every girl I looked at I fell in love with. The best dressed individual strutting the halls of Northern was a Brewster project dweller named Nate Gennings. Nate's main lady, whose nick name was Lady, was Nate's female equivalent in the fashion game. Lady also called the Brewster projects home. Both of them had smooth, pretty dark skin, that meshed perfectly with their high-end, well-cordinated attire, from the top to the bottom. Nate and Lady, (Whose real name is Deniece Martin) were always fabulously attired, like a king and his queen surveying their fashion domain as they catted through the hallways of Northern High School, like royalty. They never seemed to wear the same outfit twice. Nate owned every flavor in the Hi-lo shirt collection, the virgin-wool, high-end version. There were at least a dozen different colors with the hand-stitched pockets and collar. If you didn't own a Hi-lo, you couldn't call yourself a player. Nate owned every style of shoes that Ben B. Burkes sold. There were leather and cashmere coats for the winter. Nate even sported a black-and-white Palamino horse-hair coat, which was unheard of at that time by a po' fella' like me. Nate was a trend-setter and the most fashion-conscious fellow's at Northern tried to copy his style, but, to no avail. They were just copy cats. Nate was the genuine article. There were others who had style, finesse, and could dress with the best. One such student who answered to the name of Frog, wasn't the best-looking fellow at Northern. What he lacked in looks, he made up for with style. Frog's real name was J.C. Holiman. He was one of the first fashion guru's that I noticed at Northern, sporting custom-made Hi-lo shirts, with leather trim on the pockets and collar. Frog represented well. Smoky Robinson's nephew, Billy Burston was to light-skinned dressers, what Nate was to dark skinned dressers. Billy's sister, Jackie, was reed thin and as cute as a button, with her sparkling big green eyes. Jackie, was on par with Lady when it came to her attire. (Rest in peace Miss Burston.) The unique thing that all the dapper dressers had in common, was they kept their well-coifed hair laid to the bone at all times, especially Nate...Never a hair out of place, ever. If you ever wore a process, then you know where I'm coming from. You could always tell when Nate was strolling the halls, because there was always an entourage of young girls trailing him to his class, vying for his attention. That made most fellows jealous and envious of him.

During summer break, I found myself sitting under a shade tree in front of the Detroit Bank and Trust, then located on East Grand Boulevard, contemplating something stupid. I wanted to be a fashion icon, too. I sat under that shade tree day-dreaming about shoes (Gators and Lizards), and the slick-looking duds I saw being strutted about in my new school. When school starts back in the fall, I'm going to be in the fashion parade too. If I can only hit a good lick. My young dumb-ass thoughts were about to lead me straight to the pokey for the first time in my life. I must have been pretty obvious sitting under that tree casing the stream of bank customers coming in and out of the bank. My big plan was to snatch someone's money and haul ass back to the neighborhood. Lucky for me one of the bank's patrons got suspicious and alerted the bank personnel, who promptly called the police before I could do anything that would land my stupid-ass in prison or worst. As I was about to strike, the police rolled up on me with two cops ready to pounce. They jumped out of their squad car and began quizzing me regarding my intentions. My reply didn't jive. I had no I D on me and the cops couldn't confirm my age. They hand-cuffed me and hauled my ass off to the 13th precinct on Woodward and Hancock. I think they arrested me to teach me a lesson about what was in store for me if I did something stupid. After cooling my heels for a few hours in lockup they cut me loose with a stern warning. "Let that be a lesson to you, son." I felt relief as I galloped across Woodward, looking back at the 13th precinct, where I was temporarily detained. I was glad to be making the half-mile trek back home.

When school resumed in the fall my usual group of school chums: Ken Taylor, Steve Walker, Cricket and Romy waited for me to come down to join them for our mile-long walk to Northern High. During the first week of the new semester, I noticed the girls were noticing me. There was this one sweet young lady in particular who found me quite appealing. Her name was Renee Bell. I liked Renee; but, she made me nervous as hell when she chased after me up and down the halls of Northern, whenever our paths crossed. I just couldn't handle her attention. This little cat-and-mouse game went on for most of the semester in the fall of 1964.

I was growing up fast and at fifteen years old, I began to venture further from the nest to experience some of the popular spots for youngsters in the city. One such venue was the Arcadia skating rink, located on Woodward near Alexanderine. It was located in a big, old brick building that held one of the best skating rinks in the city during the times in which it flourished. Friday nights the Arcadia was the place to be to get your skate or dance on. You could bop to the beat of all the hip music of that era. You could bring your own fancy floor-master skates. If one couldn't afford his own pricy pair of the skates with the rubber and plastic wheels, one could always rent a pair of beat-up wooden-wheel clunkers. You could slow jam with your girl, (if you had one) to Little Anthony and the Imperials, "It Hurt So Bad." My all-time favorite skating record was "Green Onions," an all-instrumental piece by Booker T. and the MG's, that packed the rink with a flurry of happy feet.

All the action wasn't on the skating rink floor. There was a show going on off to the side of the skating rink. Where the older cooler Macks, with their bevy of beauties were smilin,' stylin' and profilin' in their finest hook-up's. With their freshly-whipped, waved-down, pumped-up in-the-front doo's. One player in particular stands out. Arthur Baby, was a Detroit, over-the-top superstar Macaroni, hooker-booker, supreme. When the pimp God's made the baby, they broke the mold. Arthur was hip. His trusty sidekick was a bullwhip and he drove a pretty, cream-and-bronze drop-top convertible Eldorado. Arthur, was labeled the best dancer in Detroit at that time. His outfits were custom-made and fit the baby to a "T." Arthur Baby, was charismatic as hell and he wore it well. I was much younger than Arthur Baby; nonetheless, I admired his style. I overheard him and another player talking. Arthur's friend asked Arthur why he carried a bullwhip? Arthur called it his pro-tamer. That got a good laugh out of Arthur and his pimp friend. The bevy of beauties chuckled along with the two Macks styling, smiling, and profiling off to the side of the skating rink. Arthur Baby, attracted game like Profit Jones, attracted worshipers. Profit Jones, was a flamboyant evangelic who attracted thousands of worshippers. Arthur

Arnold "Fass Cass" Hannon

could start a stampede in his direction with his dance moves. Arthur had a magnetism about him that pulled throngs of partiers in his direction.

The Graystone ballroom and the 20-Grand were his stomping grounds. Nobody dressed like the baby. He was miles ahead of his time in that department as well. The 20-Grand was an entertainment mecca. located on 14th and West Warren. The 20-grand was to dancing, what the Arcadia was to skating. The Temptations, Miracles, Four Tops, Walter Jackson, Chuck Jackson, and many other entertainers of such caliber, performed at the 20-Grand. The big headliner acts would play the Driftwood Lounge. The Driftwood was the night club portion of the 20-Grand, where older patrons came to eat, drink and enjoy a great live show. The younger set danced the night away in the attached Gold Room Ballroom. On occasion the big acts would come over to the gold room and pantomimed their act, as a promotion between their live set.

One Saturday night in the mid-1960's, I was groovin' at the Grand, suddenly there was a roar from the crowd. I thought the Temps were about to perform. I looked toward the entrance and I could see the top of someone's head moving slowly in my direction, when a phalanx of admirers swarmed him like he was some long-lost Messiah. As the crowd parted to let the source of their adoration stride in with his entourage. There he was in full view shinning like new money, Arthur Baby, in his glory. Draped in an all-white cut-to-the-bone, custom-made pimp, jump suit, sporting a pair of white Stetson shoes to complement his attire. He wore a slant-back process with enough waves floating through his hair to make a nigga' sea-sick. He was a young pimp at the top of his game. Arthur Baby's outfits were custom-made by the designer to the players during that period named, Bubba. Arthur Baby, was about to get his swerve on and give everybody a taste of his fancy footwork on the dance floor. J.J. Bond's hit, "Its All Right" filled the Gold Room with it's catchy beat. Arthur Baby, started shaking his right leg to the catchy beat. Elvis Pressley, knew how to shake 'em down; but, Arthur Baby brought it to town. The Baby couldn't be touched when it came to that thing called dancing. On cue, Arthur, broke out in dance doing the jerk. This was Arthur Baby's night. He didn't need a dance partner he brought the house down going solo. After the Baby's finale, a cluster of dazzled damsels rushed him with their handkerchiefs drawned to wipe his sweaty brow. The Temps may have been the headliners on stage, but, Arthur Baby was the star on the dance floor. Arthur Baby, was in his pimp prime, at that place and time. Arthur was what the game referred to as eight or nine pros deep. The Baby didn't only turn out young pros: he turned out young pimps as well. Every square, from nowhere wanted to be like the Baby.

Later that same year at Diamond Jim's annual "Mack of the year" gala, where all the elite players involved in the black underworld gathered to honor their own; The night lifers, D-men, number men, pimps, pros and charlatans of the night, partied the night away at Diamond Jim's after hours spot, adaptly referred to as the P and H Club. The Club was located on Second and Delaware. One had to have a V. I. P. ("Very Important Pimp"), invite to get in. The only message written on the invitation was; "Select few Diamond Jim's, 2 a.m." Diamond Jim, was famous for his raffles whenever he gave one of his parties. The raffles consisted of a giant sheet-cake all decorated up with icing. It was cut into small squares. Inside one of the squares was placed a diamond ring. The cake, when portioned off would yield about a hundred squares. You bought a raffle ticket with a number on it, and depending on your number, you chose a square in that order until someone picked the right sqaure with the ring inside of it. Legend has it that most winners bit down on the ring while eating their cake. The squares were ten dollars a pop. Later on that night, Arthur Baby, was crowned Mack of the Year, circa: 1965.

I wonder why nobody else had a gun. They searched everybody who came in the joint. In a moment of solidarity, I asked Dave why that dude was the only person not searched. David explained, "That's Tom Morgan. Ain't nobody crazy enough to search Tom Morgan." Later in my life, I would come to know the trials and tribulations of the notorious, Terrible Tom Morgan.

Hamp's after hours joint: circa 1964

Chapter 7

INTO THE COLD HARSH, DETROIT NIGHT

On a cold December night in 1965, outside it was showering frozen rain and snow to create a frozen sleety terrain. The streets were slippery and slick. On that cold December night, Beanie, was hot under the collar. Was it something I said ? All I said to her was that. "I think it's about time we discussed my father's identity." That terse little statement ignited a firestorm in my mother. Then I heard the two chilling words that I dreaded on that cold, blustery winter's night. "Get out, Get out," she shrieked with an icy tone. I wanted to plead my case; but, I chose not to. I grabbed my coat and hit the streets. That would prove to be the first of many similar actions directed toward me. I was a confused 15 year- youngster and I didn't understand her actions or attitude regarding my concerns. This was not normal. Something bad had to have happened between, Beanie, and my biological father. My curiosity was heightened due to the secrecy surrounding my conception; maybe when I'm older the truth will emerge. At that moment I had other pressing concerns.

Outside I was met with icy layers on top of snow. Into the icy tundra I go. I was out there now. If I don't find some heat real fast, I'm going to freeze to death. It was late and everything was closed. I wandered our neighborhood broke and weary. I thought: "what a fine mess" I've gotten myself into. I had too much pride to turn back now. That was my inspiration as I trudged through the snow and ice. When I approached Clay and Oakland Street, I spotted a shadowy figure headed in my direction with his hands planted firmly in his pockets; walking menacingly toward me. My heart pounded as the stranger got closer. I relaxed at the sight of David Tate. (Little King David was his street name) There was the older original King David, who was a major playa' in the game during that time. David

Tate, claimed Little King David as his moniker in homage to the older established King David. David was a wee-bit older than me. His uncle, James Tate, owned the apartment building across the street from where my family lived.

We greeted each other and he asked me what was I doing out at that time of the night. David, sensing that I was going through something, motioned for me to follow him. I was game for that, as long as we were going some place warm. David was a dark-skinned muscular fellow who was a cross between James Brown and the future rapper, Shaba Ranks. David could be a loose cannon at times. He could be temperamental and the kid could fight like "Dolimite." But, on that wintery night, he was in good spirits as we plodded our way through the icy snow. David, the wayward man child was as usual at odds with his well-to-do-mother. David, knew how to navigate the back streets and was on a first-name basis with all of the night lifers, pimps, pros, you know the usual suspects whose day didn't start until 2 a.m. The kid knew his way around. I've never known David to attend school. He operated in the fast lane of ghetto life. The seasoned players, such as Diamond Jim Riley, Wonder Ray and Sundown, are but a few who took David under their wings as mentors.

David led me to Clay Street, where I noticed a fleet of Cadillacs and other nice rides parked under street lights glistening from the snow that fell quietly on their hoods, on the otherwise deserted street. David knocked on a door. I wondered where in the hell were we going at that late hour of the night. A man opened a slot in the door and peeped out. "Open the dooh, nigga,'" David barked. "Don't you recognize game nigga'?" The doorman opened the door and said. "Who that?" While looking at me. David shot back. "He wit me," then we scampered up a set of stairs, passing decked-out men and women coming and going. The further we got up the stairs. I could hear music coming from the entrance at the top of the stairs. I was about to enter a world I had only heard about. I was entering a blind pig or as some called it, an after-hours joint, owned and operated by an old school player named Hamp. When we entered the foyer, we were met by plumes of cigarette and marijuana smoke, laughter and cheer could be heard all around me. The lights were low, I felt like a voyeur in a strange new-world. There was a long glossy bar with long-legged sharp-dressed pretty women, sitting with crossed legs in high-backed bar stools. Sharp dressed dandies entertained them with cocaine and drinks. James Brown's, "Pa Pa Got a Brand New Bag" whaled from the juke box, while other patrons danced the night away. I was all eyes and ears trying to absorb the action attacking my virgin senses. Behind the bar on a shelf, sat a gaggle of bottled liquor standing at attention like soldiers waiting to be called into action. The bartender looked at me and spouted, "What you drinking?" Since I was broke and didn't drink, the answer was easy. I just shook my head "no." I was too nervous to speak. I must have looked like a fish out of water. David came over and whispered. "Act like you belong here nigga.'" That was easy for him to say; but, this was all new to me. I walked over to an open door where a bunch of loud men shot dice around a converted pool table clutching fists full of money..."Nina, in the funk house, nine." One shooter shouted. I noticed one fellow in particular who had a big pistol perched in front of him while he shot dice. He wore a doo rag on his head. I wondered why nobody else had a gun. They searched everybody else who came in the joint. In a moment of solidarity, I asked David why that dude was not searched? David explained. "That's Tom Morgan. Ain't nobody crazy enough to search T T." As Morgan's reputation grew, I would come to know of the trials and tribulations of the notorious, Terrible Tom Morgan.

Further in the back there was a kitchen where an older women fried chicken and french fries. David, noticed me checking it out and asked me did I want something to eat. I repeated what I heard one of the pimps say, "I ain't turning down nothing but my collar." With that, he ordered up a batch of chicken wings and shared them with me. David was an only child and probably looked at me as a little brother. We finished eating and headed back into the main bar area. At that precise moment in stepped this ultra-cool, slow-limping-pimp, draped in a fabulous black-mink coat and a matching black-mink hat. He had on a blood-red, silk suit, with matching accessories under the mink. I looked down and spotted his red Gators, that matched his suit. Three, fine, curvy honeys were trailing him, draped to the bone as well. Pressed in the middle of his red-and-black stripped neck tie was a huge diamond stick-pin spelling out "Delicious" in diamonds. For that moment in time, he owned the night. He was a sight for sore eyes, pure decadence. Everybody wasn't impressed. One such female patron who had a little too much to drink, stood in front of the red-suited dandy, pointed at the centerpiece hugging his neck tie and declared, "Delicious, what kind of name is that for a man?" At that moment the music stopped and the bar got real quiet. All eyes were on the red-suit, waiting on a response. Pimps lived for those types of moments. Delicious looked around, then hunched his shoulders like the gangster movie star, James Cagney, looked the woman dead in the eyes and proclaimed. "Well, I'm not a faggot, I'm not a whore, so I must be a pimp bitch, now buy me a drink fo' I sic' these whores on yo' monkey ass." With that, the music cranked up, the laughter flowed and the bitch ordered a round of drinks for Delicious and his entourage. Delicious was on point that night, with no doubt. I was getting tried and home sick, After losing sight of David, I went in search of him. I noticed a back room off the beaten path and eased my way over to it. Looking inside, I spotted David, fast asleep sitting on a couch with other wayward souls scattered throughout the dimly lit room. I found me a seat and joined the sleeping horde. I was good for the night.

After slumming around for the weekend. I found my way back home in one piece to our apartment on Bethune, just in time for school on Monday morning. Beanie, in her own way was trying to teach me a lesson. The lesson was a moot point to me at that time. At the time I was still trying to figure it all out. Was it a lesson on not to be curious about my own lineage?

Back at Northern, our school had a very distinguished visitor. Martin Luther King Jr.. Most of the student body was assembled in the auditorium to hear King give us an uplifting rendition on making right choice's regarding our futures. King went on to tell a story about the wise man who lived in a village. Everyone in the village would go to the wise man seeking knowledge and guidance for their everyday lives. There was a jealous man living in that same village. He was envious of the wise man's gift of delivering his fellow villager's the knowledge to help sustain their daily lives. At every opportunity the jealous man would try to foil the wise man. So that the villager's would turn on the wise man. The jealous man saw an opportunity to make the wise man seem less credible. He concocted a scheme where he would put a live bird in the palm of his closed hand, then he would ask the wise man, what did he have in his hand? Of course being a wise man, he would know it was a bird. Then the jealous man would ask the wise man, if the bird was dead or alive? If the wise man said that the bird was dead, the jealous man would open his hand and let the bird fly free. If the wise man said that the bird was alive, the jealous man would then squeeze the bird to death. Either way, he would have proven the wise man a fraud. T jealous man marched down to the wise man's hut, and of course all the villager's followed him to witness the jealous man's latest ploy to unravel the wise man. When the crowd reached the wise man's hut, the wise man stepped out to meet his adversary. Now face to face, the jealous man asked the wise man what did he have in his closed hand? The wise man replied. "A bird my son." The jealous man then said to the wise man. "Is the bird dead or alive?" The wise man looked that jealous fool in the eye and proclaimed, "It is up to you my son. The bird is in your hand, it is up to you whether it lives or dies." Then the wise man turned his attention to the crowd, he pointed to the crowd. "You, you and you: your lives are in your hands, it is up to you whether you live or die." The fool scuttled back to his own hut, to try and device another scheme to prove the wise man unwise. The fool's life was in his own hands and he was crushing the life out of his own existence with foolishness. So remember, if you're reading this, your life is in your hands. It is up to you whether you crush it or let it fly.

I tried out for the Jr. Varsity Basketball Team. The coach was a short, bald-headed man, named Mr. Taylor. He sort of resembled Wig. Coach Taylor put us through some rigorous workouts and drills at tryouts. Unfortunatly, I didn't make the team. I was rejected, but not defeated. Hey, life goes on. Northern was one of the powerhouse basketball teams in the early to mid-sixty's in the Detroit Public School League, with some great basketball players. Northwestern had Curtis Jones, whom, some believe was the greatest point guard in Public School League history. Curtis wasn't just a great player, he was a magician with a basketball. His ball-handling skills, and patent moves made Northwestern High a powerhouse team as well. Pershing High had one of the best power-fowards in Willie Iverson. Pershing was coached by the legendary, Will Robinson, who holds the High School League record in a multitude of categories. Coach Robinson, in this year 2006, is ninety-four years old and I'm proud to state that he is one of my neighbors. Most mornings I can look out my front window and see coach going on his daily walk through the park. Northern rounded out the top three teams in the league with three All-City and All-State, first-team players: small foward, Zo Banks, who would be killed in an automobile accident shortly after he graduated from Nothern High in 1965; center Chuck Tolson, and the other best guard in the state, Bill Talley, who was the heart and soul of our team. Talley, as everyone referred to him, had one of the sweetest jump-shots in the state, and he had blinding speed and quickness to compliment his shot. He was a very exciting player to watch play. Talley was unstoppable and our games were always filled to the rafters at home and away games." The big "N.O. whoop, whoop" was our school chant. The games were a platform for Nate Gennings and Lady (Denise Martin) to flaunt their smooth style, they were the trend-setters when it came to high fashion. When they made their grand entrance into the games. All eyes were on them, even the players on the court would acknowledge those dark skinned fashion icons in their matching color-cor-dinated outfits, striding devilishly to their seats inside the packed gym. In our school there was an unspoken caste system. It depended on one's per-sonal fashion sense. Many dressed well. Only a handful possessed real style. Students who had their own style, and backed it up with consistency were at the top of the caste system. No one was more stylish than the two Brewster project dwellers, Nate and Lady. That is until a dark-toned, straight-back-process wearing transfer student from Northeastern, showed up at his new school threatening to uncrown Nate as the top cool cat player at Northern. The tall new arrival had a fancy, French sounding name, Franshot Westbrook. This cool cat was sitting stretched-out in his seat in my study hall, room 308. He was wearing a green iridescent suit, complemented with a crisp white dress shirt, with cuff links and a match-ing stick-pin planted in the heart of his money-green neck tie, with a tooth-pick dangling from his mouth, sportin' a pair of black Nettleton loafer-gators. He made quite an impression on a square like me, he re-sembled a young, Otis Williams of the Temptations. He looked more pimp-like than student. I overheard his friends calling him Fran. It didn't take long before the slick girl-wanna-be's were clamoring for his attention. Whenever I passed him in the hallway, he would have some cutie carrying his books. When Fran made his way to class he strutted like a young Macaroni-in-training. Northern had a reputation for turning out players and hustlers. After being acclimated into my new school, I must admit there were an awful lot of player types making their way around our school. Early in the new year, 1966, Northern went on to become "State Basketball Champs," defeating Flint-Northern at Jennisen field house in East Lansing, home of the Michigan State Spartans. It was party time all over the northend.

Another friday night at the Arcadia, I was shootin' the breeze with some of my mellow constituents, when someone tapped me on the shoul-der. I turned around and was greeted by Renee Bell, smiling and batting her eyes at me, sparkling with affection. She had on a mini-skirt and a pair of shiny white patent-leather boots. The girl was looking swell. She had my full attention. I found Renee to be quite appealing that night. She slid into the seat next to me, revealing even more skin. After some small talk she invited me to walk her home. She grabbed my hand and led me out onto Wood-ward Avenue. She lived a few blocks away on Warren and John R. When we approached her and her sick mom's apartment, she asked me if I wanted to come up for a minute. "Hell yeah," was my reply, and I followed her up the stairs to her apartment. She offered me a seat in the living room, where

I waited anxiously as she disappeared into another room. When she emerged, she was wearing a baby-blue sheer see-through nighty. If she was trying to seduce me, she was doing a damn good job. I was good to go. Renee strutted over to me, sat on my lap and begin whispering sweet nothings into my ear as she stroked the baby hair on the nape of my neck ever so gently. Up to that point my sexual experience was limited to bumping and grinding to the beat of a slow record, kissing and rolling around on a couch or the floor with some of the young girls my age. This was different. She removed my hand from my lap, exposing my excitment. That must have ignited her passion even more. She placed my hand in hers and delivered it between her hot thighs. Then began rubbing her fingers across my fingers, which made me softly stroke her bushy moist "pudding." That's what I called pussy in my youth...while I stroked her gently, she kissed me like I had never been kissed before. She placed her soft, succulent lips on mine, then slide her tongue inside my young, moist mouth, and I returned the favor. Our young tongues met. The kiss was long, hard and wet. Both of us were hot and excited...excitment we could not contain. She placed her hand in my lap and began gently massaging my full-blown manhood, it was harder than tungsten steel. Before I knew it, my pants were off and we were on the floor making juice popping love. I had heard about the nasty, now I was doing it. Just writing about that night long ago is turning me on. We both were 15-years-old at the time, and that was the last time I had me some 15-year-old-pudding. I still break-out in a cold sweat reminiscing about that night, it was that damn good. When I left, I was on cloud nine and so was she. I could tell because she had that big, I'm satisfied all over-grin on her face, which spoke volumes. I could tell she had a good time too. And, that's the truth, Ruth.

Cool ass Pigeon, was over in a quiet corner dazzling a pair of cuties with his pimp charm as Marvin Gaye, crooned in the background on the juke box. Vince the prince six-foot eight frame was reared back in his seat soaking up all the game coming his way; while his pros attended to his every need. Vince, was a mellow-yellow, good pimpin', fellow with green eyes. Vince was all about the pimpness. I spotted Thomas Patton, whose game was silky satin draped in a brown virgin-wool expensive over coat holding court with Pretty Rick, looking pretty slick in the center of the action.

Stoke's after hours joint: circa 1968

Chapter 8

A TASTE OF HONEY

One of the tenants in our building on Bethune, was having a dispute with a stranger in front of our apartment building. The stranger was wielding a big stick with a nail protruding from the end of it. The stranger was shaking the stick menacingly at Mr. Gillum. Whistling Bob, was playing peace-maker. He stood between the two men. I knew Billy Gillum. He lived in our building; but, I didn't know the stranger. He was new to our block. I asked my friend, JoJo, who was one of our neighbors, what was that all about? JoJo noted that the stranger was trying to screw one of Billy's daugthers. Billy caught the stranger leaving his apartment when he came home from work. The girls were not exactly the virgin types. They were what the guys referred to as "loose booty" in the neighborhood. The girls probably enticed the stranger. That was my un-informed take on it anyway.

Later that night at home, I overheard Wig and Beanie discussing the incident between Billy and the stranger. Wig, went on to state that the stranger's name was Honey, and he also confirmed what JoJo had told me earlier in the day. The two men had got into it over Billy's daugthers. Beanie remarked. "What a strange name for a man." Wig, continued to explain that he had met Honey in Bob's, bar (Not Whistling Bob.) located on Camaron and Clay. A knock-down, drag-'em-out cut-throat bar that sat on the edge of the northend. Wig continued that Honey, had wandered into the bar a week earlier. He came in bare-footed and raggedy. A wino in the bar started teasing Honey about his appearance. The skinny dark-skinned fellow, had had enough of the wino's ribbing. He spoke up in a slow southern drawl. "Mista, I walked from Alabama bare-footed. I'm a bad motherfucker. I will bite your head off. You don't want to fuck with me. Now buy me a drink." The wino extended his hand, then proclaimed, "I'm from Alabama too. That's a long ways to walk. If you walked from Alabama bare-footed, you damn right. I don't want to fuck with you. Give that man a drink on me." From that point on, Honey, attracted people to him like bees to Honey. Bob's bar was one of the toughest bars on the northend. On that night, Honey the bare-footed stranger had 'em eating out of his hand. Wig went on to state that someone asked Honey, how did he get a name like that. Honey explained, as he sipped his drink that his grand-mother use to call him. "The sweetest little nigga' in the world." Thus, mem-bers of his family started calling him Little Honey. The drinks didn't stop. The more he drank, the more shit he talked. Drunk now, Honey, went on about how he was the low-downest nigga' in the world. "How so?" A voice shouted through the laughter. Honey shot back. "'Cause I peeped at my grandmother taking a douche when I was a little boy." The way he ex-pressed it made the bar patrons roar with laughter. Honey, was their kind of nigga.'

By the time I was old enough to kick it with Honey, he had established himself as a shit-talking pimp, who had an uncanny resemblance to Bootsy Collins, the flamboyant entertainer. Honey, the loquacious pimp, bragged openly about his escape from Atmore prison in Alabama. He came to De-troit, in search of his brothers. Whiskey, the oldest, and Bubba, the youngest, they had settled in Detroit, years before Honey made it here. I found out through the grapevine that Honey, was telling the truth about Atmore. He was sentenced to life in prison for killing a White man. I never knew the particulars surrounding the murder or his escape.

When the law caught up with Honey in Detroit, a community activist, Dorthy Tate, James Tate's older sister and David Tate's aunt had a strong in-fluence in our community. She took up Honey's cause. She petitioned then Governor G. Mennen Williams, to grant Honey asylum in Michigan, as long as he stayed in Michigan. The asylum was granted on the basis that Ala-bama, was a hot bed of racial injustice, and sending Honey, back could be a death sentence. As long as Honey, stayed in Michigan, he was free from extradition back to Alabama. One must keep in mind that those were the early 1960's, and the country was in the throe's of a major civil rights move-ment. Honey, bailed me out of some tight situations. For instance, Beanie, had thrown me out again. Like always, I was caught at the worst possible time. I was broke; but, I had one ace in the hole: I had a job at the Recess Club. Honey, would let anyone and everyone hang out in his tiny basement apartment on Chandler and Beaubein Street, smoking weed and drinking. There were always women and girls around. I caught Honey, in a pensive mood and asked him if I could rent his couch to sleep on for a few weeks. Honey agreed and we decided on fifteen dollars a week rent. It was tough trying to go to high school and work. Sometimes my girlfriend, Brenda, would join me on the couch for an overnight rendezvous. Honey didn't mind. He entertained women on a regular basis. I think he was trying to pump every woman on the northend. Usually, I could hear and see the whole show. That thirty something year old love machine took on all female (pardon the pun), comers. He didn't call his lady friend's by their name. He referred to them as "bitch," when addressing them. I never heard any of them protest; matter of fact they seemed to relish in it. I figured that it wasn't what you said; but, how you said it. If, I or some other square would have called a Black woman a bitch to her face without Honey's glib gift of gab, we probably would have gotten checked real good or worst by the offended.

One evening, Honey shared his good fortunes with me. Women of all ages seemed to love that obnoxious shit-talking Negroe called Honey. Two young sisters knocked on Honey's door one evening. When Honey opened the door the sisters were standing there wigglin' and gigglin' ready for some action. Right there in front of the girls, Honey, asked me did I want some pussy. All I could say was "uh, hum." He asked me. "Which one of these bitches did I want?" I went for the younger sister. Honey and big sister didn't waste much time. They got naked and before I knew it, Honey, was stroking big sister like it was the last piece of ass he was gon' get. I was still sitting on the side of the bed trying to help my date take her boots off. Honey, had big sister moanin' and groanin.' I hadn't hit a lick. I was still struggling to take my partner boots off. Honey, without missing a stroke with big sister's legs love locked around his neck looked over his shoulder at me and said in an agitated tone. "Fuck the bitch with her boots on man." So I did as I was told. I fucked the bitch with her boots on. When I would run into Honey from time to time we always had a good chuckle about the boots incident. It's been quite a few years since I've seen Honey.

The last time I saw him was at least a few dozen years or so ago. He had some wacky broad (not all women are broads, but this one was), with him and they were having a lover's spat. Honey, used one of his patented lines whenever he wanted to humiliate his woman at the time. He'd bark. "Shut up bitch. I brought you to town. If it wasn't for me, you'll still be fuckin' yo' stepfather in the back of the barn down south." Though fabricated by Honey, that line hit a nerve everytime. Then he would break out in his stellar cackle. That always made the offended laugh along with him. That was Honey's way of having fun at his woman's expense.

I met my first serious girlfriend in the fall of 1964, in the hallway at Northern High School. Her name was Brenda Knight. Brenda was a year older than me. Her main focus at that time was her singing career. Brenda worked very hard at becoming an entertainer. She had two girlfriends who shared her dream of stardom: Marlene Kareem and Brenda Rolland. They named their trio, The Sequins, and performed locally at cabarets and other small venues in the mid-1960's. They even managed to cut a record, titled "Try My Love." It was a nice-sounding record; but, ultimatly it died on the vine due to lack of exposure. Brenda and I became close. I was even tight with her mother, whom, everyone called Rabbit. I had found new allies. At one stretch whenever Beanie kicked me out, I could always find refuge at Rabbit's house. That gave me a breather from the streets. I appreciated Rabbit for her hospitality. Brenda got pregnant and gave birth to a daughter. She named her Lydia. I could never understand why Brenda, didn't consult with me regarding the childs name or surname. Brenda, didn't press me for child support either. That made me skeptical. Evenually, we went our separate ways, leaving Lydia in the lurch. Brenda passed away in the early 1980's as a young thirty something year-old. Whatever Lydia's aspirations are in life, I bid her God's speed. With Brenda's passing went all her secrets.

I found myself on the outs with Beanie, more and more frequently. I had to adjust accordingly to the situation at hand. I was getting crafty at finding places to lay my head cheaply. During one of my excursions from home once again I ran into David Tate, still lapping up the night life. We hooked up again and I found myself at another after-hours joint that I had heard about; but, had never ventured into. The P and H club was its name and its claim to fame. The blind pig was operated by the infamous, "Diamond Jim Riley," whom, David affectionatly called. "Pappy." Jim Riley was old-school. He was cut from the same swath as the 1940's pimp, Monkey Dee. Legend has it that Monkey Dee was the ugliest, and baddest pimp in Detroit's history. Urban legend has it that when Monkey died a hundred prostitutes took off their underwear and threw them in his grave before they lowered his casket into the ground. Jim Riley, with his trademark big cigar, and gaudy diamond jewelry; he even sported a diamond between his front teeth, long before today's rappers made it a trend. Diamond Jim's name fit him to a "T." As I watched the glitzy patrons flowing through the club, I remarked to David. "Theres a lot of playboys in here." David, spouted. "White boys are playboys, nigga's are pimps. Then he started pointing. "That's, Danny Boy Moore, Sundown, Sunday Morning, Bell Starr, Pretty

Curtis, Maurice Downs, (the older) King David, Jimmy Joy, Buddy Rose, Ted White, and Horse Collar." He went on and on dropping names on me. The night belonged to them. Looking back, I'm always amazed about how no one hardly ever questioned my age. I guess the game is different. Normality becomes obscure, non-normality becomes the norm. Jim wore many hats. He was a numbers man, boxing promoter, record company owner and an after-hours-joint operator. Jim's specialty was hooker, booker to the ladies of the evening, an entrepreneur extra-ordinare. Diamond Jim, with his slicked-back hair, broad shoulders and mighty girth was handsomely attired at all times, he was a mighty figure to behold. Mr. Riley exuded moxie. Unfortunately, Jim was shot to death in front of Watts Club Mozambique, in the late 1970's, by some rancid-minded oaf striking down a home-town legend. He was then carted off to jail for the rest of his miserable life, never to be heard from again... what a loser.

By the time I had turned seventeen, I was all over the place: here, there, everywhere. The more I hung out, the more Beanie threw me out. It kept me on my toes. If I wanted to compete. I had to think fast on my feet.

The Jordan family down the street had moved out of their huge house on Bethune. A single man, whom, I would come to learn was from Saginaw, Michigan, moved into the big house without a family. Mr. Jordan had 8 or 9 children, so it was understandable for him and his family to live in such a big house. The new tenant's name was Fred. That's all I would ever know about his name, just Fred. I've never known his last name. Fred welcomed anyone deemed a hustler. I started hanging out at Fred's pad as well as other nefarious haunts, when I was on the lam from my family's humble abode. Others hung out at Fred's too; Jerry Ross, Steve Walker and his brother, Antman, Bop, Eddie Will; even Calvin Judkins, Stevie Wonder's brother and their father. Whom, I knew by his street name, Scar, along with a host of others from Saginaw and Grand Rapids. Fred was the man. He had only one rule. He was the boss. Fred, was a big strapping man in stature and he garnered much respect. He was one of those manly men, like whistling Bob; but, with a teddy bear's disposition. Fred, if I had to guess was in his mid-thirties at that time in the mid-1960's. He wore his hair in a JFK process. Fred's main money-maker was selling beans. That was the street term used in the 1960's to describe barbiturates whose brand names were Secos, Decks, Speckled Decks, and Black Beauties. Fred put the young stragglers to work catching the door for his clientele. The core of Fred's clientell consisted of underworld types and night lifers who parlayed from mid-night to dawn. The usual suspects included pimps, hookers, gangsters and other unsavory figures who downed his products to stay up and energized through the night. The beans left one high as hell. The drug also, kept one talking all night long. Children of the night loved their beans. Soon as night fell, Fred's door was like Grand Central Station. Don't let us run out of beans, you'll get cussed out fa' sho.' Customers were always ready to get energized. Without beans, most of the game couldn't function at night. Without beans, your game suffered ten-fold. If your competition had dropped their beans, and you hadn't dropped yours, they were running in the fast lane and you were half-stepping in the slow lane. The cost was two pills for a buck. The average sell was for about ten dollars worth or more. If one were a pimp copping for his pros, depending on how deep his stable was would determine his tab. Some pimps had 5, 6 ,7 or 8 hookers to look out for. They could spend some serious dough. It didn't matter, they were checking off money hand over fist.

At age fifteen, I got to meet and greet a Pantheon of pimps; the night riders and rulers from 12th street, Mack Avenue, downtown, and the northend. I served players from all over the city. I'm telling you, there were a boat load of pimps out there. Night-time action was nothing like daylight action. There's a whole new dynamic at night, a paradigm shift. You had your day people and your night people. Guess what? They were as different as day and night. The bean house operated 24-7, doormen changed shifts, catching the door and selling the product.

I remember one bright, sunny day in about 1965, the yellow Cadillac Deville turned off Brush Street onto Bethune, with its black convertible top dropped. Diamond Jim Riley, was the driver and his passenger was the then new, Heavyweight Boxing Champion, Cassius Clay. Everyone on the porch stood tall as Jim's car cruised by. Jim blew his horn at us. Everyone on the porch waved their arms in unison. Clay glanced at us and waved back. I felt like I was witnessing something special. Clay, (His name before he became Mohammed Ali.) was an imposing figure, even from the porch you could feel his power.

Looking back, it was unbelievable the number of people out after 2 a.m., sporting their fly-ass-ice-cream color rides, with the "Impressions" and "Temps" seeping from their radios. Most playa's found their way to the bean house. Back in the day, beans were the fuel that super charged the night lifer's in the 1960's. After night lifer's had copped their beans, it was time to hit the pro stroll's, or after hours joints.

Stokes was legendary for his after-hour joints in Detroit. I tried to get in his first joint way back in 1964. He ran a joint on Eulid near Hamilton. I was turned away. I was too young and nobody knew me. A few years later me and Brenda managed to get in his after hours joint on Woodward and Holbrook, located in the basement of the long demolished, Mt. Royal Hotel. Stoke's name rang like a bell in the underground night life set. If Stoke's name was associated with a blind-pig, it was instant action. Charles Stokes was a big, chiseled muscled man. Everyone affectionately called him Stokes. He was an ex-simi-pro-football player, and he was anointed mayor to the players. He ran a big-time operation where the party people found good times after the bars closed at 2a.m. You could always find a steady stream of shiny new rides lined up on Woodward and Holbrook, for blocks in both directions. Shit talkers and street walkers lined Stoke's basement bar; the joint was always on jam. I remember one weekday night, it was around 1967, and all of the true playa's were on board at Stoke's that particular night. I overheard one conversation where two true pimps were kickin' it about how "only the real ones come out on week nights." One of them re-marked that. "Only squares go out on Saturday night." They had a good chuckle over the comment, then started slapping each others hand. Cool ass Pigeon was over in a quiet corner dazzling a pair of cutie's with his pimp charm as Marvin Gaye crooned in the background on the Juke Box. Vince, the Prince six-foot-eight-frame was reared back in his seat soaking up all the game coming his way; while his pros attended to his every need. Vince, was a tall, mellow-yellow, good pimpin' fellow, with green eyes. Vince was all about the pimpness. I spotted Thomas Patton, whose game was silky satin draped in a brown virgin-wool expensive over coat holding court with pretty Rick, lookin' pretty slick in the center of the action. Rick was draped in a red-leather coat with a red Barsileno hat perched a-top of his well coifed doo. Two pimps on the prowl, standing in the mist of the action trying to catch a steppa' winking and blinking their way. So that they could spring into action and reel 'em in. Stokes was slowly moving through the crowd with a fist full of money as if to imply, come get some of this as he manuvered his way over to the crap table. I spotted Esquire coming down the stairs into the fray draped in a white mink coat, with a matching white mink hat, that mother scratcher was a real cool cat. That was standard pimp attire at the time. Squire, (as everyone called him) spotted one of his pros at the bar. He proceeded to check her about not being on her job. She reminded Squire that it was raining outside. Squire went into a reactive tirade spouting. "It may rain on the game; but, it don't rain in the game. Get your ass out there and get my dough, dodge the rain drops bitch." Pimps like Esquire loved to show off on their game in a crowd of other pimps. It's a pimp thing. Playa's call it pimpin' on a bitch. I've witnessed that scene numerous times with other pimps and their game. While Squire was going through his changes, someone in the joint shouted. "Raid." Everyone but the cooler playa's started rushing the exit. The exit was plugged with bodies. Some of the panicked patrons began breaking out the windows and climbed up out of the joint. Once outside, everyone had a good laugh about it because it was a false alarm. What a night on Woodward and Holbrook, where the party continued on the sidewalk at four in the morning. I just finished reading Stoke's obituary in the Michigan Chronicle, and I conjured up images from the past. The obituary went on to say that he was seventy years old when he died on September 22, 2005. It went on to state that he wasn't only a celebrated night-life entrepreneur; but, that he was known to give from his heart. He helped the needy, he gave barbeques and cook-outs for his community. He didn't smoke, drink or do drugs. So long, Mr Stokes, you showed Detroit how to have a good time, while in your prime.

Stoke's wasn't the only game in town after hours. The competition was thick. In mid-town on Garfield off Woodward, sat the Ponderosa. At the time it was operated by an old-school pimp named, Jimmy Jones and later by Doc Holiday. Jones was in the same league as Diamond Jim, that was at the top of the game food chain. Other top notch playa's in that league were Adolph, Buddy Rose, Chick Springer, and of course, Charles Stokes, Mr. Kelly and Maurice Downs. All of the above-mentioned were old-school playa's. By the time I came along their pimping was just a hobby, something left over from their glory days. When I grew up to them, they were basically businessmen who reigned over the night-spots where playa's hung out. Most of the above-mentioned are either dead or out-to-pasture.

The Democratic Club was located on Mack and Beaubein Street, housed inside of a big mansion, where I had the pleasure of rubbing elbows with Arthur Prysock, the jazz singer who was hanging out with the player's. Upstairs was the bar area and on the main floor was where you could order food and just hang out styling. One night I was leaving the bar area. As I began my descent down the huge winding staircase. I spotted her sitting with her legs crossed. Her jeweled-laden wrist was dangling like a curved-neck Swan. She was as dark as night and had an air of majesty about her. Girlfriend was stylishly attired, all the way down to the snow-white fluffed mink coat that draped gingerly around her shoulders, with a white matching mink hat that sat nestled gently on top of her freshly coifed jet-black hair, with flecks of blond highlighting her bangs. My eyes perused her all the way down the stairs. Looking her over, I knew she was special. Her darker-than night-skin was shimmering like a black diamond caressed in mink snow from head to toe, it gave her an aura of mystery. Every stitch gracing her svelte figure was custom-designed, styled for her personna. She appeared to be my age. After looking her over. I felt that she was extra special. Over the years, I would run into her from time to time at different venues throughout the city. She was forever on point. Sista' love changed minks and expensive cars like some folks changed shirts. I thought I had witnessed one of the classiest-dressed Dame's to come down the pike in Lady; but, even Lady was no match for that fine feline, black-pantherist who exuded class and dazzle, whom, everyone affectionately called, Black Patty.

Down on Woodward and 7 mile stood the 19th hole across the street from Palmer Park golf course. It was a quaint little after hours spot where you could get your goody or Mack on. The joint was run by Rockhead, a westside numbers man who was much older than my set; nonetheless, Rock was Brenda's singing mate, Marlene's sugar daddy. I would see him at their apartment when I visited Brenda. The 19th hole was popular when the movie "Deep Throat" was out. Over the bar of the 19th hole was a sign that proclaimed. "I made Linda Lovelace gag." Linda Lovelace, was the star of the porn flick "Deep Throat." Mr Kelly's was over on Chene Street, as was Stoke's years later. Yep, them were the days my friend, I thought would never end. And that's the truth, Ruth.

There were all types looking for their treats. Pretty pimps and pros decked out in slick colorful clothes. Players and Playettes of every shape and hue. From the yellowest of yellow, to the darkest of night and every shade in between. Some handsome pimps could cold-stare a pro down at the dooh, stop 'em dead in their tracks. You had the smooth shit-talkers who could talk a pro out of the loot in her boot. Pimps called it trickeration.

The Game: circa 1966

Chapter 9

HOOKER BOOKERS

Back at the bean house, it was business as usual. I was fifteen years old and didn't need much sleep. During my tenure as a doorman at the bean house, I served some of the mightest Macks in Detroit, at that time. Jimmy Diamond was good at talking with his hands. When he spoke he was like a Maestro conducting an orchestra. For instance, when he delivered his trademark. "I got two barbers...one to lay 'em down, and one to lift 'em up" line, his hands are making sweeping motions as his words flowed swiftly from his mouth. Thomas Patton, (better known as T P) was a smooth brown-skin twenty-something-year old, 12th Street Playa' during the 1960's and 70's, he often hit the bean house door. He drove a new 1965 brown drop-top Eldorado. Over the years more than a few of T P's Caddies were brown convertibles. Brown became his trademark color. On that night outside in his drop-top sat a fine-ass beauty ready to get busy on her job. All she needed was the beans T P, was coppin' for her and her wife in-laws, who were already on their job. How do I know all that you ask? Well, I would always quiz the pros about who their man was and what stroll did they work? T P's pros would all have the same pat answer. "I'm with the almighty T P, and I got to get his dough, ya' know." The same scripted dialogue. T P, had a boat-load of honeys testifying with his name dripping off their luscious lips. One night, Thomas, was leaving the bean house and one of his pros came struttin' in. T P, reminded her about his trap. She replied. "I ain't broke luck yet, Baby." T P, wasn't one of those slap 'em down vicious dog matic type pimps. He calmly told her that. "I'm doing real swell, ya' know, if you wanna' keep latchin' on, you gotta' keep my traps strong, 'cause I got some fresh young gamers waiting on yo' spot." The pro' replied. "I'm all over it, Baby. Come by the stroll in a couple of hours, Baby." Now, that's pimpin' to an eager-eyed fifteen-year old wanna-be. That was my awakening to that game thang. If, I as a young man would have had any scruples or

guidance toward a saner endeavor, I could have pursued a scholarly journey early on. It just wasn't laying like that at that particular juncture in my
life's journey. I had to play the hand that I was dealt. I just wanted to make
that point for my critics.

Things were not always honky-dory for T P. Some jealous simp, (That's
not a typo.) I said. "Simp," shot T P five times over a renegade (running
wild) pro.' T P, survived the ordeal and is out-living a boat-load of ex-play-
ers from his era. Wonder Ray, was always freshly pressed and he drove the
best. He favored La Baron suits that were sold exclusivly from Kosin's back
room. He always had a squad of pros fawning over his mellow-yellow, good
pimpin' ass. How would I describe Wonder Ray? Ray was a wonderful pimp.

Allen Underworld, was a pimpin' gangster. I called him a pimpster who
tried unsuccessfully to muscle his way into Fred's bean house action while
Fred was locked up for a brief time. When Fred was sprung he put a stop
to all of that. I must say, Underworld did take liberties with Fred's women
when Fred was in the pokey.

Johnny Red was a downtown pimp, whom, were the most-dedicated
to the game in Detroit, they played by the old-school rules. If you were a
straggler pro' working the downtown strolls without a downtown pimp to
speak up for you. You couldn't survive the downtown pro' houses or
streets. Other pros and stick-up artist would take all stagglers money without retribution. Pros had to choose up or get up. Johnny Red, was shot
down on Woodward and Columbia in downtown Detroit, by another pimp
named Miami Kid. It was all over a pro.' Miami's game got in Red's face and
Red pulled her. The Kid couldn't handle it. I guess he said, fuck the rules and
gentlemen agreements amongst pimp's when it came to knockin' a pro'
off. So Miami, shot that po' pimp down to the ground right out on the sidewalk, circa: 1968.

Sweet smellin' Sam, another regular visitor to the bean house was a
sharp dude and he was always fresh. He lived up to his name, but there was
one problem: He was always walking and I never saw him with a pro.' I
guess one could call Sam the pro'-less wanderer. Fishman was a frequent
drop in. He was always on his way to or coming back from New York.
What I learned dealing with those charlatans of the night, is that they could
make their mouth's say anything.

"Hawk," was a pimp's pimp. Hawk was what other pimp's strived to be:
a true player. Hawk, made pimpin' look easy. They say that true pimp's are
born; not made. Hawk was a born pimp. He had the look-down pat and no-

body hooked up a suit and tie like the all-mighty Hawk. He was always freshly pressed, and he drove the prettiest sky-blue, pimp-Deville, with a navy-blue drop-top. That was in 1966, the game was good to those who were good to the game, and Hawk fit that phrase to a "T." He was a low-key pimp. When asked how he was doing. Hawk would curtly reply. "Doin' what I can, until I can do what I wanna." Hawk, had a deep voice and he was somewhat a singer. If a fresh stepper got in his ride, she was good to go. In the mid-1960's, some players had little record players mounted under their dashboard upside down, that played 45 records. That was before eight-track tapes and cassette players. One crisp sunny day, Hawk, eased to the curb in front of the bean house, with the top-dropped on his pimp Deville, crooning along as the Impressions, "Keep on Pushing" played on his portable record player. When the Impressions came to the chorus, "Keep on pushing." Hawk would ad lib, singing in unison with the song to the cutie riding shotgun. "Keep on Pimpin.'" His name fit him snug like a glove. He sorta resembled a Hawk.

There were plenty of white hookers coppin' beans, but, I only saw one white pimp. His name was White Folks. He wore the big-brim gangster hats. If Folks wasn't white, you would think he was your average shit-talking, charismatic, black pimp.

Another one of our clients was Donald Johns, known on the streets as D J. He was more to do about gambling in the night spots than pimpin.' At time's D J, would show up at the bean house around 2 or 3 in the morning with nice jewelry on. D J, was also a sharp dresser...he had his own style. D J put me in the mind of Humphrey Bogart, with his mannerisms...the black Bogart. Once after a night of gambling he showed up at 7 or 8 in the morning with no jewelry and high as hell off of beans. That night he had gambled his jewelry away at the Ponderosa after-hours joint. D J was and still is a cool brother as of this writing.

Jimmy Joy was a Macaroni off of Mack Avenue and he had one of the deepest stables in Detroit at that time, 12 and 13 pros deep. Joy's game was tight. He had pros from all over the city coppin' all night praising his name.

Prez' and Chocolate were pimpin' dykes. They were two pretty stud-broads, and were finer than most of their pros. Prez' and Chocolate out-pimped a lot of their male counterparts. Chocolate owned a hotel on West Grand Boulevard, across the street from Northwestern High School. It was called Chocolate Hotel. I figured that whenever they went pro-less they could always just put on a dress and sell their own pussy.

Esquire was a white pros desire and a legend in his own mind. Squire was the perfect dapper pimp: flamboyant, slick-looking, gift-of-gab. He had all of the bells and whistles. Squire would banter that he didn't pimp hoes, he pimped pros. Most of his women were white pros with big blond hair; except for a couple of black boosters. The girls would scrap over who was going to ride in the front seat of his royal-blue-and white-Eldorado convertible. I would often spot Squire cruising out Woodward in his Eldo,' with the top-dropped on warm summer evenings with one or more of his white pros. All leaning like gamers rode back in the day. Squire hung out in the In Crowd Lounge, on Woodward and Kenilworth Street. The In Crowd Lounge, was where players came to shine among their peers before the after-hour joints opened at 2 a.m. Other bars in that vein were The La Players, on Joy Road, The Disc Jockey Lounge, over on Livernois in northwest Detroit. A decade later in the late 1970's it became the home of Chick Springer's Lounge. Henry's Lounge, was on Fenkell Avenue, The Burning Spear, was on Puritan Avenue. There were a host of other spots sprinkled throughout the city. Most, catered to the fast crowd.

Squire was holding court in the In Crowd one slow pimpin' night. As usual, he drew a crowd. Squire was on a shit-talking roll. He was going on about how he didn't have no pepper in his game (meaning black pros), and that he was a white pros pimp. Squire could afford to talk shit. He was always freshly-pressed and could back his talk up with game. Ice cream-colored suits, freshly minted Caddies to lean in while he checked his traps on the various strolls around town. Good things don't always last. Squire went on to get beat-down by Doc Holiday, in the Ponderosa after-hours joint. He did a bit in Federal Prison, and had fallen on hard times. So boys and girls contemplating similar lifestyles, I want to remind y'all that it only lasts for a hot minute, in the overall scheme of thangs, pimpin' ain't easy, and neither is hoein, so be very carefull of what you ask for, ok.' I'd like to remember Squire, in his prime. The life of the party, holding court in his favorite watering hole surrounded by other pimps in his colorful attire, talking shit with the best of 'em, with his jewelry flashing, and laughing the night away.

If you can imagine a tall, young James Brown, with bigger hair, dressed in a blue sport coat, orange pants, with a green scarf tied around his neck like Roy Rogers; then, you would have Willie the Weeper. As strange as the man dressed he looked good in that shit. He was so ugly that he looked handsome. Weeper ran his pros out of a little motel bar across the street from Dodge Main Auto Plant, on East Grand Boulevard. His pros catered to the factory workers. They would catch their tricks in the bar, then they took care of their business in the attached motel. If the average Joe dressed like the Weeper, they would be labeled as a clown. Yeah, Willie the Weeper, was one of the parade of pimps hitting the bean house door on a regular basis.

There were all types looking for their treats. Pretty pimps and pros decked out in slick colorful clothes, players and playettes of every shape and hue. From the yellowest of yellow, to the darkest of night and every shade in-between. Some handsome pimps could cold-stare a pro' down at the dooh, stop 'em dead in their tracks. You had the smooth slick-talkers, who could talk a pro out of the loot in their boot. Pimps called it "trick-eration." There was a loose group of dope men masquerading as pimps who used their drugs as a lure to get strung out pros into their clutches. During my exploits and dealings with pimps and pros, I found it to be a cutthroat vicious dog-eat-dog existence. Even if pimpin' didn't exist there would still be pros workin' it. Tricks reign over their family's, pros reign over their tricks, and pimps rule their pros. If there were no pimps, pros would rule the world. Pimps keep pros true to the game. It's just a natural attraction, like birds of a feather. It's a sick, sad dance that has gone on forever; way before I was born. I didn't understand all the dynamics surrounding the pimp-whore syndrome then and I certainly don't understand it now; nonetheless, the eternal marriage between pimps and pros still exists to this day. I'm just trying to put it out there...Those scandalous types of relationships that endure not only in Detroit; but, throughout our country and the world.   I wouldn't want a child of mind too ever have to experience the lowest display of self-worth known to human kind. I had to clarify that point for the record.

I met Little Mike, who was a regular visitor to the bean house. Little Mike, was another one of those downtown pimps. Mike was a mean, hard street pimp who ruled his roost with an iron fist, and I mean that literally. As beastly as Mike was to his pros, some loved him; others loathed him; but, they all respected him. Most downtown pros didn't fear easily, but regarding Mike, it was a different story. Little Mike, was the evilest bastard in the valley called John R and Columbia Street. He handed out vicious punishment to pros who got out of order. Mike was the kind of pimp who relished in showin' off on his pros in front of others for sport. Mike had some big-time, psychological baggage, He was a borderline maniac. Mike, would be the kind of patient who drives the psychologist crazy. For instance, one night I was hanging out in the Ponderosa, Jimmy Jone's after-hours spot on Garfield in mid-town Detroit. Little Mike, was holding court with some of Detroit's low-downest pimps and pros at the basement bar. This was the hard core set. The Ponderosa was an anything goes kind of joint. Down-town pimps hung out there. Mike was talking shit and to liven things up, Mike spotted his pro that he had brought with him, with her chin buried deep in the palm of her hand looking bored sitting on a bar stood. Out of the blue, Mike cold-cocked her in the jaw like he was hitting a man. Bam! He knocked the startled women off of the bar stool. She hit the floor, stunned. My initial instinct was to come to her aide; but, I understood where I was; besides the pro' would have turned on me anyway to appease Little Mike. It just wasn't prudent to come between a pimp and his game. I would have gotten shot if I had intervened, and I'm sure the other pimps present felt the same way. Mike, shaking his big black fist at her lying on the floor half-conscious, shouting at her with his black gangster hat broke down over his brow." Get up bitch, and straigthen up, you better smile, bitch." Mike was pure evil. I thought about my own mother and I wanted to kill him. Mike drove a big four-door blue Fleetwood. He loved to drive up on the sidewalk chasing pros in his car; just showing off. Mike didn't play, and the pros knew it. Two things pros ran from when working the downtown strolls and whorehouses; one was the police and two was Lit-tle Mike. Little Mike was a short, dark-skin muscular man. I'm talkin' peni-tentiary muscles. Mike had a thick bushy mustache and possessed a bullies disposition. There was a saying on the downtown streets. "If you worked the streets where Mike roamed, you better have his dough or he'll crack your doom." If there is any solace for the women he victimized. Mike died broke and alone.

There wasn't just one type of pimp. Pimps were as complex and multi-dimensional as the whole of society. There were many styles and many personalities. Westside was a pimp-in-training back in the mid-1960's. Dur-ing the 1970's and 80's, his game sky-rocketed and he became a major player in Detroit's game. When Westside, was out and about with others of his ilk, he would greet 'em with policing the game, got to keep it sucker free. Side was a tall light skin-pimp with a passion for white pros and white pros had a passion for Westside, the crafty pimp. His stable of fancy white pros could work where black pros dared not tread. When I lived on the westside, he lived a couple of blocks south of me over on Sturdevant and Lawton. While passing his house one hot summer's day. Westside had all his girls outside in front of his pad in tight skimpy tops and shorts washing his Cadillac. Pony from Palmer Street was another frequent visitor to the bean house. I didn't know Pony's game. He was a quiet fellow who could have been a D-man or a stick-up artist. He fit the bill for both. Now that I'm older, I realize the danger that I was in as a youngster. I shunder to think about how I spent my precious time. One slip and I could have been history. I guess God wanted me to write this book. Another major bean popper was David Ruffin. Yeah, that David Ruffin. If one didn't know he was in the "Temptations." He could have easily been mistaken for a pimp.

Hooker or not, Bootsy, was one of the finest women anywhere; bar none. She was a golden, bronze-green-eyed Goddess, who reeked with sex appeal. She was slew-footed and fast walking. Bootsy, did not look for tricks; oh no, tricks looked for Bootsy. I would often see a line of white tricks in cars following her down the street. She looked like a pork chop to hungry dogs. Men have started wars over her kind of appeal and beauty. Here she was strutting her stuff up the bean house stairs; there to get her daily dose of stay up. Bootsy, didn't wear panties and she loved her pretty skirts. She would tease us youngsters at times, by sitting on the porch's banister with her legs slightly parted; just enough for us to see that she wasn't wearing any panties. Just as quickly, the show was over. She was off-and-running, leaving a trail of aroused young men in her wake. I suppose it would take a gang of psychiatrists to unravel her attraction to selling pussy. Rich men would have married and cared for her. Although, Bootsy would have probably only treated them like tricks. Some people needed the street action to feel like somebody. I would venture to guess that Bootsy was one of them. Fred's business was unique. Every bad ass sold coke and boy. Very few sold or could get their hands on a batch of beans, that required a big pharmacy connect. A lot of slingers dropped beans, (swallowed like regular pills) there were a lot of top notch slingers also masquerading as pimps. Such as, Adolph, Memphis Slim, Cincinnati, Milwaukee Jack, Butch Harris, George Hall, Bobby Neely, who the rapper Ludacrist looks like. Marzette, was the top dog of all the slingers and let's not forget, Slim Goody, the ex-12th street pimp, turned slinger. They're all dead now. May these words immortalize their existence. Some of the slickest playa's out there were the Davidson Street Stuff Players, some would call 'em Flim Flam men. For the laymen, that's "Con men" to you. Their specialty was the pigeon drop. They had a bag of other tricks that are only privy to their little click in Conant Gardens. Ty and Ron did their thing. Those two were smooth operators. They would communicate with their eyes when working a mark. (Victim of their con.) See fellows, I was peepin' y'all's game; while y'all were working y'all's mark. Somebody was studying y,all. Me. Suckin' up all that game. Richard Dee, Curtiss Reed and Gerald Watts were off Davidson too. They were more hustlers than con-men. Then you had the cream off the top: Donald and Ralph were young, tricky and slick. Shake one of their hands you better count your fingers. Both drove big fancy rides. Donald, drove a black Continental and Ralph, used to ride Woodward in a big brown, (what they call in today's vernacular) tricked-out Fleetwood Cadillac. Ralph's, Caddy was a 1969 in 1969.

Recalling, Reggie Harden, the 7 foot tall, High School phenom from Eastern High School. The then fresh out of High School, draftee of the Detroit Pistons. I looked up one day and there he was banging on the bean house door. He was a far cry from the Reggie Hardin, I had met from the paper boy banquet at Roma Hall, some 5 year's earlier. Reggie, couldn't stay out of trouble and was evenually kicked off of the Detroit Piston's Basketball team, Reggie was now a bean head and Heroin junky, snarling on the other side of the bean house door. Reggie went on to get himself in a bit of a fix. He would go on to get murdered on the mean street's of Detroit. Reggie could have been a contender. Rest in peace my brother. Those my friend's were just a sampling of some of the bean house carnivores.

August of 1966, Beanie was plotting our escape from our third-floor roach-and-rat-infested apartment on Bethune, unknown to Wig or us. She was planning our escape to a better life and Wig wasn't a part of the equation. At about 8 p.m. on a week night, while Wig was working the afternoon shift at Acme Quality Paints. A truck pulled up in the back of our apartment building on Bethune. While Beanie quickly packed, we were instructed by her to carry packed boxe's and bags of our belongings down to the waiting truck. She ordered us to move quickly. It suddenly dawned on me that we were moving and without Wig. Wig, wouldn't arrive home until after midnight. As we loaded the truck some of my friends stopped to help us out, and a wave of sadness engulfed me. I figured Wig, would get the bad news from some of them before he made it upstairs. I waved goodbye to Steve, Antman, Cricket, and Ken Taylor. We also bid farewell to the rats, roaches and memories that are firmly etched in my mind's eye. "Untill, the day that I am no more."

Where we were headed, I did not know, and how was Beanie, going to pay for it without a job? My concerns would soon be answered as we pulled up to our new flat. It was a large brick building with four units. We moved into the upper right-hand unit. Our new address was 2918 Monterey, off of Lawton, on the westside of Detroit. After hauling our belongings up two flights of stairs. Inside of our new flat we were awed by two large rooms, consisting of a large living room, a dining room and a kitchen. Down a long hallway there were two large bedrooms, and a moderate-sized bathroom. We were only renters, but it didn't matter, because it was home. Our new living room was bigger than our old apartment on Bethune. Soon after we arrived there was a knock at our door. When Runt opened the door, two men carried in a new couch, followed by Mr. John. I was perplexed, to say the least. My first thought was, what is he doing here? It was an awkward encounter. Then my mind flashed back to the meetings between Mr. John and Beanie in the dark hallway on Bethune.

Mr. John couldn't read or write; but, somehow he managed to land a job at a Chrysler assembly plant. He had the right name. John Henry, and Mr. John, definitely was a steel-driving man. What Mr. John, lacked in intellect he compensated for it in brawn and good old-fashioned hard work. His work ethic was second to none. As a young child, Mr John, cut his teeth in the cotton fields of Mississippi. I'm talking 1930's Mississippi. All he's ever known was racism and hard work, especially during the brutal days of Jim Crow. Blacks were more valued by how much cotton a black family could pick. The lessons I learned from Mr. John, the quiet unassuming man who fell in love with my mother, is that you never know a person until you know their plight and the trials and tribulations that delivered them to this place called now. Mr. John was the catalyst that transformed my mother's life.

Soon after we settled in she began training to become a nurse's aide at Providence Hospital, then located on 14th and East Grand Boulevard. I transferred to Central High School, located on Linwood and Tuxedo. It was a new beginning for my family, and for Mr. John, as well.

I was sixteen and in the tenth grade when I dropped out of high school. My stomach was growling and I needed money. One day I walked in the front door and straight out the back door of Central High, in search of fame and fortune. It was tough going after dropping out of high school. I began spending more and more time in the streets. When you're young, every experience is new. I didn't realize that at the time, I was driven on impulse. I was all about survival... no child support, no family support. I thought I was a hustler. I didn't realize it then that I was only throwing rocks at the penitentiary.

Arnold Hannon

Chapter 10

THROWING ROCKS
AT THE PENITENTIARY

Slim, had dropped out of school and was running wild in the streets. At times he landed in juvenile detention, and was constantly living on the lam. Runt, was enrolled in Durfee Jr. High School, next door to Central High. Runt, was a good student up to that point in time. The short time that I spent at Central was enlightening. Central was a square's school, compared to Northern and it wasn't as competitive as Northern, in the fashion department. The students at Central seemed more academically inclined. A good deal of the students in that westside school had a solid family structure, which is conducive to enhancing cognitive skills. That's my observation on that. I used to play pee-wee football for the Westside Cubs, and I was pretty good. I decided to try out for Central's football team. My position of choice was wide reciever. I thought I had a decent game and a chance at making the team. There was only one problem. I wore a process and the coaches wanted me to get a hair cut. I, being a young jerk rebelled. Maybe a little parental guidance could have stepped in and saved me from myself; anyway, I was cut from the team. I was devastated. My stubborn dispostion and mis-aligned principles would not allow me to relent. When I played for the Westside Cubs, I would strut around my neighborhood on the northend after practice in my uniform proud as punch. I must admit that I was disappointed when I was cut from Central's football team. I suppose that my priorities were discombobulated. If I could do it all over again. I would have gotten the damn haircut. That hair doo thing was baggage left over from my days living on the northend. Slim, and I would separately trak back to the northend, to hang with our old friends on the end. He had his core group of friends, and I had mine. When at times, when I had trouble regarding lodging. I could always turn to Brenda and Rabbit. I was always welcome. Most of my time was spend working the door at the bean house.

The police had been hassling Fred, about all the comings and goings at the bean house. One summer evening in the mid-1960's me and some of the my young co-horts, along with Fred, were hanging out on the front porch of the bean house, shooting the breeze when four of my old friends rode up. They stopped and parked in front of the bean house. Once again, they unfurled their tall, huge bodies out of the black sudan, then they strolled long-legged up to the front porch. Fred was sitting down, while The Big Four hovered over him. Chew Tobacco, asked Fred did he live there? Fred nodded his head, affirming that he lived there. Rotation Slim ordered Fred to stand up. Fred complied and was promptly hand cuffed and placed under arrest. This time Rotation Slim and his crew didn't look too inviting on the business end of their raft. I had grown up a bit. I don't think they recognized me as the kid who had rode with them a few years earlier, in search of a butcher-knife weilding robber on East Grand Boulevard. As they lead Fred away, Rotation Slim, glared at about a half-dozen or so of us gathered on the porch and warned in his southern drawl. "If y'all keep hanging out here, y'all gonna' end up at 4000 Cooper Street." I didn't know where 4000 Cooper street was. I was soon enlightened by one of my co-horts that 4000 Cooper Street, was the address of Jackson Prison. The regulars still made their pilgrimage to the bean house; but, an old drug was fueling their Jones; boy, mixed jive, scag, penny caps. Heroin had many names; but, the results were the same: self-destruction. I was green as grass and didn't realize the magnitude of those deadly drugs. I was a kid caught up in someone else's nightmare. Mixed jive was a concoction of Heroin, lactose and quinine, packed in gelatin capsules and sold for a dollar a cap. Thus, they were called penny caps, and that my friends was the beginning of the demise of many in the black communities in the great City of Detroit. You could always tell the size of a junkie's habit by the size of their swollen-needle marked, riddled hands; which were left scarred, and swollen from daily injections of that toxic blend of tragic magic. Thank God, I never used it, or sold it.

From time to time, I ran into Slim and his merry band of thugs: Barkley, Country, and Malon Mckinney's psycho' cousin Derrick Smith. They were a young, ruthless bunch whose only mission in life was to create havoc in the community.

Mr. John helped Beanie buy her first car. It was a shiny new 1965 Mustang, that just happened to be the hottest new set of wheels in the country. Every young women wanted one. There was even a song named after the hot new ride. "Mustang Sally," song by the incomparable Wilson Picket. The gravely voiced soul singer from Detroit's Eastside.

By 1970, Beanie, had completed her nurse's aide training and was working at Providence Hospital, which had by then moved to Southfield, Michigan. When we were tired of running the streets we found our way back home on Monterey. Runt, played basketball for Central High and he was a mama's boy. Me and him got along swell. It was a different story between Slim, and I. One night all three of us were at home on Monterey. Beanie was at work, of course that was a recipe for disaster. Slim, was agitated about some petty disagreement we had. I think it was over who ate the last pork chop, or some stupid crap like that. An argument ensued and it escalated into violence. Slim, grabbed a broom and broke it across my back. Then he grabbed a butcher knife and chased me out of the house into the front yard. It was night-time and no one else was around except, me, Slim, and Runt. I stood in dis-belief as he waved the knife menacingly at me. He turned to Runt and ordered Runt to attack me. He threatened to cut me if I fought back, but, Runt, refused his order. I ventured over to Richton Sreet, where Brenda and Marlene had an apartment. I stayed there until I could figure out my next move. I didn't mention it to Beanie, because I wasn't exactly the favorite son. I could never figure out my Mother's bias toward me when it came to me and my brothers. That wasn't Slim's first attempt to commit bodily harm against me. One evening when we lived on Bethune, me, Slim, and Runt were at home when me and Slim, got into an argument, that was a usual occurrence. I've forgotten what we argued about. We wound up tusslin' in the living room, where he slung me into a sharp-edged, end table. It tore through my pants leg and left an inch-long gash down to the white meat on my shin. I walked the fiftteen-odd blocks down Oakland Avenue to Brenda's Mother's house on Russell, where I found refuge.

I could always depend on Brenda and her mother, Rabbit, in times of need in those days. They were always there for me. The scar on my leg will forever remind me of how much disdain I have for my brother. I don't hate him. I just don't like him very much.

I was sixteen and in the tenth grade when I dropped out of high school. My stomach was growling and I needed money. One day I walked in the front door and straight out the back door of Central High School, in search of fame and fortune. It was tough going after dropping out of high school.

I began spending more and more time in the streets. When you're young, every experience is new. I didn't realize that at the time. I was driven on impulse. It was all about survival...no money, no family support. I thought I was a hustler. I didn't realize it then that I was only throwing rocks at the penitentiary.

My mellow man, who lived down the street from us on Monterey, had an unusual name, Tea Garden. I never knew if that was his first, or his last name. Everyone just called him Tea Garden. Tea, was one of the first dude's that I met when we moved to the westside. He lived with his parents in one of the nicer houses on the block. His parents owned a dry cleaners on Oakman Boulevard. Tea and his Mellow man Norman, would get dressed up and cat up and down Monterey in search of game. There wasn't much game around there, so they were just walking to the corner and back. Both fellows sported pumped-up doo's. They weren't as slick as northend doo's; but, they were all right. Tea and I were about the same age and would kick it from time to time.

One evening we were riding out in Tea's mother's car. I think Tea was a mama's boy. We were going no place in particular, when out-of-the-blue he asked me if I wanted to go to Toledo, with him too hang out with his girlfriend and her cousin. I agreed to his proposition and we made the trek toward Toledo, Ohio. On the way to Toledo, we talked about different things that men have in common. The subject turned to pussy. Tea started elaborating about how he would never make love to a woman who was on her period. Tea was quite adamant about it. He went on to degrade such an act as too nasty for him. I agreed that it indeed was nasty. When we arrived in Toledo, we were met by two cutie's. One for him and one for me. Tea introduced me to the two women. Then we went out to get a bite to eat. When we finished eating, we made our way over to Tea's girlfriends house. After a bit of small talk, we paired off. Tea was making out with his girl and me with Cuss.' We were kissing, hugging, and rubbing. The mood turned serious. Tea got a blanket and made a pallet on the floor. He and his girl got down on the pallet, while me and Cuss' took over the couch. Tea turned out the lights. That's when the humpin' started. I was humpin' Cuss' and Tea was handlin' his business with his girlfriend. We were young and the humpin' lasted most of the night. When the humpin' was over, we all fell fast asleep.

As the morning sun streaked through the window shades, I was awakened by the Sun rays in my eyes. Tea and his girl were still sleeping. I looked over at Tea and his girl laying on the pallet. The covers were pulled off of them, exposing them. Tea was lying there in a pair of bloody draws. A big circle of blood surrounded his crouch area. My first thought was, you lying motherfucker, so much for you not making love to a girl on her period. I never let on about seeing him lying there in his bloody draws, it was my little secret. On the ride back home, it was all I could do to keep from exposing him. We made it home with my secret intact.

The westside had a lot more violent thugs and stick-up artist than player types. There were some, but, the D-men controlled the majority of the street action, with the power and lure of drugs. In essence, all the good steppers were overwhelmed by the easy accessibility of the all powerful narcotic. That was my 16 year-old-observation of unfolding events. I was a little older then, and so were the thugs. The child in me had lost his innocence. I begin to see and hear about more gun play, who shot John, that kind of shit. The streets on the westside were wider and bigger than the streets on the northend. So were the guns: 357 magnums, .45 automatics, and sawed off shotguns. I'm not suggesting that the guns were not as prevalent on the northend: but, I just didn't see them as much as I saw them on the westside. On the westside, every fool was totin' a pistol or sawed-off shot-gun, including my brother, Slim. Slim was way out there. He was consumed with life on the dark, rugged side of the streets. I saw a lot more rollers openly plying their trade,(drug dealers) and stick-up artists who specialized in robbing them. They all managed to co-exist while preying on each other. Among the baddest of the bad asses was a fellow named Donald Banks, AKA, Shady Six. Six was a medium-height, thin-built, light, brown-skin Puerto Rican, looking gun-totin' black gangster. Shady's younger brother, Bojo, had the foulest mouth on the westside. When he called you a bitch or punk, you felt it reverberating in your bones. That was about all he was, all-talk, no bite. He survived off of his brother's reputation. On the other hand, Donald Banks alter ego, Shady Six, was the real deal, Jackson Prison alumni. During the time that I lived on the westside, he was a twenty-something year-old, big shit-talking fool. His specialty was sticking up dope houses. He left a long string of shot-up, pistol-whipped desperadoes in his wake. He too was known to sling that tragic magic. One of Shady's road dog's was a felllow called Big Son. Big Son, became a major roller on the westside, in the mid-1970's. He left his mark on the westside as a big fella' in his trade. Unfortunately, Big Son's fame was cut short by the blade of a northend roller named Bill Talley. Yep, the same Talley who starred on Northern's championship basketball team. Talley did a pretty long stretch in the pokey for that crime. They settled their beef in a motel room on the westside...one brother dead and one hauled off to jail. In this case, like many others before them and after them. The system got two for one without any casualties amongst their own ranks. Shady Six, was shot to death in the early 1990's. I guess one could say. Shady went to the big shoot 'em-up in the sky. His shit-talking younger brother, Bojo, became an alcoholic.

There were whole family's caught up in the vortex of fast money. The People family included the patriarch and matriarch-Pop's, his wife and two son's; Ricky and Billy People, and their sister, whose name escape's me, and their cousins Gully and Normy. Pop's died in prison. His wife and daughther are doing some major time in the pen as well. Billy, was murdered and so was Gully. Normy died in a dope house fire. Ricky, the sole survivor of the men in his family was paroled after a seven-year bit in prison. I wondered was the price that family paid worth it for their 15 minute's of fame. Those are just a small sampling of my brother Slim's click. Along with his little rappy, Victor, who as of this writing has been tucked inside the penal system for at least the last 20 plus years. God only knows when he'll be cut loose. When a women birth's a child. I wonder does she sometimes envision the plight of her offspring? Can mother's and father's envision a time when their little bundle of joy could be staring back at them once a month, sometimes for the rest of their lives through plexi-glass and steel bars. Can she ever envision watching her child begging for forgiveness and mercy, only to fall on deaf ears. Well, it is my belief that the time is ripe for Black American adults, (Men and Women) to give their children the benefit of their insight and intelligence. It is no longer a stretch to envision our youth incarcerated with basketball scores for their sentences. It is a reality being played out a thousand fold daily, in Black family's throughout the good old USA.

Occupying the apartment next door to ours on Monterey was a member of the 1950's and 1960's singing group The Falcons, his wife and two children: a young son and daughter. The Falcons were a local group who hit the charts in the early 1960's with "I Found a Love." The late, great, Wilson Pickett, was a member of The Falcons, before he hit it big as a solo act with "Mustang Sally." The Falcon's follow-up hit "You're So Fine" helped establish the group's sound. Directly across the street lived the legendary Marv Johnson, whose hit in the early 1960's "Come to Me" helped put Berry Gordy and Motown on the map. Mr. Johnson owned the four-family flat. He occupied one of the units and rented the others out. In the large apartment building next door to Marv's property on the corner of Monterey and Lawton, lived one of the pimps who frequented the bean house, Joe Martin. From our balcony, I saw Joe squire a bevy of beauties in and out of the building. Joe was a tall soft-spoken cool as they come, pimp. Who on occasion rolled dice on the bean house floor with Hawk and other Macks, stalling to catch one of the many loose pros who hit our door in search of the almighty beans. Some pimps made the bean house a rendezvous point, where they could check their traps in the wee hours of the night. Those were the cream-off the top pimps, who relished in kicking it with their peers. They were always freshly-dressed and groomed-to-the-bone. Flash Beaver was a tap-dancing pimp type who plied his dancing skills at venues all over the country. He appeared on the hit television program, The Gong Show. His signature finale when ending his routine, he would pull out his handkerchief then proceed-to jump rope with the short handkerschief, that always brought the house down. By the way, Beaver went on to win first place on The Gong Show.   Monterey was a long, wide street. Our building was bounded by Dexter, two blocks to the west and Linwood, one block to the east. Monterey consisted mainly of two, four, and six-family units; with a smattering of huge apartment buildings and single-family houses. Most of the dwellings were big and well-maintained. It definitely was a step-up from the northend. The westside was built by Jews, who migrated from the northend in the 1930's, 40's and 50's. Anglo's were spead out in Northwest Detroit. They had very strict convenants built into their deeds and by-laws, prohibiting whites from selling to blacks. Jews didn't adhere to the covenant practices of the Anglo's; thus, when Jews moved from the northend, they sold or rented their property to black people, who were pushing their way out of "Black Bottom." Blacks have always supported the Jewish business's, located in our communities. When Jews moved from the westside to Southfield and Oak Park, blacks bought or rented their properties on the westside, and that migration pattern continues today. With Jews moving to more affluent areas, such as Franklin and Farmington Hills, blacks continued their move further out into the suburbs. Now we're spread throughout the surrounding regions. Of course, as blacks moved west and northwest, the Anglos changed their tune regarding their covenants. They sold out to black's in the early 1970's, then abandoned Detroit, establishing new covenants as they fled further from Detroit. Blacks have always been a source of revenue for Jews seeking to upgrade their lives. In essence, blacks and Jews were partners in the progression of each other's people, and that's the truth, Ruth.

The westside was cool, but, I longed for my old stomping grounds on the northend. I was torn between two sides; north and west. I often visited Brenda on the northend. On occasion, I would stop and kick it with some of my old co-horts. On one such occasion, I rode the Dexter bus to West Grand Boulevard and Cass Avenue, across the street from the General Motors Building. I was sixteen and could go for days without much sleep. I had on a sharp-ass sports coat, dress slacks and dress shoes. After exiting the bus, I walked the remaining blocks from Cass Avenue. I walked one block east to Woodward, north on Woodward two blocks to Horten, then, east on Horten past Brush Street. Down to Beaubien Street, then one block south to Custer Street, where I ran into an old acquaintance, Jarome Morgan, one of the guys I grew up around on the northend. Every since Jarome was a teen he slung that tragic magic. Jarome did his thang and he was in and out of jail. He never hit it big in the classic sense as a major roller. He did have one thing going for him in his trade of choice: he was-consistent. That's why it's hard for me to understand why he didn't get over. The culprit probably was that he "got high on his own supply." That's not carved in stone: that's the only rational thing I could phantom. From time to time, I'd run into Jarome, here and there. We would speak, that was the size of it; but, on that day, he caught up with me. He was in good spirits and he seemed to be doing well. Jarome and I were the same age. We never were running buddies; but, we respected one another. Years earlier, Jarome and Jerry Ross had a beef over a young lady on the northend. Jarome subsequently was pistol-whipped by Jerry. In 2001, Jarome was murdered over crack territory on the northend. He was shot-gunned to death on Oakland and Bethune Street. Rest in peace, Jarome, and may your lord and savior be your guide.

Lets back up. I crossed Beaubien Street, after kicking it with Jarome. I took a short cut through my old elementry school, Palmer, where a group of my old chums were playing football: Junie boy, Isadore Turner and five or six other dudes. They needed another player, so I volunteered despite the fact that I was nattily attired. My stay didn't last long. Our team kicked off to Isadore's team. Isadore was a strapping well-built lad, he was a little younger than me. He was set to receive the kick off. Palmer was a small play field. As soon as the ball was in the air, I raced down-field and timed Isadore's reception perfectly. As soon as he touched the ball, I was on top of him. As he readied to shift his right foot into foward motion, I hooked him around the neck with a clothes-line tackle, jarring him to the ground...No gain, much pain. Without missing a stride. I dashed out of the gate and on over to Oakland Avenue, one block east. Then north on Oakland, a dozen blocks or so, then east over to Russell and Kenwood, up the stairs into Brenda's mother's house. Right into Brenda's arms, thrilling her with all my charms. Still freshly-dressed. Boy, I enjoyed being a young man.

Now that I had dropped out of school, I became more adventurous, exploring different venues, as long as I was working and hustling good, and paying my own way, I was good to go with Beanie. That was until I managed to say something she deemed off limits. Then it was, "Hit the Road Jack." They call it tough love in todays vernacular. I've always paid my own way since I was about eight or nine years old, beginning with my first job. I didn't know it at the time; but, paying my own way at an young age reaped me residual effects. It taught me independence and self reliance. As I got older we started calling it rent. By the time that I had turned seventeen, I had worked many dead-end jobs. I didn't have much of a choice. It was swim or sink...no middle ground. Grown-ups, I knew didn't encourage me to go on to higher education. That is not an indictment; just the facts. It was all about getting a job and helping out. I worked everything from bus-boy to warehouse worker, and a host of other menial jobs in between. I even worked a girl or two. I was learning how to survive until some older, more experienced pimp knocked 'em off. Some pros became wise to the fact that I was green as grass, then they ran off, or got knocked off. One day I had 'em, the next day I didn't. Shy of my seventeenth birthday, I landed one of the best jobs of my young life. I landed a summer job with the Federal Housing Administration (FHA) located on the famed Washington Boulevard in downtown Detroit, as a summer intern in the mail room. That was big shit for a po' black teen in a white-dominated Detroit. The FHA was a federal agency that regulated housing in big cities. The agency was located in the Book Building. It took up two floors on the upper levels of the building. Working on Washington Boulevard, meant that I could window-shop until I dropped. It was one of my favorite past-times. With my meager wages, I couldn't buy much, so I let my imagination run wild as I drooled over the stylish threads in the windows. During that time, downtown was spectacular and exciting. Washington Boulevard, was the crowning jewel, in an oasis of jewels. It was a wide boulevard, with a flower laden island separating north and south traffic. In my short travels through the city, Washington Boulevard, was the cleanest street I had ever encountered. I didn't see a lot of Black people working in positions of authority downtown. At the FHA, there was one other black working there besides myself. He was a long-time employee, exiled to the mail room until retirement or death, whichever came first. Back in the 1960's, I thought it was a good job; but, later in my life's journey, I came to realize that I was only a token working in the mail room. I'm left dumb-founded as to how my people survived the blatant racism and disrespect bestowed upon us as citizens of these United States of America. No wonder there's so much carnage in our communities. We take all our frustrations out on each other.

The most embarassing thing to happen to me in my youth on a job was, when I was employed at a small lunch and supper club on West Six Mile Road, between Woodward and Second Avenue, in Highland Park. The club was owned by a white couple. At that time, Highland Park, was a mostly upper crust enclave; peppered with well-off black and white family's. The owners of the club were friendly and upbeat. I got in their good graces and enjoyed working for them. One afternoon while working the lunch crowd busing tables, they had a live band playing soft standards, the band was fronted by a singer. The crowd was majority white. There was one problem: the band showed up, but the singer didn't. That left the club owners in a lurch. One of the owner's jokingly blurted. "Arnold, go find us a singer." Me, being the dip that I was at that time in my youth. I blurted. "I can sing." I couldn't believe that came out of my mouth. It was a reflective, spontaneous type of response...no rhyme or reason to explain it. I never even considered that someone would take me serious. The wife's eyes lit up, she smiled at me, then said. "Oh yeah." She then grabbed me by the arm and led me to the front of the stage and announced to the audience. "Our busboy, Arnold, would like to sing us a song." She then handed me a microphone. She had just shoved a foreign object into my hand. Then she walked off the stage and left me "Bewitched, bewildered and bothered." I was floored. I had a little secret no one else knew. I couldn't sing. It was one of those precarious moments you experience in life, where you just want to shrivel up and disappear: pouf, transported into another place and time. I was stuck and had no place to hide. I sheepishly turned to the band and nervously spoke. "Do y'all know "Stand By Me;" praying they didn't; but, they did. Then the band struck the first chords. It wasn't long before my little secret was exposed. I just dropped the microphone, walked off stage, out of the door, and then down the street, where I disappeared out of sight; never to be heard from again. I didn't even go back to get my last paycheck. I sent my brother, Runt, to pick it up. That's how embarrassed I was.

THE HANNON FAMILY

Ora West-Hannon,
my grandmother died in 1946,
two years before I was born

James Hannon, my grandfather
circa 1930's

Ora and James Hannon
On Belle Isle early 1930's,
my grandmother and grandfather

Bennie Mae Hannon/Moore and her
husband William "Wig" Moore
1956, mother and stepfather

Me and my brothers
at Christmas 1955
Arnold, Runt and Slim

"Fass Cass" - 1968

Arnold "Fass Cass" Hannon
and Debra Ross - 1971

Arnold "Fass Cass" Hannon
and Debra Hannon,
my first wife - 1972

FAMILY AND FRIENDS

Slim Hannon and Arnold Hannon
1968

Arnold and Friend
The Burning Spear Lounge - 1977

Arnold and Brenda Knight
The Burning Spear Lounge - 1977

Malon "Mack" McKinney, Friend and Arnold - 1972

Friend and Arnold
1971

Arnold, Henry's Lounge
1975, on leave from Army

Arnold "Fass Cass" Hannon and Friend
Chick Springer's Lounge - 1979

Darlene, Handsome Harold and Dell
1970's

Handsome Harold's Serville. Note license plate, DST111
Dell stole this one too - 1978

Jimmy Blue, Sir Gabe, Game,
Friend and Broadway Cornell
New York - mid 1970's

Jimmie Blue and Ronnie Rico
New York - mid 1970's

Blue, Friend, JM and Arnold
Green Party, Burning Spear Lounge - circa 1979

Arnold "Fass Cass" and Friend
circa 1968

Friend, Arnold and Friend
circa 1995

Debra and Arnold
circa 1979

Arnold and Sugar - circa 1978

Arnold and Deb - circa 1972

Arnold and Friend - circa 1979

Arnold, Todd's Mens Wear - 1974

Arnold and Penny
Chick Springer's Lounge - Circa 1980

Lydia and Arnold - circa 1970

To Second Left:
Bobby Jackson,
Wonder Ray in Shades,
Thomas Patton,
Allen Underwood, Hat
Top Back:
The All Mighty "Hawk"
Kneeling D. J. and Joe Martin
Detroit Playa's
circa 1963

Wonder Ray, Joe Martin
and Thomas Patton
Playa's To The Bone
circa 1966

Playa's
King David, Hooker,
Booker, John Blunt's
nephew, Johnny Mapp,
Thomas Patton, Joe Martin
a host of
Mellow Mackaroni's
circa 1964

The Democratic Club
(Blind Pig)
Syracruse and Game
Panama Red and Game
Which one is Fass Cass?
circa mid 1970's

Detroit Playa's workin' it in New York
Franshot, Frosty, Blue, Syracruse,
Handsome Harold - circa 1969

Standing: Ronnie Love,
Handsome Harold, Syracruse,
Bobby Gibson, JP

Playa's Round Table
Micheal Brance, Syracruse,
Friend, J.M., Ronnie Love,
Handsome Harold
Bobby Gibson (Back)
circa mid 1970's

Mack of the Year Gala - circa 1981
Chick Springers Lounge
Standing left to right: Thomas Patton, Danny "Boy" Moore, Curt, Panama Red,
Chunchy (Philadephia), friend and Perry Adams
Sitting left to right: Pimpin' Dee, Florida Bobby, Friend, Reggie and
Arnold "Fass Cass" Hannon

My Lovely Wife
Terry Hannon and Arnold Hannon
circa 1996

Arnold Hannon
1998

Arnold Hannon
Army - 1974

Arnold and Terry
Las Vegas Wedding - 1997

Terry and Arnold
Wedding Day, Las Vegas - 1997

Terry's Graduation Party
Terry and Arnold
University of Detroit - 2001

Arnold and Terry on vacation, Niagra Falls - 1999

Vintage Game
Haygood & Company Cabaret
Thomas Patton, Arnold Hannon and
Arthur "Baby" circa 2006

Terry and Arnold
circa 2006

Arnold Hannon Graduating
Wayne County Community College
circa 1988

Arnold Hannon
Graduating University of Detroit
circa 1990

Terry and Arnold Hannon
1999

Arnold and Shannon
1998

Walter and Patty Shannon
Terry's Graduation Party - 2001

Arnold and Terry
circa 2006

Terry and Arnold Hannon
Terry's Graduation - circa 2001

Arnold and Terry's Garden
2005

PART TWO

We must find ways to make education glamorous to at risk urban youth. For those students who embrace academics, our society must invest the resources to help them achieve their goals. We, as a society, must find ways to tap into our young men and women's intellect. They have so much more to offer the world than Murder, Madness and Mayhem.

Arnold Hannon

Chapter 11

MURDER, MADNESS AND MAYHEM

In my mothers new neighborhood on the westside, Black men and women marched off to work mainly in the auto plants and sub-par-menial-waged jobs; while others hung out on street corners. Some ran their own business. In many cases that business was illegal street numbers or the usual underworld occupations of the non-conforming types. There were also men and women going about their daily grind of just trying to survive life's march.

At that particular juncture my march through life lead me to a company named Super Toys, located in the old Packard Auto Plant, on East Grand Boulevard, and Conner; More than a quarter century earlier my grandfather toiled on the assembly line for the Packard Motor Company. During the time of my employment, the plant was sectioned off into warehouses for individual businesses, basically wholesale distributors and small manufacturers. Lou Katz, and Al Pitt were the Jewish owners of Super Toys. My job was to fill orders from the various department stores like Sears and Kmart, who ordered their toys and pet supplies from Super Toys.

It was during that time my girlfriend Brenda, had moved to Richton Street, one block from where I lived on Monterey. Brenda, Marlene and Marlene's sister, Nene, rented a huge apartment in one of the biggest apartment buildings on the westside. I now had a place to hang out on the westside. Marlene, was going with an ex-convict named, Stacy: who also became a regular around the apartment: as well as Nene's man, Reggie. Stacy was a singer and ex-con with a glib attitude, whom, I gave much latitude. Reggie was a well-kept, young man with well-to-do parents. There was a lot of comings and goings at the apartment; especially with rehearsals for the girls singing group and their friends from the entertainment field. One such visitor was a singer by the name of Joby and his wife. Joby, was the first cousin of Eddie Kendricks of the "Temptations." Joby would go on to become a member of the R&B singing group, "Enchantment." Joby's wife threw him a birthday bash at Eddie's Palmer Woods mansion, one of Detroit's swankiest neighborhoods on Belmoral Street. All the regulars were invited to the party; including me and Brenda, along with Marlene, Nene and Brenda Rollins, the other Member of the Sequin's. It was a snazzy beautiful house, with all the amenities of the lush life. The party was held in the basement, it was decked out to the hilt. I had a few harsh words with one of the partiers weeks earlier. He wanted to settle it right there in the basement. Marlene sensed what was about to go down and pleaded with us not to spoil it for everyone else. We obliged. I was relieved dude was way bigger than me.

A year or so after hanging out at the apartment, I got the notion to sell some beans. Nene and her cousins, Charlie and Fred, were bean heads. A few others were users as well. I saw a golden opportunity, so I thought. I copped from Jerry Ross and David Tate. Business was pretty good, until the night I peeped out the peep hole and saw two White cops strolling down the hall, headed in my direction, looking like they meant business. I panicked, then I promptly threw my stash out of the eighth-floor window; then I waited for the two cops to come kick the door down. It turned out that the cops went right pass our door and around the corner to another apartment on a domestic call. Needless to say, when David and Jerry came by with the new product, I couldn't cop, because I had thrown all of the beans out the eighth floor window; thus, ending my little business venture. It started getting wild around the apartment. Nene, Charlie and Charlie's brother, Freddy, were dropping beans everyday. All kinds of shady types were hanging out. That pushed all the square regulars away; including Marlene, who moved out. I too drifted in a different direction.

Back at Super Toys, I began buying pet clipper sets wholesale from Al and Lou. The only thing that distinguished pet clippers, from human hair clippers was a plastic label with "Pet Clippers" embossed on them. I just peeled off the label and presto, I had human hair clippers. I then took them back to the hood and made a killing selling them as home barber sets. I bought them by the case and sold them retail. No one got wise to that little ruse. The pay was low at Super Toys and the turn over rate was high. There was a lot of hiring and firings of employees; subsequently, I met a lot of people down-on-their luck, trying to scratch out a living. I met some real characters. For instance, a fellow whose parents were determined to have a successful son, whom, they hoped would become the first college graduate in their family, so he said.. He was a fifty-year-old warehouse worker, who didn't quite live up to the name his parents had anointed him with. His name was Lawyer Jones.

Another fella' that stands out in my mind was a white drifter from North Carolina, named Grady. You know the type: pale, white, with no color, big Adams apple and beady blue eyes. My first impression of him without knowing him: I wrote him off as a racist, or some kind of serial killer. I was guilty of pre-judging him because of the way he looked. When I did have an opportunity to have a conversation with him, it didn't take long to decipher that he was just a lonely, poor, illiterate man, somewhat slow in his southern ways. As Grady begin to open up, (speaking in his native North Carolina drawl) I realized how wrong I was about him. He was a nice, humble guy in need of friendship. He was alone in Detroit, for whatever reasons, and he had no family or friends; so we started hanging out, mainly at the Roxy Bar near the downtown area around Erskine and Woodward. I wasn't old enough to patronize the bar, but it didn't matter, as long as I was paying, I was staying. The Roxy is long gone today; but, back in the 1960's it was a low-class, anything goe's type of establishment that attracted patrons on the low-end of the social structure. Grady, liked the Roxy because of all the loose prostitutes who patronized the bar. I was along for the ride. I was just glad that I could sit in the bar and not get hassled because of my age. On one particular payday evening, Grady, was feeling horny and wanted to hook up with one of the hookers that plied their trade in the Roxy. He asked me to hang out with him. I agreed and we caught the bus down to the Roxy Bar. When we arrived at our destination, Grady, entered the bar. I stopped out front to kick it with Panama Red, one of my buddies from downtown. When I finished my business with Red, I entered the bar, where I spotted Grady sitting at the far end of the bar facing me. A pro,' who had her back turned toward me was standing between Grady's legs, up close and personal... with a yard of tongue down Grady's throat and rubbing him down. Grady saw me, then came down to where I was standing and told me that he was going to pay the pro' twenty dollars for sex. I reminded him that he could get a cheap room around the corner. He agreed and went back to retrieve his date. As he and the pro' were walking toward me, I got a good look at the hooker and it became clear that Grady had bitten off more than he could chew. His new-found love was a fag' dressed in drag. I pulled Grady over to the side and warned him of my suspicions. He slumbered over to the fag' and grabbed his crotch to check out my suspicions. Grady's buck-eyes confirmed that he had indeed grabbed a dick. He was furious and ready to fight. I pulled him to the door. His rage was obvious. I gave him a stern warning: "That motherfucker will cut your throat." Grady went unfulfilled as he huffed and puffed on out of the door. Grady sulked all the way down Woodward Avenue.

We hung out most of the remaining evening in the downtown area. There were a lot of folk's out and about. The night life was booming with a lot of places open late at night: the White Caslte restaurant, on Woodward near Elliot, across the street from The Dessert Inn Motel, that was owned by Sam Gant and Mac Pye, two Black businessmen who owned property throughout the Detroit area. It was rare for the times for blacks to own prime commercial real estate in Detroit. Down the street from the Dessert Inn was the Stone Burlesk, then owned by Italian mobsters. A few doors down was the Roxy Theater, an all night movie theater, where homeless types and other shady individuals, for the price of admission could have a warm place to rest their head. I spotted a familiar face in a rumpled old pimp suit, going into the show with a couple of broken-down old whores trailing him. He was an old customer of the bean house, Shelly Bomen, the aging downtown, down-on-his-luck pimp. Shelly ran his whores, (Shelly, pimped whore's not pros) out of downtown whore houses, right about where Comerica Park stands today, on the John R side. There were some bars at downtown locations that were strictly trade bars: that allowed prostitute's to ply their trade. The Columbia and Purple Onion bars were the most prominent in that regard. When Shelly came to cop his beans, he was a big shit-talker and whore-stalker, that's what he called himself anyway. He would often brag about how he would pimp anything breathing: Hoes, fags, kids... he didn't care... if they got with him they had to go. I came to the conclusion that Shelly, was a man void of conscience or pride.

Working at Super Toys was all right; but, not very profitable. I was never going to get rich working there, as Beanie used to say, it'll keep you out of the poor house. Back on Monterey, the mailman had brought me some good news in the form of a $90.00 income tax refund check. Before the check arrived, I got up the nerve to ask my mother about that father thing again. I got the same negative response as always. I wondered to myself what was the big secret regarding my conception. I always felt like shit after one of those exchanges with my mother. It was as if I had done something grossly wrong by seeking that knowledge. As usual, I was left perplexed. I pressed the issue, which, as always ended with me getting tossed out of the house. Somewhere down the line I had hoped that she would eventually share her secret with me. Anyway, when the check came, Beanie, had intercepted it, she opened it up, and saw the $90.00 check and asked me if she could have it for groceries and bills. I was already the only kid in the house paying rent. She didn't ask Slim or Runt for a dime. I refused her request, then an argument ensued. Once again, I was rendered homeless. The last words I heard were, "Get your ass out." With check planted firmly in hand, I hit the road. I made my way over to Richton Street, to hook up with Brenda; but, no one was at home. I had to find shelter for the night. It's a hell-of-a-thing when you're suddenly tossed out there. Desperation creeps in. Once again, I was in a desperate situation. My mind was working over-time trying to find a solution to my dilemma: Maybe I should have given in; naw, it was never about the money with me, it was more a matter of principles. I worked hard for my meager wages and I was entitled to my earnings; especially when I was already paying for my own upkeep. In the eyes of the law, I was still a minor. My immediate problem had to be addressed, I had to go to work in the morning. Grady had given me his address over on Trumbel. He didn't have a telephone, so I took my chances and caught the bus over to his flat. He was at home. I told him of my dilemma. He was glad to see me and welcomed me with open arms. We had agreed on rent, for now I was good for the night. Grady didn't have a television or telephone; just a small radio. White people were poor, and Black people were po,' even though Grady was white he was nonetheless, po' like some po' Black folks. I stayed there for a couple of weeks, long enough to get myself together. I wanted my own place. During my short lay over at Grady's, we spent a lot of time in the streets, looking back, we must have been the oddest looking pair of running buddies out there. Downtown was our stumping grounds.

I eventually hooked back up with Brenda, and moved in with her. Living with someone ain't like going to visit them, where you'll have to leave and go home or whatever. Living with someone is like visiting and never leaving. You will come to discover some unpleasant realities about your mate's routines and life-long habits that aren't going anywhere. I would have to leave before she'll relinquish her habits. Some habits are purely psychological idiosyncrasies, buried deep in one's sub-consciousness.

Back at Super Toys, I was beginning to get tired of the low pay and tedious monotonous work. Before I quit, I was determined to get something out of my stay there. I came up with a little scheme. It was the late 1960's. Me and Grady, were in the back section of the warehouse putting new stock away, when I looked up and noticed that the ceiling was peeling, with thick chunks of plaster loose and hanging down. I got a long pole and poked the ceiling out. When the plaster fell to the ground. I laid down and had Grady cover me with the debris. We were only trying to get the rest of the day off. After covering me with the debris, I instructed Grady to run out and get Art, the big White, Polish foreman. I thought Art was going to send me home with pay; but, instead he sent me to their medical clinic. I got a clean bill of health and was sent back to work. Grady soon moved on. He led the life of a nomad. Thinking about it now, I think Grady may have been a wanted man, a fugitive who just drifted around the country in search of self. I got fired from Super Toys and Beanie was getting ready to move into her own home for the first time in her life. Once again, I'm on my own. Little did I know then that the little ruse with the falling ceiling would prove to be a God send.

Early in 1969, I was sitting in the same courtroom that I had testified in against the young armed robber some twelve years earlier, before Judge Davenport. That was a few years before they tore down the old court house to make way for the new Frank Murphy Hall of Justice, a bigger and more efficient court. During my early teen years, I would sit in on some of the trials that took place in the old Recorder's Court. It was fascinating to observe how the system operated and the different characters on trial.

On one particular day in court, standing before Judge Crockett Sr. was a young man I knew from the streets. He used to hang out around Kirby and Beaubien Street, near the local outdoor swimming pool, operated by the Detroit Recreation Department. All the kids in the area used Kirby's pool to cool off from the summer's heat. Most of the younger kids made their way down to the pool in groups. It was only a mile south of where I lived on Bethune. On one such outing after my dip in the pool. I was ready to leave. Everyone I came with wanted to stay; therefore, I had to go it alone. As I passed Kirby and Beaubien, a few yards away I spotted a young dark-skin man with a gun in his hand. The subject of his attention was an older fellow pleading for his life. Bam! The young man with the dark sunken eyes had just shot the pleading dude in the leg. The gunman glared at me and then ran off, disappearing down a nearby alley. I never forgot the dark-eyed young man with the smoking gun in his hand. Many years later we meet again in Judge Crockett's Courtroom. I was one of seven people in the courtroom and the charge against the young man was murder. With a charge of that magnitude, the defendant's family was nowhere in site. Also present were: the bailiff, the prosecutor, a court reporter, two stern-looking cops and a court-appointed defense attorney. David Armstrong, the defendant stood before the Judge looking grim and defiant. He glanced over his shoulder and saw only me as he awaited his fate. Not much had changed about him. He was a little older and bigger now. I wondered if he recognized me from our last encounter years earlier. I heard the Judge bellow. "Murder." I don't remember in what degree. On that day, David Armstrong, a few years my senior and still a very young man looked up as the judge barked. "Bound over for trial; No bond," as he slammed down his gavel: Bam! The two officers quickly hustled Armstrong, out of the courtroom. Through my youthful vision it was quite a sad scene. Armstrong's cold, dark eyes revealed a tragic saga of hurt, neglect, abandonment, let-down and rage. I felt that David Armstrong, had experienced more than his share of tragic events in his young life. Jail was somewhat of a step up for Mr Armstrong. As grim as things appeared, David Armstong, will be heard from again on the mean streets of Detroit; where his alter ego, Buck Dave, would emerge and rain havoc on Detroit's underworld.

During our last years on Monterey, I labored at many jobs, including a stint at the long-defunct "Dodge Main Auto Plant," on East Grand Boulevard. The old, now-torn-down plant made Dodge and Chrysler cars. My job involved pulling car frames onto the beginning of the assembly line with a long metal hook. It was tedious, hard work. That was not the direction that I envisioned my life going. I hung on for a few months, then I was out of there. During the summer of 1967, I worked as a desk clerk at a motel on Woodward near Canfield. It was after midnight, July 23, 1967. I don't recall the motel's name; but, I think it was the Downtown Motel. I was the late night clerk. I faked a robbery because I wanted out. It was a dangerous situation with me renting motel rooms to all types of shady characters late at night on Woodward Avenue. I felt like a target sitting in my little enclosed-cubical with whores, stick-up types, and junkies peering in at me. I devised a plan. An exit strategy, the poor man's severance package. I came up with a fake robbery: I called the owner of the motel and the police to report that a woman had ran into the motel's lobby, screaming that her boy friend was beating her. She pleaded for me to open the door to hide her behind the enclosed plexi-glass office area, where I did my business. Just as I opened the door to help her escape from harm; a man rushed in and produced a gun. The woman hit the cash register and they were off and running. Leaving me afraid and shaken. That was before the advent of security cameras and the like. That was my story and I stuck to it. When the police arrived, I put on an act worthy of an academy award. I pretended to be afraid and nervous, hoping they wouldn't suspect me, or discover the stolen loot in my shoe. The cops bought my story and reassured me that the robbers were not coming back. When the owner arrived, the police filled him in on the situation, then they told him that I was lucky because a rash of armed robberies were happening in the area. Hell, that wasn't news. Everybody knew that. That's why I did it. I rationalized it as my severance pay. I quit the job on the spot, then headed out onto Woodward Avenue.

I didn't have a car and the buses were almost non-existent at that time of night. I proceeded to walk north on Woodward in the general direction of Beanie's flat on Monterey. Some 3 or 4 mile's to the west. As I walked, I prayed for a bus to catch up to me. I moved toward my destination. It was whichever came first, the bus or home. I was hitting my stride and I was determined to walk, come hell or high water. You'll never know who or what, you might run into on the mean streets of Detroit, late at night. A few blocks into my journey, I reached into my sock and retrieved the stash of cash from the heist. I continued north on a stark, desolate area of Woodward, (The area around Horten and Smith Street.) that I knew very well. I was just a block away from where I grew up at on Bethune. There was as I remembered, no street lights on in that stretch of Woodward. As I continued my trek toward Monterey and Lawton, things were livening up as I approached Clairmount Street. As I neared Reggie's Barbershop, on the corner of Clairmount and Woodward, there were a lot of people out and about. The Caddys were on pimp patrol for loose game, the glamorous set were piling into The In Crowd Lounge, a block away on Kenilworth and Woodward. The In Crowd Lounge, adopted it's name from a hit record at the time. The song was by the one-hit wonder, Dobie Gray, who made. "I'm in with the In Crowd" a top-ten hit in the 1960's. Instead of turning west on Clairmount, the quickest route to my destination. I decided to go down and check out the night-lifers. I felt like a young groupie, as I drooled over the beautifully-coifed players and playettes strutting their stuff in and out of The In Crowd Lounge. Then someone spotted him, the out-of-place white drunk staggering down Woodward, headed in our direction. When the impostor staggered by, everyone knew he was a cop in that infamous police squad called "STRESS," that was an acronym for "Stop The Robberies Enjoy Safe Streets." It should have been called the hit squad. Here's how "STRESS" operated: they would send undercover, White cops into high crime areas. One plain-clothed cop with gas can in hand pretending that he was...out of gas and drunk. Muggers would make him as an easy mark; then, attempt to rob the wayward White fellow. There was only one problem, the White cops were setting up Black men and gunning them down in the streets. In some cases blacks were shot while running away, (or) with their hands up. It didn't matter because the White "STRESS" officers used Black men as live target practice. One of the reasons Coleman Young, became the first Black Mayor of Detroit, is that he vowed to abolish "STRESS" if elected. It wasn't the only reason Mayor Young was elected, it was just a part of his overall strategy to help get him elected as the Mayor of Detroit. In the early 1970's, Detroit, was on the brink of exploding again. Well, let's get back to the the white cop staggering past The In Crowd Lounge, pretending to be lost and drunk. The cops didn't know that this was the "clever as ever set" out that night. They were not buying it. The bar was on jam. There was a heavy over-flow out front kickin' it when that white fool came slumbering by with a gas can dangling from his hand. The crowd started laughing and ridiculing him as he passed a gauntlet of revelers. Someone in the crowd shouted. "Get your po' white ass away from here, everybody know you "STRESS." "Mahfucka." Then everyone, myself included, started chanting "STRESS, STRESS, STRESS, STRESS" in unison. What started out as a one voice chant, became a chorus of echoing voice's that trailed the hapless cop down the street. The cop's face turned Cherry red, as his undercover operation was uncovered. A parade of passing pimps in their "fly" rides, started honking their horns at the hapless intruder. By the time he reached Clairmount and Woodward, everyone on the street knew who he was. Finally, his backup team swooped him up. With their tails between their legs, they sped off in a cloud of embarrassment to more fertile hunting grounds. I wouldn't be surprised if that little episode didn't cause some unsuspecting brother some grief that night.

After the scene had normalized, I headed back toward Clairmount and Woodward, still no bus in sight. I was half-way home. I crossed Second Avenue, then Third Street, walking on down pass the Lodge freeway over pass. Just as I was approaching 14th Street, a long sleek black 1967 Cadillac Deville, convertible with the top dropped cruised by. I recognized the sporty dude who was driving. He was the westside player and hustler known as Pigeon. He was out and about, doing it with style. Pigeon, was younger then me and I was barely nineteen. "Baby, boy" was doin' it. I guessed that he was headed to Melvin Franklin's, (Temptations) mother's house, where Pigeon's wife, Tootsie, Melvin's little sister resided. He had made a turn onto Clairmount from Linwood Street, headed in that direction, I assumed that's where he was headed. I felt down in the dumps as I walked. It seemed as if everyone and their mother was out sportin' slick rides, and I was humpin' down the street all alone. I imagined me griping my own "Super fly" ride someday. Boy, my priorities were screwed-up. I should have been gearing myself for a quality education.

When I approached 12th Street, I noticed a crowd of people gathered around the corner of 12th and Clairmount. Cops were raiding an after-hours joint, and roughing up the patrons as they prepared to haul them off to jail. A crowd of locals had gathered to witness the proceedings. The crowd jeered at the rough-house tactics the cops were employing. As I stood there watching the unfolding drama. I spotted one of the fellows from my westside neighborhood, Gregory Smith, who was being man-handled by White cops. I too became incensed. It was a hot muggy night and the crowd's blood was boiling. Insults were hurled at the cops, followed by bricks, bottles and anything else the crowd could get their hands on...400 years of pent-up rage was unleashed. The cops hurried to complete their mission and get out of there with their hides still intact.

I didn't know it then; but, this was the spark that ignited the infamous uprising of July 23, 1967. The first store hit at that wee-hour of the night was Esquire's Mens Wear, on the corner of Clairmount and 12th Street, across the street from the raid. At that precise moment, the Clairmount bus had arrived and I hopped on it to complete my journey. I really was torn between jumping on the bus or joining the uprising. I opted out for the bus. As I hopped on the bus, a mob of marauders poured in behind me, snatching the lone white rider, dragging him off the bus like prey into their deadly clutches. It was ugly. Even though I wanted to intervene, I felt like the others on the bus, it would only bring some of that our way. We were simply out-numbered. All I could think was: "Poor fellow, may God be with you." The bus driver beat it out of there. Leaving the badly-beaten ex-rider, who disappeared into the night in the bus's rear-view mirror as the bus fled swiftly down Clairmount. When we got to Linwood, (several blocks away) the driver jumped off the bus and called the police from a nearby pay phone. Cell phones were decades away. As the bus riders haggled about what had just happened, the bus driver was heard struggling to explain to the cops over the phone what was unfolding on Clairmount, on that hot, steamy late July night in Detroit, in 1967. I decided I was better off walking the mile or so trek home. The more I walked, the more cop cars I saw flying in the direction of the melee. Word was out on all fronts, and the dam was about to burst. When I made it home it was nearing 4 a.m. and I was dog-tired. What a night. I crawled onto the couch and fell fast asleep.

A few hours into my nap, Slim and Runt were waking me up all excited, like the circus or something had come to town. They riotin,' they riotin,' blurted Slim, as he and Runt rushed out into the fray before I could join them. They were just too excited and couldn't contain themselves. I stepped out onto the front balcony and heard the screaming sirens coming from the east and from the west. I could smell the parched, smoky air and I saw huge clouds of black smoke soaring above the trees off in the distance. I couldn't wait to get out there. I had no fear. There was an overwhelming adrenaline rush. I hustled to dress and fled out into the pandemonium. As I ran toward Linwood Avenue, I saw other young people coming out of their houses, going in the same direction... there was an air of festivity. The smoke and sirens were like magnets pulling throngs of people toward its epicenter. In my young, mis-guided mind, I thought: "The shit is on, Jarome." The first action I saw as I neared Linwood, was the meat market on Monterey and Linwood, being gutted of its bounty. The looters stripped the market bare like a pack of Piranha fish stripping a dead carcass, then someone torched it. Even though it was owned by a Jew, on that day, if it was white, it would ignite. I headed for the liquor store on Linwood and Sturdavent. I was 19 and as fit as a fiddle. As I approached the liquor store, the looters were already at work, stripping it of its liquid gold, booze. I rushed in, amidst elbows and shoves. As I battled for entry at the front entrance, shards of broken glass and a short step-down were the only obstacles between the looters and the storage area, that held cases of liquor stacked tall against the wall. I grabbed a case of Hennessy. A couple of doors down an older gent who was to shy to participate, was standing in the doorway of his business and called me over. He said. "I'll buy all you can get." He handed me three fifty-dollar bills, and I headed back to get more liquor. I plunged in several more times, until the store was wiped out. I ran down Linwood with about five hundred dollars to the good. I went in search of more. I ran across a clothing store being gutted, and I grabbed all I could carry in my arms. I ran down Linwood, amid broken glass, sirens and screaming, frenzied mobs of looters, and burned-out buildings. It was madness in motion, and I was having a ball.

Once back home, I asked Beanie to drive me over to the Algiers Motel, where I thought I would party with the cash that I had made off the liquor sales. As we weaved our way through the dense traffic flow, I saw firsthand the destruction sparked by the early morning raid on 12th Street. It truly was a grim scene with people being trampled, police cracking heads and burned-out buildings everywhere I looked. I didn't know it at the time that Slim had gotten busted. Once again his big foot had been eaten by yet another security gate, while trying to crawl out from under a looted store. The cops busted him as he laid on the ground writhing in disgust. Runt, made it through the carnage and so did I.

When we arrived at our destination, Beanie, let me out on Woodward and Euclid Street. The first person that I saw that I recognized was one of the Davidson Street Stuff players. Donald T, was training his little pro' Blinky, in front of the Algiers Motel. He was schooling her on how to catch a trick's eye. I nodded hello to him prancing on the sidewalk in his black nylon wife-beaters tee-shirt, with his doo rag tied tight around his Tony Curtis styled doo. Twenty-year-old Mack in training, schoolin' his game. It really is too bad that our young energies couldn't have been funneled into a more positive sphere. Hind-sight being 20/20. Back in the day, it just wasn't laying like that for some of us, for a myriad of reasons. The game was glamorous to po' young inner-city youth. That's the closest many of our urbanite's would get to some semblance of success. For many inner city youth, that way of living was a rite-of-passage. The game was supposed to be our ticket out; unfortunately, it was just a mirage, the beginning of self-destruction for many. The street creed has left many young lives in shambles. The fast-life was the beginning of the end for most: Monkey see... Monkey do. The youngsters learning how to screw their lives up, from their elders. Let's stop the vicious cycle. We must stop the madness! May the next generations learn from our successes; not our failures.

The action around the motel was fast and furious. I rented a room and with my young ignorant way of processing things, I thought I was gon' find me a pro' and pimp my ass off. When I look back on that period of my life, I was lucky to have survived it all. I was lost and way out there, just like my mis-guided brothers and sisters who were living on the fringes of our society. One had to be crafty and street wise to navigate his or her way through the crap, and live to write about it. If only we would have attacked the universities and colleges, with vigor and vim, the way we attacked each other with guns and knives, and the way we attacked the penitentiaries with our young lives at stake. And, oh my how we attacked the dark corners of the streets and morgues with wasted lives. Maybe we could have helped to build a better and stronger people. Like I stated, hind sight is 20/20.

I was pumped and my adrenaline was flowing. Hell, I had forgotten that there was a riot going on around me. At the time, I wasn't mature enough and I didn't have that vision thing. That's when the guidance thing should have kicked in; but, again, you play the hand that you are dealt. I had a pocket full of loot to front with. I was determined to come up with some fresh game. I can't believe I was that naive. It's almost deplorable for me to think that the character that I'm describing was actually me. I suppose when one grows up in the concrete jungle, surrounded by urban predators, one can easily become imprinted into the fabric of that environment. If one doesn't know ones inner-self, one could easily get caught up in the vortex of the so called game. This is my assessment, through my own experiences growing up po' in Detroit. There's a need for young people to have visible, positive role models to contrast the visible, negative role models running rampant in our communities. We need conscientious, professionals who have overcome many of the same obstacles facing today's and tomorrow's generations to step-up and be proactive role models in our communities. Our communities must find the means to expose today's youth to positive role models. We must find ways to make education glamorous to at-risk urban youth. For those students who embrace academics, our society must invest the resources to help them achieve their goals. We, as a society, must find ways to tap into our young men and women's intellect. They have so much more to offer the world than murder, madness and mayhem. Everyone wants to live the glamorous life without breaking a sweat. It ain't gon' happen if you're born poor. The subliminal messages to our youths in the hood has been in my estimation, that positivity can be deemed negative, and negativity can be deemed positive. For example the sharp ass pretty people "driving their fancy cars and living it up like movie stars, with fancy women in fancy bars." Most players lead negative lifestyles; but, in some circles in our communities they were held in high esteem. Some players had a way of making being bad look good. A lot of impressionable youth want that swagger, that thing that attracts money and women in droves. Impressionable youth only see the glamour. Its a crying shame that more aren't exposed to the swagger of the doctor, lawyer, or other educated-types working in the neighborhoods, doing positive deeds to off set and defame the so-called game. It's a vicious cycle, a cycle that is un-ending, learned behavior.

"Human's are a sum total of their heredity and environment." All do not fall into those well-placed traps. Many heeded to the positive elements, also permeating throughout our communities... there's just not enough. There are those who had great parents, who steered their young in the right direction. Things worked out well for many of them. Those are the brothers and sisters who are thriving, with thriving children and grand-children, who will become the glue that holds the urban communities to-gether... the true keepers of our future.

I did manage to knock off a young tender hanging out by the swimming pool. Most of the young women were hanging out looking for some at-tention. You don't hang out around pimps, and wanna-be-pimps, wheelers and dealers and other unsavory characters seeking attention. That is a recipe for disaster. Oh, you'll get attention alright. In most cases, it won't be the kind that you bargained for.

The street's action around the Algiers Motel, was fast and furious, awash with a cast of shady characters, with the police searching for some of them. I was too young and green for it to faze me. They say, God, looks out for kids and fools. I'm guilty. I was a big time fool, and without God, watching my back. I wouldn't be here writing these words. I thought I was having fun; never realizing that the external stimuli, was causing internal psychological discord that clouded my perception.

Later on that night it got real ugly. There was a lot of gunfire in and around the motel. I had stashed a fifth of Hennessy under the bed in my room, and invited other nervous motel guest over. I figured that there was safety in numbers. We laid on the floor to prevent us from catching a stray bullet through a window. We could hear the cops and robbers running all over the complex, with the strained shouts of angry cops as they pursued their prey. Suddenly, with lightning force my motel door was kicked open, then a barrage of threatening cops poured into a screaming, fearful audi-ence of young Black men and women. With guns drawn, the cops searched my room from stem to stern. One of the fully-armored, white cops bel-lowed. "Where's the looted goods y'all stole?" In unison, we belted. "Ain't nothing in here." I spoke up. Only thing in here is this half-empty bottle of booze, y'all welcome to some." One of the helmeted cops stifled a laugh. They were satisfied that we had nothing of value, or any looted goods. They warned us to stay in the room because there was a curfew in effect. "Ok," we responded, with relief. The cops left and repeated that scenario throughout the motel complex, until they hit pay dirt, catching a brother with hot goods. There were plenty of heads to crack. As the drama un-folded outside, we laid on the floor passing the bottle of Hennessy around inside. It suddenly dawned on me: what the fuck am I doing in this motel crawling around on the floor? That was a long night. I laid there in the mid-dle of the ghetto, with looting by day, and shootings by night. Behind the main motel was the motels annex. A huge white mansion with a ton of rooms for rent. It was dubbed. The annex. The main motel and the annex, were separated by at least 20 yards. We could hear the loud, bullying voices of cops belting out commands. Every gun shot, every siren, every foot step and every loud cops voice echoed its way into our room. Then we heard it: Boom, Boom, Boom, the blast of big guns. Then we heard the sirens whaling in the background. That made us lay flatter on the floor with our hands over our heads, It was a very intense situation. We survived the night. Later on I found out what happened in the annex on that horror filled tense night. A squad of racist, rabid cops, "Ronald August, Robert Paille, and David Senak" had stumbled on three Black teens, "Aubrey Pollard 19, Fred Temple 18, and Carl Cooper 17" entertaining White girls in their room. That proved to be a combustive mix. The planets were aligned. It was the right place and time to ignite and assert the cowardly cops racist rage. All the evil forces of nature were in motion at that particular place, at that particular moment in time. It came to be known as "The Algiers Motel Murders." The three cowardly White cops murdered three un-armed young, Black men, because they could. I guess the cops couldn't contain their hate. The fuse was lit. When the morning sun streaked through the curtains, I breathed a sigh of relief. I peeked out of the window and saw cops rounding up looters, and throwing them into paddy wagons.

Then I spotted him: the big black, bully cop, who went by the name of Black Diamond. Black Diamond was assigned to my high school as the cop in residence. He was a head cracker and enforcer for the police department; like the legendary cop from the 1940's, Ben Terpin. As big as Black Diamond was, I had seen him chase down and catch some fleet-footed brothers. If he had to chase you, and he caught you, that was your ass. You'll get a royal ass-whoopin' on the spot.

Meantime, me and the young woman I had met by the pool earlier, decided that it was a safe bet to get out of there while the getting was good. She said we could go to her small apartment over on Ferry Park and 14th. We made a break for it, ducking and dodging roaming gangs of thugs, looters and the police. We walked south on Woodward, a half dozen blocks or, so, to the Grand Boulevard, then we proceeded west on Grand Boulevard, about a quarter-mile, until we got to 14th Street. From there, one block south to Ferry Park, then we were there. She was right, it was a small apartment all right; but, it was cozy. She lived in a three-family building. The sun was beginning to set and I was about to get my Johnson wet. Just as I was about to get cozier, there was a knock at her door. When she opened it, there stood a young dude who lived on the first floor. We had passed him in the hall on our way to her apartment. Dude peered in and saw me laid back. He pushed the door open. I looked down at his right hand, where I saw him gripping a snub nosed 38. I braced myself, waiting to get shot, and I didn't know how to stop it. He stood to the side, and made a sweeping motion with his gun hand and head in unison; which meant, get to steppin.' I was well aware that a riot and curfew were in full effect. When staring down the barrel of a gun, you get to steppin,' and that's what I did. I fled out into the night with the National Guard and police ruling the streets. There I was, making my way down dark and empty streets, with nary a soul in sight. I walked north in the middle of the street, with my hands held high over my head to disspell any notion of a perceived threat coming from me. As I traveled north on 14th Street, I was hoping to make it home in one piece. I was in no mood for a confrontation with the authorities. I heard a heavy, rumbling noise off in the distance. It was a slow moving procession with it's heavy, armored vehicles clawing at the asphalt. The closer the rumbling got, the more fierce it sounded, grinding my nerves down. As the rumbling got louder, I knew that soon I would be face to face with whatever it was. Then, I saw the heavy vehicles rolling straight for me. As the convoy came into eye sight. I recognized that it was the National Guard. I was now in the eye of the storm. There was no need to alter my route, there was nowhere to go but straight ahead. "Nowhere to run; nowhere to hide." I trudged along in a slow death march, toward the blinding lights of the guard's mighty machines. The closer I got, the faster my heart beat. I was now face-to-face with glaring lights blinding me. The roar of tanks and troop-carrying vehicles were rolling toward me in full battle gear. I had gotten damn-near-naked to let them see that I wasn't armed. They seemed startled, like a Bull-Elephant, stumbling upon a Mouse. Hands up, eyes closed I awaited my fate. Then, a booming voice barked. "State your business a curfew is in full effect." Humbly, I replied. "I was stranded and I'm trying to make it home on the westside." The voice bellowed. "Keep moving with your hands up and you might make it home in one piece." I slid to the side and let the mighty convoy pass. I was so nervous that I suddenly became patriotic and started saluting and waving my ass off at the rumbling convoy. Walking with my hands up down a dark, shattered inner-city street, was a surreal experience. I felt as if I were the only person in the world in that much danger on that hot, July night...nary a soul was stirring.

As the landmarks became more familiar, my anxiety began to subside. I could almost smell Beanie's home-cooking. When I entered our flat,

Beanie and Runt were glad to see me. Beanie, went on about how they were all worried about me. They had heard on the news that three black youth were murdered in the Algiers Motel. Beanie thought one of the murdered victims was me. She had informed everyone concerned that she had dropped me off at the Algiers on the day of the murders. My presence dispelled their concerns. I told them that I had heard the gunfire all around me that night as I laid stretched out on the motel's floor. That was the first time that I had heard about the murders.

In the meantime, me and Deb, were ready to get busy after weeks of sexual fore-play. Milton was staying downstairs with Deb's God-mother for the night, and Deb was looking quite delectable in her cute little sheer pajamas, with her soft pubic hair shining through. She was nestled in my arms, playing footsie with me on the couch, smooching and making small talk. Then she looked up at me with that... come hither look in her hazel eyes. She grabbed my hand and led me to the promised land...

Fass Cass and Deb: circa 1969

Chapter 12

BIG MAN, AND TRINA
FROM NEW JERSEY

Late in 1967, I landed a job at the prestigious law firm, Honigman, Miller, Swartz and Cohn, as a messenger delivering important documents to other law firms and courts located in the downtown Detroit area. I also cashed checks for the firm at the First National Bank, on the first floor of the First National Building. The same building the law firm was and still is housed. I remember that on one occasion, Mr. Jason Honigman, endorsed a check for $5,000, then he instructed me to go get it cashed, and to bring him the money. With check in hand. I headed down to the first floor bank as instructed and got the check cashed. The teller that waited on me never questioned me about credentials. I concluded that Mr. Honigman, had special arrangements for that to happen. When the teller handed me the cash back neatly packaged in one hundred-dollar bills inside a bank envelope, it was tempting to keep on stepping out through the front entrance. Hell, that was more money then I had ever had in my possession in my life up to that point. I thought about it for a hot minute, then I proceeded back up to Mr. Honigman's office and handed his secretary the cash-stuffed envelope. To me, it felt like a million bucks. I worked for the firm for under a year.

Once again, me and my mother clashed. I wound up moving in with Brenda, at her mother's house on Russell and Kenwood. I could always find a hot meal and a place to rest my body during those perilous times. I was working at Dodge Main assembly plant and wasn't exactly broke. I had to submit to working in the auto factory, because there wasn't much else out there for a high-school dropout to make a decent living at. Working in the auto plants was considered a good job. I was transferred over to the Mound Road engine plant, where I worked on the assembly line, pounding dampers on engine blocks with a rubber mallet. To look down the assembly line at an endless parade of engines rolling in my direction was an exhausting endeavor. That wasn't exactly my ideal of the American dream. It was hard, boring work and I couldn't envision doing it for the rest of my life, like Mr. John. Speaking of Mr. John, he and Beanie had been (unknown to me) house hunting. I wasn't home a lot at her westside flat. I was too busy running the streets and chasing a dollar. I was out of touch with home life. I wasn't aware of the impending move until I saw the movers. I didn't want to move with her. I wanted my own place; so, I stayed behind until the landlord put me out. I didn't have a key. I had to climb up to the balcony where the balcony door was left unlocked. I lived rent-free until I was discovered, and then I was sent packing. I was adamant about not following Beanie to her new digs on Stoepel, near Six Mile Road, on the northwest side of Detroit. Beanie and Helen brought a two family flat. In the beginning, Beanie and Runt moved into the lower flat. Helen and her two sons (Micheal and Lamont) moved into the upper flat. Slim was doing his thing in the penitentiary. When I was thrown out of the flat on Monterey by the landlord, I headed for familiar grounds on the northend, where I rented a hotel room by the week, at another one of Sam Gant's properties, the East Grand Hotel, located on Brush and East Grand Boulevard. The East Grand Hotel, was a pimp and pro' haven. It used to be one of the stops on my paper route. When I was a ten-year old delivering papers in the hotel, I came upon two sporty young playa' types, they were about 19 or 20 years old. As they scampered down the steps, one of the young men crudely remarked, that he had been in the House Of Corrections for the last 30 days and he needed a shot of hot pussy. I had heard the word before seeping from Mr. Gillum apartment; he made it sound yummy to a 10-year-old. Now back to the subject at hand. During that stretch of my history, I rented the hotel room by the week. Drugs were beginning to enter my life. I used a little weed, beans and wine...nothing heavy. Most weekend nights, I could be found hanging out in The In Crowd Lounge. I liked the In Crowd, because you could rub shoulders with the major players in Detroit's night life. I even managed a pro' or two. Drugs, pros, and bars. I was twenty-years-old and on my own with no rules. The In Crowd had a D J who went by the name of Soul Finger. His name rhymed with the James Bond movie. "Gold Finger." Soul Finger was a tall, mellow, yellow fellow who wore his hair whipped, dipped and flipped. Playboy, could talk the talk from his lofty loft, above the stage where the Go-Go dancers did their thing to the beat of all the hot tunes of the day. "Going to a Go-Go" by The Miracles, "Bumping on Sunset," by Wes Mongomery, "Jimmy Mack," by Martha and The Van-della's, and of course. "I'm In With The In Crowd" by Dobie Gray. The In Crowd was a cozy little bar. A steady stream of pimps and pro'-types strut-ted their stuff through the front entrance of the bar. Soul Finger, would greet each major player with prose and verse as he spit out his signature rhymes. For instance, when Ali Kahn, the pimp, made his grand entrance, Soul Finger would bellow, "Ali Kahn, the ladies man, pimpin' good in the neighborhood." Everyone would turn to acknowledge Ali Kahn's presence. That homage was bestowed on all true players...male and female. There was a lot of powder (coke) floating around. Crack was eons away and all the women looked good...none of that emaciated, drawn, burnout-looking hags crap. Most pros took pride in their appearance. Both sides of Wood-ward was loaded with street walkers. Woodward was a major track back in the day. It was packed with hookers and hooker bookers; from south on Woodward and Watson, to north on Eight-Mile and Woodward Avenue, with The In Crowd Lounge, tucked smack dab in the middle of the action, where the players made their rendezvous, to kick it with other players, check their traps, drink, show off, that kind of shit during their down time. Polished players such as Arthur Baby, Hawk, Both Jimmy Diamond, and Di-amond Jim Riley, Jimmy Blue, Nate Gennings, Franshot Westbrook, Dennis W., (AKA "Frosty, the Snowman.") Handsome Harold, Aubrey, Billy the Kid, Sryracuse, Joe Cash, Ronnie Love, Pigeon, Bell Starr, Wendy, Thomas Patton, Bobby Jackson, Esquire, Ron Alexander, and a host of other true polished players and playettes who hit the In Crowds door, all to be hailed by Soul Finger.

Mentioning Bobby Jackson, conjures up memories of an older playa,' older than me. He would blow into the In Crowd wearing his freshly-pressed suits, and sporting his trademark derby hat, dancing on stage with the Go-Go girl's having way to much fun. Years after the In Crowd had shut its doors for good, I was reading an article in Hugh Hefner's ("Play-boy Magazine" fame.) new magazine at that time, it was based in France. It was titled "Qui magazine." The cover story was about an ex-pimp from Detroit, who found redemption from his wicked ways and deeds. The in-terviewer quizzed him about his tranformation, from a pimp to a man of God. Bobby Jackson, was the source of the interview. Jackson responded, that, "I was sitting around when Jesus came down. I just grabbed hold of his coat tails, and he pulled me up out of that life." That was the last thing I heard or read about the pimp, who liked to jump on stage and dance with the Go-Go girls In The In Crowd Lounge. That's how I remember Bobby

Jackson... in a place and time that seems eons ago.

I did something really stupid when I was fourteen years-old. I smoked my first joint with some of my knuckle-headed friends. We were standing out in front of Jake's Shoe Shine Parlor, on the corner of Bethune and Beaubien Street. We were just out shooting the breeze, when somebody pulled out a joint, lit it, hit it and started passing it around. When it got to me, I didn't have the nerve to turn it down. I didn't want to look square in front of the fellows. You know that peer pressure thing. I took the joint, hit it a couple of times and passed it on. Now, one has to keep in mind that I was young and fresh. Before I knew it, I was laughing my ass off at everyone and everything. I was floating on cloud nine. I wanted some more of that shit. It was down hill from there, so far as drugs were concerned. The Genie was out of the bottle. For quite some time it went from weed, to beans, to cocaine, to pain. I once got so wasted that I almost didn't make it back to this world. I dropped a handful of beans and headed to Brenda's house. Shortly after arriving, I passed out cold. It was all they could do to revive me. I was flirting with the grim reaper. They put ice on my balls and slapped me hard in my face. Brenda, said that I didn't move. When I gained consciousness a couple of days later, I was still high and groggy. It took me a couple more days to get my head right. Brenda and Rabbit saved my seventeen-year-old-life on that night a ton of years ago.

Beanie and Wig were separated, and from time to time, I would see Wig staggering through the streets around Oakland and Clay Street. His alcoholism had hit full-throttle. I really felt bad for Wig, knowing his plight in life. Young country boy scurried away in the night to the big city, seeking a better life... only to find pain, strife and an unhappy wife. There was an old, smelly flop-house that sat on the edge of Bethune Street, behind a barbershop, that stood next door to the La Rosa Hotel. One had to go around back to gain entrance to the smelly rough-house, with winos and drunks as its occupants. An old man named Lyle, who was a businessman and hustler from the old south, ran the gambling and flop house. Lyle sold corn liquor to the flop-house dwellers, who were mostly transients from the south. That was the bond Lyle had with the down-and-outers. He would befriend them on a daily basis. He even provided work to the more enthusiastic among them. Lyle converted old trucks into ice cream trucks, then he employed those flop-house dwellers, (who wanted to work) a job driving his musical treat trucks, through various neighborhoods in the city. The transients would sit around drinking and playing coon caine, a card game they played in the south. Wig, from time to time was one of Lyle's flop-house occupants. All one had to do was to find a musty corner to rest one's head... a predicament that many unemployed, illiterate men found themselves in. Due to their lack of education and, (or) the lure of cheap wine and corn liquor; many found themselves living on the rugged edges of the black community. Let's put it like this... There are well-off blacks, middle class blacks, poor blacks and po' blacks. Then you had Lyle's patrons, who were poorer than the regular po' blacks on the social ecconomic scale. Wig and his cohorts were sub po.' Wig was the only piece of father I've ever known; even though we didn't have blood ties. I felt that Wig and those of his ilk got a rotten deal in life.

The spring of 1968, Beanie and Helen, were settling into their new digs on Stoepel. It was a joyous occasion for our family. Beanie's and Helen's new house, like all her other dwellings had only two bedrooms and I would have been the odd-man-out, relegated to the couch. I wrote down the new address. I also had given Beanie my new address at the East Grand Hotel. One evening I heard someone honking their horn downstairs. I looked out and saw Beanie beckoning me to come down. She was driving her new car, a navy blue Buick sedan. I admired her new ride for a minute, then I hopped inside and off we went. She drove me to her and Helen's new home. It was a nice little two-family house...nicer than any place we had ever lived in before. Beanie lived in the lower flat and Helen in the upper flat. The floor plan was identical in both units, and oh, did I mention that there were only two bedrooms? There was also an unfinished basement that was small and damp; but, funtional. Beanie asked me had I found a place yet? I told her that I was planning to stay at the East Grand Hotel, until I could find something else. She offered me refuge... if it was nessasary. Months passed before I had to take her up on her offer.

After I moved into her new house, that damp unfinished basement would prove to be a sanctuary from the sometimes rat race upstairs. Slim, will be paroled soon, and Beanie was working at Providence Hospital. Helen was working at the Post Office, and I was migrating between Beanie's house and the streets. Runt, was living the life of Riley. Micheal and Lamont were in school. On the surface life was good; but, there were underlying elements bubbling beneath the surface. I was still searching for my identity. The longer I stayed there, the harder it got to cope with my family. I was ready to move on. I needed my own piece of the rock.

On a hot summer's night when I thought Beanie was in a good mood, I ventured off onto shaky ground and brought up that father thing. Once again, that set off a familiar refrain; the fuse was lit, Beanie exploded. I don't remember the exact exchange; but, it ended with Beanie proclaiming. "Get out of my house." Once again, I had to vacate my mothers diggs in the middle of the night. Always defiant, I must admit that I was a rebel... against everything and everyone. All one had to do was to tell me that I couldn't; then I would, tell me that I could, than I wouldn't. I had an innate ability to screw myself...again I'm homeless.

I stepped out into a mild breezy fall night, with plastic bag in hand with some of my belongings inside it. Suddenly, I remembered that Mr. John had bought Beanie a pistol to keep in her car. Beanie worked the night shift at Providence Hospital, and Mr. John was concerned for her safety. At the time, I feared for my own safety at night on the mean streets of Detroit. I opened her unlocked car door and removed the gun from the glove compartment. Than I made my way up the street to Livernois and Six-Mile Road, where I waited on the Dexter bus. I put the gun in the plastic bag with my other traveling gear. It kept shifting in the bag, so I had to keep positioning the gun so that its print wouldn't show through the plastic bag. When I look back on that mess, I can't help but to shake my head in wonderment. I was one stupid youngon at that point and time in my life. Walking around with a loaded gun in a plastic bag was a recipe for disaster. Beanie never knew, or found out what happened to the gun. Even after it was long forgotten, I couldn't bear to tell her, and I've been feeling guilty about it ever since. I hadn't decided on where I was going until I was on the Dexter bus. I decided on the Mt. Royal Hotel, where I hoped that Wigs look-a-like son, Steve, was still staying there. Steve and his white girlfriend came to Detroit from Tennesse in search of his biological father, Wig. Steve was a splitting image of Wig, down to his half-moon bald head. When I arrived at the hotel, I pulled out the room number that I had written on a slip of paper. When I found the right room, I knocked on the door. When it flung open, standing there was Steve's white girlfriend, Tammy. Steve was glad to see me and recieved me with open arms. When Steve first got to Detroit, he managed to look me up, and we hit it off from the get go, like real brothers. Steve was on a mission. He asked me to help him find Wig. I warned Steve, that it wouldn't be a pretty picture. He was good with that. He just wanted to see his pops. I knew where to look on Clay and Oakland, on the northend. Thats where we spotted Wig and his wine-head buddies. We watched from a distance. We stood there in icy cold silence and we were saddened by what we saw. Steve and I felt that we would spare Wig, the humiliation of us seeing him at his lowest point in life. We turned and walked away with our heads bowed down...hurt and dejected. "Self preservation is the first law of nature." I vowed to myself at that unpleasant moment in time, that my own life would not wind up like Wig's.

When we got back to the hotel his girl was making them lunch, which consisted of a slice of onion on white bread, splattered with mayonnaise. They offered to share their staples with me; but, I declined. It was all that I could do to keep from gagging; while watching them devour those disgusting sandwiches. I could tell that Steve was po,' and that he came from a long line of po' folks down in Tennesse. That sandwich thing was a way of life for them. I was broke, but, I had the gun. I didn't want to rob anyone, I decided to sell it. I went across the street to the gas station, on the corner of Hazelwood and Woodward. I approached the station owner, and told him what I had, and that I would sell it for a reasonable price. He looked the gun over, and offered to buy it for about forty dollars. I thought about it, then, I took him up on his offer. I went and got Steve and white girl, and treated the three of us to some hamburgers and french fries. I can tell you now, that they ate it like it was the last thing they were going to eat. Steve was a southern boy catching hell in the big city. Steve didn't know how he was going to pay his hotel rent. I proceeded to pull Steve's coat. I went on to tell him that his money-maker was lying next to him. I had become abreast of the wicked ways of the streets. I could spot a potential hooker a mile away. Steve's woman was a pro,' they just didn't know it. The time was ripe for enlightment. Hey, I was sleeping in a damn chair and they were starving to death on the bed. I wanted to slow roll with Steve; but, since he was a square, I didn't want him to take it the wrong way, like most squares would have. I went on to tell Steve, that if he swallowed his pride, he could make a boat-load of money. His raised, eyebrow-response spoke volumes that he was interested, or pissed. I told him he could lay there and starve to death and get put out, or he could start using his money-maker. Then I nodded in his girl's direction. Steve wanted me to elaborate further. I went on to tell him that I knew a couple of spots where white girls thrived, making three-or four-hundred dollars a night. He started smiling, and quizzed me about the what, where, and when. I told him about The Last Chance Bar on Eight-Mile and Woodward, and Jumbos Bar on Third, in the Cass corridor. Both spots were white pro' havens where they didn't have to worry about cops. I told him to instruct his woman not to fuck with "black tricks." She asked. "Why, don't their money spend ?" I had to really school those two green horns; about the ins and outs, the outs and ins of the game. To answer her question about not tricking with blacks, I told them what I had heard a pimp tell his game; that black trick's dicks were too big, their money was too short, and they fucked too long. They got the point. I also pointed out that most of the working pro' bars were long established, and that as long as you were making money, they had your back. Those types of pro' bars were located in the unofficial red light districts in Detroit. After explaining the deal to Steve, he was good to go, all I had to do was point them in the right direction. I put the plan in motion. I asked Steve did his woman have any clean clothes and makeup. He produced a matching set of semi-clean duds. She didn't have any makeup, so the three of us marched down to Woolworth's Department Store on Woodward and the Boulevard. I had a little loot left over from the gun sale. After she got her stockings, makeup, a few pair of undies and rollers for her hair, I had two dollars left. I reminded Steve, that it was a loan; not a gift. He agreed and we were ready to roll. I schooled white girl on how to catch a trick's eye and how to reel 'em in without saying a word. I then explained that all she needed was a wink and a come hither with her fore finger; while the other hand rested on her hip. After she got all dressed up, I gave them a prep talk, y'all ready to get paid ? Let me hear you say, "Yeah." "Yeah." they shouted in unison. Just before we hit the streets, I delivered last minute instructions, blow jobs and jack offs, ask for a hundred dollars, but accept fifty dollars, if necessary, fuck and or "around the world" ask for two hundred dollars. This left white girl puzzled. She asked me what around the world meant? I simply stated that's where you do it all. I had already got all the logistics down: hotel locations and the best hotels for short stays. There was a lot of competition, whore houses, street walkers and bar pros. She was clean enough, young enough ; plus she was white, that meant gold. Before she entered the bar. I told her to go get 'em for Steve, Baby! I then told her to "break luck." She had no idea what I was referring to with that last line. It meant, turn your first trick of the night, and the rest of the night will be all right.

Looking back, I can't believe that I was using my mind for that crap. At the time, it was a good move. Under different circumstances, it might have been different. White girls feathers wasn't ruffled by her new occupation. She took to the stroll like a duck takes to water, I wondered if she was pretending to be green. That was just a thought...I had no real validity to support my suspicions. After all the kinks were worked out, the cash started rollin' like, Nolan. Suddenly, everybody was eating steaks and shit like that. I had schooled Steve on how to protect his game from predator pimps and pros working in concert with their man, trying to knock off new game for their own stable. White girl was raking it in like a master steppa,' regardless, they were still green as grass about the intricate nuances, surrounding that twisted lexicon called the game. I had to pull their coats to the code of conduct of the game. I simply told her, Don't get in a pimp's face or his ride, and don't get personal with other pros. If they persisted, let it be known that your man had your back and any conversation they had for you, tell them to run it though your man, and no half-steppin.' Of course, I had to explain what half-steppin' meant. "Let them know that you are about business and yo' man don't play." I reminded them to stick to the script, and they'll be ok. I knew in my mind that if a pro' was caught slippin' she could be swooped up by some crafty pimp. A lot of rookies would deliver their game to the stroll and when they came back to check their trap, some slick ass pimp, or his woman done got yo' game and gone, Jarome. There were a lot of cat and mouse games being played out there on the pro' stroll. If you didn't know the terrain, "yo' action could be put into traction." I was determined not to let that happen to Steve. That was a lot to put on my young 16 year-old ass. Hell, I needed her just as much as Steve did.

Back at the Mt. Royal Hotel, I'd run into Steve's next door neighbor, a big, black fellow and his razor thin, but, cute money-maker, whom, I would come to know as Big Man and Trina from New Jersey. So they said, once we met. Big Man, was a big black brother who wore his hair in a process. It still looked nappy, even after being freshly whipped, Big had some bad hair and big pink lips and he was tangle eyed; nonetheless, he still possessed the panache of a pimp.

One day in the hallway of the Mt. Royal, we kicked it about some street shit, and made our introductions. Big, told me a little bit about himself, and I told him a little bit about me. He said, they came to Detroit, to get a fresh start. He said it in a tone that made me suspect about it's validity. It made me wonder if there wasn't more to the story. Were they running from a shady past? Big was about 6' 5" and weighted about 330 pounds. Looking back, Biggy Smalls favored Big Man. During the time I knew Big Man, I don't think Biggy was even born yet. Big's woman, Trina, was slim, cute and all street. Big had the last word on everything. If it didn't have Big's seal of approval, it didn't go down. The more we kicked it, the more we hit it off. They were at least a good six years my senior, and way more advanced in the game than me. I became Big's guide through the maze of Detroit 's night life. We hit all the bars and after hours joints. Trina, was usually on her job trickin' and slickin.' One night we were hanging and swinging at Hamp's after hours joint on the northend. All of the fly playa's and playette's were on board that night in the late1960's. I looked down the bar and spied Steve and white girl, sitting at the bar having a good old time, wearing new duds and sucking up cognac. I waltzed on down the bar to where they were sitting and gave them a big hug. Then, I complimented them on their new look. In my mind I was thinking: Steve, you fool, exposing a vulnerable white girl to this much game. I didn't speak on it. I let it be. Steve was going to have to learn his own lessons concerning this wicked lifestyle, called the game. Big spotted me kickin' it with Steve and moseyed his way down to where we were to acknowledge Steve's presence. Big said to Steve, that he was glad to have a fellow player for a neighbor. I sensed that Big had ulterior motives, and the white girl was the mark. Big gave me a sense of fellowship, so I thought. With Steve's new-found wealth, the drug dealers had reeled him into their grasp. Along with Steve's drug use, he and white girl were clashing.

I Ran into Steve one day at Jumbo's Bar, on 3rd Avenue. He was in a desperate way. He had run out of money and white girl had disappeared. He told me that she went to work last night and pouf, she was gone. I realized then that it was time for me to make other plans regarding lodging.

One gray, cloudy day, I came to the room and a maid was busy cleaning the room. When she looked up and saw me, she asked me my name. After telling her my name, she handed me a plastic bag with my belongings in it. She told me that Steve had checked out, and he said, that he was going back to Tennessee. I was back at square one.

Big and Trina's door was open. They too were moving on. I told Big about my dilemma. He promptly asked me to help him move to his new digs on Euclid and Second Avenue. That was music to my ears, I was hoping that maybe he would have an extra room for me. When we arrived at our destination, we confronted a four family dwelling, big and sturdy... the building loomed large before us. Trina blurted out. "That's our new home," with joy in her voice. The porches were huge, with each flat having it's own balcony. Euclid was a busy bustling street, with traffic and pedestrians movin' and groovin.' Woodward Avenue, was just a stone's throw away to the east. The neighborhood, had a eclectic mix of working types. ADC and Welfare recipiants were sprinkled together in the community; as well as hustlers and the usual criminal elements darting in and out of the fray. One of the most eccentric personalities to pop up now and then on Euclid, was an old-timer who peddled all kinds of merchandise on his bicycle, riding up and down the street, howling. "I got it;" meaning, if it was for sale he had it. He was dubbed. "I got it." That's what everyone called him. Of course he answered back. "I got it, got it." With Big's blessing, I was hoping to join in the mix, along with Big and Trina. No way was I going to go crawling back to Beanie's house. I finally got around to cracking on Big to rent the spare room he had. Big didn't hesitate. "Thirty five dollars a week and you pay for your own food. Or you could pay an extra twenty dollars a week and eat with us." I agreed to pay fifty-five dollars a week room and board.

While Big and Trina were plying their trade, I got a job selling Black History books door-to-door. I saw an ad in the Michigan Chronicle. "Outside sales Black History books." Then it gave a phone number and address. I applied and was interviewed by an African brother who spoke with an African accent. His name escapes me, but, he had a nice office downtown in the Guardian Building. I did well enough in the interview to land the job, it paid only a sales commission. He had to explain to me what "commision" meant. That was the first job that I had worked, other than a paper boy, where I had to sell something in order to legitimately get paid. The gig consisted of young college aged men and women being dropped off in neighborhoods in northwest Detroit, where blacks had begun to settle in droves. Pride and knowledge of our heritage was beginning to take root. Our mission was to sell as many books as posible in order to make a decent commission. Each team member was given a Black History book and a scripted format that we had to memorize, then off we went knocking on doors. We also carried a stack of contracts. The books were as thick as a small phone book, loaded with Black History facts, events and figures that left their mark on "Black American Culture." Our scripted format worked most of the time. I ad-libbed from time to time, depending on the customer. The books cost $39.95. One could purchase the book with $10.00 down and three weekly payments of $10.00. Easy as pie. One must keep in mind that it was the late 1960's and that was decent money for a teenager. Our sales pitch went something like this; this is my ad-libbed version, inserting the name of U of D in my revised version of the original format. "Hello, I'm a student representative from the University of Detroit, and we are in your community promoting Black History. Our mission is to get Black History into the homes of progressive black people. We are a growing community separated from our past. We must preserve and instill that vast reservoir of knowledge to the future generations of Black men and women." Then I would insert the price and terms for purchasing the history book. Then I flipped through some of the highlights contained in the book, I closed the sales pitch with. "With your purchase of this book you will help supplement black students at the University of Detroit." That was a bunch of bull, because I was decades away from attending U of D. Most of the time the pitch worked. To get my commission of five dollars per-book, I had to sell a lot of books to make a decent buck. I was young, energetic and bubbling over with personality. When we had hit most of Detroit's, black, middle-class neighborhoods we took our show on the road to Jackson, Kalamazoo, and Lansing, Michigan.

Between, small time jobs and managing an occasional hooker or two, life was a series of ups and downs; more downs than ups. I learned a valuable lesson from Big Man, about diplomacy: Most men have a jealousy button when it comes to sharing their woman with other men. I noticed that Trina would go off on occasion with some young fellows that she found appealing and have a fling or two. I knew, so I figured that Big knew too. I conjured up the nerve to ask Big. "What's up with Trina, laying up with squares for free?" Big informed me that Trina was a seasoned pro' and you can't cage a seasoned pro', let them have their fun. Big rationalized that "they gettin' the honey, I'm gettin' the money." Big spouted, that. "Pros can only pay one nigga', that's the nigga' they love and that's me, Baby!" Big expounded further. "Don't you believe for one minute that Trina's fuckin' for free; you just ain't privy to the prize, nigga'." Then he repeated himself. "They all suckers; no one fucks for free; but, me."

I managed to get the African to purchase me my first car. I reasoned with him that if I had a car, I could cover a greater area; thus, sell more books and make more money for him and for me. It worked. A week later I was sporting a 1962 Chevy Impala. The car was old and rusty, but it didn't matter, because it represented freedom to me.

Euclid was a tough street. Tension and danger were by-products of the enviroment. I distinctly remember one incident when two fellows down on their luck were arguing on Big's front porch about some stupid shit. Gary, who was a regular porch-dweller, was threatning this other stoop-dweller, named Cowboy. Gary, was up close and personal in Cowboy's face selling wolf tickets. Cowboy, who was smaller in stature than Gary, sat passively as Gary hurled insults and threats his way. On the corner of Euclid and Second sat a supermarket. The armed security guard who worked at the market was passing by the altercation between the two men when he left work. The security guard who was in full uniform had a holstered pistol dangling from his hip. Oblivious to what was transpiring on the porch.

Cowboy peered around Gary, who had his back turned. Gary didn't notice the guard's passing. Cowboy pushed Gary aside, then rushed toward the startled guard and snatched his gun out of his holster. At the sight of that, Gary's eyes lit up. When he saw an armed Cowboy headed in his direction, spewing bullets from the stolen weapon at him, Gary threw his beer bottle at Cowboy and broke wide toward Woodward Avenue. Cowboy fired at Gary, empting the gun of its hot lead into Gary. When the noise had settled. Cowboy burst through a cloud of gunsmoke weaving his way between dilapidated dwellings, disappearing into a blighted ghetto-scape, with the smoking gun still in his hand. Gary, laid on the littered field gasping for breath. I just knew the poor fellow wouldn't make it. Soon the familiar sounds of sirens screeched toward Euclid. Months later I ran into Gary on the street. I was surprised to see him still alive. He was wearing a colostomy bag at his side and he had lost a lot of weight; but, he was able to live another day on planet earth, instead of being buried under it. Euclid, was a hot-bed of excitment, if shoot 'em-ups was your thing, and I ain't referring to television. That action was live and-in-living color.

I can recall another diabolical portrait of inner-city madness involving a fellow, whom, I went to elementary school with. His street name was Tank. I never knew his real name. He was about 17-years-old at the time. Tank was always in trouble with the law. He had a reputation as a stick-up kid. He and his rappy, Ronald Holmes, were two of many, young, stick-up artists in the neighborhood. Tank and Holmes used to stick-up mom and pops stores and dope houses on the northend. Between stick-ups. Tank would rob gay white dudes who frequented a gay bar on Second, near Philadelphia Street. On a hot, muggy night in August, Tank was on rip-off patrol on Second Avenue. When he spotted a white fag coming out of the gay bar, he crept up behind the unsuspecting mark and ripped his back pocket, pants leg and all, right off of him. Tank ran into Big's building for refuge. The bar was a block away. He still had the pants leg in his clutches, with the wallet still intact in the back pocket. Now back to the madness that I was referring to. It started with Tank, limping down Euclid from Woodward. Tank, limped past Big's building and entered the dope house that was located on the westside of Big's building. Everyone in the neighborhood knew that it was a shooting gallery, where junkies went to buy and shoot their heroin right on the premises. It was a horrible place with junkies in and out all day and night. Jack Walker was an ex-con junkie, who operated the joint. Jack and Tank had some kind of running beef that I wasn't privy to. That beef thing proved to be a dangerous proposition on that hot summer's night.

Me, Big, and Trina were out on the front porch kickin' it when Tank came limping by. Our eyes followed him up the stair's into Jack's place. Then, we heard gunfire. It was loud and nasty, followed by Tank exiting the shooting gallery running past us headed toward Woodward Avenue, brandishing the now exposed rifle, that was responsible for his earlier limp past us. He had the gun hidden down his pants leg. He had just murdered Jack Walker. As Tank made his escape, a horde of junkies poured out of the shooting gallery...some with their needles still intact, dangling from their arms and necks. I watched as they disappeared into the night, like Zombies, followed, as always by the sound of screaming sirens.

Nearing the end of 1967, I was still hanging tough with Big and Trina on Euclid, selling Black History books was now a thing of the past. I had to come up with a new plan to make ends meet. A mellow, young playa' by the name of Ron Alexander, was a crafty fellow who lost his life in the late eighties. Ron didn't pimp prostitutes. He pimped square girls, who had good jobs. He corralled a stable of square working girls, scattered throughout the city. Ron didn't drive the traditional pimp's ride: he gripped a pretty, lime green '98 Olds, with all the pimp trimmings. Ron walked like a pimp, and talked like a pimp. he just didn't deal with street pros. One evening, I ran into him hanging out in the In Crowd Lounge, and flat out asked him what was the secret of his success? He gave me one of those; Negro are you serious looks? Then he spoke. "Find yourself a gimmick to keep you going until things start poppin' your way." I took his advise and found me a gimmick. My gimmick was simple. I remembered how I would get hit-up by people selling raffle tickets. I could never make it to any of the raffles. Most of the time, I never knew who won the raffle. At the bottom of the tickets in fine print, was. "Need not be present to win." The raffle drawings were always months into the future. Hell, by then I had forgot about the raffle, or I had lost the tickets. I figured that there must be others out there in the same predicament as I was. I took my cue from my experiences of buying raffle tickets from others. I never won, or, I never showed up for the raffle; I didn't know if the raffle was legit or not. I grew up knowing the owner of a print shop on Oakland and Bethune. When I was ready to make my move, I looked him up. He still had the print shop on Bethune. I hustled on over to the print shop and ordered up a thousand tickets, for about fifty bucks. I sold the tickets for 50-cent a ticket, or five dollars for a book of twelve. The customer would sign their name, address and phone number on the stub. Supposedly, If the customers ticket stub is drawn at the raffle, the ticket holder would be called. The format was designed to sell the ticket. It simply stated, "We're having a raffle to help build the first black dormitory at the University of Detroit." I inserted a phony address on the ticket, and dated the drawing for the raffle six months into the future...plenty of time to build up a bankroll and for the raffle to fade into oblivion. The caveat was printed at the bottom of the ticket in big, easy-to-read-print. "Need not be present to win." The prizes were listed in chrono-logical order: 1st prize $500; 2nd prize, $250 and third-place prize, $100.00. After I sold all out of the tickets, I would order a thousand more. I would find a major avenue, like Mack or Dexter. I hustled every business on the avenues. When I got to the end of the block, I would cross over to the other side of the street, then I proceeded to work my way back to the end of that side of the street. Once finished, depending on the time, I would hit another avenue. Each avenue was good for fifty or sixty dollars per run, on bad days, I made half of that. On great days, I would sometimes double or triple my bank. My objective was not to con people out of a few dollars; but, rather to keep myself from starving to death. At that time in my mind, it was better than robbing and possibly hurting someone in the process. When you're young and no one's looking out for your best interest, you had to be crafty to survive without getting locked up, or worst. It was all about survival. I had to depend on my own initiative to survive.

During the spring of 1968 I met my future, first-wife, Debroah Ross. On a sunny afternoon, me and some of the regulars were hanging out on Big's front porch shooting the breeze. Big hunched me in the side to get my attention. He nodded toward the honey-brown cutie getting out of her shiny new 1968 Firebird, headed into the two-family flat on the eastside of Big's building. She was smiling, and she waved at us with one hand; while clutching the hand of a little boy about five years-old, with her other hand. They disappeared into the lower flat. My full attention was shifted in her direction. From time to time, I would spot her coming and going. I would make it my business to be seen by her. She was always smiling and bubbly. I found out through the grapevine that the two-family flat was her aunt's house. Her aunt and her aunts sister shared the lower flat, while Deb and her son lived in the upper flat. Later I found out that the elderly lady was actually her God-mother. The two old, childless sisters had helped Deb's mother raise her. Deb's mother had ten other kids. It was a big relief to Deb's mother and a blessing for the two sisters. That all started when Deb was a baby, so they were quite close. When Deb graduated from North-ern High School, in 1966, she moved into the upper-flat of her God-mother's house, fate had me showing up at that place in time on Euclid; or

I never would have met her. Deb was all the two sisters had and they spoiled her rotten. I was always looking foward to seeing her. Deb struck me as being out of place on Euclid. She was fresh and friendly, in a geniune way and she was most definitly a square. I had to keep my appearance on point. I was smitten with Deb, and I wanted to meet her in the worst way. Deborah, was her name. I referred to her as Deb. She was about my age, 20 or a year younger. I couldn't help but notice the cleanliness and neatness of her appearance. There was a rosy youthful glow about her cheeks. She walked with a confident gait in her stride, and she was as cute as a button. Deb, was a square from nowhere to me. That was one of her unique qualities: a rose amongst the weeds. To put it more succinctly, Euclid was in black and white; while Deb was in color. One fine summer's day, her son Milton, was playing in front of their house with his little ball by himself. I just happened to be leaving Big's house at that moment in time. I heard a little voice. "Hey Mister, can you get my ball?" His little ball had rolled into the street. How could I refuse that? I retrieved Milton's ball, and I asked him "What's your name?" In his little voice he said. "Milton." I tossed him the ball and he tossed it back. That turned into a game of catch. Before long, I was twirling him around in circles. He was laughing out loud, and it made me feel good. Now it was time to end our little game. I had to continue on my mission. As I turned to depart, I hadn't noticed his mother standing behind me, grinning, watching her son have the time of his life. She extended her hand and said. "Hi, my name is Debroah. I'm waiting for my turn." Then we laughed. I looked over and Milton was laughing with us. I exchanged greetings and asked her did she mind if I played with her son? I apologized for not getting her permission; but, it all happened so spontaneously and that no harm was meant. Deb replied that it was all right. She was watching from her window. We said our goodbyes and off I went feeling mighty spiffy. I gave her my street name, "Cass." Arnold just didn't cut it in the streets. The ice was broken, and it was now time for me to get to know her. Slowly, but surely, we began to chat. She began to open up more and more. She talked about her job at a Chrysler's Auto Plant. She even made me privy to her situation with her God-mother, and about how her life had come to be at that point in time. She went on to tell me about Milton's father. She offered all of that information voluntarily. I was a good listener and prodded her on with "Yeah." "You kidding," and "Talk to me Deb." She would go on and on for hours. I didn't mind, because I enjoyed being with her. I asked her about Milton's father.

Deb said that Milton's father was murdered and that his street name was Red. I thought Milton had looked familiar. I informed her that I knew a Red, a fellow who ran with a tough bunch on the lower westside around 14th Street, and Mcgraw. I quizzed Deb about Red, and she decribed him to a "T." We both concluded that it was a coincidence that I knew Milton's father. I looked her in the eye and proclaimed. That maybe God, sent me to be Milton's Guardian Angel. Deb, looked up at me fluttering her eye lids, intently staring into my eyes. Then she spoke the exact words that I wanted to hear. She nodded her head in affirmation and said. Yes, maybe God did. At that moment I felt that Deb would soon be mine, because I had made a connection. There was only one small problem...there was another guy smitten with Deb as well. He worked with Deb at the auto plant and he was in the picture before me. I would see him visiting her house. He was about her age, he was short, wore glasses and he had an intense stare. I must admit that I got jealous when I saw them together. It was time to step my game up; while, I still had wiggle room to maneuver my way into her heart. I ran into her one evening when I was leaving Big's house, and I felt that it was do or die; "Shit, or get up off the pot." To break the ice, I curtly asked her if she dated only short guys? She seemed puzzled by my inquisition, and asked me why had I asked? I replied that I saw her boyfriend, and she answered. "You mean, Denny." "Yep, is that his name?" I said. "Oh, he's just a friend," was her reply. "So he wouldn't mind if I asked you out for a date?" Just before she stepped into her gleaming new fire-bird, she replied. "No, he wouldn't. I ain't got no ring on my finger." She then sped off with a smile so warm that it could melt an iceburg. I stood there with my heart in my hand, beckoning for her to take it. By the time, I saw her again it was October. The Tigers had just won the World Series, the city was going nuts. I spotted Deb, leaving her house, and asked her about our date. I asked if we were still on? She wryly replied in jest, "If you promise to play with my son." I quickly agreed to her demands. Then she suggested that I come over to her house for dinner on the upcoming Friday night. I hugged her and said. "I'll see you Friday night. Is eight okay?" She replied, that it was a good time as I walked away. In my mind, I started counting the days. This was on a Tuesday or Wednesday. I had time to prepare myself. I was on cloud nine, feeling pretty damn good. Then I heard Big shout. "Let's go party with the Tigers."

We followed the excited throngs of fans down to Woodward Avenue, where the party was in full bloom, no looting, no shooting; just good old-fashioned hoopla. Euclid is about half-a-mile from West Grand Boulevard, where the lion's share of the celebration was happening. It was a good time for the citizens of Detroit. The next day's newspaper coverage of the World Series was extensive. Buried on the back page was a story of a young, Black man, found dead behind a store in a downtown alley. He had been shot to death. He was identified as: "James Evans, of Detroit, was found shot multiple times in a downtown alley. No one has been arrested for his murder." The northend was only one block east across Woodward, and about six blocks south was my old stumping grounds on Bethune. I decided to investigate whether or not it was the James Evans that I knew. He was the ex-leader of the gang called the Casinos. After kickin' it with some of my old chums, my suspicions were confirmed. It indeed was the notorious gang-banger, dead at 21, just like "Billy, the Kid," the infamous killer from the old west. As far as I know, no one has ever been arrested for my old nemesis death. I was saddened by Jimmy's murder. He was just one of many troubled youths from my past whose personal demons led most of them to their demise. Now it was time for me to turn my full attentions to the golden cuty next door.

Big and Trina, were plotting their next caper as well. Trina wasn't your ordinary mud-kicker (street prostitute). She was more or less, a wanderer. She caught tricks wherever she found them. One day, she was passing through a local restaurant to grab a bite to eat. While eating, out of the corner of her eye she caught a homely-looking little, light skinned fellow staring her down. She made eye contact with the little fellow, he was wearing coke-bottle thick lenz eye glasses, sitting at the counter pretending to sip his soup; while eagerly eye-balling her. Trina was ready to reel him in like a big old fish. Most seasoned pros have a good intuition about who's a potential trick. Trina, on cue, slid up next to the shy little fellow and struck up a conversation. Trina went on to explain to us that he was mentally slow; not retarded, but slow. She told us his name was Damon. He was 30-years-old, and was under guardianship to his parents, who were loaded. Big and Trina, decided not to come at Damon like a trick-thing. They decided to slow-roll him and then, set him up for the home-run. It was a delicate dance that would take time to develop. By the time that I was let in on the scam, they were well on their way to knocking off some major dough from the slow little high-yellow, fellow called Damon. They had set him up like bowling pins and they were ready to knock him down. After bedding Damon down a few times, Trina, managed to get inside of Damon's head. Pulling a hundred here, and a few hundred there. She was working her way up to the big score. The plan had to be fool proof. It was a one-shot deal. It had to be played just right. Every human on the planet is sexual, no matter one's station in life. Regarding sex, the mentally-challenged are no different. When sexual frustation, coupled with loneliness and mental issues, a person like that; in the hands of crafty urchins like Big and Trina, that spelled disaster for a poor fellow named Damon, and I wanted nothing to do with their little scam. Trina, worked her whore magic and got Damon to fall in love with her.

It was now time for me to get cooking with Deb. I arrived on time for our dinner date at her place. Money was tight, and I was relieved that she was cooking us dinner. There was one little hitch. She wanted some wine to go with our dinner, so I headed out into the night in search of wine without a dime. I could have gotten some loot from Big or Trina, but, they were not at home. So I walked toward Woodward. I thought hard on the dilemma, and came to the conclusion that I had to come up with my own scam if I wanted to save face. No way in hell was I going to tell Deb, that I was broke. I also felt that she may have been testing me. I was dressed to impress, and in distress. Then it came to me. I remembered Tank's encounter when he ripped the pants off of a dude during a street robbery; while going for the dude's wallet. I decided to improvise and create my own victimization. I ripped my pants leg wallet pocket on my perfectly good pair of mohair pants. Then I came running back to Deb's house, faking like I was out of breath, banging on her door. I was not going to let this fine feline get away. When Deb opened the door, she found a wide-eyed me with panic in my voice. "Call the police, call the police." With panic in her own voice. Deb, screamed. "What happened?" "I just got robbed, call the police." She hustled me inside and slammed the door. She grabbed my hand and hurried me up the stairs, where I proceeded to call the police. I had to play it to the bitter end. It even helped my cause. Deb, apologized profusly for sending me out into the night like that. I thought to myself; "It worked," as she pampered me with comfort and food. We sat and talked until the cops arrived. When the cops got there, I repeated my story to them. They took the report, then reminded us about how dangerous it was on Euclid at night, and that one must take extreme caution, when venturing out at night. I replied, that the next time I'll be more careful. We bid our good-byes to the officers, then I turned my full attention to my new girlfriend. Sorry Deb, if you're reading this. I just couldn't bring myself to tell you that I was broke. As the night progressed, we talked, laughed and kissed between our conversation. I learned that she was an alumni of Northern High, class of 1966, that would have been my class if I hadn't dropped out. She seemed surprised when I told her that I went to Northern. I told her that was the second thing we had in common. The first being that I knew her son's dead father, Red. I didn't crack for the booty that night; even though it was mine for the taking. I think this impressed her. I kissed her goodnight sofly on her lips, then I left, surely to return for my just rewards.

When the new week began, Big and Trina, were stepping up there con on Damon. By the end of the week, Trina, had gotten hundreds of dollars from Damon, and I was embarking on my second date with Deb, at her place again. I learned more about her during another long talk, while ogling each other as the conversation flowed. She told me about her job at a Chrysler Auto Plant. She revealed that she got the job right out of high school. In the following weeks, Trina, started bringing Damon around and introduced Big as her brother, and me as her cousin. Damon, none the wiser took the bait, hook, line and sinker. I didn't like the idea of them working such a vulnerable individual. It was not my place to intervene. Big and Trina, were going to be who they are, regardless of how I felt. Hell, I was living on borrowed time myself, so it was best that I kept my opinions to myself. The big payoff called for Trina to get Damon to propose to her. He did, and she accepted. Big faked his congratulations and warned the sheepish, little man. "You better take good care of my sister." It was all I could do to keep from laughing out loud, at the absurdity of it all. Their song and dance continued for weeks while they were planning their so-called marriage. In the meantime me and Deb, were ready to get busy after weeks of sexual fore play. Milton, was staying downstairs with Deb's God-mother for the night, and Deb, was looking quite delectable in her cute lit-tle sheer pajamas with her soft pubic hair shining through. She was nestled in my arms playing footsies with me on the couch, smooching and making small talk. Then she looked up at me with that... come hither look in her hazel eyes. She grabbed my hand, and led me to the promised land. Her bedroom was cozy and inviting. The lights were low. She lit some incense, then put on some soft music. If my memory serves me right, I think it was Roberta Flack's, "Killing Me Softly with His Song." Outside, the rain splashed off the window pane. Inside, it was warm and cozy. While I sat on the edge of the bed, she stood in front of me with her now hard-nipples bristling gently against my moist mouth, while stroking the nape of my neck with her fingertips. I placed my hand inside of her P J's, and rubbed her soft, baby smooth naked ass. She pushed me back on the bed, then laid on top of me, gently rolling her moist, inviting pudding on my man-hard shaft. Then we locked lips. Her kisses were as sweet as honey. I don't remember ei-ther of us removing our clothes. They, somehow found their way to the floor. We whispered sweet nothings into each other's ear, as Roberta Flack crooned in the background. I whispered in her ear softly, that she might get pregnate. She whispered back in mine. That, she didn't care. With that, she grabbed my throbbing rod and slid it into her moist, hot, trembling pudding. The bed started squeeking, and the room was reeking, juices were popping, and I was not stopping. When the smoke cleared, she wouldn't let me up. She wanted me to just lay there inside of her. I was 21-years old, and my Johnson could stand at attention for days. She fell asleep on top of me. A few minutes into our sleep, she woke me up stroking and cleaning my shaft with a warm cloth. When she finished, she disappeared into the bathroom. When she returned, she crawled in bed and snuggled into my arms, and together we fell fast asleep to the beat of the rain splashing against the window pane. Several hours had passed. Then, we were awakened by someone pounding on Deb's front downstairs door. She panicked. "It's Denny. Go out the back door." I told her that I wasn't going to run from no pip-squeak. I got up, put my draws on, went downstairs and confronted that fool banging on the door like he had lost his mind. I opened the door. When Denny saw me standing there in my draws smelling like Deb's pussy, he freaked and started crying out Deb's name, like a wounded man. I told him he better get his ass off the porch. Deb, belonged to me now. He bristled up like a porcupine, ready to bogard his way in. He was too light to fight and too thin to win. As he persisted, I had had enough. I cupped my hand like I saw Rotation Slim, do when he pimp-slapped the guy who robbed me on my paper route. "Kapow." I slapped Denny in the chops just like Rotation slim. It worked. He shot off the porch, jumped in his ride and burned rubber all the way down Euclid. We had to take the phone off the hook due to his persistent calling. I whispered in Deb's ear. "You got to tell that fool that there's a new sheriff in town." With that, we bid each other goodnight. The next day, I was standing on Big's front porch when I saw Trina and Damon coming down the street, with Damon lapping at her heels. Trina, walked fast. She, had Damon hobbling to keep up. That's the way Trina wanted it...a female power play. Whatever deep-seeded, twisted sentiments Trina had against men, she took them out on Damon. She humiliated him and he gladly accepted it. As a matter of fact, I think he got-off on Trina's abuse. I dared to venture into Trina's business. I got up the nerve to ask Trina, why was she so hard on Damon. Trina, leaned back on her heels, looked me over with her hand planted firmly on her hip with her mouth twisted wide open, like she couldn't believe what she was hearing. Trina, pointed at me and said. "I've been watching you sniffing around next door. You better watch yo' ass and hope that the bitch don't play your square actin' ass." Uh, oh, I done lit Trina's fuse. She pointed at Damon and said. "I got this here. Keep your square actin' ass out of my business." With that, I apologized. I should have known better than to come between a hooker and her trick. You just don't go soft on a seasoned pro' like Trina. It was crunch time for Big and Trina, to wrap up their little caper with Damon. They had already fleeced him out of God knows how much money. It was time for the big pay-off. Trina, had already told Damon to keep their love affair a secret. She rationalized that if he told his parents they might make him stop seeing her. It made sense to Damon, and that was good enough for me. Trina planted in Damon's mind that they would need $5,000 to move and get married. In the late 1960's that was considered good money. I realized that after the big score Big and Trina, were moving on. I had to step up my game because I didn't want to get caught half steppin.'

Big wasn't around much the last couple of weeks. Something was definitely up. From Deb's window, I saw a red and white used Cadillac Deville pull up next door. Big jumped out of the Caddy. I ran downstairs and proclaimed, "You done laid, nigga." Big, with a big watermelon-eating grin on his face, said. "Hell yeah, Baby." He swiftly began moving his and Trina's belongings out. Big told me there was a couple of weeks left on the flat, then he threw me the keys. When he was finished moving his stuff, I said. "Slow down, man, what you rushing for?" He looked at me like. "You just don't understand." Then he spoke. "If you see dude Damon, tell him that we had an emergency back home and we had to hit the road." I shook my head ok, knowing damn well that I wasn't going to tell Damon no shit like that. As a matter of fact, I didn't want to have nothing to do with that mess. As Big was ready to leave for higher ground, he turned toward me and gave me a big bear-hug. Then he got into his Cadillac. I leaned in to shake his hand for the last time. Guess who I saw sitting in the back seat, crouched down peeping out of the back window? Tammy, Steve's white girl from Tennessee. "Now ain't I slow," was all I could mutter. Big, had copped the white girl and stashed her away in another spot. Now there were three: Big, Trina and white girl, Tammy. I knew one thing, wherever they were headed it was going to be quite an adventure. I sashayed back up to Deb's and told her about my dilemma. She insisted that I move in with her. She didn't have to say it twice. Deb also told me that she was glad Big and Trina were gone. Deb thought that they were a bad influence on me. She didn't get an argument out of me. I wasn't turning down nothing, but my collar.

Six months later, me, a pregnant Deb, Beanie, Runt and Deb's God-mother's, were standing in the middle of Deb's God-mother's living room taking our vows from Deb's family preacher. I found a job with a wholesaler who sold lady's wigs and hats to retail outlets such as Hudson's and Crowley's. It's name was Hart Milinery Company, located in Harmony Park in Downtown Detroit. On the quiet tip, I would buy wigs wholesale from Hart and Company, then take them down to the Purple Onion and the Columbia Bar, then sell them to the bar pros. Sorry Deb, I had to supplement our income. That was one of the few jobs that I held down during my marriage to Deb, which would turn out to be quite an adventure itself.

Poor Damon would sulk past Big's and Trina's used-to-be home every day for months looking hurt and dejected. I felt so bad for the man. It wasn't a damn thing that I could do; but, wish him God's speed. After seeing Damon from Deb's window make his pilgrimage past Big's old address for months. One cold, fall day, I watched poor Damon disappear down the side-walk, with his head bowed down low for the last time, never to be heard from again. Love and tragedy seem to go hand-in-hand. God bless you, Damon. May the memory of what they did to you haunt Big and Trina, long after the money and love they swindled you out of is long gone. Yeah, I guess one could make the case that poor, Damon, got played by the game of life.

I jumped my 23 year-old young ass into my fresh, gleaming white El-dorado; with aqua interior, ready to make the suckers feel inferior. I felt mighty spiffy. My virgin ego was bursting at the seams. I rolled down my power windows, looked over at Kosin's shoe store with it's wide glass win-dow, I peeped Westside and the other seasoned Macaroni's reared back on their heels, with their arms folded and their heads cocked ace duce, off to the side peering out the window, checking me out. I felt that I had arrived to Mackdom. That sounds really trivial to me now; But, back then, it made sense to me. Westside stuck his head out the shoe store door, and bel-lowed to me, "Welcome to the game, young blood." And that's the truth, Ruth.

Westside, anointing Fass Cass: circa 1971

Chapter 13

WELCOME TO THE GAME YOUNGBLOOD

My new family's adventure began to unravel when me, Deb, and her son Milton moved out of her God-mother's house in 1970. We settled in our new digs on Tuxedo and Lawton, not far from my mother's old address on Monterey. We moved into the lower flat of a two-family flat. The owner of the dwelling, a Muslim gentlemen lived in the upper flat with his wife and kids. We didn't have much when we moved into our new digs. Our only possessions were: a small 19' portable TV, a second-hand bedroom set for me and Deb, and a bed for Milton. Deb had her Firebird, and I had my beat-up 1962 Chevy, that ran when it felt like it. Regardless of our humble beginnings, we loved and cared for each other. During the early days of our marriage, I held down several jobs at various times, in small factories and other dead-end jobs. We spent time with both of our extended family's during the holidays. Deb's mother's home on Thanksgiving, and my mother's new home on Stoepel, at Christmas time. We were your ordinary, just-starting-out-young couple. I dare to write that if we had been white, at some point in our early marriage, we had our "Rockwellian" moments. Norman Rockwell was a great white American artist, whose paintings were pure "Americana folklore" steeped in the American tradition of "Flag, Country, and Mom's Apple Pie." Yep, Mr. Rockwell, you did your fellow Americans proud. Now back to reality, we were not "Rockwellian." We were "Blackwellian."

The westside was vicious at night. It could be likened to walking through a hostile territory. If one wasn't bad out on the mean streets at night, you had to act like you were bad. The streets on the westside were long and wide. A lot of dope fiends scurried about, looking for money to feed their drug Jones, and of course, I got caught flat-footed at times, without a car to navigate my way at night in the dark, concrete jungle called the westside. I didn't have the luxury of sitting in the house. I had to take care of my family...car or no car.

After about five months in our new flat on Tuxedo, Slim, had just gotten paroled from prison. He hung out on the westside with the local thugs doing his thing. He found out that I was living on Tuxedo and paid me a visit on an overcast summer's evening. He knocked on my door, and I let him in. We kicked it for a minute, then I replied to him that me and Deb, had to make a run. He asked us to drop him off on Linwood and Tuxedo, a block away. We agreed, and dropped him off. To make a long story short, me and Deb took care of our business. It took about an hour and a half. When we returned home someone had broken into our flat and stolen the only source of entertainment for our family, our 19' television set. That was all we had of value, other than Deb's car. We stepped out on the front porch. One of our neighbor's kid came over to us, and said that he saw who broke into our house. The kid went on to describe the burglar. "He was a tall, dark-skinned nigga,' wearing a green shirt." Deb and I had just dropped off a tall dark skinned nigga,' wearing a green shirt. The kid also stated that the culprit covered the television set with a sheet. Upon hearing the damaging testimony, I called Beanie, to mediate the situation. I knew that if I had called the cops, Slim, was headed back to prison. If I confronted him personally it could get real ugly, where one of us would have gotten hurt. Beanie, came over to my house. She had Slim with her. Slim, upon being accused of breaking into my house, brought tears to his eyes, which he was good at. I saw him use those fake tears too many times over the years to be moved by his convoluted drivel. I listened, as Slim put on an act worthy of an Oscar. He not only brought water to his eyes; but, he also swore before God in heaven that it wasn't him. When my neighbor brought the kid who saw him over to my humble abode, Slim's eyes got big as silver dollars. That was a sure sign that he was guilty as charged. Whenever he bucked his eyes like that, then would follow his contrived tirade professing his innocence. Beanie bought it... hook, line and sinker. Beanie, turned to me and said. "I don't think he did it." Needless to say, I was flabbergasted by her reaction... more hurt by her remarks than the break-in itself. I don't remember responding. I just opened the door and bid them goodbye. Our sanctuary had been breached. It was time to move on. I spoke with the landlord regarding my options. He balked at my mention of him returning our security deposit. The dispute lingered on a bit longer then I had anticipated, we were ready to move on.

I sought out the advise of an attorney, whose ad I saw some place. His office was located downtown, in the Guardian Building. The attorney's name was Stephen Reddish. I would come to discover through my conversation with Mr. Reddish, that I was his first client. Mr. Reddish was young, eager and hungry: A formula for success. I explained to the attorney about the security deposit dispute. Mr. Reddish went on to explain to me that the landlord was in the right until final resolution of the lease and, or final inspection of said premise's. He went on to explain too me that it wouldn't be beneficial for him to pursue this matter. Then he changed the subject. He asked me if I, or did I, know of anyone injuring themself at, or on their job. I thought about it for a minute, then I remembered my little doo-hickey at Super Toys. I told him about the time the ceiling had fallen on me. I had poked it out, and crawled under the debris; but, I didn't tell Mr. Reddish that. He will have to read this book to find that out. I also told him that I had gotten fired shortly after that incident, which was true. He took all of the relevant information and said, that he was going to proceed with a workmen's comp case. I was all for that. I really didn't know what the hell he was talking about. I gave him my mother's phone number and address. I could always get my messages that way. I wasn't very stable and moved around a lot. Beanie, could always get in touch with me. I signed some papers confirming Mr. Reddish as my attorney. He said something about pro' bono, then shook my hand. Then we bid each other goodbye. I never expected anything to come of it.

A few weeks after my meeting with Attorney Reddish, Deb, and I found an apartment on Hazelwood, near Second Avenue. It was a step up from our last rental. The apartment was a super nice place with plenty of room for the three of us. Deb, and I had a bedroom and Milton had a bedroom. The apartment also had a living room, dining room, kitchen, a bathroom and the usual amenities; but, it was much bigger than what we were used to.

I had to hook back up with the African and started selling Black History books again. That time around, I had to commute between Detroit and Lansing Michigan. During our trek to Lansing, we hit all of the small towns along the way; like Kalamazoo, and Muskegon. Once there we would find the black communities and then go to work selling Black History books, making money on the road. Some of those communities had black's living on one side of the road and whites living on the other side of the road. I could see barriers, such as fences, brick walls and dead-end streets separating the races. It struck me as odd to see segregation staring me in the face. Lansing would be my last trip out of Detroit to sell books. Deb, was getting suspicious about me being on the road. I had met a little cutie in Lansing. She happened to be of the Caucasian persuasion. Before I could strike gold, Deb, had drove up to Lansing to try and catch me with my draws down. After selling white girl a Black History book. I went back to the hotel that me and the African were staying at. Guess who was sitting on the bed grinning like a Cheshire cat? My adorable wife, Deb. I got the last laugh; she didn't catch me with my draws down. Nonetheless, she demanded that I drive her back to Detroit, and to forget about life on the road.

Back in Detroit, with a wife and step-son, I had my feet planted firmly on the ground. I hated it. I longed for the night life. I had to revitalize the raffle scheme to keep pace with my bills. Most of the low-wage jobs that I held down just didn't cut it. Deb, was holding up her end, so I had to keep my end of the bargain up. "By any means neccesary."

About that time in 1970, Mack was being assimilated back into a free society. He was at home, fresh out the pen. I ran into Mack's brother, Jerry, who had a girlfriend living down the street from me on Hazelwood. Jerry, informed me that Mack was on parole, then, he drove me over to their mother's house where they had a small party for Mack. Mack looked fresh and healthy. He had a baby-face, youthful glow when he went into the pen 5 years earlier. He now sported a thick bushy Mustache and thick sideburns. He spoke with a husky tone out of the side of his mouth. I attributed his new look and sound as baggage picked up in prison. Mack was now officially a tough guy.

After a few hours of hanging and riding with Mack and Jerry, it was time to get back home to Deb, and Milton. My car was out of commission, so I had to rely on Deb's car. I would take her to work and Milton to school. Then, I was off hustling or working some piece of a job. Mack hadn't been home a good month and he was having a hard time finding employment. Being on parole, Mack, was on a short leash. I decided to ask Mack, if he wanted to hustle some raffle tickets with me until something else opened up for him. He agreed. I taught him the ropes and we were off and running, with Mack working one side of the avenues, and me on the other side. Woodward Avenue, Mack, Grand River, Livernois... all the major avenues. We would meet up at the end of the block and count our loot. Mack, took to his new game like a duck takes to water. Mack was good, and he adapted quickly to the format. We had relatively, young-looking mugs so that student rep line from U of D went over swell. Nearing the end of 1970, Mack, and I had just about depleted most of our customer base of the business's on the major streets. Mack got bored and was contemplating his own new ventures. I began staying out late, running wild in the streets with the wrong indivisuals, and I didn't contribute much to our household expense's. Then, I got some good news, and some bad news in the same package. The good news was that, Deb, was pregnant and I was going to be a father. The bad news was that, Deb, was pregnant and I was broke and immature.

Fast forward eight month's...I'm sitting in the 8th precinct lock-up peering through iron bars trying to get a glimpse of the High School Basketball Championship Game, on the small television sitting on the sergeant's desk. I had gotten caught stealing a pair of pants from the long-closed, Federal's Department Store on Grand River. When someone calls you on the phone in lock-up, and the cops let you speak to the caller: Then, you know it's abut some serious shit. A doctor on the other end of the phone explained to me that my wife, Deb, had just had a mis-carriage and that she was doing fine. "However, we couldn't save the baby." The doctor went on to assure me that they had done everything that they could to save the baby. The doctor asked for my permission to dispose of my son's remains. I was broke, distressed and in jail; so I agreed to their inquiry. Looking back on that situation, I don't think that was the prudent thing to do. I would like to have given my son a proper service and a decent burial. Soon after Deb's mis-carriage, me and Mack, were hanging tough again.

Another northend acquaintance had just discharged from prison. Sonny Jackson, was sentenced to 2-5 years in the Michigan penal system as a feisty 17-year old. Sonny showed his ass so bad in the penitentiary, that instead of being paroled at the end of his minimum sentence, he went on to do the whole five years. Sonny, in prison jargon maxed out. The penal system couldn't hold him past his maximum sentence. Sonny, was a troubled kid who became a monster as an adult. Sonny fought, robbed, threatened and assaulted outside of, and inside of prison. He was an angry, vicious predator. He was Mack's main man. Me, Mack and Sonny knew each other from the streets of the northend, as children. Mack and Sonny crossed paths again inside of Marquette Maximum Security Prison, located in the Upper Peninsula. Marquette was the last stop in the penal system. Prisoners who were too violent or unmanageable were sent to Marquette. Mack, told me that he was sent to Marquette for starting a riot in Ionia Reformatory, a maximum security prison for youthful offenders. Mack stated to me that he had run into Sonny in Marquette. Sonny, was there for committing violent acts inside of Jackson Prison. Mack went on to state that his first day on the prison yard, Sonny and another inmate from the northend, Ronald Green, (May his soul rest in peace.) were attacking an inmate. Sonny was clubbing him in the head with a iron pipe, and Ronald was stabbing the inmate. That was the last time Mack, said, that he saw Sonny during his stay at Marquette. Sonny was locked up in a segregated cell, in a segregrated cell block located underground. They called it "X " Block, where the authorities controlled the lights, temperature and water, and the inmates were locked in their cell 23 hours per day. Sonny would remain in "X " Block until he was discharged from prison a year later. As fate would have it, Mack, and Sonny hooked up on the outside. This would prove to be the beginning of havoc being rained down on the mean streets of Detroit. From two of Detroit's meanest son's, straight off the streets of the northend. At times, I was a witness to their carnage. I'm the soul survivor of those turbulent times. My prayer is that God, spared me to get this story out to enlighten; not to frighten, some young person or persons contemplating doing something destructive with their lives.

Eventually, Deb left me. It all began to unravel on a beautiful summer Sunday. I came home after being away from home all weekend, without a word of where I had been. I came in, flopped on the bed and fell fast asleep. I was tired and out of it. I had not a clue, as to what was happening in the rest of the apartment. When I laid down it was daylight. As I began to awake, I peered through sleepy eyes into the dark room. I was thirsty, so I got up and slumbered through the living room into the kitchen, I got a drink of juice from the frig,' then I slumbered back through the living room and back to bed. I laid there for a few seconds. Then it came to me. I jumped out of bed and rushed back into the living room. My subconscious mind had picked up something out of whack the first time that I walked through; but, my conscious mind didn't register it. I was wide awake now. I discovered that the apartment had been stripped clean of our furnishings. Then the phone rang. Deb, was on the other end informing me that she had left me, and that I had to get my shit together before she would come back. Later, I would find out, with the help of her brothers and sisters, they had moved everything out while I slept. It was looking bad for the kid. I was broke. Deb, also took most of the food. On top of all that, I didn't have a car. I didn't feel like dealing with it right then. I went back to bed and fell fast asleep.

The next morning I was awakened by a screaming telephone. Madder than hell about my immediate situation, I answered the phone harshly, thinking that it was Deb. On the other end of the phone was a voice that I didn't recognize. The voice spoke in an elegant tone. "Hi, my name is Steven Reddish. May I speak to Arnold Hannon?" I stated. "This is Arnold speaking." (The voice on the other end refreshed my memory.) "I'm your attorney. I filed a law suit against Super Toys on your behalf awhile back. Well, I have settled your claim." I nearly fell on the floor in shock. I bummed bus fare and rushed downtown to Mr. Reddish's office. When I arrived at his office he had me sign some papers. While I signed the papers, he informed me that he had called my mother's house to reach me and she gave him my number. After signing the papers, he told me that Super Toys insurance company wanted to settle out of court for $30,000. His fee would be a third of that, that would leave me with $20,000. He went on to explain, that it would take 15 days for the insurance company to process the check. Fifteen days couldn't come fast enough. They were the longest days of my young, broke life. Just like that, I had $20,000 waiting for me. That was more money in one lump sum that I had ever had. I felt a renewed faith in God. It was as if the almighty was embracing me. There to pull me out of yet another tight jam.

On the 14th day of waiting, the rent was way past due, the frig' was empty and so was my stomach. I sat on the kitchen table all night waiting on the morning sun. I fell asleep on the kitchen table. Someone was buzzing the buzzer to my apartment. I went down to the front door to see who was buzzing my apartment. When I opened the door, Mack was standing in the foyer. He had come by to kick it with me; not knowing that this was my big pay day. I let him in. Then, I asked him to loan me bus fare for me and him to go downtown. I told him, that I would fill him in later about what's going on. I had to share my joy with someone. Mack was the only person available at the time. When we arrived at our destination, Mack, waited in the lobby of the bank; while I took the elevator upstairs to the insurance company. I signed more papers. Then a thin White man, wearing a short-sleeve white shirt and a thin black neck-tie. He had one of those plastic, pocket-protectors stuffed in his shirt pocket. He had pens and pencils protruding out of the pocket protector. The thin White man, handed me a check for $20,000. Then, he stated. "Don't spend it all in one place." He shook my hand, then he disappeared back into his work area. I hopped on the elevator, and went back down to the bank where, Mack, sat patiently in the lobby. The grin on my face spoke volumes. Mack asked me. "What's up?" I told him to wait right there. I walked over to a teller's window and opened a bank account. (my first) I put $12,000 in the account, waved Mack over, then handed him three, crisp $100.00 bills.

I hailed a cab on Woodward Avenue, and then told the cab driver to take me to Dalgleish Cadillac, on Woodward and Piquette. Upon arrival at the dealership, I paid the driver. We hopped out of the cab, then we strolled through the used Cadillac lot, located out front on Woodward Avenue. The new-car dealership was located in back of the used car lot, on Cass Avenue. At that moment my mis-guided thoughts raced back to recall the days and nights that I slumbered alone through the streets of Detroit. Walking and feeling left out everytime a slick Caddy, with it's top dropped cruised by with a shotgun-seat-riding beauty, smugly giving my walking ass the dead eye. I spotted other mis-guided young playa's, driving hard in their "Super fly" rides. Now it was my turn to join the midnight riders and rulers. I had arrived. Boy, I was one screwed-up kid. The way I saw it, I was about to put the missing pieces together. I was young and eager. Caddys, fresh duds and pros were on the horizon. I was a race horse pumping with adrenaline, chomping at the bit of life, ready to hit the tracks. It pains me to admit that shallow thinking person that I'm describing was me. I didn't know it then, but, that could have been my golden opportunity to go to college, invest in the stock market, maybe real estate or some other kind of business venture. That was my chance to do something long-term and positive; while still a very young man, and I blew it. At the time, I wasn't aware of any of that. I had no mentors to guide me through the maze of real opportunity, so I invested my time and money on something I knew. The game. As we searched through Dalgleish's lot, there were two Caddys that stood out and caught my eye. One was a 1969, royal blue Eldorado, with a white vinyl top for $4,000. It was 1971, and $4,000 was some good dough. The other car that caught my eye was a 1970, white Eldorado, with aqua interior, for $5,000. I wanted the white Caddy; but, I chose the blue one to save $1000. I paid the salesman in cash, got my license plates and keys. Then I drove off the lot feeling pretty spiffy. I was going to drop Mack off at his parole office. During our ride to Mack's parole office we noticed that the ride was a little rough. Mack and I looked at each other, then said, in unison. "Got to go back and get the white one." I made a u-turn on Woodward and headed back to Dalgleish. We spotted my salesman, a fellow by the name of Leo Deroucher, same name as the Los Angeles Dodger's manager. I told Leo, that I wanted the white Caddy and that I was willing to pay the extra grand. "No problem." Leo exclaimed. We changed paper work, tags, keys and cars. Then off we went.

I dropped Mack off, then headed downtown to Kosin's clothing store. Kosin's was my favorite store to window-shop as a teen. Here I was, strutting my raggedy ass into Kosin's, with a pocket full of loot, ready to dress with the best. Inside the store, I was hastily greeted by one of the two black salesmen, who at the time had no customers. I didn't know his name; but, I did know of the other black salesman. He was one of the regular, pimp-type passing through the In Crowd Lounge. His name was William Outlaw, better known as "Billy, the Kid." "Billy, the Kid" was a pretty, baby-faced, Latin-looking sharp-dressing playa,' salesman. Billy, was busy with a customer; otherwise, I would have given him the action. I guess because of my appearance, the brother waiting on me tried to give me the bum's rush. That made me feel slighted. He turned his attention to another customer who had just walked into the store, leaving me stranded. I spotted who I thought was another salesman; but, later I found out that he was actually one of the owners, Ben Kosin's. I asked him if he was available to help me. Mr. Kosin's said. "By all means." Then he proceeded to show me an array of various outfits. Mr. Kosin's gave me big time prop's; even though I wasn't nattily attired. I appreciated that. I then began picking and choosing a variety of expensive outfits. Ben, then ushered me into Kosin's famous backroom, where all the expensive top-shelf suits and sports coats were located. I tried on a few pieces. Then, I decided on two La Baron suits, they were high fashion at that time. When I was ready to cash out, the black salesman, who had slighted me, eagerly eyed me as I peeled off hundred dollar bills, from a big wad of cash and paid for my purchases. The bill came to about a couple of grand. As I stepped out of the door with my purchases, I winked at the black salesman, who had blew me off. He was steaming. He couldn't be mad at me; he had only himself to blame. Kosin's shoes was located next door to the clothing store. I ventured inside the shoe store and picked out a pair of brown gators, and a couple of pair of glass-heeled shoes. Glass heels were popular in the early 1970's. I had seen a playa' named, George Hall, sportin' a fresh pair and I thought that they looked slick. Before, I left Kosin's shoes, an up-and-coming tall slickster, who went by the name of Westside, came in. Westside, had his ruffian running buddy, sidekick named Bobby Neely, with him. I mention that moment in time to illustrate the slick, quick wit being spewed by playa's like Westside. A short in stature playa' named, Shorty, was already inside the store when Westside, and Bobby Neely came in. Shorty was about 5' 3." Everybody knew each other, but, not me. Westside, quipped to Shorty. "Hey Shorty, I heard they got a sale on elevator shoes down the street." For anybody else those were fighting words. Westside, grabbed Shorty and gave him a big bear hug. Shorty, hugged him back and they had a good chuckle over the line. When I left the store, I walked across the street loaded down with shopping bags full of goods from Kosins. I jumped my 23 year-old young ass into my fresh, glemming white Eldorado; with aqua interior, ready to make the suckers feel inferior. I felt mighty spiffy. My virgin ego was bursting at the seams. I rolled down the power windows, looked over at Kosin's shoe store with it's wide glass windows. I peeped Westside, and the other seasoned Macaroni's reared back on their heels, with their arms folded and their heads cocked ace duce off to the side peering out the window, checking me out. I felt that I had arrived to Mackdom. That sounds really trivial to me now; but, back in the day it made sense to me. Westside, stuck his head out the shoe store door, and shouted to me. "Welcome to the game, youngblood." And that's the truth, Ruth.

When you're looking at the Sharks from the shore, they seem pretty docile, with their mighty fins gliding smoothly across the ocean surface. It's another story when you jump in there with them. Suddenly they seem fierce. It's the same way with pros, when you jump into their element, you better know how to carry yo'game, pros eat weakness alive. Most of them were slicker than Goose shit... and that's the truth, Ruth.

Fass Cass: reflecting

Chapter 14

THE AMERICAN SCHEME

Now, that I had acquired all the bells and whistles to perpetrate my game with, I was ready to roll. All I needed was a pro' or two on board to take up my slack. First I had to tie down some loose ends. I went back to my apartment and put my new duds away, then, I paid the rent up to date. I called Beanie and told her of my good fortune, and that I would be paying her a visit soon. I took a shower and hurriedly dressed. I was like James Brown. "I was on the good foot, and I felt good" in my new pimp duds, I couldn't wait to hit the streets. Then, I remembered that I was due to take my G.E.D. test in a couple of days. I promised myself that I would study later for the test.

I walked outside into a warm summer's evening, it felt as if everyone was looking my way. I jumped in my new Caddy and headed over to Beanie's house. Beanie, and Runt were at home. I gave Beanie $500,00 and Runt a $100.00. As I was about to leave, I gave Beanie a $100,00 for Slim. They followed me outside to admire my new ride, then, off I went in search of game and fame. I didn't have to worry about staying out too late. Deb, had left me on her own initiative, hence, leaving me with no one to answer to, plus, I had the apartment to shelter me. The first stop in my 23-year-old quest for game wasn't too far from Beanie's house: Baker's Keyboard Lounge on Livernois and Eight Mile Road. Baker's was and still is as of this writing a cool, Jazz club, where all the top-notch Jazzmen, played their good music live. There was only one problem: there were no pros in Baker's, Just sophisticated men and women, out enjoying the melodic sounds. I got up out of there and made my way over to Fenkell Avenue, to Watt's Club Mozambique... no action at Watt's either. So I huslted across the street to Henry's Lounge, where there was tons of action; but, no game. That little cat and mouse game went on for the better part of the night. I had my choice of square's to pick up and lay down. I wasn't in that frame of mind though. I wanted a pro'...I was ready to do some pimpin.' Don't ask me why, because, I don't know why. It could be that it was a rite of passage for mis-guided urbanites, or an outlet to boost my self-esteem, or even a way of stroking my over-inflated ego. Some mis-guided brothers and sisters are plagued with that stupidity. "Every person starts out in life as a blank slate, their slate gets imprinted as an individual develops; cognitive developement can depend on one's heridity and environment." With most indivisuals "heredity and environment will determine whether an individual will be groomed with positive stimuli, or negative stimuli." Far to many of my fellow urbanites blank slates (including my own) were imbrued with significant amounts of "nagative stimuli"...the type of learned crap, that keeps one confused and discombobulated. Crap that's passed down through the generations. The key to enlightment is to eradicate the bullshit imbrued upon one's life's slate. Indivisuals, must somehow replace the "negative stimuli" with "positive stimuli." It's taken me a lifetime to grasp that concept. Even today I'm still grasping after a half century of living.

That pimpin' thing wasn't working out to well for me. Hell, I didn't even know where to find a pro.' Some pimp I'm turning out to be. Then I thought about it. Pros hang out in pro-bars, whorehouses, the street's, hotel's, motel's and after hour joints, the usual night haunts. So that's where I started hanging out. All I had to do was follow the Caddy's and Duce-and-a quarters (that's Electra 225 to all my young bloods.) perched at the curb sides; where I would then park my own slick ride. Then I proceeded into said establishments in search of game.

During my search for self, I often referred back to some of the maxims that pimps like Hawk, used to banter about as words of pimpisms to up and coming young playa's. One of the local bean heads was walking up to the bean house, where, Hawk, was standing outside kicking it with others playa's. The local asked, Hawk, how he was doin,' Hawk replied, with his patent line. "Doin' what I can until I can do what I wanna." From the master's mouth. That's what I was doing out in the streets. "Doin' what I can, until I could do what I wanna,'" and that's what I'm gonna' to tell a pro.' If I can ever find one.

When you're looking at the sharks from the shore, they seem pretty docile with their mighty fins gliding smoothly across the ocean surface. It's another story when you jump in there with them. Suddenly, they seem fierce. Its the same way with pros, when you jump into their element, you better know how to carry your game. Pros eat weakness alive. Most of them were slicker than goose shit...and that's the truth, Ruth. I wasn't about to get in a pros face if she belonged to another pimp, because that could lead to violence. You could be attacked by the pros pimp, or both of them could double team yo' ass. You'll be lucky if you don't get shot or stabbed in the process. That's why it's best not to fraternize with someone else's game. Now if she get's in a pimp's face, it's up to her man to check her. If not, it's open season on that pro,' because, no one stepped up to speak for her. The game had a lot of unwritten rule's and I violated damn near everyone of them. Nonetheless, I was young, eager, and determined to make this playa' thing happen. I had to be a little bit lost to entertain such thoughts. To tell you the truth. I had no idea what my young ass was doing at that time. Basically, I tried to emulate the many older playa's I've seen in action during my teen years, hanging around the gamers. Little did I know at that time, this little ritual has stifled my race's growth for far to many generations. I was just another young victim of that vicious cycle. Even through I had all the tools: clothes, ride, jewel's and swagger, I was still striking out at every turn.

After days of searching the tracks and strolls. One evening I was out cruising the the streets of downtown Detroit, in the shadows of the Ponchartrain Hotel. I spotted two fine pros strutting into the hotel. One of the pros spied me making a u-turn back toward the hotel, and slowed up. I eased up in front of the Ponchartrain Hotel and parked. The pro' who had stopped came up to my car. I rolled down the power windows on her side, and said, as she stood there. "Y'all lost?" She said. "Naw, I saw that pretty Caddy, and wanted to get up close and personal." She looked young, around my age. I began to think another square. Then she said. "Mind if I get in?" My reply. "Be my guest, but what about your friend?" She answered. "She's tired, and went up to our room to get some rest." I replied. "Well, get in or get in the wind." She slid in, and off we went. I had to protect my image. Before we got too far, I reminded her. "You know you in a pimp's ride? Brashly, she shot back. " I ain't no motherfuckin' square. I know what you is." My ears perked up right then and there. With her words, "I ain't no square," was my cue to get busy with some game. I proceeded with caution. I wanted to know more. I began by asking her name? She replied. "My name is Joann." Then I wanted to know who her man was? She answered all of my questions. She said, that she didn't have a man, and that she was a stepper (meaning hooker) and her last man was a lame. She stated, that she had to get away from "that stiff ass motherfucker." I asked about her girlfriend and did she have a man and a plan? She informed me that they were a team..."You knock one, you get two." Then it was her turn to quiz me, starting with my name. I needed a street handle. I was torn between calling myself Cassanova or Fass Cass. I told her my name was, "Fass Cass, comin' at yo' ass with a blast." She chuckled and wanted to know more. Starting with how many girl's did I have? The answer to that question was none, but, I didn't tell her that. I told her that I had two pros on the road getting my traps cross-country. Then, I told Joann, that it was no guarantee that they were going to work out, but, I could always use a backup. I spurted. "When I knock you and girlfriend off, then I'll be ridin' fo' deep." Pimps talked like that back in the day. Riding out Woodward, we came upon the Monterey Motel, then located on Monterey and Woodward, in Highland Park. Attached to the motel was the Howard Johnson Restaurant, where pimps hung out. It was a rendezvous point to check their traps from their pros. I pulled into the lot, then asked her if she was hungry. She gave me one of those why not shrugs. We went inside, and slid into an empty booth to continue our chit-chat. I watched her while we ate, trying to detect some semblance of the truth. One thing I had come to realize about the game: everybody lied a lot; and not just about major shit, but, about everything...from big lies to the simplest of lies, and every kind of lie in-between. When, I got ready to pay the bill, I pulled out a Missouri bankroll. (show me) Like a good pro,' she peeped the bankroll, out of the corner of her eye, and was impressed. She grabbed my arm, than we sashayed out of the restaurant into the night back to the Rada. She hinted to me that she was ready to choose, then she asked me. "You got a spot for two new wife-in laws?" My reply was. "If y'all paying, y'all staying." I don't know where that came from, but, I just felt kind of pimpish at that moment. When we got back to the Ponchartrain, she asked me if I wanted to come up to meet my new people. I reminded her that she was moving too fast. "I ain't got my first trap yet." Pros like to test playa's to see if they're real or fake. One of the cardinal rules of the game is that real pros, choose real pimps, with real traps (cash). She gave me her room number and asked me to call her. I played hardball and said. "Naw, you take my number and call me when y'all break luck." I was schooled by some major players who would lament. "Don't go weak on a pro,' that's their cue to try and work you." So, I kept my game strong. I went home, fell asleep and waited for the phone to ring.

When I woke up the next day, I checked the calender and noticed the date. It was the day that I was suppose to take my G.E.D. test. I hadn't studied, and was bent out of shape about it. Regardless, I headed over to Grand River, near Livernois, to the Adlai Stevenson Building, to take the test. I worried for naught. I aced the test and was told to watch the mail for my G.E.D. certificate. I left the testing sight feeling pretty good about that little achievement. When I got back to my apartment, my phone was ringing off the hook. I could hear it from the building's lobby. I hurried in and answered the screaming phone. The voice on the other end sounded soft and stressed. It was Joann. She said. "Baby, I been calling you all day. My girlfriend Cookie, stole all my shit." I said. "You mean the bitch you wanted me to bring to my crib?" Joann replied. "Yeah, I didn't know the bitch was that scandalous. She ran off with some dude down the hall." Then, in a pleading tone she said. "Baby, I'm ready. Come get me and take me to my new spot." I didn't know if she was trying to work me or what. Then, I reminded her about that other thing. Joann, with confidence in her voice said. "Baby, you chose, I got yo' trap. I'll be waiting for you in the lobby." That was good news. My paper was getting short, and I didn't want to hit my bank account. I barked. "Be ready. I'm on my way." When I got there, I had a chance to see her in the sunlight. She was sexy as hell. She was a thin light-brown-skinned beauty, with long pointed boobs. She had big succulent lips, with slightly protruding front teeth and round brown eyes...eyes that were looking for me. Hot damn. She looked like a completely different girl. I almost slipped out of my pimp mode. I wanted to lay her fine ass down. I had to contain my composure. I remembered a pimpism, I picked up from gamer's. " If you get her mind, you get the money and the honey." As Joann slid in the front passenger seat, I asked her where was her luggage?" She replied. "The bitch stole everything I had." Then, she grabbed my hand and pressed a Jr. wad of cash in the palm of my hand. It was about a hundred and seventy dollars. I then said to her. "It's light; but, all right, it's a start." Joann didn't know it; but, after seeing her, I really wanted to lay her fine ass down. A move like that, to a pro' like her would have been considered a sucker move. Fellows, if you ever needed a ego boost, you'll never get an ego surge like the one you'll have when a pro' greases your palm with pro' dough. It's almost as good as having an orgasm. That's when the pimpin' takes over yo' soul, baby. You start to acting pimpish, talkin' pimpish, and walkin' like a pimp. That shit is contagious. Greasing of the palm will transform a little ole' square into a big ole' pimp. I thought about it for a minute and came to the conclusion that I can't take her home. What if Deb came by; after all she was still my wife, and she still had a key, I respected her. I informed, Joann, that we were going to parley at the Monterey Motel, closer to the stroll. I explained to her that I had to see if she was for real or not. I told Joann, the first thing we had to do was to get her some fresh duds and toiletries...I can't have my pro' looking like a tramp. That made her smile. Most pros need a pimp to take charge. They always had to take charge when dealing with tricks. Pimps were the perfect balance to contrast that. Pimps understood that; after all, beneath a pros thick exterior beats the heart of a little girl, seeking Daddy's approval. Smart pimps know that too. I would come to learn that, Joann, wasn't your ordinary street whore. She was much more. She plied her trade in the glitzy hotels downtown: the Statler, the Ponchartrain, the Book Cadillac Hotel, and other upscale hotels. Baby girl, knew how to work 'em to. Every night the trap got bigger and better. Joann worked late into the night. The only places open were Ted's restaurant on Woodward, in Palmer Park, Howard Johnson's in Highland Park, and a few others...were open late to serve the night lifers.

When we weren't at the restaurants, we were frequent vistors to the various blind pigs located throughout Detroit. One of our favorite spots was a joint located on Linwood and West Grand Boulevard. It was run by a major roller named Jack Crawford. Jack was a classy, sporty fellow whose patrons consisted of major rollers, such as Butch Harris, another Northern alumni. Butch was a tall, movie star handsome chap, and a super sharp dresser. Butch played football for Northern High, and was considered a playboy with a lot of young tenders nipping at his heels. I would categorize Butch, after he left school, as a gentleman gangster who took care of his business, and his business took care of him swell. Bobby Neely, George Hall, Cincinnati, and Texas Slim, were all gangsters. Let me rephrase that: They're all dead gangsters. Jack's was their spot, and of course players, shared the lime light, rubbing elbows at the bar and talking shit.

One late night me and Joann, were hanging tough, chatting up a storm at Jack's place. I saw out of the corner of my eye, George Hall, and Eddie Jackson, checking us out. George looked like he was agitated about something. George was a ill- tempered, pimp / D-man, who was no joke when it came to getting in scraps. I was well aware of his reputation. I had met, George, during my nights hanging out with David Tate. George didn't say anything to us that night. But, he did put some money in the juke box and played James Brown's "Talking Loud and Saying Nothing" while eye-balling me and Joann. That was my cue to get up out of there, before this thing escalated. D-men of Georges caliber would often test young pimps. If they smelled weakness, they would try you. Plus, Goerge carried a big 357 magnum pistol and he loved to crack a nigga's head with it. One must keep in mind that it was the early 1970's, and the advent of Crack Cocaine was a decade away. Even though, it was a different vibe, the murder rate was off the charts. My generation was coming of age during that time. We were fresh and in some cases friendly. "I'm fresh and friendly" was a line I used on pros. After we left Jack's place, it was approaching 4 a.m. and I was headed back to the Monterey motel; when Joann asked me to drop her off downtown at one of the big hotels. She said, she had an out-of-town trick lined up at the hotel earlier in the day. I figured mo' dough, why not? Besides, I could go home now; not back to that cramped motel. I dropped her off, then I headed home.

When I got home, I went straight to bed, I was wasted. A few hours into my sleep, I was awakened by the screaming telephone, ringing non-stop in my ear as I peered out of one eye. I could glimpse streams of sunlight pour into the room. I got up and slumbered to the kitchen to answer the phone. It was Deb, on the other end. She was in a bubbly mood. She said, that she wanted to see me later on in the day. I told her that I would try to accommodate her wishes, and that I had a busy day ahead of me. When I hung-up, I called the motel to give Joann her instructions. Pros love to get instructions from their pimp. Joann, answered the phone, still half asleep. She asked me what time was I coming by the motel? She sleepily said. "I got something for you." I said. "See you for breakfast in an hour." We then ended our little chat. I hurried to get dressed. I was curious about Joann's surprise. When I got to the motel, I walked into our room sharper than two tacks on a toe nail (something I heard Honey say once.) I came into a clothes-strewn mess. Joann was half-dressed. I asked her what was my surprise. She threw a wad of big bills, knotted up with a rubber band at me. I quipped. "So this is my big surprise?" Joann said. "That's yo' trap, Baby. Here's yo' surprise, come on out Sandy." The bathroom door was opened and out stepped a green-eyed, tall, young blond cutie pie. My first thought was. "I done hit the jack pot." I had snow in my game and she was bearing gifts of the green-back kind. She said. "Hi Fass Cass. Jo' been schooling me about yo' game. I had to see for myself. I couldn't wait to meet you. I'm your new wife, Sandy, if you want me." Sandy leaned into me and kissed me on the cheek; while pressing a choosing trap into the palm of my smooth, pimp hand. I was in pimp heaven.

I stepped out into the sunlight, draped with two prime pros dangling from each arm; I just wanted someone who knew me to see me at that moment in time. We ate real good that morning. During our conversation over breakfast, Joann filled me in on what had transpired when I dropped her off last night at the tricks hotel. The trick already had Sandy, in the room when Joann arrived. I'm guessing that Sandy, was the trick's back-up if Joann didn't show. The trick paid Joann, to join the party, and the girls got paid royally for their litte threesome. Sandy, was from Windsor, Ontario, and drove over from Canada to Detroit, to turn the trick. Joann found out that Sandy loved her some nose candy (cocaine) and that she didn't have a man. Joann had more talent than just selling flesh. She was a knock-off artist. (cop other pros for her man's stable.) She bought Sandy, a blow and did whatever pros do to each other sexually. Now I had a new addition to my game. My ego was uncontainable, damn near off-the-chart. After we ate, I dropped the girls off downtown. Sandy, left her car back at the hotel's lot; while they did their thing on foot. They were just what a pimp likes to see when I dropped them off, giddy and happy; they were young and they had good game.

I cruised down Woodward, to the Flamingo Barbershop, then housed inside of a store-front located in the Mt. Royal Hotel. I had to get my hair freshly whipped. I chose the Flamingo, because that's where the top-notch playa's got their hair done. That was the same Flamingo Barbershop, from the 12th Street, days. The 1967 riots drove most of the business's from 12th street. They were either burned out or looted out. Most of 12th street business's had to relocate to other parts of the city, or to the suburbs. We didn't have cell phones or beepers back in the day. If one wanted to communicate with someone, they had to use a pay phone or someone's house phone. Life was much slower in that respect. The Flamingo was the perfect place to socialize with others in your trade. There was always a lively, spirited atmosphere for slick players..."Birds of a feather flock together." Whoever coined that phrase should be rich. The barbershop was busy on that particular day. I didn't mind. I wanted to show off my slick new duds. There was another reason pimps patronized the Flamingo, other than to get their hair whipped and a manicure. There were always pros coming and going on the corner of Holbrook and Woodward. Pros were in and out of the barbershop, checking out the playa's, or getting their flirt on. There was always some game being spewed. That gave the pros a chance to brush up on their own game. The anchor of the complex was the Mt. Royal Hotel, where some of the pros resided. It was a busy little corner. When, I finished getting my hair laid, I ran into one of my old acquaintances, Junie Boy. He went on to tell me that, "Mack, and his crazy cousin, Derrick, was robbin' and shootin' up nigga's left and right." Junie, also stated that the cousins were feared on the northend by squares and gangsters. Then the conversation turned to me. Junie Boy stated. "Yo' hare is laid, and you're sharper than a Rat's turd." (That was no typo. He said "hare," instead of "hair.") When he saw me headed to my Eldorado, he said. "You pimpin' hoe's and slammin' Rada' dooh's now nigga.'" I answered. "Yeah, the game finally caught up with me." We laughed and waved goodbye. Junie Boy, wasn't doing too bad himself. He jumped in a new, yellow Fleetwood. I relished in the fact that his wasn't a pimp's ride. That was a dope man's ride. Pimps are at the top of the game food chain, they're what most gangsters were perpetrating to be. Hey, I didn't invent that madness, that was the climate I was indoctrinated into. I was a unenlightened victim, like the young people before me and the young people after me. In my case shit happened so fast that I didn't realize that I to was being victimized. I was played by the game of life. I just happened to be amongst the the lucky few to survive that madness. And I lived to write about it.

I finally made it back to my apartment on Hazelwood. When I entered the foyer of the apartment building, I could smell home cooking. I thought somebody was going to eat good. As I got closer to my apartment, the more intense the mouth-watering aroma became. Then I thought I heard my television set. I eased my key into place. When I opened the door, the aroma exploded in my nose. The television indeed was on and back in it's place. Deb was sitting on the couch sewing, and all the furniture was back in place. It was as if she had never left. When I saw Deb sitting there, I knew she was a day late and a dollar short... I had gotten a good whiff of pro' dough and it was intoxicating to the point of no return. I was lost and turned out. Arnold, lay dormant somewhere inside of my subconscious mind. His alter ego Fass Cass, had emerged from the depth's of my id. The strongest love on earth couldn't stop that urge to pimp. When I think back on that, I can only surmise that I was mentally-ill, because sane folk's don't rationalize like that. After a little bit of how you doing and I'm so glad to see you bull; it was time for the hard questions. First from me, "Where you been, why you back, what's your plans. Will you leave me again at the first sign of trouble?" Deb chimmed in. "I see you done got your stuff together," followed by laughter. Deb, bless her soul, that's how she talked. She never cursed. Deb continued. "You got a new Cadillac, and new clothes, and you're acting like some kind of pimp. You ain't no pimp. You're a married man, with a family." At that moment, I felt love for Deb, and strong regards for our relationship. Thoughts of our lives together consumed me. I thought back to our humble beginning's. I thought about our first encounter and our first kiss.

In that moment, I reminisced about the times when she would take me to rehearsal for a theater group I had joined. It was called Metro Art's and was located near Wayne State University. It was a city-funded program for inner- city youth. There young people could study music, fine arts and the theater. I had always wanted to try my hand at acting, and had seriously thought about relocating to California to give it a try. Now that was in the late 1960's. The only movies I saw with people that looked like me were what was referred to as, "Black-explotation-movies." We would rehearse in the evening for our first production at Metro Arts. It was a three-act play by Ray Bradberry. Ray Bradberry, was the creator of the future television show "Star Trak." That show would go on to propel, Bradberry, into cult icon status. The play was called, "1999" a futuristic play. I can't recall when he wrote the play, but, 1999 was a couple of decades in the future when we presented it at Metro Arts, in the late 1960's. I played the lead role George, a father of means. The play's theme centered on a super dynamic playroom that rich people installed in their homes for entertainment purposes. A whole wall was transfixed into a giant video screen. All one had to do was imagine a place on earth and the system would transform your thoughts onto the screen. To make a long story short, my children played by other cast members, devised a scheme to have Mom and Dad consumed by the playroom. They imagined the African Plains, and locked us in the playroom with the sound effects of wild animals attacking us. The curtain came down with me and my stage wife screaming with fear. When the curtain came up the small audience, Deb, included, roared with approval. We got a standing ovation. It felt good looking out into that audience seeing my pregnant wife, proud as punch cheering for her husband, with a look of sheer love and adoration on her glowing face. Reminiscing about the past softened my heart.

Now, back to the present. I answered Deb's question with. "You married a broke man." Deb, went on to state that we needed to be together. Deb knew how to bring the square in me out; whenever she got mushy with me, Arnold would re-appear and my alter ego, Fass Cass, would disappear. I asked Deb to fix me some of her home cooking. After I ate, Cass reared his flighty head, and I hit the street. Whew, she almost had me. Before I left, I told Deb that I was going to think about it. Then I dashed out of the door. I knew one thing: if the pros knew that I was keeping company with a square broad, (That's what pros called women like Deb.) I wouldn't only lose the pros; but, my credibility in the game would take a good lickin.' Pros would spread that kind of gossip to anybody they thought knew me in the game. It just wasn't prudent for the two cultures to clash. The struggle between good and bad had begun. The good-bad paradox weighed heavily on my shoulders. On one shoulder I had Deb the good, and on the other shoulder, I had Joann and green-eyes, representing the bad. Which would I choose? I imagined Joann representing the bad, whispering in my ear. "Pimping is yo' calling, Baby. Let me take you there." I do believe that the minds of young people are the devil's playground, where he tempts, entices, then seduces individuals to do devious deeds. With my situation, the devil's way was irresistible to my youthful mentality. The notoriety of being a big Mack overwhelmed me. I choose the pros over home cooking, back rubs and good, clean loving and living. Again don't ask me why. Its beyond my intellect, I don't know why it turned out that way. I guess I didn't want to spend my life second-guessing myself. I had to find out first hand if I had what it took to make it in that game thang, was I as crafty as my mentor pimps. That's just the way the devil wanted me to think. At that moment in time, I chose the jealousy, the petty gamesmanship played between so-called playa's and pros, with an assortment of other fools thrown in the mix. The shady characters you had to rub elbows with, the plain old loathsomeness of having to deal with someone who provided sexual favors for a living, all in the name of fame, fortune and game. Too bad it took a good chunk of my life to figure it all out. I informed Deb that I was moving on.

I rented an apartment downtown, in the Town Apartments on First and Michigan. I had Sandy sell her car. I didn't want her riding out into the sunset. Pros moving around on foot are more reliable and stable, easier to track. Two or three months after moving into the Town Apartment, I ran into an old friend who everyone was suppose to be scared of. I can't recall the place we crossed paths. When we saw one another, we both broke out in a big grin and bear-hugged each other. Mack was getting plenty of money. He told me his cousin, Derrick, had gotten cracked on a murder case, and was on his way to the pen. Mack had a new running buddy, Sonny, who had some rag-tag, white broad with him. Just before we said our goodbyes, Mack said to me. "Remember that $300,00 you gave me when I was struggling?" Well I'm paying you back. Then he pulled a knot out of his pocket and peeled off three, one-hundred dollar bills, and pressed them into my hand, with a handshake. That wouldn't be our last encounter, there was more to come. Much more.

The next thing I knew, I was being shaken awake. We were teetering on the edge of Grand Rapids. I had fallen asleep. I thanked him again, and just as quickly, I was back out in the frigid night looking for a sign of life. I spotted a neon sign blinking in the distant, beckoning me toward it's glow. My cold legs and feet couldn't move fast enough. The blinking light led me to a Pool Hall. When I walked in from the cold into the warmth of the Pool Hall, all eyes were fixed on me, standing near the front entrance, shivering like a wet dog on a cold night, with only a thin suit and shirt to protect me from the frozen tundra of the winter's night.

Grand Rapids: circa 1972

Chapter 15

THAT THING IN GRAND RAPIDS

Me and my duet of pros were still kickin' it strong two months after we moved into the Town Apartments. The girl's were spending more time together than I was spending with them. Hey, they were keeping each other happy with licks and tricks. The tricks supplied the dicks. I know it sound's sick; but, the game is a sick endeavor. I was good with all of that. I didn't like sexin' pros anyway. Most pros are suspect of pimps who do mo' fuckin' than pimpin'. When one of my pros cracked for sex. I curtly reminded them that they had a wife-in-law for that, and to get their dick's from their trick's who had cash. Pros loved that kind of talk. Regarding sex, I would generally go into a tirade and lament. "If you fuck me and don't get paid, then you a trick bitch." I hated to use that language; but, sometimes pros like to test playa's. For most pros that's the only language they understood. Pros called it being real. Pimpin,' It's just a dirty little game, invented by a deprived soul eons ago and evolved into what it is today. As a young man I was restless: here, there, everywhere, every night it was rest, dress and read the "Free Press," (Detroit Newspaper) was a pimp's motto in Detroit. When the pimps who live and die by that motto lose their pros, they damn near starve to death. Because it's hard to rest, dress and read the "Free Press" without dough coming in to relieve the stress. The only thing that motto is good for is keeping a man lazy and dependent on a pros ass to fuel his insatiable ego. While I was busy checking trap's and dealing with all the crap. I should have been checking business accounts to help secure my family's future with a long term game plan. Once a playa' get's knocked out the box, it can be a motherfucker getting back on your feet. You can pimp if that's your thing, but, always be prepared for the fall, so you won't have to linger in despair. You can pick yourself up and move on to something better for your life. Life don't begin and it don't end with pimpin' off of a pros ass. Life begins and ends with one standing on God's stage alone and naked.

I ran into Mack and Sonny again; both were ex-convicts. They were still partners in crime. Mack wanted me to drive them to Grand Rapids, to drop some beans off to a fellow he had met in prison. I don't know where Mack got his supply from; but, he had at least a few thousand beans in his pocession. I declined his offer, until he made me an offer I couldn't refuse: Cash. I figured why not? I could always relate to extra dough. Joann could handle my business while I was away. I agreed to Mack's offer. We planned to leave in a couple of days. Just enough time to school the pros on how to handle my business. We left on a Thursday. Before I left, I told Joann, that she was in charge of the day-to-day activity. I made it clear to both girls that I wanted my paper stacked tall against the wall. They understood. I kissed them on their cheeks and bid them farewell. I really had confidence in my game to leave two prime pros behind like that. They were now prime targets for predator pimp's on the prowl for new game. Mack and Sonny had what they called a hideout; a vacant flat over Mack's mother's (Tina) house on Oakland and Smith Street. Sonny had a white girl named Laura, with him. Mack brought along a young lady he met while we were selling raffle tickets in the foyer of the long-closed Sears Department store, then located on Grand River and Oakman Boulevard. Her name was Diane, and boy was she fine. She worked at Sears as a sales clerk. I didn't know that the girls were going to be on board with us. Also unknown to me, Mack was planning on marrying Diane in Muskegon, Michigan. Diane was an intelligent good-looking square. I wondered what attracted her to a thug like Mack. They say opposites attract and some nice girls are attracted to dangerous men. On the other hand. Sonny's girl was just someone he could use and abuse. To satisfly his warped ego. He would back-hand her in the mouth; whenever the mood struck him. He talked to her like she was a dog. Laura, never protested and cowarded under Sonny, like a frightened pet. I figured that some people's lives were indoctrinated with abuse early on in their development. Being abused is entrenched deep in their psychological makeup. Laura and her whole demeanor struck me as such an individual. We stopped in Muskegon, where Mack knew a preacher that would marry him and Diane. They already had their blood tests and marriage license. Sonny and I stood in as his best men. We were back on the road to Grand Rapid's after Mack's and Diane's marriage. After a few hours on the road, we eased into Grand Rapid's. We found a motel to check into. I was the only one without companionship. Sonny had Laura, and Mack had his blushing bride, Diane. I had zilch. After dining on the local cuisine, it was time for us to deliver the package to Mack's mellow man. The girls waited at the motel, while we made our move.

When we reached our destination, we scampered up a flight of stair's to the second floor flat of a two-family flat. Mack and Sonny were strapped. They didn't leave home without their hardware. I was along for the ride. I wasn't into carrying guns, it just wasn't my style. What I was doing with those two ex-con gangsters remains a puzzle to me. Even today. On that day everything went smooth. Mack's mellow reassured him that he would have the goods flipped in a few days. Diane had to get back to Detroit. She had a real job. Mack stayed behind while me Sonny and Laura delivered Diane back to Detroit. I handled the driving.

When we got back to Detroit, we dropped Diane off: then, I paid a visit to my apartment to discover that the pros were handlin' my business. I checked off a trap or two, then I hit the road back to Grand Rapids, with Sonny and Laura in tow.

We made it back to Grand Rapids. After dropping Sonny and Laura off at the motel. I decided to hang out at one of the local downtown bars where I got lucky and knocked off a hip-square girl. She was sexy and cute, and I was horny: a volatile mix. I eased on over to her and bought her a drink to break the ice. After a few more drinks, and a little chit-chat. She was good to go. Before she knew it, we were back at my motel room rolling around on the bed, having a good time. Back in the day we didn't have to worry about Aids, because it wasn't around then. The worst you could catch was the claps. We had a pretty good time enjoying each other's warmth and passion. In other words, we had a one night stand. Everything was developing smoothly. Mack had delivered the last batch of beans to his mellow man. The money was flowing. There were two little problems: we were running out of beans and my white Eldorado was drawing too much attention. We decided that I should go back to Detroit and drop my car off. I had called Slim and pre-arranged to trade my Caddy for his clunker for a few days. I had no problem getting him to agree with that arrangement.

The moment I arrived back in Detroit, I headed striaght downtown to my apartment. I checked my traps, changed clothes, fooled around with the pros, gave them instructions and then promised them a grand outing when I got back.

When it was time to hit the road back to Grand Rapid's, I had Slim's jalopy and he had my Caddy. I was well into my journey when I discovered that I had left my over coat in the Caddy. All I had on was a two-piece bur-

gundy suit, dress shirt, and a burgundy Dobb's hat. It was in the dead of winter and I was too far outside of Detroit to turn around. The heat in the old
station wagon worked; but, not as well as the heat in the Caddy. I was traveling on a long stark stretch of highway, light flurries of snow flickered
across my headlights. The only images visible in the pitch-black night, were
the shadowy silhouettes of naked tree branches and foliage that lined the
highway. I was freezing, because the heat was barely registering in the old
clunker I was driving. Suddenly, I heard a gurgling sound coming from the
motor. I tried to ignore it, by pretending that I didn't hear the sound. Just
as suddenly, the car started shaking and the motor begin to sputter. Then
the car came creeping to a stop. "Oh shit." I'm in big trouble in the middle
of nowhere, on a highway somewhere between Detroit and Grand Rapids.
It was pitch-black outside and the temperature was below freezing. I had
a major dilemma on my hands. I could sit in the freezing stalled car and possibly freeze to death; or, I could take my chances walking in hopes of getting help from a passing motorist, who would have mercy on me and stop.
I chose to walk. As I scuttled up the road. I was nervous and colder then
a well-digger's ass in Brute Montana. Images of me splayed out on the side
of the road frozen in the morning sunlight, flashed in my mind to help keep
me motivated and moving. My ears were numb and tingly, so were my feet.
Then I spotted a beacon of lights moving toward me down the highway...
a sign of hope that I would get help. Whoever it was had to pass the abandoned station wagon. I waved frantically at the approaching headlights. As
if God had placed the order himself, the headlights came to a screeching
halt at my frozen feet. I spotted a shadowy arm montioning for me to open
the back door. I opened the car door and flung my heat-deprived body
into the warmth of the back seat. The guardian angel came in the form of
a young White man, with three sleeping toddlers huddled together in the
back seat. Another toddler was stretched across the front seat. I took my
seat beside the sleeping tots. I recall profusely thanking the young man and
assured him that he may have saved my life. He stated that he saw my
stalled vehicle in the middle of the road and figured that whoever it was,
was in trouble. He asked me where was my coat. I told him that it was a
long story. He then asked me where was I headed. I replied. "Grand
Rapids." The young gentleman then said. "You're in luck I 'm going past
Grand Rapids." As we conversated more during our ride. He went on to
explain that he had just left his cheating wife and was now headed to his
mother's house with his kids. The next thing I knew, I was being shaken
awake. We were teetering on the edge of Grand Rapids. I had fallen asleep.

I thanked him again, and just as quickly, I was back out into the frigid night looking for a sign of life. I spotted a neon sign blinking in the distance, beckoning me toward it's glow. My cold legs and feet couldn't move fast enough. The blinking light led me to a pool hall. When I walked in from the cold into the warmth of the pool hall, all eyes were fixed on me standing near the front entrance, shivering like a wet dog on a cold night. With only a thin suit and shirt to protect me from the frozen tundra of that winter's night. A voice in the pool hall, said. "Man, where's your coat?" I promptly replied. "It's a long story." I asked. "Where's the pay phone?" one of the patron's-pointed me in the right direction. I called the motel and told Mack of my dilemma... then; I told him, as soon as I can get a cab, I'll be on over to the motel. It wasn't long before the cab arrived. I hopped in and off we went. When we got to the motel, I paid the driver and went immediately to Mack's motel room. Mack opened the door. He, Sonny, and Laura were sitting around eating Kentucky fried chicken and watching TV. I grabbed a piece of chicken, then proceeded to explain my ordeal on the road. They all said that they were glad to see me without much enthusiasm. They were gangsters. They didn't hug. I was dealing with ex-cons who were programed not to show their emotions. I wasn't indoctrinated with that penitentiary stimuli. I did expect at least a handshake. Now we didn't have a ride. I was too tried to deal with it. I went to my room, and fell fast asleep.

The screaming telephone woke me up at about 5 o'clock in the evening. When I answered it, Mack was on the other end stating. "We gon get something to eat, and then catch a cab to pick up the rest of the loot." I said. "O k." I got up, freshened up; then met up. Laura waited in their room; while the three of us kicked it in the motels lobby contemplating our next move. After we ate, we called a cab to transport us over to Mack's cellie's house, to collect the last payment for the beans he had left with him. Mack and Sonny were still strapped, just like the "American Express" television commercial, they didn't leave home without them. (pistols) As stated I did-n't carry a gun, it just wasn't my style. Knowing Mack and Sonny were packing heat made me nervous. When we arrived we knocked on the front door. A little boy answered it. Then, we proceeded up the stairs into the living room, where we were met by a somber audience: Mack's boy, two other kids and Mack's boy's woman. It just didn't feel right. There were too many sad faces. Mack's boy was sitting at the kitchen table with his head held down. He couldn't even make eye contact with us. Mack and Sonny, with the brims of their big gangster hat's broke down in front over their brow were glaring menacingly, with their hands planted firmly in their pocket's. I hovered in the background disbelieving what was about to tran-spire. Mack's boy broke the silence with. "I ain't got yo' money man. I got robbed." Ex-cons like Mack and Sonny learned in prison to communicate with their eyes. Mack looked at Sonny, Sonny looked at Mack, I looked at them both intently hoping like hell, that they didn't do something stupid. Just as Mack and Sonny were about to make their move, there was a loud knock at the downstairs door. I felt relief; only the police knocked like that. I felt the police's presence would quell the impending turmoil. With Mack and Sonny, we could have easily caught a murder case. In retrospect, the po-lice saved us from ourselves. Looking back I'm mighty grateful that they showed up when they did. In the time it took the cops to get upstairs, Mack and Sonny had slid their hardware under a sofa, then we raised our hands. The kid who let us in had slipped downstairs and called the cops. The same kid was now leading the cops up the stairs. When they made their entrance the kid pointed at the three of us and blurted." They was gon' rob us." That's all it took. We were searched and hand cuffed, then carted off to the hoosegow. Mack's buddy from prison sat at the kitchen table with his head again held down. He said nothing; nor, did his woman say anything in our defense.

When they got us to the police headquarters, we were separated and interrogated one at a time. We didn't answer any questions. We were charged with armed robbery and we were due for arraignment in the morning. When morning came we were hauled over to the court house and placed in a holding cell to await our fate before a judge. Then we were marched into the courtroom and stood before the judge. I can't recall the Judge's name; but, he was white and stern-looking, looming large behind his tall massive bench. I felt a craw in my throat as the old, white, bushy-eye-browed judge glared at us like we had a foul odor. This was my first ar-raignment on such a serious charge. Knots were beginning to form in my stomach and I wanted to go home. The judge assigned us a court-appointed attorney, and a $50,000 bond. The judge asked us if we understood. In uni-son, we managed a weak. "Yes sir." The judge set our next court appear-ance, which was referred to as a preliminary examination. Mack and Sonny, had been through this little ritual before. They knew what to expect; I had-n't, and I didn't know what to expect. I was worried. I saw my whole life going down the drain. I hadn't bust a grape to be in that much trouble. We were all handcuffed together and then carted off to the "Kent County Jail." Our bonds were to high to make bail. We would have to stay locked up until our next court date, about three weeks down the road.

When we entered the jail, I realized how serious things were. After being processed and issued jail garb. We were escorted to an elevator and informed that we were going to Maximum Security, due to our high bond and the nature of our charges. They called us a security risk. As the elevetor made it's slow decent down to our new home, my spirit began to wane. Mack and Sonny, were refugee's from one of the toughest prisons in Michigan. They looked grim and defiant, talking out of the sides of their mouths. I followed their lead and wore a mask of grim defiance; then, I started talking out of the side of my mouth. When the elevator came to a halt, we stepped off into the corridor of the Maximum Securiy section of the "Kent County Jail." We were met by a horde of massive steel doors on each side of us. One of our deputy escorts asked Mack (who was using an alias Fred Brown.) which rock did he want. Mack nodded in the direction of the rock to his left. Cell blocks are referred to as the rock. Then Mack nodded to the right looking at Sonny, meaning for Sonny to choose the cell across from him to the right; but, the deputy called my name first and asked me to choose. I chose the rock that Sonny was supposed to get. Then they escorted Sonny around a bend to the only cell left. It was away from our area. The massive steel doors opened and I was staring at about a dozen other grim defiant faces, talking out of the sides of their mouth's. We were locked up tighter than Dick's hat band, to await our next court date. I was surprised to find a clean dormitory-style setting, with about a dozen other inmates, all of them black. I would come to find out that my armed robbery charge was the least charge on the rock. All the inmates were in various stages of their court process. Some had been in a state of limbo for as long as a year or more. If we didn't do well at our next court date, we could be in for the long haul. The only entertainment was an intercom that pumped in a radio station. To punish us even more, they had it set on a white rock station. We heard rock, news and weather from the time we got up, until the time lights went out. I heard the song,"Horse With No Name" riding through the dessert, by a white rock band called "America" so much that even decades later when I hear that song, I'm immediately transfixed back to the "Kent County Jail" in my mind. That was the longest I'd been locked-up in my life. Time crept by. When our next court date was finally upon us, we were relieved that we were going to have our preliminary examination hearing. The prosecutor will present his case, along with the evidence. Our stay in the county jail was incident-free. Me and Mack had visitors. Slim came to let me know, among other things, that my car was in good hands. Deb, came to see me and Diane came to see Mack. Sonny, didn't get a visit. His girl, Laura (I guessed) went back home wherever that was.

While sitting in the court house lock-up, the court-appointed attorney assigned to us was an African-American. He was there to prepare our case for our prelimanary examination. He was one smart cookie. He asked us point blank were there drugs involved? We came clean and told him that this was not about a robbery; but, about barbiturates. We were there to get paid for our product and dude got scared, because he didn't have our money. So he got the law involved. Then, our lawyer confronted our accusers, who were already in the courtroom, waiting to testify against us. Our lawyer told us that he told our accusers that if they lie about what happened, then, he had no choice but to introduce drugs into the equation, and they would be implicated and placed on trial with us. He warned them that they might even be locked up with us. I told you that he was one smart cookie. He saved our ass. Even though I don't remember his name, I owe my freedom to him.

When the proceedings started, the prosecutor called his first witness to the stand. She was one of the plaintiffs, the girlfriend. After being sworn in, the prosecutor proceeded by asking her did she get robbed? She dropped her head and mumbled. "I take the fifth amendment. I don't want to incriminate myself." Needless to say, the prosecutor was not amused. Matter-of-fact, he was livid and threatened his witness with perjury charges. He called his next witness and got the same response on down the list of witness's. It was clear that his case had fizzled. Every single witness took the fifth amendment. Our lawyer moved to dismiss, and the motion was granted. The prosecutor was determined to get something out of this. He informed the judge that me and Sonny, had misdemeanor warrants back in Detroit... me for traffic tickets, and Sonny, for urinating in public. Fred Brown, Mack's alias was cut loose. Me and Sonny, were escorted back to jail to wait to be transported back to Detroit, by the Detroit authorities a day or so later. A couple of days passed when two white plain clothed cops showed up to deliver us back to the big D. On our ride back, me and Sonny, were hand-cuffed in the back seat. The cop on the passenger side was looking over our rap sheets. He noticed the disparities in our rap sheets. He turned to me and asked me. "What in the hell was you doing with a loser like him?" (pointing at Sonny.) While Sonny smirked and rolled his eyes at the cop's comment. I just shrugged my shoulders and said. "I grew up with him." The other cop said. "Yeah, you almost got a life sentence fucking with him." All I could do was hang my head during the long ride back hand-cuffed next to a psycho-path in the back seat. Not a word was spoken from that point on during our journey. Once in Detroit, we were taken to the 12th precinct, until we cleared our warrants. Sonny's court date had come. He was cut loose with time served the next day. They could hold me 72 hours without charging me, and that's what they did... two more days of sleeping on a wooden bench surrounded by filth, with the drip of a stinking, nasty toilet to wear me down. After three days of scratching my dirty ass, and eating foul baloney sanwiches. I heard the keys clanking and my name being barked by a sultry guard. I knew that I was either going to another jail; or I was going home. My hair was nappy, my breath stank and I hadn't had a drop of water or soap on my ass in days. When the turn key opened my cell door and said you're free to go. I felt fresh and friendly. It was a cold March, afternoon in 1972, there was ice on the sidewalks, and snow flurries were fluttering down. I felt like a kid again. The fresh air, the gray sky, even the cold felt good. I slid playfully along the sidewalk on the ice. I was on my way to catch-up to Slim, to claim my ride and my pride.

Cornel, was a fast polished brother... game wise, to the hilt. Cornel led me to a shoe shine parlor. He hopped up in the shine chair, then he mentioned for me to join him. He said, the shine was on him. I thought: nice fellow, until he lead me into a steak house. I understood that it was my turn to pay. I think, I got the sucker end of the deal. I told you that I was learning. The shine was about $3.00, the steak was $20.00. I didn't mind. I took it as another Manhattan, lesson on trickeration.

Fass Cass and Broadway Cornell, New York City: circa 1972

Chapter 16

STRAIGHT FROM
THE HORSE'S MOUTH

The nightmare in Grand Rapids, was behind me. It felt mighty good to be a free man. Now it was time to reclaim my life and my Eldorado from Slim. My first stop was Beanie's house, where I elicited her services to get in touch with Slim, so that he could deliver my ride to me. She got in touch with him. Slim, was there lickety-spilt with the Caddy still intact. Man, was I glad to see it. Beanie offered me food and a shower. I opted out of the shower; but, I couldn't resist my mother's home cooking. I wanted to take a shower in my own apartment, where I could change into fresh duds. I didn't call the pros, I wanted to surprise them, catch 'em off guard. When me and Slim finished eating, we hopped into my ride. I dropped Slim off and headed downtown. I needed some water on my ass in the worst way.

When I stepped into my apartment, it looked like a tornado had passed through it. Clothes were strewn everywhere, and dirty dishes with days old crude caked on them were stacked high in the sink to the point of overflow. That is another reason why some pros don't make good wives. They have no sense of order. When left unattended, some pros just don't give a fuck about trivial matters, like cooking and cleaning. Joann, and green eyes were not at home. I figured they were on their job, handlin' my business. I cleaned up the place a bit, then took a long, hot shower. I slipped on my silk pajamas and slid into some big time lounging and relaxing, watching television and trying to get acclimated back to being a free man again, and comptemplating my next move. I nodded off watching television. When I woke up, I was being straddled by Joann, facing me with her dress up, and her panties off, kissing me on my neck, beckoning me to wake up. Sheepishly, I said. "What you trying to do, turn a trick?" Then she planted a wad of cash in my hand and said playfully. "Hell, yeah. I want to trick with you,

Baby." letting me know that she missed me. After she got her goody on, I chastised her about her messy house keeping. Defiantly she whined. "I didn't know you were gonna' be here. I been busy taking care of yo' business." I thought about it, then I said. "You don't get it, it's about having some pride in where you live." Then Joann, said something that ended that conversation. She said. "If I had any pride, I wouldn't be sellin' pussy." That shut me up. Pros just don't understand; but, I ain't gon' blow my game, trying to convince a pro' to be something she wasn't. I hadn't seen Sandy, and asked about her where abouts. Joann said. "I was gon' break it to you gently, Baby. Sandy got homesick and pulled up stakes. I tried to hold on to her until you got home. She just up and ran off one day and never came back." Joann, re-assured me that she had my back and that it wouldn't be long before we knocked off some fresh game. Joann got back on her job; while I rested up for a few more days to get my mind and body back in sync.

I got bored after a few days. Before I knew it, I was back in the mix, hanging tough. I was trying to make up for lost time. One evening, I rubbed shoulder's with a fellow I knew from Northern High School. His name was, Dennis; but, he was better-known as, Frosty, the snowman, on the street. That means that he preferred white pros over black pros, Frosty would brag, "Ain't no pepper in my game," was his hook. Frosty was a charismatic, crafty pimp with tons of personality and game. His claim to fame was that he pimped white pros cross-country, with a band of merry pimps from Detroit, that included: Chauncy (Philadephia) Franshot, Diamond J P, Cornell, Joe Cash and a few others, all from Detroit. The fellows would Mack pros throughout Canada, on up to New York. They were barred out of Canada, for pimpin' white pros to tough in Canada. The Canadian law called it living off the vale. The United States, called it pandering. Frosty was back in town and he was sharp as a Rat's turd; not, Detroit, sharp, but, New York, sharp. He geeked me and Joann up. She was with me when I ran into Frosty. Frosty noted that he was in town for a few days. After he finished his business here in Detroit, he was flying back to New York. I hinted to him that I was thinking about testing the waters in New York. Frost spouted. "Well, jump in playa.' If you can make it in New York, you can make it anywhere." Before we bid our good-byes, he gave me his phone number and address in New York. With that he said. "Look a pimp up when you get there."

A few weeks went by after our little chat. I was sitting in Reggie's Barbershop on Clairmount and Woodward, waiting to get my hair done, when in stepped "Terrible Tom Morgan." Tom was a top-dog slinger, who ruled his turf with an iron fist. Lucifer, was the true devil, but, Lucifer and Terrible Tom went to the same school. "T T" as Tom was often referred too had taken over the northend and proclaimed it T T's territory, putting all dealers on notice that if they plied their trade on the northend, they had to go through Terrible Tom. Tom was a major bully, who traveled with a gang of penitentiary hard hench men. They specialized in intimidation, they were at T T's side when he strutted into the barbershop. Reggie, the shop's owner; was straightening a customer's hair when Tom walked in. Tom stood in front of Reggie's customer, who was getting his hair done by Reggie, and snatched him out of the barber chair. then he threw him to the floor, with the burning konk still in his hair. Tom sat down in the barber chair like it was his turn. Poor fellow who was snatched out of the chair sat on the floor stunned and too afraid to protest. Reggie, ordered another barber to finish that unfortunate patron's hair. Terrible Tom mumbled. "Sorry man, I had an appointment." He then reached into his raise, pulled out his bankroll, then peeled off a $50 bill and flipped it to the humiliated customer. Everybody, including the victim, had a hardy laugh about it. End of story.

When I finally got my hair finished. I stepped outside into a radiant bright day. I spotted a tall, strapping fellow that I knew from Northern, he played on the football team when we were in high school. At 6' 8" and about 270 pounds. He was an imposing figure on the football field. Now, as a young man, he is an imposing figure on the pro' stroll. He had one of his pros hemmed up, checking her real good. We called him Big Greg' in high school. Out here on the stroll, he was referred to as, Syracruse. Long man, long name, long game: most people just called him Cruse. Cruse grew up in the Woodward and Clairmount uptown area, along with Frosty, Chuncy, Cornell, Fran, and Handsome Harold. They were a close-knit core group of pimps, who attended Northern High and grew up in close proximity to each other. Oh I can't forget J P. During the time they were in high school, they were future pimps in the making; who brought new blood to the game, not only in Detroit; but, cross country, as well. When Cruse was finished handlin' his business with his pro' out on the sidewalk. He slid up to me and said."White pros paying nigga's real swell in Toronto." Looking over my ride, he suggested we hook up and check it out. While me and Cruse continued to kick the game around, a caravan of pimps eased down Woodward and honked their horn's as they paraded past the barbershop in their ice cream colored Fleetwoods. Westside, was leading the pack in his red Fleetwood. Gene Smith was gripin' his brown Fleetwood, and Eddie

Bee was holding down the rear in his emerald green Wood. Westside, and Eddie parked their rides, got out and kicked it with us. When we finished talking shit and telling war story's me and Cruse exchanged phone numbers. I told him that I'll get back at him later.

A few weeks down the road I ran into Cruse at Pretty Curtis, after hours joint, off of Joy Road. I also ran into Jimmy Blue. Who was better known as Blue. He had a brown eye and a blue eye. We were like family. Blue's mother and my mother were childhood friends. Blue also was a Northern High alumni. He was a couple of years older than me. Blue had a propensity for white pros. He was one of those pimp-or-die type brothers. While kickin' it in Pretty Curtis's makeshift after hours joint in the basement of his house, me and Cruse got back to the subject of Toronto. That was on a Thursday night. We agreed to make the trek up to Toronto, the next day, Friday. Once again, Cruse, geeked me up about all the untapped snow action in Toronto. Blue asked me to drop him off at home. I obliged him. On the way out of Pretty Curtis joint we ran into David Ruffin, of the Temptations, with an entorage of friends, heading into the after hours joint. Blue ran over to David, and shook his hand; while I laid back in the cut. I didn't know David personally, and I didn't want to appear like a star-struck groupie. After dropping Blue off at his place, I went back to my apartment to prepare Joann for Toronto. Then I thought about it. I didn't need any distractions. After all, me and Cruse were going to Toronto, seeking snow action. Cruse was traveling solo, so I decided to leave Joann at home. She had plenty of work in Detroit. I explained to her that I was headed to Toronto, and that I would be back early next week.

The next evening, Friday. I called Cruse up and told him I was on my way to swoope him up, then we could hit the road. This would be my first trip to Toronto, and I was anxious to hit the road. Toronto was about a 5-hour drive from Detroit. Cruse knew the terrain in Toronto. He had run pros up that way on several ocassions. I followed his directions. We hit the tunnel over to Canada, then we hit highway 401, and then we were on our way. I drove straight through to Toronto. When we rode into Toronto, some 5 hours later, we made a bee-line to Young Street. We cruised Young Street, for a hot minute, then Cruse spotted a young pimp from Boston, named Byron, whom he met during one of his previous jaunts to Toronto. Cruse pointed at Byron walking down Young Street, and asked me to pull over. I pulled my ride over to him. Me and Cruse got out to greet the young Mack from Boston. After Cruse introduced us, we kicked it with him for a minute. He put us up on where the players from the states gathered for the night action.

After checking into a hotel and getting a bite to eat, we hit the night spots. One spot stands out in particular: located on Young Street, an after-hours joint, Canadian style; where the fast-set hung out to let their hair down. No matter the place or occasion, it's always a treat when real play-ers meet. I felt out of the loop, I didn't know anyone in the joint. Cruse knew a few playa's from different parts of the States; but, no pros, whom, were mostly white.

Then I spotted a dashing figure, draped in a leopard-skin coat moving with much panache in our direction. That was the early 1970's, when per-colating strobe lights were a fixture in most clubs. As the dashing figure got closer, I noticed a horde of cuties trailing him. He was a smooth, dark-skinned dandy with his hair neatly whipped. Cruse looked up and recog-nized an old friend from Detriot, approaching him with open arms. Cruse returned the gesture, and they greeted each other with bear hugs and slaps on their backs like they were long lost kin. I recognized the slick-looking brother from Detroit; but, I couldn't recall his name. Cruse introduced us by saying, "George, meet my main man, Fass Cass." Then he turned to me. "Cass, meet George Murphy." Instantly his name rung a bell. George was a major player from Detroit. I only saw him in passing down in Detroit. George was international, so far as the game went. He asked Cruse had we knocked off any game yet? Cruse said. "Naw man, Cass carrying me until I knock some game off." With that, George, reached into his raise, pulled out a wad of bills, then peeled off a few funny-looking bills and slid 'em in Cruse's hand. The funny-looking money turned out to be Canadian $20.00 bills. Cruse thanked George, then me and Cruse went in search of fresh game. We came up on "E." The only action we got was drinking partners; no real coppin' action. Sunday afternoon we were headed back to Detroit. All things being equal, it was a good experience.

Back in Detroit, it was business as usual. Joann had my back and I was still married. One afternoon, while riding out taking care of my business, I looked in my rear-view mirror and spotted Deb's car on my bumper. She started beating on her horn, signaling for me to pull over. I pulled over, got out of my ride and headed her off; before she could rush the passenger side of my car where Joann was sitting. Deb, was pissed at the sight of Joann, rid-ing shotgun in my ride. With her hand on her hip, she went into a tirade about me being a married man running around entertaining whores. I could stay there and become a part of the spectacle or I could get out of dodge.

I choose the latter. I
blurted. "I'll call you when you calm down." Then, I was out of there. That little scene didn't faze Joann one bit. She had been checked by some seasoned pros about their men. When I got back in the car, Joann, calmly said to me. "That's what you get for fuckin' with square bitches." I felt bad for Deb; but, she left me at the worst possible time. I felt betrayed by her actions and I couldn't trust her any more.

Joann and I kicked it in some of Detroit's finest bars and restaurants, and we hit all of the top notch after hours joints. That shit can only take you so far. We were young and restless, and in need of adventure and excitement. Joann had several wife-in-laws along the way. She managed to run them off. In some cases they ran off on their own. I could always count on my bottom pro,' Joann. She was in it for the long haul.

One late night, we were hanging tough at Stoke's after hours spot on Chene Street. That was in early march, 1973. We were sitting at the bar, when in walked Frosty and Chuncy (Philadelphia) smoking big cigars and sporting fancy, gaudy jewelry. They made sweeping hand gestures when they spoke. This was designed to showcase their flashing jewelry. They stopped and kicked it with me. After complimenting them on their jewelry, Frost quipped. "Pimps trophy: they giving 'em out in New York to Macaroni's. That New York, shit geeked my young ass up. I forgot about everything Detroit, at that moment. I was in a New York, state of mind and I was ready to roll. Chuncy went on to state that they had just flew in earlier in the day and were flying back to New York, in the morning, I took down their phone numbers and address in New York. Frost and Chuncy lived in the same apartment building in New York, same building, different apartments. They reminded me that if I was going to drive, the best route to take was 401 through Canada. It was the same route to Toronto, so I knew it well. It would take them 45 minutes to fly to New York, from Detroit. I would find out that it would take me about 15 hours driving. I was feeling bored with Detroit, and I wanted a taste of the apple. So, I made my mind up right there on the spot. It was three in the morning and I was ready to roll. I grabbed Joann's hand and escorted her out of Stokes. Then we headed back to our apartment, we grabbed a few garments and some cash to make the dash to New York. Gas was only sixty- two cents a gallon in 1973. Anything else we needed I'll get it on the road.

We loaded up the trunk with our outfits, then I drove to the gas station, got a fill-up and hit the road over to Windsor, Canada. Then we made our way over to highway 401, we were on our way to New York City. We were at the point of no return. There was no turning back now. I would have to do all the driving. I was determined to ride into Manhattan in record time. As we rolled along the Canadian highway, daylight slowly began to pierce the darkness. As night began to fade, we got a panoramic view of the early spring, Canadian landscape, that loomed large before us, around us, and behind us, as the Caddy purred on all cylinders.

Five hours into our journey, we made a pit stop to freshen up, get something to eat and use the bathroom... that kind of thing. Then, it was time to gas up again and get back on track. We were young, fit and sleep was not an issue for me at least. Joann cat napped most of the way. About 10 hours into our travels, we came upon the bluest body of water, that I had ever encountered. I was riding in the mist of the Atlantic Ocean. It was a grand experience. The caveat came in the sighting of Niagara Falls, pouring tons of ocean over it's horseshoe- shaped bluff, with sea gulls and rainbows flashing across the royal blue sky; matched only by the true blueness of the great Atlantic Ocean. We came upon our first set of toll booths, as we were making our descent into the good old USA. At our last set of toll booths, we entered downtown Buffalo, New York. Joann pointed at one of the hotels in downtown Buffalo, then gestured for me to pull up in front of it.

Joann, exited the vehicle with her money-making face on. She ordered me to take a nap. She wanted to check out the town. Joann was woke now. She slept a lot during our long drive and was eager to stretch her legs. My own take on that was that, Joann, was on some kind of pro-ego trip. She could always brag that she sold pudding cross-country. Whatever her motives, I was tired and I was good with whatever, as long as she brought me some breakfast back. Joann wasn't a flamboyant pro,' so she could ply her trade with the slickness everywhere she traveled. I figured Buffalo, was a good proving ground for New York, for me and Joann. From what I gathered from Frosty, the action was fast and furious on both sides of the game, so I had to brush up on my Mackin,' because in Manhattan, the playa's ain't slackin.' Sorry folks, but, thats how some young knuckle heads communicated in 1972.

Soon after Joann left, I fell fast asleep on the front seat of my car parked across the street from the hotel that, Joann, disappeared into on that bright, beautiful, spring day in Buffalo, New York, with a pristine blue sky overhead. A few hours later I was being shaken awake by Joann, who was chewing gum and smiling like a "happy hooker." She was in pro' heaven. You can always tell a "happy hooker" by the fullness of her pockets, and the brightness of her smile. While I rubbed the sleep out of my eyes, Joann, handed me my carryout breakfast of bacon, eggs, hash browns and toast, with orange juice to wash it down. I belted. "You got the money, Baby?" Joann shot back. "I got the money, Baby." Then she reached into her raise and handed me the catch of the day, followed by a big ole' I hit a good lick grin. It was a nice little stack of $20.00 bills. While we ate, Joann filled me in on what had transpired while I was in dreamland. She told me that she had caught a couple of white tricks in the hotel's restaurant. She made a couple of hundred dollars and they paid for the breakfast. Teasingly, I told her that she was ready for the big-time. She smiled and nodded her head in the affirmative. It was time to hit the road again. Not long into our journey we got lost. While gassing up, I asked a trucker for directions to Manhattan. He told me to follow him, because he was headed that way. We trailed the trucker straight into Manhattan. When we crossed the Manhattan bridge, some 15 hours after we started our journey, it was 8 p.m..

We were greeted; not by a city, but by a monstrosity... it was instant culture shock. I was a speck, awash in a sea of specks. Suddenly, the world seemed hugh. I felt lost and excited. Riding into Manhattan for the first time, smacks you in the face with its energy. All trip long, Joann, was a picture of composure, sitting back stoically checking out the scenes along our route. Now she was sitting up wide-eyed, with her head damn near hitting the dash board, with her mouth flung open in awe. Joann, seemed excited and nervous, and so was I. I think Joann, and I were in a New York state of mind. I had no idea where I was on this massive island called Manhattan, the pimpin' capital of the world. I was in search of 51st, between 2nd and 3rd Streets. That's the street Frosty and Chuncy lived on. I was sitting at a red light, contemplating our next move. When suddenly, out of the millions of people in New York, I spotted one of Frosty's pimpin' buddies from Detroit, walking across the street in front of my car. It was Franscot, the suave sharp cool player, I knew from high school. He was with a pimp that I would come to know as Kelly, from Boston. After getting Fran's attention, I pulled over to the curb. He came over, recognized me from Detroit, and introduced Kelly to me. After minimal chit-chat, I asked him what was the best route to Frosty and Chuncy's place. He obliged and pointed me in the right direction. He said, that he knew exactly where it was. He had a spot in the same building. I found a telephone and rang Frosty up. He was his same jovial, pimp self. Before we hung-up, he invited me to come by and kick the game around with him and the fellows. As I manuvered my way through the swiftly-flowing Manhattan traffic. I spotted a pro' stroll about a block from my destination. I looked over at Joann. She knew what time it was and said. "What time you gon' be back?" I told her about an hour and a half. She slid out of the car into the fray. She looked nervous. I reassured her that she would break luck in the Big Apple. She said. "Ok Baby," and hit the stroll in full stride.

When I got to Frosty's apartment, he was pimpin' on one of his snow pros about his paper, (money) he walked me upstairs to Fran's apartment. It was really a hangout joint for pimps. Fran' had a penthouse at another location in Manhattan. When we entered Fran's apartment, a crew of Detroit, Macaroni's were sitting around playing spades. I knew everybody: J P, Marcellus, Fran' and Jimmy Blue. They all had their pimp face on, sitting around waiting for their pros to check in. After kicking it with the fellows for a minute, Frosty, then marched me around to Chuncy's apartment. When we walked into Chuncy's apartment, it was show time. Just what Chuncy needed: an audience to do some pimpin' on his white pro.' I quote Chuncy, when he delivered this stinger to his game, regarding his paltry trap. "Bitch you gon' bring a pimp some change. Get yo' ass out there and bring a pimp a real trap." Followed by a wink of the eye, directed at me and Frosty, to indicate to us; how you like me now? Being young and fly, I was impressed by the audacity of his tirade. As I was leaving their building, I ran into Jimmy Blue, who was also making his exit from the building. Me and Blue were play Cousin's back in Detroit. Blue was doing his pimp thing in New York. He had a couple of white pros in his stable. Since our teenage years, Blue was down for the game. Blue had his bumps in the road along the way; but, evenually, he lived out his fantasy of pimping white pros all over the country, including Hawaii. I have never known, Blue, to have a black pro.' He had a black girlfriend in high school, named Marsha, who died in her early 20's. All of his gamers were fine ass white pros. Anyway, after running into Blue, I told him of my dilemma. I needed a place to stay. He guided me to a local hotel, a block or so from Frost's apartment building. I rented a room, then I thought about it. I was riding and everybody else was walking. New York, wasn't a riding town, it was a walking town. I was beginning to feel that driving to New York was a big mistake. My Eldo was too cumbersome to maneuver in Manhattan. Hey, I was in a learning mode. I went back to pickup Joann. She was standing in the door way of a store. When she saw my ride pull-up, she made a mad dash toward my car, nervously she jumped in, then blurted out. "No more corners, I'm not a street pro,' from now on I'll work it my way." I decided to call it a night and headed back to the hotel that I had rented for me and Joann. It wasn't much; but, it would have to do for now.

The next day, I got up early and left Joann in bed, while I checked out the daylight action around town. I decided to travel on foot. After slumbering around a bit, I headed back to the fellow's apartment building, since they were the only folks I knew in this crowded metropolis. When I got to their building, another home-boy, who was also a part of the Detroit, contingent of pimps. He was Blues ex- square girlfriend, Marsha's big brother. He was in front of the apartment building, sitting on the stoop, putting two young white hookers through their paces. He had 'em in training for the New York, stroll. Cornel's lesson went something like this. "Now walk to the corner, turn around, put that hand on that hip and work that shit." Then he looked my way and spotted me. After we greeted, he grabbed my arm and said. "Come on, let me show you New York." He told the girls to keep practicing, while he lead me down Second Avenue. Cornel was a fast talker and walker. He also possessed a quick wit, with his verbage. As we strolled along the avenue he took me to school and said. "While you looking up at the tall buildings, midgets are in yo' pockets, robbin' you blind." We got a good chuckle from that exchange. I knew he was bull-shitting, but, he looked dead serious when he said it. On every street that we passed, there were tons of people all over the place. I made the comment. "Damn, there's a lot of people here." Cornel rebutted. "This is Mahattan. There are people on all fronts. You ain't down on Woodward in Detroit." I noticed he put emphasis on this being New York. Cornel, was a fast, polished brother...game wise, to the hilt. Cornel led me to a shoe shine parlor. He hopped up in the shine chair, then motioned for me to join him. He said, the shine was on him. I thought: nice fellow, until he led me into a steak house. I understood that it was my turn to pay. I think, I got the sucker end of that deal. I told you that I was learning. The shine was about $3.00, the steak was $20.00. I didn't mind. I took it as another Manhattan, lesson on trickeration.

When me and Cornel parted ways, I headed back to the hotel thinking, Joann, was out getting busy. Boy, was I wrong. She was still in bed, curled up in a fetal position. I watched as she flung her head over the side of the bed, and threw up some green slimy shit in an ice bucket. My first impulse was that this bitch is bold, meaning she was kicking a Heroin habit. I prayed that wasn't the case. Someone was knocking at the door. When I opened it, Blue, was standing in the doorway, waiting for me to invite him in. I invited him in. When he spotted the gook in the ice bucket, he acted concerned and asked if he could help. I asked, Joann, if she wanted to go to the hospital. She replied. "No" and insisted that all she needed was some rest. "It'll be all right," she said. I left it alone. Me and Blue headed out in search of good times. We ended up at a players bar called "Charlie's Two." There were some fast Negros up in there. They were New York, sharpies on top of their game. Some of the slicksters spoke in what was referred to as New York fly, the language of the players. There was one pimp who stood out. He was clever as ever with his verbage. Blue noticed me checking the scene out and said. "Y'all got the same name." My birth name is Arnold, and I always thought it wasn't slick enough to use on the street; but, that slick-talking New Yorker, was wearing the name well. His name was Arnold Stang. I liked that, it had a rang. New York, fly was really what we called pig latin back in Detroit, but, with a slicker twist. I looked down the bar and spotted an old nemesis from Detroit, named Sugar Hill. I had knocked off one of Sugar Hill's pros back in Detroit. Sugar was a pimping dyke, who got mo' pussy then most men. Sugar spotted me and ambled her ass down to where me and Blue were kickin' it. When she got in front of me, she pulled her bull-dikey pants up with one hand like she was a natural man, then grabbed her pussy with her other hand like she had a dick down there. She spurted. "You still got my game you knocked me off for down in Detroit." Then, trying to be clever at my expense, she blurted. "I can have a Gorilla, and nigga's want to fuck behind me." She got a good little chuckle from the crowd out of that little riff. I couldn't let that dickless wonder pimp on me in New York, City. Oh, no. Shit like that spreads like wild fire throughout the game. I grabbed my own real dick, then reared back on my heels and repeated something I heard Rudy Ray Moore, say on one of his comic albums. Well Sugar, I don't think you were doing much fuckin,' the bitch told me that y'all were "belly to belly, skin to skin, a whole lot of lickin' wasn't a damn thing going in." That was followed by a roar of laugther from the packed pimp bar. Then Sugar Hill ambled her ass back down the bar to fuck with somebody else.

After a few days of partying mightily, my bankroll was flat. I had money in the bank back in Detroit. Those funds were deemed untouchable. Joann would have to step up now fa' sho,' until I could knock off her some help. New York was beginning to saturate my mentality to the point of obsession. I still struggled with why Joann was sick. I could speculate all day; but, I wasn't sure about the root of her illness. It would take me damn near 9 years after the last time I saw Joann to figure it out.

I was fast asleep in my bed one night, long after me and Joann had departed, and it just came to me out of the blue. My eyes popped open and I uttered these words."The bitch was kickin' a habit." I know she didn't shoot dope. But, looking back, she was always wiping her nose and sniffling. There you have it folks. There is only one monster that could transform a vivacious engaging pro' into a run-down, burned out scag. That was the almighty boy. She was snorting Heroin, and it all came down on her in "The Big Apple." She wasn't the Joann, I knew. She had become a liability. Joann, managed to kick her habit due to the fact that she couldn't get her hands on the drug at the time. My naive-ness lead me to believe, that she had gotten over a normal illness. Maybe our little trip to New York did her some good. It enabled a young woman in distress to get that monkey off her back. In spite of everything else that went down in New York, looking at that situation with fresh eyes, I was saving Joann, from the scourge of drug addiction without realizing it. It took me years to come to that conclusion. In the meantime, Joann, was beginning to get her strength back. Another good night's sleep and a good shit won't hurt. I figured, we'll be back in the saddle again soon.

Early the next morning, I heard noise in front of the hotel outside of our window, it woke me up. I couldn't believe my eyes. The city was rigging my car up to a tow truck. I started shouting out of the window. "Hey, what you doing to my ride?" One of the riggers, referring to my Michigan tags, hollered. "You ain't in the motor city. Break our parking rules, you get your shit towed." All of that time, I was parking in a no-parking zone. I thought, the worst they can give me is a ticket. Boy, was I wrong. I would have gotten a ticket in Detroit, but, in New York, they just haul your car away. I couldn't get downstairs fast enough to try and stop them. I made it outside half-dressed, just in time to see the tail end of my beloved Caddy racing out of sight. I was stunned. I didn't have a clue as to who to contact in this big metropolis called Manhattan. I asked some of the hotel staff for help. They provided me with information and pointed me in the right direction. I contacted the Manhattan department responsible for towing and impounding vehicles. They informed me that I would have to pay a parking violation, as well as a towing and impound fee, That came to more than I had. The fee would damn near wipe my bank roll out. That was one of those moments in life where one has to pull a rabbit out of the hat. A clerk at the impound lot suggested that I contact one of the Cadillac dealers in Manhattan, to sell my car to them. Otherwise I would be charged a daily fee for storage. Then she rationalized, the dealer would take the fines and other fees out of the selling price. I was caught between a rock and a hard place. I had few options. I contacted a Cadillac dealer and made arrangements for them to see the Caddy at the impound. They liked what they saw and made me an offer of $3,000. I countered with a $5,000 offer. We settled on $4,000. After I paid the impound fee and fines, I was left with $3500.

When I got back to the hotel, Joann was still in a funk. It didn't matter. I had $3500 and I was going shoppin' in New York. I took a long look at the situation and decided it was time to get out of dodge. I had seen the bums of New York, who stayed a little too long in the Apple, and some of those bums used to be mighty Macks. I wasn't about to join their ranks. I went back to the hotel early in the evening, Joann, was still in bed, with Blue sitting in a chair beside the bed comforting her. Blue, said, that he thought he would wait on me. I said, that it was cool, and besides her action was in traction, so there wasn't much for him to cop there. I didn't tell him that; but, I sure thought it. I was loaded down with packages of fresh duds. When I got dressed, I primped in front of Blue and Joann, then asked her how I looked, forgetting she was sick. I called myself being coy. Blue, was a crafty pimp and opportunist. I wasn't sure if he wasn't trying to console her right into his stable. I put a stop to any of that by showing up when I did. I waltzed him right out into the Manhattan night, where we made our rounds. This was my farewell tour, before me and Joann made it back to Detroit. The first stop on my tour, with Blue in tow was Frosty's apartment, where I bid the home team, adieu. Oh, yeah. Cornel went on to become a lawyer. He put his gift of gab to good use. I guess he decided to do some legal pimpin.' (I told you he was slick.) In a couple of days, Joann, had pulled herself together, and we caught a flight out of La Guardia airport...two one-way tickets, $70,00. We were on our way back to the big D. I rode out, now I was limping back in.

Ah, it was summer time in Detroit, when our plane touched down. Then it dawned on me, I'll be walking again. Suddenly, the blue sky seemed gray. I had to slow my game down in Detroit. Everything seemed slow: the cars, the people, and definitely the players. I hadn't quite adjusted back to Detroit's speed. I was still talking fast and walking fast. I was still in a New York, state of mind. Looking back, I was in critical mental condition. I must have freaked a lot of people out with my behavior. I made a quick pit-stop over to Beanie's. As soon as me and Joann stepped out of the cab, the neighborhood stragglers were out and about. The first thing out their mouth's, after saying their hello's was. "Where's your ride?" That little re-frame would be echoed by aquaintances who knew me when I was sporty,

Fass Cass, in the Eldo. I perceived that to be a way of putting me down for limping back to Detroit. It was ok, I'll come back bigger and better, I thought. Hell, I was still only 23 years old. Damn, what if I had lost something significant like a million dollars, or a house: I would have been ridiculed out of town. In today's vernacular there's some hater's out there. You think you have friends when you have ends; but, when you lose your ends, you lose your friends, and that's the truth, Ruth.

After Beanie asked me. "Where's your ride?" I told her my version of what had happened to it. Then she went on to tell me that, Wig, had died of cirrhosis of the liver. He drank himself to death. I asked her about the funeral. She and Wig had never divorced. Beanie, informed me that Wig's sister, Katherine had called her up and asked her to relinquish Wig's Social Security, so that they could bury him. Beanie, was a bigger person than I would have been. I would have said. "I'll bury him myself with the Social Security money." But Beanie being the prideful person that she was, signed away her rights to Wig's Social Security... that shows you the character of my mother. Beanie, caught major hell from Wig. I couldn't understand it at the time. I understand now that it was all about pride. Me and Joann, ate some of Beanie's home cooking, then I handed Beanie $500 on my way out of the door. A chorus of "Where's your car?" followed us up the street, as me and Joann, made our way through a gauntlet curious George's to Six Mile Road and Livernois, where we caught a cab downtown. Joann went to the apartment and I went to the bank to replenish my bankroll. In the coming weeks, I jacked off a lot of loot frontin', smilin', stylin' and profilin' in the night spots around town. Joann, had gotten lazy. She may have been chasing a blow. She was on her way out of the picture. I told her. "I can starve by myself." It ain't no joke trying to pimp when you're walking. The only thing keeping, Joann, half way in check was the prospect of me getting back on my feet. It didn't happen soon enough. I got flat broke, up the creek without a paddle. This dogged me all the way home. When I got to the apartment building, with the rent due, Joann, was waiting in front of our building, sitting in a cab. She handed me what would prove to be my last trap from her. When I got up to the apartment, and saw her things gone and the apartment pristine clean. I knew what time it was. I was now flying solo. I leered at the lonely $100.00 bill, Joann, had planted in my hand and went to bed. I'll deal with it in the morning, and that's the truth, Ruth.

When I sprung out of bed on the day of deliverance, every fiber of my being was charged up. Humming, on all cylinders ready to super charge my world. Isn' it ironic how material goods can transform a young po' black guy like me, from a lowly dispensable twerp, to Superman, ready to take on the world. I would like for my readers to look past the superficiality of my actions, and probe a bit deeper into the human condition, and explore the psychological dynamics: that's what makes us, and drives us for better or worst.

Fass Cass, comin' at yo'ass with a blast: circa 1979

Chapter 17

NOWHERE TO BE A SQUARE

Joann, had, done run off and my bankroll was beginning to stank, and nary a pro' was on the horizon. I was twenty three and fancy free. It was time to diversifly my options. It is my contention that when one is financially strapped, that is when one must be at the top of their game. It's about how well one handles adversity, that will ultimately determine one's fate. Sometimes it means changing one's game. You have to find the means to rise above the fray. "It's crowded as hell at the bottom, but, there's plenty of room on top." Handsome Harold, would often quip, "The cream always rises to the top." In my case. I was the crud slinking to the bottom. I still had one thing working in my favor: I was still a very young man. Now, all I had to do was to figure out which direction I was going to pursue. Was I going to crush my life in my hands, or watch it soar? At that juncture in my life, only time will tell.

Once again, unknown to me, Beanie, was getting ready to move on up to higher ground. Mr. John, who had been working steady, long hours, had been saving his money for years. I got a call from Beanie with her good news. Mr. John, had bought a big ranch style house on Burt Road near 8 Mile. That definitely was a step up for my mother. She was now officially middle class. Mr. John, was divorced from his wife of many years, persuaded Beanie to move into his new home with him. Notice that I said. "His new home." She took him up on his offer only if my brother, Runt, was welcomed to come with her. Runt, was still in his early 20's. It made sense. Then she said that I was welcomed too. I appreciated the gesture. I asked her what was she going to do with her house on Stoepel? She replied. "I'm going to keep it and rent it out." Before we hung up. I told Beanie that I would keep her offer in mind.

My first order of business was to find me a job...something soft. I had cided to try sales. I liked to dress well, so that's where I chose to pursue employment: men's clothing stores. I submitted applications to all of the clothing stores downtown. I had grown accustomed to their merchandise when window shopping as a teen, and patronizing them as a young man. I submitted applications to Sherman Men's Wear, Todd's, Huhges and Hatcher, and a few other clothing stores, darting the landscape of downtown Detroit. During that time, Todd's Men's Wear was opening a new store in the Northland Mall in Southfield. I was hired and placed at the Northland store. I took to my new profession like a duck takes to water. I incorporated my street verbage into my sales pitch and it went over swell with my customers, who were mainly African Americans. I would add a little spice to keep my female customers shopping for their husbands and boyfriends. For instance, one exchange would go like this. "Hi, I'm looking for a suit for my boyfriend and I don't know what color to get him, can you help me?" My response would be. "Right this way Miss, would you like a down brown, true blue, or a mean green? By the way, is red ok? I've got a mellow yellow for your fellow. If you'll step further down the rack, I got a cold-blooded black." This is just a sampling of the many pitches I used to reel in the sales. A few of the other salesmen tried to steal my thunder, with their own version of rhyme. I wasn't bothered by that, after all imitation is the best form of flattery. I always kept in mind that they were copy-cats. I was the genuine article. You got to keep in mind that this was in the early 1970's and hip youngsters communicated in that fashion. It made for an interesting day. Todd's was a fun place to work. I enjoyed working there and I enjoyed selling clothes. The owner and founder of Todd's was retired. His son, Phil Elkins, ran the day-to-day operations. Old man Todd, the 80-year-old Patriarch, spent the majority of his retirement in Florida. On occasion he would come to town and hang out in one of his stores. During one of his excursions to Detroit, he decided to hang out at the Northland store. I was working three customers simultaneously, and eveunally made a sell to all three. Old man Todd, was laying back in the cut checking me out. When the customers left, he ambled over to me and said. "Good job, young man. I liked the way you handled that." I told him that I was a fan of his, and that I used to patronize his downtown store as a teen. I didn't tell him that I mostly window-shopped. I said, "I was a wide-eyed kid then." Old man Todd, interjected. "Hell, you're still a kid. I'm 80- years old, so, you're still a kid." He wasn't going to get an arguement out of me. If the old man says that I'm a kid. Then I'm a kid. I got a good, silent chuckle over that line.

While we were cozing up to each other, I asked him how did he get started in the garment business? Without missing a beat, the old Jewish merchant said. "Your people are the key to my success. Let me tell you, back in the 20's, I would take my push cart and load it up with shirts and pants, then take my cart down to the Colored people's section in Black Bottom." Yeah, he said. "Colored." That was not a typo. Old man Todd, was old, old school. Then, he went on to boast with great delight. "Your people bought all the garments that I could peddle. Hell, I could hardly keep up with the demand, and today I own three stores, thanks to your people." Then, his little praise to himself was followed by a healthy, hardy laugh. I couldn't tell if old, Todd, was laughing at us or with us. I thought about that for a minute, and came to the conclusion: damn black people can make a Jew rich, who didn't even live in our Community. Then, I rationalized that a brother should be able to clean up. Shortly there-after my brother, Slim, put me up on a wholesale clothier connect, located on West 8 Mile Road, outside of Livonia, Michigan. It was called Martin and Ross, a Jew who had survived a Nazi concentration camp. Now that I had connected with a wholesaler, I was in business. I began to invest my pay checks on cases of designer geans and shirts, just like old man Todd. During my off-days and down time, I'd load up my trunk and go straight to the ghetto. Where I proceeded to make money hand over fist; doubling, and sometimes tripling my investment, just like old man Todd. A few months prior to me getting the gig at Todd's, I went into a downtown recruiting office and signed up for the Michigan National Guard. Just when I was about to make a killing hustling clothes, I got a call from Beanie, who was living in Mr. John's house at the time. She called me with the news that there was a telegram there from the Army, ordering me to report for active duty. It had a plane ticket and an itinerary with it. That military notice came in June of 1974. I was due to ship out at the end of July of the same year: destination, Fort Dix in New Jersey. Before my departure date to Fort Dix, New Jersey, I began closing out all of my affairs. I closed down my apartment and sold my furniture. Then, for the remaining few weeks that I had left before reporting for duty, I moved into Mr. John's house with Beanie, and Runt. Even though I joined the National Guard, I still had to do 6 months of basic training and A.I.T.(Army Intelligence Training) with regular army troops. I decided to make a little romp through my old neighborhood on the northend, to connect with some of my old acquaintances. Those who weren't dead or locked up, or were too emaciated on drugs to care. I was 25-years old, getting ready to possibly embark on a life- changing endeavor, and I just wanted to share it with my old buddies if I could find one. I was driving Beanie's Buick through the old hood, looking for a semblance of the past; but, there was hardly a trace of anything familiar to me. The old apartment building I grew up in at 405 East Bethune, was gone. As a matter of fact, the entire community in a two-block radius was razed to make way for a new park for the aging community. Even my old childhood buddies, the few that I could recognize were drawn and steely-eyed. Heroin and alcohol coupled with a dose of poverty were the main components responsible for destroying young lives and an entire neighborhood. I wondered if Beanie, hadn't moved, would this too have been my fate? Naw, I don't think so. I've always been about

surviving. I would have found a way out. I believe that an individual must look inward to find their true self-worth. I couldn't find the courage to face my old friends at their lowest. As I scurried through my old turf, I felt that I wasn't recognized. I waved anyway. My waves were greeted with uncaring glances, most barely raised their heads in my direction. It sure didn't feel like home. I hit the gas and got up out of there. I guess that old saying is true. "You can't go home again."

In retrospect, I was fortunate that the military pulled me in at that juncture of my travels through this miracle called life. It allowed me an opportunity to discipline myself and it separated me from the carnage in the streets of Detroit. My time for departure to Fort Dix was at hand. I didn't have to pack much. Everything I needed would be provided for me by the army. A couple of outfits, some toiletries, and I was good to go. Beanie drove me to Metro Airport, where I boarded a flight to Philadephia. In Philly, I boarded a bus to Fort Dix in New Jersey. On the flight to Philly, I was surprised to see the Detroit Pistons boarding the plane. There was Dave Bing, and Bob Lanier, whom, loomed larger than life as he passed my seat with the rest of the Pistons in tow, filing past me to take their seats. It was obvious that I was a fan. I kept turning my head around to gloat at the team. When I arrived at Fort Dix, it was a warm, fall day and recruits were in the midst of their military drills. All around me, recruits were marching, running, shouting and grunting. I got a good look at what was in store for me. I wasn't in the greatest shape and watching all that physical activity made me nervous and somewhat apprehensive about the grueling training that I was witnessing. Once I got into the daily grind of being shouted awake at 4 a.m. by the drill sergeants and acclimated to what the army referred to as hurry up and wait. (Translated it meant move your ass, then wait for your next set of orders.) I survived 13 weeks of boot camp. It was physical and mental training from dawn to dust, after 13 weeks it was over and it left me in the best shape of my life at 25-years old. After boot camp, I got to go home for a week. On my return, I will start my A.I.T training. I will be training to be an infantry gunner. It involed weapons and munitions training.

When I came home on leave, while out and about I ran into Jerry Ross, the ladies boss. He had opened a record shop on Fenkell. He was making loads of money and I don't think he got it slinging records and 8-track tapes. It wasn't my business, so I kept right on stepping. What I really wanted was female companionship. I'd been sweating and grunting for 13 weeks with males. I was good to go. I rented a car. Beanie, and Runt barely saw me while I was on leave. I did learn that Slim, was back in the penitentiary and Runt was still living the life of Riley with Beanie.

On the day that I was to fly back to Fort Dix, Beanie again drove me to the airport. During our ride to the airport, I ventured off into that father thing, Beanie, was a captive audience. She couldn't put me out of a moving car. It didn't matter. She still treated it like a trivial matter. She mumbled, that it wasn't important. She said it without the usual scorn. I begged to differ. She knew both of her parents. As a matter of fact, me and my cousin, Louise, were the only family members not privy to our biological father's existence. I can't speak for Louise; but, did the powers that be ever consider how I felt all those years, watching others celebrate Fathers Day, without a hint of my own father's existence. The rest of the ride was spent in icy silence. There were chilly goodbye's exchanged when we got to the airport.

I boarded a plane, headed back to Fort Dix, to complete my training. Recruits had a little more freedom during this phase of training, and A.I.T. training wasn't as physical and draining as basic training. There were thousands of male recruits and only a few hundred female recruits. For entertainment we had an NCO club, (Non Commissioned Officers) located on base, or we could go to a little town just off base, called Rice Town. In Rice Town, recruits could hang out on the weekend and mingle with the locals. Where there's soldiers and money, the pros will follow. I was fortunate. I knocked off one of the female recruits. She was a blond, blue-eyed snow girl from Boston. Her name was Lisa, and Lisa was real good to me. I was the envy of my fellow recruits, when me and Lisa would strut our stuff around base. On most weekends, we would have our little tripst at a Rice Town motel. The Black female recruits wouldn't even dance with me at the NCO club. During our leisure time, in most cases they wouldn't give me the time of day when I spoke to them, trying to break the ice. Then, they had the nerve to roll their eyes at me when they saw me squiring a white woman. I don't know why most of the sisters would shun me. Those same chicks would get upset when they saw a brother cozing up with females of another persuasion, go figure. I will always have much love and respect for my sisters, and they will always be my first choice; but, I love my penis more than I love them. If the sisters won't serve it, you best to believe it's gon' get served.

I, being the player that I was, was knockin' off all of Lisa's military pay. There were other black player recruits checkin' traps at Fort Dix, especially the brothers from New York and New Jersey. Brothers came from all parts of the USA: Washington, D.C. Florida, Chicago and most other parts of the country. Most of them brought their urban lifestyles with them. Same thing with the white recruits. You had southern white recruits who openly displayed their distain and prejudice toward minorities; like the white First Lieutenant assigned to my unit. During orientation, he went into our daily itinerary, explaining what was expected of recruits. Such as what we would wear, when and how long we could sleep, etc. Then the subject turned to our lodging and nutrition. The Lieutenant went on to state that recruits would have. "Three hots and a cot. There will be pop, juice and milk." Then, he said, while looking me in the eye. "I like white milk, that chocolate shit makes me sick." Needless to say, that statement left a bad taste in the mouths of the black recruits who were present. Our body language spoke volumes. We picked up on the coded inference. It wasn't about milk, it was about white people and chocolate people.

The army was truly a melting pot, with many varieties of flavors in the mix. Ex-Kronk boxer, Caveman Lee, was in my platoon years before he got with the Kronk boxing team. In the army, recruits didn't refer to him as Caveman, we addressed him by his given name, William. Lee, was an extraordinary gentleman and an all around nice guy. On occasion, Lee, would take some recruits home with him to Philly, on weekend leave. Caveman's home in Philadelphia was only about an hour's bus ride from Fort Dix. Lee's family lived in the projects in a tough, inner-city enclave. Lee's family struggled. Regardless, they remained a close-knit family. About a dozen recruits shared the barracks I was assigned to. Most of my bunk mates were African-Americans from across America. Even though we didn't come from the same geographic area, we shared a common bond, pigmentation. During our down times we devised ways to amuse ourselves. One way was to have little boxing matches, with toilet paper wrapped around our fists for padding. During one of our sparring sessions I was pitted against Lee. Now, Lee, was built like a very muscular Baby Bull: the only reason that I gave it a shot was that I didn't know he was a boxer, and there was no hitting in the face. The boundaries were: body blows only; chest, abdomen and ribs. Well, anyway, while mixing it up with Lee, I threw a shot and it glanced off his arm and caught him square on the jaw. He didn't even blink. I thought to myself, damn, this mothers gone kill me. Before that happened I started apologizing profusely. What made me end our little boxing bout was what came out of Lee's mouth. He looked at me, still in his fighter's stance and said. "That's all right man. You can hit me in the face." I then realized that I was fighting in the the wrong league. Every recruit in my platoon made it through basic training and A.I.T.. Upon completion of our training we were given a ceremony where recruits received a certificate and a graduation year book with photos of our unit going through our drills, along with group photos of the recruits in my platoon. Lee, was younger than me by a couple of years.

A few years after completion of my military obligations, I was reading the sports page of The Detroit Free Press. I came across a story about a new, middle-weight boxer from Philly, who had just joined The Kronk Boxing Team. The article went on to state that he was making his debut on a fight card coming up at Cobo Hall. His name was William "Caveman" Lee. They didn't have a picture printed in the paper of the new Kronk stable mate. I wondered could this be the same William Lee, from Philly, whom, I used to spar with in the barracks at Fort Dix. I had to check it out for myself. I bought a ticket to the fight at Cobo Hall, in downtown Detroit. On fight night, I recognized the fighter as the William Lee, I used to body punch with in the barracks. "I'll be damned." I blurted at the sight of Lee entering the boxing ring, draped in Kronk red and gold boxing gear. The fight fan sitting next to me said. "Excuse me, did you say something." I answered. "Oh, I'm just excited. Me and Caveman were in the army together. We used to spar together in the barracks." The guy looked at me suspiciously and said. "Yeah, right." Lee won his fight that night and would go on to win enough fights to get a shot at the middle-weight title, that would pit him against "Marvelous Marvin Haggler. The Middle-Weight Champ Of The World" at that time. The fight was broadcast on national television; unfortunatly, this wasn't Lee's night. Marvin knocked Lee out in 63 seconds of the first round. It was ugly.

My stint in the military didn't end with basic and A.I.T. training. It was only the beginning. I had two more years of National Guard duty to complete. When I returned home from New Jersey, I had saved most of my military earnings. It would come in handy. I needed everything: living quarters, automobile, the works. Beanie, and Mr. John, along with Runt, were dug in on Burt Road, at Mr. John's new house. Helen still lived on Stoepel in the upper flat. Beanie had rented out her lower flat to a young couple from Washington D.C.. Slim was still in the penitentiary. My Aunt Ida, had passed away. Ida's death devastated my mother. She took her oldest sister's passing hard. Whistling Bob, had succumbed to diabetes. I heard that Mack and Diane had separated. Surprisingly, Mack had left his $100,00 house to Diane and their young son and daughter. I was only gone for 6 months. I still had to get acclimated back to civilian life. That meant that I had to find a job. I wasn't feeling that pimp thing. That's the main reason that I ditched the white girl Lisa, from Boston. I really wanted to get serious about my life. I gave it a shot at being square again.

First things first. I began scouring the want-ads. Then, I started knocking on the doors of potential employers. One of those ads lead me to The Thunderbird Motel, located across the street from the Main Post Office, on Fort Street in Detroit. At the time, the Thunderbird was owned by two Jewish businessmen, Sam Breaverman and Don Nushuo. Don's, son Bobby, ran the day-to-day operations. He would check in once a day, or when we needed to exchange larger bills, (generated throughout the evening) for change and smaller bills. The majority of the time, I didn't bother Bobby. I just reached in my pocket and made change. Yeah, I was getting it like that, once I became familiar with the routine. The Thunderbird had the dubious distinction of being the first x-rated motel in Michigan. They also owned The Viking Motel, on Grand River, The Sands Motel, on Michigan Avenue, and The Cranbrook Motel, on West 8 Mile Road. They also offered x-rated flicks on their in-room televisions. All you had to do was just turn on a particular channel, and walla, x-rated movie's. That was a big deal in 1977. The motel also offered a wide array of sex toys with a display case right in the lobby. Where there's sex, money will follow. My job was the afternoon desk clerk, renting rooms and supervising a small cleaning and maintenance staff. Rooms were rented for overnight stays and short stays. My base salary was slightly above minimum wage. Hey, I would have done it for free. With thousands of dollars going through my hands each week, I made it my business to find a way to make some of it stick. I called it supplemental pay. I made mine and the motel never came up short. Everybody was happy. it was steady employment, and my little ploy didn't interfere with the motel profits. I worked alone in my small cubicle. There was a lot of trickeration going on, on all of the shifts, by all of the clerks. Everybody did their own thing, without snitching on each other. It was a gravy train.

After being employed a few months, I started working more hours and double shifts, seven days a week at times. It didn't take much time to build up a thick bank. I once again was able to invest in ladies and men's fashions. This was jumping off in the late 1970's. Martin and Ross, were still my primary wholesalers. I expanded my inventory to include jogging suits, short sets in summer and coats in winter. In early 1978, I purchased a two-year-old Toronado, gray with a bright red, vinyl top. Between the motel and my side hustle, selling clothes from the trunk of my car, business was booming, popping on all cylinders. I was pulling down more than a grand a week, and that was just the beginning. Most of my customer base for my fashion ware was the same type of customers as old man Todd's during his street hustling days. I took my business straight to the ghetto and got paid.

During that stretch of history, The Burning Spear Lounge, had opened on Puritan and Stoepel, a couple of blocks south of where Beanie lived. The Burning Spear, was the new in-crowd spot where all the top-notch gamers made their nightly pilgrimage. I threw my 30th birthday party there. The theme was. "You got to be seen in green, know what I mean?" I got the idea from the movie, "The Wiz," which had made its debut during that time, the best green outfit won $500.00. Of course I won for the sharpest, green hookup at my own party. I was voted in by the partiers. I bought champagne for my guests with the prize money. I just reached into my pocket and gave it to the bar maid. Let the champagne flow. Month's after my birthday gala, I ran into the last persons I thought I would see hanging together in The Burning Spear; Jerry Ross, was throwing his own birthday shindig. On board to help him celebrate were: his brother, Mack, Jackie B, Clifford, Billy B, Black Patty; even Terrible Tom was on board, with more than a few road dogs to watch his back. Jerry had a lot of friends...to many to rattle off; but, you get the picture. Everybody was there. It was supposed to be a private party, celebrating Jerry's 32nd birthday. I just happened to be in the bar, and stumbled in unaware who the celebrants were. To see that many different clicks together: players, rollers, squares and killers, all paying homage to the once little frail kid, freezing in the winter of his adolescence, wearing a thin, blue jean jacket, while blooding and chasing the big bad bully down the street. Jerry's little gathering was only something that Jerry, could pull off. I hadn't seen Jerry or Mack, in a long time and they were glad to see me. We embraced and kicked it about old times. On that day, I was having the time of my life laughing and reminiscing with two childhood friends. That would prove to be the last time I would see one of my child-hood friends alive. Shortly after Jerry's affair, his brother, Wizard, shot him to death after an argument. He shot Jerry, down like a dog in their mother's house on Oakland and Clay. The least ambitious son struck down the most ambitious and prosperous son. Once the trigger was pulled, there was no putting the genie back in the bottle. There was no way to make it stop. Jerry, lay dying on his mother's kitchen floor surrounded by his family. Mack, wasn't there and Wizard, better be glad or there would have been two murders in their mother's house that night: Jerry's and Wizard's.

The news of Arthur Mckinny's (Better know as Jerry Ross.) demise spread through the throngs of the underworld like wild fire. I spoke to Mack at Jerry's funeral. He spoke on what he would have done if he had been there. Mack said, that he would have killed Wizard on the spot. Mack was hurt, as tough as Mack was, and all the drama he had lived through, I had never seen him so shattered in all the time that I've known him. He was hurt for Wizard, as well, knowing that, that act would crumble what-ever self-worth Wizard had left. Then Mack said, misty-eyed. "I'm gon' beat Wizard's ass. I ain't gon' kill him." Just as Jerry drew throngs of people to him in life like a magnet; he attracted even more in death. Jerry's funeral was on jam. As I looked around at the sea of hardened mourners, there wasn't a dry eye in the house; except his mother, Tina, who stood strong and regal, alone in her thoughts and grief. God bless you, Jerry, on your journey home. Hopefully, there are no bully's to be dealt with in heaven. No one was ever prosecuted for Jerry's death. The family closed ranks to pro-tect Wizard from the law. Tough bunch those Mckinnys.

Mack, went on a reign of terror, shooting and robbing his way through life. Mack lurked in the shadowy crevices of the ghetto, striking like a Cobra at his dope-slinging adversaries. Mack's name rang like a folk hero in the val-leys of Detroit's mean streets, and the law was hot on his trail. Mack's cousin Derrick, had managed to weasel his way out of a life sentence on a legal technicality. He prepared his own briefs while in the pen. Somehow, that cold-blooded snout found his way out. He soon hooked up with Mack, who was now known as Mad Mack on the street. The two of them created a third personality that was so sinister that it left hardened criminals trem-bling in their boots. Mack met his demise the same way that he lived his life: violently. The story goes that Derrick, and Mack were on a dope house stickup. Derrick provided the guns. Mack got caught in a shootout with a gun that jammed on him. The other bad guys who were being robbed had guns that worked. Derrick managed to get away. Mack was shot down in the foyer of the dope house that they were sticking up. I didn't even know Mack, was dead until a week after his funeral. I read about his death in the obituary section of the Michigan Chronicle. The last thing that I would like to write about Malon Mckinny (Mack), is that the world missed a world class artist. It's too bad that life got in the way of his talent.

By the spring of 1978, I was hitting on all cylinders. I added a new twist to my game. I started meeting all kinds of freaks who were attracted to the porn we offered on the television in their rooms. The VCR video-feed was located in the office, and the desk clerks changed tapes when needed. Truck drivers, out-of- towners, and an assortment of lonely types staying overnight would crack on me to arrange company for them. In other words, they wanted prostitutes. Initially, I played it down and didn't get in-volved. The longer I worked the desk, the more money I made. Time al-lotted me the opportunity to get acclimated, and the experience that I needed to bring the pros on board and set them up in vacant rooms ready to serve Johns, in need of companionship. In the beginning, I hired two young pros that I knew from around the way. They were really pros dis-guised as maids. The plan was for them to clean the rooms. When their fe-male services were called for, I would buzz them up in whatever room they were in. I would tell them that a gentleman was expecting them. Then I'd give them the John's room number. They, then would ease into the room, do their pro' thing, when finished they sashayed on down to the desk and peeled off my cut. They loved it. They were making loot doing their maid thing and sellin' flesh to supplement their income. I was their eyes and ears, so they didn't have to worry about a lot of bullshit. Now I was a triple-threat: I had the desk action, the clothes action, and the pro' dough coming in. I was getting paid hand over fist. Reflecting back on that time, between 1975 and 1981, those were some big street money-making years for me. When you're young and fly, big money breeds big fun and bigger envy. Suddenly, everyone wants a piece of you, trying to figure out the source of your cash flow. During those times, making money was never a point of contention for me. What to do with it was at the root of my woe's. I was too cocky to invest. I spent money like there was no tomorrow. At times, I was rendered financially inept. I blew too much cash on cars, clothes and good times.

The second coming of my presence to the game started with the pur-chase of my second Rada,' a 1976, mint green, with a white drop-top, with white interior. Once again, I was ready to make the suckers feel inferior. I put a nice down payment on the ride and I was good to go. I had my hands in so many pockets that I was running 20 hours a day, 7 days a week. A lot of pros wanted to latch on; but, I didn't think that was the prudent thing to do at that particular stage of my run. I didn't want to get too greedy. On my return from New York in 1973, I was laying low, seven years later. I was ready for the show. You ask, what show? I say, the show in the streets, where all the real players meet. That shit sounded clever back in the day. Today I can't believe that kind of crap was part of my daily rap. It is only by the grace of God that I out-lived that malarkey and am still around to talk about it. I was rollin' like Nolan, and the pros took notice. I was once again, on their radar. My reputation was solid from the early 1970's. Most of the players and playettes knew me on a first name basis and knew my game was good. In other words, I got my props in all the right places. Word spread like wild fire among the ladies of the evening looking for a spot. Whenever I ran into a pro' that knew me, they always cracked. "You got any work at the motel?" It always blew my mind that everyone seemed to know what was going down. I thought it was my secret. I turned down most of them. I wanted to control who I dealt with. In early 1979, I relinquished a bit and recruited two top-notch pros out of The Last Chance Bar out on 8 Mile and Woodward. Unlike the maids who moved around cleaning rooms in between tricks, the fresh new recruits laid back in their separate rooms and waited for me to send them the John's. I wanted to keep our relationships strictly business, because there were too many headaches having a pro' claiming my name. Like everyone else, there was a 60-40 split...40 for them and 60 for me. Whatever spin you want to put on it, I was still pimpin.' Every night we all made dough. If I could find the right mix of girls who were all about business, and knew how to lay low and handle their business; then, there was room for expansion. When dealing with pros, this could be a tall order. With most pros it becomes a competition. They not only want to knock off more tricks than their competition; but, they would probably turn me into a competition to see who could knock me off first. I didn't want it like that. The perfect alliance would be no emotional ties for me or them. Now that the pros were hanging out, my pimp peers started coming out of the woodwork, hanging out in their fancy rides trying to knock off a pro' or two for their own stables. After a while, I had to put a lid on the action in and around the motel. Too much was going on. I had to find a way to tone it down. I let all the pros go, except for the maids. I had to do it delicately. I didn't want to leave the pros with an attitude, so I had to devise a plan. I concocted a story that the vice-squad was on the prowl, locking up pros and pimps. That spread like bad news throughout the game. Pros would spout. "Girl don't go down to the Thunderbird, they locking bitches up." There's one thing about the game: when you put something out there, it speads through the grapevine with the speed of light. I learned from that experience that pros don't only attract Johns. They also attract pimps, slingers, stickup types, muggers, and an assortment of all types of other freaks, and let's not forget the police. If I don't stop it, our neighbors, the "Main Post Office" will. Then, it wouldn't be long before the motel owners were put in the mix, and I couldn't let that happen. My little ploy worked. It wasn't long before the action dried up. I didn't knock off as much money; but, that was ok, I wasn't putting myself on front street. I had stacked some major dough for a desk clerk. I wasn't pressed. From time to time, I would hit the night spots, keeping the lie alive, spreading the word that the heat was still on at the motel.

In the summer of 1978, after 3 years, I was honorably discharged from the National Guard. There was no more once a month training, and no more once-a year-active duty up north. I felt like a new me, and that old pimp bug started permeating my thoughts. I tried being a square; but, everywhere I turned, playa's my age and younger with less game than me, were the talk of the underworld. New clubs were spouting up all over town, owned and operated by seasoned veterans of the game. Veterans like Chick Springer, who bought the classy Disc Jockey Lounge, on Livernois and Pilgrim, Chick remodeled the lounge and gave it a new name. Chick Springer's Lounge. Then, it was instant action. It became the place to see and be seen. Chick Springer's was partially responsible for The Burning Spear going belly up. The Spear was located around the corner on Puritan Avenue. That was a stones throw away from Chick's. The brothers who owned The Burning Spear were some down dudes in their own right; but, they were new school and Chick was old school. His generation made the game work smoothly, like it was intended to work. Everybody knew Chick, the young and old timers, squares and playa's alike partied under the same roof. The word spread throughout the game, and the night lifers began to come in droves to Chick's lounge. One weekend night in 1979, I paid my last visit to The Burning Spear. The news circulating through the grapevine was on point. The Spear had lost its luster. Its best days were indeed behind it. To compensate for its declining popularily, they upped the ante on their drinks. I ordered one, and it was higher than a Giraffe's ass. There were more gangster types making their rounds inside the Spear. It had a bad vibe. It didn't feel like the same joint it once was. Looking around it became clear to me that, The Burning Spear Lounge, had become a haven for gangster types. I made my way up out of there.

When I stepped out into the night, I paused. All of my suspicions were confirmed. Standing out front on the sidewalk were a cluster of young men, sporting dark suits, with a shirt and tie hookup, heavy over coats, and big brimmed hats broke down gangster style over their brows. During that era in Detroit, big brimmed gangster hats were rare. Only someone out of touch with current fashion trends sported them. The three young men were looking grim and defiant, like convicts. I recognized the dude who was the center of the other's attention. As I passed the trio, trying to pretend that I didn't notice them. I sneaked a peek into the same sunken, cold, dead eyes of someone I had seen decades earlier standing before, Judge Crocket, on a murder charge. He was peering over his shoulder at me. I was the only spectator in the courtroom observing his fate. This time, he was a free man and all grown up. He and his co-horts had that fresh. I just got out of the pen look. David Armstrong, was standing in front of The Burning Spear Lounge, holding court, looking grimmer than the Grim Reaper. I would come to learn that Armstrong, was paroled a year earlier after spending over a decade behind bars. He was now in his early thirties, and was going by the name of, Buck Dave. He would go on to unleash a reign of terror throughout Detroit's underworld in the late 1970's and early 1980's. Armstrong was an enforcer, hit-man, and dope slinger. He was a dangerous, vicious predator. He had racked up quite a reputation in the criminal world. He would have the dubious distinction of being placed on Detroits Most Wanted List, for a slue of crimes, including murder. Armstrong, was feared throughout the mean streets of Detroit. One day, while partaking of my daily ritual of reading the newspaper, I came across a story about a shootout involving undercover cops, who were trying to apprehend one of Detroits most-wanted criminals, David Armstrong. Armstrong, was struck down by a hail of bullets, while fleeing from two undercover cops, looking over his shoulder as he ran with his weapon blazing bullets at them. The cops returned fire, they had a better shot, ending the tumultuous career of Mr. Armstrong. The night that I saw David Armstrong, kickin' it with his mellow's in front of The Burning Spear. I also spotted O'dell, the older brother of the slain parolee, Al, another gangster of Armstrongs ilk, perched on the hood of his car, fingering his pistol. I knew then that was my last visit to The Burning Spear Lounge. The gangsters had taken over the Spear, while the players made their exodus and invaded, Chick Springer's Lounge, and so did I. All that hanging out showed me how rusty I was. I had to step my game up to compete for name recognition. I was driving a year-old Toronado. That was no match for the newly-designed Caddy's, Benz's, BMW's and even Rolls, making the scene. Yep, it was 1979, and that old feeling was creeping back in. Back at the Thunderbird, I was still cruising along with the two maids working the rooms and me managing the cash flow on the front desk. I was still making good dough, and I was seriously thinking about knockin' off a new 1979 Eldo.' It had a new look and feel to it. I had checked one out at the auto show. They were priced at 20 grand. All of the real ones were sporting the new Rada.' Black Patty, was grippin' a pretty turquoise. Thomas Patton, sported a down brown and bold gold Eldo, with his good pimpin' self. Florida Bobby, gripped a red and black Cadillac. Westside, sported a mellow, yellow, Baritz. pimpin' Dee had his beige Fleetwood, with mink interior. Ronnie Love cruised in a pretty cream-colored Eldo. I was half-steppin' with a year old Toronado. I had to get with the flow, if I wanted to be in the know, not discounting the fleet of Benz's and other premium rides making the rounds. I'm just illustrating the caliber of game out there. Cadillac was my ride of choice. I couldn't hang with premium types driving an off-brand car, so laying fresh weighed heavily on my mind. I was Snuggled inside the confines of the security-glass-encased office of the Thunderbird. The motel now had a security system in place to capture the action around the motel. I could view it all on the security monitor perched on a shelf above the counter where I sat. The picture was grainy and I could barely make out the images. Old guys were always trying to smuggle young, under-age girls into the motel. Some male guests would rent a room, leaving their date in their car. On one particular occasion, I had an older customer who seemed nervous while renting a room. After showing his identification, I rented him a room. I watched the monitor as his date exited his car and headed to his room. She appeared to be under-age on the monitor, so I called up the room and asked the guest to bring his date to the office with her identification. He obliged and send the young lady up to the office alone. She handed me her Identification through the slot in the security glass. She was old enough to stay in the room. I noticed her address. She lived on Monica, in northwest Detroit, near where my mother, Beanie, lived, in the same proximity, about two blocks west of Stoepel. The more I studied her beautiful face, the more familiar it became. I asked her if she knew me, and explained that the reason why I was asking, was because my mother lived in her neighborhood? What came out of her mouth surprised me. She said. "Yeah, everybody around there knows Fass Cass." Then I asked. "How so?" She responded. "When I was 12 years old. I used to see you visiting yo' mother's house with yo' fine ass grippin' that pretty white Eldorado." Then she said."I heard you was a pimp. What you doing working in here?" I told her that it was a long story. Penny then said. "I'm gon' holler back when I get through with this trick, and I'm gon' keep the room all night when he leaves." I reminded her that he indeed had paid for an over-night stay. Then I remembered her. The name on her I D said, Devone, her real name. I remembered her as Penny, the cute little girl who played in the street in the northwest side neighborhood where Beanie resided. Boy she was grown now, and she was fine as hell. Regardless of her sex appeal, I just couldn't get past that cute little girl image I had of her. Now she was turning tricks. Realizing who she was, a wave of sadness engulfed me. I wanted to grab her and shake some sense into her. I would only be fooling myself. She was "lost and turned out" way before she entered my space. I could only shake my head and wish her well. I was hoping that she would holler back; not for anything personal. I just wanted to school her about the dangers of her chosen profession. As cold as the game is perceived to be, I hated seeing someone I remembered as a young innocent child, being victimized by the ruthlessness of the so-called game. It seemed like a waste of human kind for such a young vibrant woman to indulge herself in. It's one thing to have a seasoned vet with no personal history between us; but, it's another thing when you knew them as an adolecent, in a pure state of being. I just didn't feel right seeing Penny, barely 18 wasting her life with that crap. Yeah, if she hollers back, I'm going to try and give her a little insight. It was a long shot, but, I was willing to take that shot. After about 15 minutes into their stay. I noticed on the security monitor that the trick was leaving, damn, that was fast, I thought. He had rented the room for an overnight stay. It was something about the way he hurried out. When a trick has been satisfied, they don't like to linger around, and it was especially true of the white tricks. Now, I was poised to see if Penny, was going to keep her word about hollering back. About a half-hour later she was standing at the front desk, with a little sheepish grin plastered across her face. I told her that I was glad that she stopped by to kick it with me. She responded. "The last time I saw you, you were gettin' yo' Mack on. What happen Negroe?" I followed up with. "What do you know about Mackin,' you just a kid?" Penny, as I would find out was a tough-talking cutie pie. She spouted. "Man, I been gettin' paid sense I was 14." I said, "14. Where was yo' mama?" Her response was. "What mama didn't know, didn't hurt mama." I told her she was too young for that shit. Begrudgingly, she cut me off with. "You ain't my father. I thought you were a pimp nigga,' you trying to go square on a bitch?" Then she changed the conversation. She said, that her money-making road dog, Tyra was on her way down here. Then she said. "I heard you got work for a pro' down here. That's the reason I chose this motel. I been hearing about you." I replied. "So you already knew about me working here?" "Naw, she said. I just heard an ex-pimp was running pros out of here setting up dates for them, did I hear wrong?" "Maybe so, maybe no," was my reply. She spouted further. "I caught that trick and had him rent the room for an overnight. I want in on the action Fass Cass. Now you trying to save a bitch. I don't need saving. I need fast cash, Fass Cass." I told her that she was on her own. "You can keep the room as long as you're paying for it. I ain't interested in helping you screw up your life." A couple of hours later her equally- fine, young road dog, Tyra, showed up. She, too, was chasing "The American Scheme." Without my assistance the girls were clockin' tricks all night. When I reported to work the next evening, they had re-rented the room. I noticed a young, African-American male, darting in and out of Penny's room, from his car parked in our lot. I called the room and asked, Penny, who was that guy? Penny informed me that he was Tyra's man, Carl. I informed her that he can't keep loitering in our lot. At about mid-night, Penny, came by the office to kick it with me. She told me that she had thought about what I had told her about the game, and that she appreci-ated my efforts. Then, she said. "Cass, I'm a big girl, and I can handle my business." I didn't agree with her; but, I left it alone. I was kicking a dead horse. You can't save people. They have to come to their own realizations and save themselves, or reach out to others when they're ready to do some soul- searching regarding their own life. Penny then hinted to me that she didn't have a man, and whoever knocked her off could mold her into the kind of women they wanted, because, as she put it "I'm still young, and ripe for new possibilities." Then, she winked at me and purred. "You ever come out of retirement holler at me." Young pros like to bullshit a lot, and I didn't believe shit coming out of her mouth. I told her. "I think I'll pass." She seemed shocked that a man would reject her sweet, young 19-year-old action. Soon after our little chat, Penny, and Tyra checked out of The Thunderbird Motel, on jam. A few months down the road, I began noticing Penny and Tyra, when I was visiting Beanie's house. Through word of mouth, I found out that Penny's primary residence was at her mother's house. Whenever our path's crossed, we were cordial to each other. We kept our little secret about her activities at the motel between us.

Late one night, I was sitting in my Toronado, waiting on the light to change on 14th and Oakman, on the westside, when from out-of-nowhere,

I was rear-ended by some fool speeding. He couldn't stop in time to avoid hitting my car. he knocked my trunk damn near in the back seat, and smashed it like an accordion. The perpetrator looked at the damage he had caused, backed up, drove around me, then, he hit the gas and got out of there like a bat shot out of hell, leaving me to curse the night. I didn't have insurance; but, the car was paid for. I had a dilemma on my hands. I couldn't ride around with a smashed up Toronado. I had too much pride for that. My savior came in the form of my cousin, Micheal, who worked for the Post Office, as a Letter Carrier. Micheal needed a car and offered to buy the Toronado, as is. I agreed to sell it to him at a discount. I thought that he was going to get it fixed up; but, that nut drove it as is. There was no shame in cuz's game. With the two grand he paid me for the Toronado, and the money I had stacked, I was more than ready to break wide with a new ride.

Soon after selling my car to Micheal, I was on my job, doling out rooms at the motel, when in walked another figure from my past, Handsome Harold. Handsome, as he liked to be referred too as, was another Northern High alumni. Handsome, laid his first Caddy, a red and white convertible Deville. I think it was the only time in Handsome's life that he had worked. He was about 18 years old, when he laid. Handsome had a young booster, named Dell. She would go on to be his life-long companion. Dell, would prove to be a hugh money-maker for Handsome. Dell, was a booster's booster, simply the best. She didn't sell flesh. When Harold, walked into the motel, old memories flooded my thoughts. Me and Harold, shared some good times together. At times, I rode out with him in many of the canary, yellow new Caddys he sported over the years. Handsome was true to the game, down to the bone and was proud as a peacock to be a pimp, because it paid better than the assembly line. When I knocked off my first Caddy, some eight years earlier in, 1971, Harold was one of the first players I turned to for adoration. I picked Harold up in my new ride, and we rode out on several occasions back in the day. He was well-abreast of my pedigree. Game recognizes game. Standing there in the lobby, he seemed puzzled to see me working the desk. He quipped. "What's the matter, Baby, the game ain't good to you no mo' Cass?" Handsome, had an affectionate laugh that made the offended laugh right along with him. Then he said. "What's yo' angle? I know some game jumpin' off somewhere." Pimps like Handsome Harold, refused to believe some endeavors were legit, where there were no angles; but, in my case, he was right on the money. Working the desk at the Thunderbird, I was working all the angles.

Handsome, was there to rent a room for a short stay. I didn't know if he was there slickin' or freakin.' It wasn't my business. I mentioned to him that I was thinking about laying fresh. He replied. "Yeah, when you get ready, I'll take you to my man, Lou, over at Dalgleigh Cadillac. He can put you in whatever you desire." He gave me his phone number. Then I asked him what was he driving now? Handsome, would buy a new Caddy every year, starting in the early 1970's whether it was a Fleetwood, or a Seville. Outside of his first Caddy, a red and white Deville, his color of choice for his future rides was yellow. Harold, beckoned me to meet him in the parking lot, to check out his new wheels. After locking up the office, I obliged him and met him in the parking lot. I just knew it was going to be yellow. I was half-right, it was half-yellow. When I saw his ride. I said man, what color is that, blue and yellow? Handsome, in his melodramatic tone, spouted. "Naw, Cass, that's aqua running down the side and butter down the middle, Baby." Then he went on to explain the origin of the color scheme. He said, that him and his woman, Dell, were riding on the "Pacific Coast Highway," when the idea struck him. The sky was the bluest he had ever seen. It made the "Pacific Ocean" look aqua. The sun was beaming bright yellow overhead. I knew then, that would be the color of my next ride, he said. That was the ride we were admiring in the motel's parking lot. I told Handsome all he needed now was some personalized license plates. That geeked Handsome up. He said. "I already got personalizied plates." He grabbed my arm, and led me around to the rear of his ride, then he pointed at his license plate. I didn't get it. The plate read, "DST111." I asked. "What's so personalized about that?" Handsome pointed at the tag and said. "Cass, see DST111: Dell stole this one too." I said. "I be damn, ain't I slow." His woman, Dell, was one of the most prolific, skilled boosters to come down the pike. She had throughout the years, bought three house's, loads of expensive furniture for them, and a mountain of fine clothes, jewery and other goodies, and at least 10 new Caddy's in a twelve-year span. Harold, didn't have to hit a lick. All he had to do was too lay back, and live like a big Mack. Handsome, often recruited star-struck boosters, to take up Dell's slack. Before he ushered his date into their room, I told him. "You done charged me up, and I'll be calling on you real soon." He grabbed his date's hand, winked at me, then disappeared into the motel room. I bought my first Caddy from Dalgleigh; but, I didn't know Handsome's man, Lou. The next week I called up Handsome and told him that I was ready to meet his salesman. He asked me when and where to pick me up? I told him to pick me up at 9 the next morning at my place. I gave him my address and went back to work, looking forward to the next day. I ended up working a double shift. My replacement didn't come to work, so I had to stay all night. I got in touch with Handsome and told him to pick me up at the motel, instead of at my apartment. At 8 a.m. the day shift clerk was on time. I had told Handsome to pick me up at 9 a.m.. To kill time, I walked across the street, had breakfast and read the morning paper. When Handsome pulled up in front of the motel, I ran across the street and got into his car. Off we went, my pockets were on jam from the previous night's take; plus, I had hit my stash for $6,000 to pay down on my new ride. Then I remembered the winning lottery ticket from the day before, it was stuffed down in my pants pocket. I told Handsome to stop at Cunningham's Drug Store, on Griswold, downtown so that I could cash in my lottery ticket. I had hit for a grand. The number I hit was, 333. When we finally reached our destination, Dalgleish Cadillacs, Handsome, asked me how much was I gon' put down on the ride so that he could set it up with Lou Smelling, the aging Jewish salesman. I replied, about six-grand. He then asked me how was my credit? I told him. "Shot." He said, that's ok Lou will work with you for a small fee of $300.00. I agreed. Then, we proceeded into the dealership. Inside, Handsome introduced me to the balding salesman, with the prominent snout. Lou extended his hand, then, he gave me a stern handshake, as we introduced ourselves. We made some small talk, then got down to business. Lou set me down at his desk and went over the terms and conditions of the purchase price, taxes, and that sort of thing. After the paper work was completed, he asked me what color did I want? I said. "What you got?" Lou, escorted me and Handsome around the showroom floor, where I kicked a few tires on the Eldo's, Fleetwoods and Deville's that were assembled on the showroom floor gleaming brightly, under florescent lights. I didn't see anything on the showroom floor that struck my fancy. I asked Lou, if he had any two-tone Eldo's in the same style of Handsome's ride. Lou spouted. "I can get you any color you want." Then Harold, chimed in. "I got mine custom-painted. For a small fee, you can do it like you wanna do it." I asked. "How much?" Lou responded that I can have it painted for a grand. Then he ushered us up to the second floor, where they stored the majority of their rides. The showroom floor could only hold so many Caddys. On the second floor, dozens of Fleetwoods, Eldorado's, and Deville's sat in orderly rows, waiting to be claimed by eager buyers. One Eldorado, in particular caught my eye. It was a two-tone, dark-brown, with bronze running along the sides of the car. I didn't particularly like the dark brown; but, I thought I had the basics to work with color-scheme wise. I told Lou, that I liked the car; but, I wanted to change the dark brown part to another flavor. Then Handsome chimed in. "Cass, you can leave the sides bronze and paint the dark-brown, beige. Beige and bronze, Baby." I pictured the color scheme in my mind and thought Handsome, might be on to something. That computer imaginary thing hadn't been invented yet; so I had to use my imagination. I agreed on the custom color scheme. So, beige and bronze it will be. The total package came to twenty-one thousand and some change, including the custom paint job, and Lou's fee for making the deal happen. Now, it was a waiting game. It would take a week for the car to be customized. I paid six-grand down, signed some papers, then I was on my way. Handsome, dropped me off at my apartment. All I had to do now, was to wait a week, then, I'll be back in the saddle again. I couldn't help it. I was a new Cadillac junky. It wasn't the longest week in my life; but, it was in the top ten. The day before I was to pick up my new ride, Handsome Harold, showed up at the Thunderbird. I was on duty when he stepped into the outer office area. He had a big grin plastered across his chops. Then, he said. "Cass yo' car is the bomb. You gon' have the coldest ride on the street." I was curious as to how he knew what he knew, so I asked him. Handsome replied. "I went over to Dalgleigh, and went up to the paint shop. They finished painting yo' ride, now its got to dry. You'll be ridin' out in style tomorrow, Baby. You need me to pick you up tomorrow man?" I said. "Yeah, pick me up. Tomorrow, I'm taking the day off." Needless to say it was a long night. I didn't want to take tomorrow off; not, because I was a dedicated employee, but, because I was a greedy employee, and taking a day off meant that I would be losing money. But, tomorrow will be special. I'll be riding out in my dream machine. When I sprung out of bed on the day of deliverance, every fiber of my being was charged up. Humming on all cylinders ready to super-charge my world. Isn't it ironic how material goods can transform a young po' black guy like me, from a lowly dispensable twerk, to Superman, ready to take on the world. I would like for my readers to look past the superficiality of my actions, and probe a bit deeper into the human condition, and explore the psychological dynamics: that's what makes us, and drives us for better, or, for worst. "Humans are a sum total of their heredity and enviroment." There's something spiritual about standing tall on your own, and living; not just surviving like the mountain of Black men and woman, whose dead carcasses we've scaled, trying to claw our way to the top of the world. I was guilty of stupidity. At one point in my life, I was all style and no substance. I wasn't conscious of other positive options back then. I just went with the flow. When me and Handsome, entered the dealership on that glorious day for me, I felt like a kid in a candy store, and I could have any piece that I wanted. I was feeling energized before I left home, now I was feeling like a rocket, ready to take off. Lou and Handsome, were all smiles as they hustled me up to the second floor. When we burst through the outer, double-doors into the inner sanctums of the paint shop, it was the slickest, sleekest-looking combination of steel, glass, and rubber that I'd ever laid my eyes on. For an automobile it was a sheer beauty. It had an eerie aura about it, sitting there amongst the strewn old rags and other debris. I wanted to jump in and hug my new car. I glanced over at Lou and Handsome, who were grinnin' and skinnin' like hungry dogs over a pork chop. Handsome said. "We gon' call yo' ride the sho' stopper." I told Handsome. "To bad that I can't put all that on my license plate." It was a bountiful spring morning, when they whipped my new Caddy down a ramp, past an audience of star-struck salesmen, who had seen it all, giving me praise for a job well done. There was now beige, where there used to be brown, and the bronze shimmered like gold running along the sides, nothing tacky or gaudy about that ride. I decribed it as a graceful, smooth, beige and bronze ensemble that would bring the kid a ton of new action. Someone in the dealership shouted. "Who's car is that?" I stepped forward with a big, ole' cat ate the canary grin' on my face. Lou, flipped me my keys, shook my hand, and with a big smile he handed me my registration. Then said. "You got yourself a beauty kid." Lou, was about seventy years old, so he could call me a kid. When I encased my body into the bronze, leather seats and interior, I could feel the pimp God's smiling down on me. I fingered the smooth, bronze encapsulated instrument panel, with a digital display. The 1979 Eldo's were the first automobiles to offer digital instrumentation in cars. It had a C B radio and other delicate instruments... all foreign to me. Even the radio had to be scrutinized. I had hit my stash for a few extra grand. I was riding fresh, so I had to dress with the best, which I had no problem with.

I loved me some fresh duds. They made me feel legit, and clothes gave me the confidence to navigate the slick terrain called the game. You weren't going to catch me out there half steppin.' There were some spiffy young Macks, on the prowl in the motor city in 1979. They were young playa's sporting names like; Scooter, J M, Citris, Andre, Pimpin' Dee, and a slew of other real-deal, pimp-appeal playa's. Being on the shy side of 30, I had to be on first street. There was no slinging in my game; just straight pimping. I knew this was going to be my last hurrah at this player thing, so I was going to give it all I had. I didn't want to go another decade, chasing that pimp dream, that in reality is a nightmare dressed in sheep's clothing. Game was something I implored to help boost my self esteem, a way of making my life appear to be more pompus and glamorous than it was, it was a coping mechanism, designed to keep me sane in an insane society, within' the greater sociality. If adults don't give their children direction, the streets will, and that's the truth, Ruth. I was 31-years old and here I was talking out of the side of my neck, trying to harangue a pro' out of her dough. If only I would have been steered into more positive endeavors, endeavors that wouldn't prove to be advantageous to my growth. What's that famous line from the Marlon Brando movie? "On The Water Front." "I could have been a contender." I could have directed my youthful energy into law school, or medicine. I could have even plunged into writing. I could have led my family into the 21st century, with some dignity; instead of prancing in front of a mirror, practicing my pimp lines, like an actor fine-tuning his craft. I could have done better, if I had known better. Hind sight being 20/20, I had to deal with what I had become: a train wreck waiting to happen. The sad thing about it was that I didn't see it materializing. I wasn't enlightened enough to other options at the time. It ain't like people who looked like me weren't being discriminated against. I was growing up at a time when black people's options were limited; especially those born into poverty. With my fresh-purchased wardrobe, loot to boot, and a ride with glide, I was ready to hit my stride. I splurged at the major clothiers downtown: "Kosin's," "Citron's." I even conjured up the gumption to slip into "Whitehouse and Hardy," posing in the mirror, admiring the spiffy treads I had just purchased from the gliltzy haberdashery. I couldn't wait to hit the streets.

My first stop, as always was, Beanie's house. She and Mr. John had gone their seperate ways. She was now residing back at her house on Stoepel, and that's where I was headed. I had rediscovered why brothers sported fly rides: instant action. All of a sudden, I had females smiling my way on all fronts, during my drive over to Beanie's house. When I looked into the rear view mirror. I noticed a car full of young tenders trailing me, right up to Beanie's front door. Ogling and licking their sexy lips at me. I was flattered as hell, and all business, with my personalized plates proclaiming, "Fass Cass," for all to see. During that stretch of history there was a fad for drivers with children. Sweeping the urban areas were yellow placard signs, embossed with, "Baby On Board" placed in the side window, a cautionary sign for parents concerned about their childs safety. It was a way of warning other drivers to be careful. Now, some pimps found a way to exploit that for their own amusement. They put their personalized spin on the message of the sign. I spotted a young playa' with one of those signs plastered in his side window proclaiming "Pimp On Board." While we waited at a red light, he looked over and noticed me checking his sign out. I motioned for him to roll his window down. He obliged me. I hollered over to him. "Slick sign, one of a kind." He hollered back, while eye-balling my ride. " Slick ride, one of a kind." I would latter find out through the grapevine, that the pimp on board was a downtown playa' by the name of, Tommy Griffin, whose specialty was street pros and bar pros. Tommy, worked his pros out of the now-torn-down Columbia Bar, and the Purple Onion Bar, on John R and Macomb. Both bars were replaced by Comerica Park, home of the Detroit Tigers. My new girlfriends who had followed me to Beanie's house, were waving at me, beckoning for me to join them in some chit-chat. I didn't trip. I understood that it was the car that piqued their curiosity. I waved at them, and bounced into Beanie's house on that fabulous spring day. Beanie, and Runt were at home, with one of Beanie's childhood friends. Beanie introduced me to her. Her name was Burneice, who I didn't know; but, she knew me when I was a baby. Wahla. Someone from my mother's past, who says she knew me as a baby. That really made my antennas go up. "Humans inherit 46 chromosomes from their parents... 23 from mother and 23 from father." Maybe this Burneice person, could help me unravel the mystery of the missing link, responsible for the 23 chromosomes belonging to my biological father, and now to me. When Runt, stepped out onto the front porch to get a closer look at my new ride, it provided me with a moment of solitude with Beanie, and her childhood friend, Burneice. It was an opportunity to ask Burneice, in front of Beanie, if she knew my father. Suddenly, the mood went from jovial to tense in no time flat. Burneice, looked at Beanie, then she looked at me and said. "That's between you and your mother." With that, I slipped Beanie, a couple of c-notes, then I fled off into the warm spring air in search of game and fame.

When I got outside, the groupies were gone; but, my Caddy had attracted the attention of the neighbors, who were scrutinizing my ride from stem to stern. Penny, was sitting on my hood with her arms folded, trying to conceal her big luscious breast from the gawkers. She was smiling sheepishly. As I approached her, she belted. "I had to come down here to see what all the fuss was about. So this yo' new car?" I responded. "Live, and in living color." Then she asked. "You gon' take me for a spin?" I told her. "I'll holler back." Then she said. "I'm gon' hold you to that," as she slowly slid off the hood, ever so seductively.

Handsome Harold, lived about a quarter-mile west of Beanie, on Puritan and Indiana. Handsome owned a big two-family flat on Indiana. It was painted aqua and butter, same color as his Seville. When I pulled up in front of Handsomes house, he, Dell and a couple of his neighbors that I didn't know were hanging out on his front porch shooting the breeze, loud and proud, drawing a crowd. When Handsome saw me, he waved for me to join them on his porch. I parked my car and jumped out, looking cooler then a popscicle. Handsome, shouted from the porch with a little bravado. "Fass Cass, you rollin' like me now, slim in the waist and handsome in the face." That bought a big, ole' grin across my chops. I opened my arms up with love, nothing but love, Baby, as we embraced and slapped each other on the back. I introduced myself to everybody on the porch. Handsome chimed in "Cass, when you gon' take me for a spin, Baby?" I threw him the keys and off we went. I would soon find out that almost everyone I encountered wanted to go for a spin. Needless to say, I turned down a boat-load of pissed off comrades.

Handsome hit the Lodge freeway south bound, headed to our old stumping grounds, around Woodward and Clairmount, where we parked and kicked it with some of the mellow's hanging out, shooting the breeze around "Reggie's Barbershop." Jimmy Diamond, eased over to check out my ride and proclaimed. "Boy, you gon' get the gravy off the top now." After a hot minute of kickin' it with the fellows, I told Handsome that it was time to get back. I had to take care of some business. I only had one day to show off. I wanted to make the most of my time. Handsome took the long way back to his house. He cruised up Woodward, past all of the major stroll's, on up through Highland Park, down to Six Mile and Woodward, blowing and waving at pros along the way. He made a left turn on Six Mile, west to his house on Indiana. He was beaming, as he turned my keys over to me. I slid over into the driver's seat, blew my horn and bid everyone on the porch farewell. My destination was unclear. It was a warm picturous day as I woved my way through dense traffic headed downtown. I decided to hit my apartment. When I arrived at my apartment in the Trolly Plaza Apartments, on Washington Boulevard. I fixed me a sandwich and sat out on my 9th-floor balcony, overlooking the swimming pool. Then it hit me. It's spring, it's time to pay my clothing wholesaler a visit, and stock up on summer garments to hustle on the street. I was pro-less and that was a means to shore up on my cash flow.

I got up and made a bee-line over to "Martin and Rose Wholesalers" on Eight Mile, a few blocks past Telegraph. When I arrived, I was thrilled to see such a wide array of spring and summer merchandise. To do business with Martin and Rose, one had to have a tax identification number. I made purchases, and loaded my trunk up with cases of designer geans, dozens of summer short sets for men and women, and a few dozen summer shirts. I spent about three grand. When the merchandise was flipped, it would yield about a four grand profit. I liked to keep my stock low until I could feel my way through. I didn't want to get stuck with slow-moving inventory. Another reason was that I didn't want to lose an arm and leg to the stickup artist, preying on hustlers. Back then, they just robbed you. Car-jacking wasn't the phenomenon it would become in the future. I never got stuck-up; but, it was always in the back of my mind. I had to stay on my toes. You didn't want to get caught slippin.' That's when the bogeyman comes tippin.' I had to supplement my income, because I had new responsibilities: car note, a posh luxury apartment, and other amenities to keep me in the now and relevant. I had to hustle hard if I wanted to maintain my fronts. With a trunk full of new goods, and my bankroll in check, I decided to call it a night.

Un-aware that the little cutie down the hall had been checking me out. As I was about to stick my key into the lock to my apartment, I heard a dainty voice say. "Excuse me, can I borrow a cup of sugar?" Then she waltzed slowly toward me, with a coffee cup dangling from her fore finger, she was wearing a silk robe, that fluttered daintily as she moved, serving up her honey golden thighs to my probing eye's. I said. "Hell, yeah. You can have all the sugar you can stand, Sugar." She chuckled, and with that, she sashayed into my cozy abode. We got around to sharing a little wine, and a little T V. Then, we were good for the night. Hey, we were young, dumb and full of what rhymes with yum.

The next morning I hustled out of bed and begin prepping for the new day. My overnight guest was easing her way out of my bed, preparing to make her exit back down to her apartment. She cracked the door, than peeped out into the empty hallway, the coast was clear. She blew me a kiss, then scooted out of the door. I didn't have to check into the Thunderbird, until 4 p.m. I took advantage of the down time and hit the streets, hawking my wares. I liked selling from the hip, because it was all profit and low overhead. All I needed was a car and gas; then I was good to go.

When I arrived at my job at 4 p.m., my pockets had the mumps. I had bagged a few hundred dollars off of my hustle, and was feeling pretty good. To avoid being scrutinized by the owners and employees of the motel, re-garding my affordability of a new custom-Caddy. I left it parked in my apartment building lot, and caught a cab to work. I knew that if the Jewish motel owners knew that I was riding that good, I could kiss my job goodbye. With what they were paying me it would be obvious that I couldn't afford it. So I avoided the hassle that I would have endured, and left it parked.

About an hour into my shift, one of the young maids / pros came to me with an ultimatum: we were going to hook-up, as in boyfriend and girl-friend, or I was going to have to give her a raise. She rationalized that she was doing all of the work. I retorted. "Yeah, but, without my connects, you wouldn't have any work." I further explained that. "We'll talk about it later. I didn't think I was your type." She asked. "What type is that?" I replied. "The pimp type." She agreed to talk later. Just as she was stepping out of the lobby, Penny, was stepping in all gussed up. She didn't give me a chance to greet her. She went into her spill. "Cass, Baby, I know you still checkin' traps. You can't fool me. You didn't get that slick-ass ride by renting rooms." I said. "Baby girl, you're too green for me. Besides, I knew you when you were a kid, so you might as well catch up with yo' crowd." That pissed Penny off. She threw a fifty-dollar bill on the counter, and barked. "I want to rent a room." Sarcastically, she said. "I'll show you who's to young Mr. Cass. Watch a bitch get paid." I rented her a room and watched a bitch get-tin' paid without my help. I thought I might have to reconsider my options. After I got off work, I called Penny's room and told her that I would get with her on Friday. I had started hanging out at a new after-hours joint that Handsome Harold, had put me up on. It was strictly a P and H club run by Handsome's pimp buddy, Sonny Mack, an old-school player from Highland Park. Sonny, specialized in good times for players and playettes. Penny started calling me at the motel every night. I rejected her. I know pimps ain't suppose to have moral's...that's a bunch of bull. At times, the game can be complicated. I know the young girl had turned herself out, and all that. I just didn't feel good taking her money; but, if she keeps press-ing me, I may have a change of heart. I devised a plan to expose Penny, to some real game, and Sonny Mack's was the perfect place to make it hap-pen. When Penny called me early Friday evening, I told her to get ready, like Freddy, it's top shelf all the way, we're stepping out tonight after two in the morning. My shift ended at midnight. If I didn't have to pull a double shift, we were good to go to playa's row, ya' know. In 1979, I was thirty-one and Penny was a vivacious, nineteen-year-old. Young pros, liked to latch on to older name-brand player's trying to suck up to some game, to have brag-ging rights amongst their peers. I got a call from Penny, just before my quit-ting time. She wanted to know what time was I going pick her up? I told her to "dress to impress. I'll pick you up about 2:30ish, after the bars close." She said, to pick her up at her mother's house. I said. "That's a bet." Then I hung up. I was too hyped to sit around waiting two hours for the bars to close. So I freshened up, then I slid into a forest green suede sports coat, black mohair slacks, and a black silk shirt, with a pair of forest green glass-heeled lizard shoes rounding the hook up off. Glass heels were the fashion statement of the day back in 1979. It was December, close to my birthday and I was ready to hang. I topped it all off with a black Persian-Lamb overcoat, a little diddy I bought myself for a birthday present. I was looking mighty fly that night.

When I rode up to Chick Springer's Lounge, the joint was on jam. This was just a prelude to what the rest of the night held at the after-hours spot. As I looked around at all the fancy rides hugging the curbs, without a vacant space in sight, it reminded me of the good old days, when the game came together to party. I valet parked my bronze and beige beauty up front for all suckers to envy. When I stepped into the lounge, a horde of major players were on board in their own little universe. With decked-out honeys, spending loads of money, winkin' and blinkin' to get their action on. I spotted Eddie Bee, a major, major, playa.' He was a blend of old school and new school. Eddie, was decked out in a pure blue velvet overcoat, with a white mink collar. It was the real deal, sex appeal...none of that fake fur shit. He was playing hardball. He was looking clever as ever in his blue velvet coat, with the white mink collar, that made the pros come and holler. Eddie, was a bit older than my set. He preceded me in the pimpdom. It was seasoned playa's like Eddie, who had made the game so attractive to young fatherless, impressionable rookies like me. T P, was down at the end of the bar ordering up his favorite drink, along with Pretty Rick, and some of the old-school crew, who used to patronize the Bean House, more then a decade earlier. I eased my way up to the bar to order me a drink. Snow flake, the bar maid smiled, when she saw me trying to get her attention. I was a regular, so she was familiar with me. I didn't even have to order. She purred. "I know what you're drinking: Pipers Split." I said. "You know me better than my woman." Piper was a premium champagne that went for $20 a split in 1979. When Snow Flake handed me my drink, she leaned over toward me, exposing her buxom breast, and looked me dead in the eye, then proclaimed. "I'm gon' rape me one of you fine-ass nigga's tonight." Then, she gave me an ice-melting smile. I nodded and smiled back at her. I paid for my drink and made my way over to Eddie Bee, to compliment him on his one-of-a-kind custom-made coat. Just as we finished giving each other props, a tall long-legged stallion got up close and personal on Eddie, suductively stroking his white mink coller with her long sleek fingers. She commented to Eddie. "You pimpin' ass nigga.' When you gon' marry me?" Eddie paused for dramatic effect. Then he spouted over the pulsating rhythms of the kicking music. "You sure you want to marry me? You know the last bitch I tried to take care of damn near starved to death." The tall stallion almost gagged on her drink, as she tried to stiffle a laugh. Everybody in ear shot had a good giggle over his line. I shook Eddie's hand and asked him if he were going by Sonny Mack's joint? He assured me that indeed, I might see his face, grace the place. It was nearing closing time when Andre, another dedicated do-or-die pimp from my generation, stopped me at the front entrance, and proclaimed. "You know the Mack-of-the-year gala is coming up in a few weeks. You want me to put your name down?" I said. "Why not." He then replied that he was going to get a poster made with all the Mack-of-the-year candidates names on it promoting the affair. I said. "Just spell my name right, that's Fass Cass." Andre, retorted. "Nigga,' I know yo' name and yo' game." I spilled out onto the sidewalk where I mingled with a horde of revelers, Playa's and playette's, getting ready to burn the midnight oil at their favorite late-night spot. The night action was hot and heavy, squares need not apply. It was a salacious fashion and auto show extravaganza, as the patrons poured out of Chick Springer's. Sharp dandys and honeys were ready to hit the asphalt. I moved my way through a crowd of infatuated females, drooling over the slick Eldo' that was valet-parked up front. They were panting to get a look at who was driving that sweet two-tone. I felt like a star, as I collected the stack of business cards and phone numbers tucked under my windshied wipers. If I hadn't invited Penny to ride with me, I surely would have swooped up a couple of those honey-dew, dripping beauties.

When I rode up on Penny's mother's house. Penny, was looking out of the window, ready to get her party on. When baby girl stepped out on the front porch, I knew I had made a great choice by taking her with me. Fine as she looked, she was going to be representing me well. She had a succulent set of firm pointed boobs, and she was cute as a baby's poot, grinning exposing teeth that would put a set of pearls to shame. She had a bubbly personality, with a scandalous allure, she had a bounce in her stride as she moved toward my ride. looking at her with fresh vision, it wouldn't be difficult to indulge my fantasies. I didn't want to do anything to subject this wanna' be to hurt. That's one reason why I asked her to accompany me, so that she could see for herself that the real game was played much smoother than what she was accustomed to. Penny, acted like she had all the answers. I knew better, and after tonight she will to. Penny, jumped inside my ride, smelling fresh and friendly. She greeted me with. "How you doing, Mr. Fass Cass?" My reply. "I'm feeling fine my young Clementine." Of course, she didn't know who the hell Clementine was. After she inquired, I explained that it was from a folk song; no big deal. She beamed at me, snapping her fingers and said. "It's time to break out the champagne." Then she reached in her boot and pulled out a couple of crisp c-notes and said. "Don't trip, this is for the party. This ain't no trap." I told her that it wasn't neccesary; but, I'm a playa.' If I turned it down, she would think that I was a sucker. So, thank you very much. I ain't turning down nothing but my collar. Then I heard the crackle of my CB radio. "Breaker, breaker, come in Fass Cass. This is your man, Handsome Harold, here. Come back at me." "This is Fass Cass, back at you." I barked. Then Handsome chimmed in, "I'm sitting in front of the spot, in the aqua and butta. You better come on over. All the major Macaroni's are out tonight. Back at you, Cass." I responded. "Breaker, breaker, back at you chap. I'm on my way. I'll be their in a snap. Fass Cass, comin' at yo' ass with a blast, over and out, Baby." Penny got a good chuckle out of that exchange. She looked over at me and said. "You slick-ass nigga's." With that, I hit the gas. Me and Handsome liked to kick it like that from time to time, showing off for whoever was riding shotgun. C B radios were standard equipment in the new 1979 Caddys.

When I rode up to Sonny Mack's, on Oakman, near Hamilton, Handsome wasn't lying, both sides of the streets were bumper to bumper, from Hamilton down to Woodrow Wilson, about a three blocks radius, with luxury rides hugging the curbs. Fluffy flurries of snowflakes drifted down silently, as decked-out players and playetts, abandoned their parked cars and made their pilgrimage to Sonny Mack's front entrance. I waited until a parking space opened up. After about five minutes, a space became available. After I parked about a hundred feet from the front entrance. Penny, and I made our way up the sidewalk toward our destination. I pointed out all of the personalized license plates. "PFT" proclaimed one plate, I wasn't sure what that meant. I figured it had something to do with pimpin.' It was on a triple-white Fleetwood, belonging to a young Mack, named, JM. "Wes side" was on, you guessed it. Westside's yellow Baritz. Then we passed a Seville, proclaiming. "Diamond" on its plate. The blue Benz was poetic with it's proclamation. "Bnz Boy." We then came upon an emerald-green Fleetwood, embossed with "Eddie" across its plate. Of course that was Eddie Bee's ride. Parked out front like he said, was Handsome Harold's butta and aqua-colored Seville, with the familiar "DST I I I." (Dell stole this one too.) I always got a kick out of that one. By the time we reached the front entrance, Handsome had already made his way inside the joint. Penny was all giddy, and pranced with much pep in her step, as we approached the front door. I was at the precipice of my game, ready to make my presence felt where squares dare not tread. I knocked on the big dooh. The door man peered out of the slot in the door. He recognized game when he saw it. He didn't know us; but, he let us in. I guess we were representing well. He knew that we belonged with this crowd.

When we entered the foyer, we could hear cool rhythms, pulsating throughout the joint. The bar was lined wall-to-wall with Detroit's finest. There was game everywhere: coke, weed, champagne and cognac flowed like a sea of decadence. It made for a festive affair. We strolled through the joint, greeting and being greeted, game acknowledging game. I spotted Chico, the Mexican pimp, who rolled with the best of them. Ricky Champagne, was doing his thang in a full-length fox coat, cut to the bone. He was entertaining a gaggle of salaciously squirming pros, who powdered their noses with blow. Westside, was laying back in the cut, policing the game. if you were anyway shape or form square, Side, would put you on front street with his quick wit. Handsome Harold, was huddled together with Dell, Cruse, and Cruse's game. I bought a round of drinks for his party. Panama Red, was checking some mousey pro, drawing attention to himself, always looking for the spotlight. Penny, and I ambled over to the bar where I ordered a magnum of Dom Perri champayne. Eddie Bee, was surrounded like a rock star, by a horde of pimps and pros. The only visible part of him was the top of his head, weaving and bobbing to the beat of his own rhythm, as he kept his audience in stitches, while spitting game non-stop. To get Eddie's attention, I had a bar maid bring him what he was drinking. She delivered the drink to him, then she pointed at me. Eddie, looked over then raised his glass and nodded in my direction in appreciation. Eddie, reeled off one of his pimp escapades, that sent a roar of laughter across the after-hours joint. Sharp ass-pimpin' Dee, chimed in. "I just sent two pros cross country. I'm checking traps internationally." That made Eddie's antennas go up. He retored. You know you got to stay on top of that kind of action. I had one of the slickest pros' out there. I gave her a ton of game to work with. Anyway, I sent her cross-country. She knocked off a trick in Toronto. I had schooled baby girl that whenever she knocked off a trick and she didn't know how to work him, to give me a call whenever she wanted to maximize her payoff. One night she called me up for advise. She said. "Eddie,

I got this trick. How should I play him, Baby?" I said look Baby, I want you to play him like this. After giving her instructions, I followed it up with. "When you get through working the trick, go down to Western Union and wire me my trap." "Ok, Baby." Was her response. Over a period of weeks, she repeated that scenario a few more times. Everything was looking up. Then she caught the big Fish. Once again, she called me and said. "Baby, I done caught a big fat, rich, white trick. He gave me a five-carrot diamond ring and wants to marry me. Eddie, said. I told her. "Look here, Baby, I want you to play it like this. Then, I want you to go down to Western Union and wire me my trap. The pro' shot back. "Sorry, Eddie. Thanks for everything, Baby; but, I'm gon' play this one." Then I heard the phone go click. Needless to say, I never heard from that pro' again. So let that be a lesson to all of you cross-country pimps. I talked with Panama Red, on the phone recently in 2007. He informed me that Eddie Bee had passed away, and they had his funeral a few days earlier. He was 69-years old. God, bless you, Eddie. May you find an audience amongst the pimp Gods. If there is such a thing.

I introduced Penny as my little sister, which offended her. While I was joshin' with Eddie, Penny, had caught the eye of pimping J M, who was all over her with his pimp charm. That was all right with me. I still was under the notion that she was too young, which meant trouble. I was hoping that J M, came up with Penny. I had my eye on a red-bone booster called Sticky Finga's, who was throwing tons of action my way, Miss Finga's was getting her flirt on. This was a great opportunity to knock her off. Luck would have it that J M, waltzed over to me and asked if he could take my little sister to breakfast at Ted's restaurant on Woodward, in Palmer Park. That's where players rendezvoused in the wee hours of the night. I was good with J M's request. He was a safe bet to pump Penny up with game. I just didn't want to be burdened with that task. J M, was fly and good looking. I was pretty sure he'd ("pardon the pun") put her on the right track. I asked Penny, if she was all right with J M taking her to breakfast? She nodded in the affirmative, then left the joint with him. I turned my attention to Sticky Finga's. Unfortunately, I came up short. She was already spoken for by another pimp. All was not lost. I came up with a chocolate cutie named Mona. Just as I was about to get in the groove with Mona, there was a commotion in a room where the gamblers dwelled. One of the gamblers ran out into the main bar area bleeding from a six-inch scar on his face. He then ran out of the joint. I surmized that he was headed to a hospital. As the injured man made his exit, Bobby Neally, Westside's hot-headed running buddy came out of the room, holding his injured hand. It was cut pretty bad. That was my cue to exit stage left. In other words. I got the hell out of there with my new friend, Mona, in tow, followed by a horde of revelers. I found out through the grapevine, that Bobby, and the fellow with the cut face had gotten into an argument over a bet. Bobby, holding a brandy sniffer in his right hand, slapped the dude right in his face with the glass, injuring dude and himself in the process. What a way to end the morning fun. During my conversation with Mona, I found out that she was what Syracruse, had dubbed a hip square. One who liked partying with players; but, didn't submit, or commit to the code of ethics regulating the game. She liked danglin' on a playa's arm like a square. She preferred basking in the glow of a player's aura. She had her girlfriends with her, and she had to drive them home. I took her number and bid her and her friends goodnight. Then, I jumped in my Caddy, balled up her number and flipped it out of the car window when I got out on the road. Then, I fled to the sanctity of my apartment, where I called it a night and fell fast asleep.

I don't know how one would regulate the love of a father, funds can be managed. The poor child has to wait eighteen years to sort out who the real deadbeat is. Many come to realize that they've been pimped by their own fuckin' parent/or, parents. You see, there are many types of pimps in America. Society just calls them something else. We're living in a "Nation of Pimps." Only a small segment of our society is brazen enough to call it what it is, pimpin'. And tonight was our night Baby!

Mack of the year gala, Chick Springer's Lounge; circa 1981

Chapter 18

NATION OF PIMPS

Back at The Thunderbird Motel, it was business as usual. A week had passed since I last saw Penny, leaving Sonny Mack's with J M. Here she was on the phone trying to convince me to get with her for a little pow wow. I proposed that we meet at Ted's on Woodward, after I got off. She retorted. "Naw. Yo' pimpin' friend J M, that's where that fool had me down at. You can come get me at my mother's house. (pardon the grammar, but, that's how pros verbalized.) I agreed and that's what I did. When I arrived to pick her up, she scurried out of the house looking snazzy, with her buxom breast bouncing like a baby's toy. With an excited gait she scampered toward my ride. She jumped inside, without missing a stride. Than went into a snarky tirade to break the ice. She blurted. "Why you pawn me off on that pimpin' fool, that nigga' liked pussy more than he liked money?" I said. "Look, baby girl, you were all up in his face. Besides you're the one who wanted a Mack, man. I thought you liked pimpin' ass nigga's." Penny purred. "I do; but, not like that. He pimp a bitch too hard. He wants a bitch standing on a corner, while he rides by with his buddies to prove he pimpin.' I don't need that. I need a pimp like you, Baby." Then she reached in her boot and produced a choosing trap. She slid it into my pimp hand, then complimented me on how smooth they were trying to butter a pimp up. She said. "You might as well take me to my new home, because I ain't going back to J M." I looked at Penny, then, I looked at the wad of bills she had pressed in my hand, and then I retorted. "Ok Baby, let's go home, if it don't work out you on your own." With that, she broke out into a big ole' white pearl toothed grin, rested her arm on the arm rest, and then leaned all the way down Woodward Avenue, with her new Mack in his new two-tone Cadillac. I took the long way home. Her little debauchery with J M, was over. I knew I would have to deal with J M, about that. He knew the game: easy come, easy blow, no disrespect intended. The Mack of the year gala was in a few weeks. If I see him there, or before, I'll pull his coat. Now, all I had to do was to figure out what I was going to do with Penny. I didn't want her on the street. I thought she was more valuable than that. I liked classy pros. I didn't care too much for street pros. They're too much trouble, and there's too much drama to endure. After all awhile back, Penny, did say that I could mold her into the kind of woman I wanted. I decided to take, Penny, to work with me at the motel, and put her up in one of the rooms. I relayed my plan to Penny, and she was good to go with that. She had one request: that I bring her friend, Tyra, in on it. They were a team. I guess the pros that stick together, get paid together. I gave her my blessings and agreed to her request. All of Penny's traps came to me. With Tyra, I decided on a 60-40 split. All they had to do was kick back. All of the John's came through me: no muss, no fuss. Penny and Tyra were as thick as thieves. Their pet name for each other was bitch. They loved calling each other that in a loving enduring tone. I couldn't figure it out, because I didn't use that term toward them. That was something they picked up long before they got with me. Even if I had tried to sway them from using that term around me, those two hard cases would have labeled me a square ass bitch, then left my ass. You've got to be careful with pros. They're a different breed. My take on that, is that they were indoctrinated early on in life, or in the game with that self-defacing stimuli. My disapproving it, ain't changing them. The girls also had a side hustle. They served themselves up to bachelor parties, where a team of pros entertained a party of gentlemen, celebrating the groom's last night as a single man. Penny often pulled down a grand or better for a few hour's work. Tyra, and the other girls usually made the same amount. The clothes were selling swell. I was knockin' off the motel for a few grand a week then, and the two young maids / hookers were doing a 60-40 spilt with me. I was knockin' off six to seven thousand a week...not bad for a desk clerk making 5.25 an hour base pay.

During a portion of my writings, I will deal not only with the what, I will dwell on the why concerning my actions. Right now, as I see it today through seasoned eyes, I don't think for one minute that any of that crap was right. It seemed like a good endeaver at the time. Hey, I was playing catch up without a safety net. I didn't receive many positive strokes for doing things right at home. So, right didn't really matter to me then. My type of personally was geared toward being accepted by others. I wanted to be liked. That's why I blew a ton of dough setting the bar up for friends and strangers. It was my way of attracting people to me. It took me a long time to figure out why I did that sort of thing. I didn't realize it then, but, that through the early stages of my development, I developed a personality disorder, a psychological dirge born out of early childhood rejections. I had a complex view of life as a child, coupled with the lack of attention I experienced as an adolecent. That all lead to greater and more complexed psychological discord. That's my take on that. Expounding further, feelings of isolation drove me inward from early childhood, to early adulthood. Hey, I wasn't expecting to grow-up knowing what personality disorders were. I'm certain that most humans have some form of personality disorder, unless you're a perfect person. It would be incredulous of me to think that I was alone in this endeavor: however, mine are unique to me. With my understanding of self, I can work toward building a kinder, gentler human being. I chose not to perish from this great "Planet Earth" as a broken and embittered person. After all the odds of being born are so phenomenally remote. I don't think there's a number associated with it in layman's terms. I just wanted to share my thoughts with the readers on how at some point in my adult life, I became the twisted ego-maniac who craved adoration. All of that was born out of my early childhood indoctrination into becoming a not-so-well-adjusted human being.

Penny, and Tyra were in like Flynn, steppin' in and helpin' out. The Mack-of-the-year gala was upon us, and I knew I had to be on point. All of the leaders and greeters of the pimp and pro' league were gon' be on board. The affair will definitely be "Nowhere to be a square," and that's the truth, Ruth. I decided to take Penny, with me to deal with that J M, situation. I think she would have left me if I didn't take her. That was our night to shine. First order of business was to go shopping for our hookups. Kosin's was the store for me. With hundred-dollar bills stacked back-to-back in my raise, it was top shelf all the way. Penny headed to Northland to get her hookup. She was new school... that's where they shopped. On a cold crisp winter's afternoon, with the Mack's ball on the horizon that night, it will surely be a festive occasion. At Kosins I was feeling giddy and sadidy. From the rack in the back, my eyes scoured the fine array of top designer-wear for men, including sport coats and suits, with a wide variety of silk and fine linen dress shirts and neck ties to compliment one's cool outfit. I decided on a three-piece ensemble, consisting of a plush chocolate-brown velvet sports coat, with a light-brown tweed vest and matching tweed slacks. I completed the hookup with a pair of brown suede Johnson and Murphy loafers, brown silk socks, and a beige silk dress shirt with monogrammed sleeves and a dark brown silk neck tie. I was good to go, to the pimp show.

My hair was laid to the bone. I was ready to get it on. I know that might sound a little flamboyant, because it was. It was 1981 and flamboyant was in. Penny surprised me. I thought she would glam it up hooker-style; but, she looked all business in her two-piece pure crushed-velvet beige hook-up, to compliment mine. She looked finer than a tall glass of fine wine. We were good to go. When J M, see's that Penny ain't starving, that gon' rile him up. I'm gonna' be ready like Freddy, for all verbal joustings.

When it was time to step out into the night, I pulled the mink collar on my brown gabardine overcoat up around my ears. Penny was sporting a beige Persian lamb coat, with a beige Russian-type, Persian lamb hat trimmed in dark brown mink. Penny, was so radiant that I had to kiss her before I played gentleman, and opened her car door. As she slid into the beige and bronze beauty, I almost forgot she was a pro.' In my mind, pimps are gentleman. The problem is that most pros don't respect gentleman; unless they're tricks and Johns. The moment that a pimp starts treating pros gentlemanly, pros start angling on how to work him. Nonetheless, Penny seemed flattered, she had never been treated like that before by a pimp. Hey, that was a special night. Most of those so-called playa's didn't allow their game to attend those types of affairs, because there was to much game on board. It was safer to keep them away. In other words, their own insecurities cast doubt on their own game. A lot of fake playa's can't stand up to the real deal. If you were caught half-steppin' yo' game could come up lame. I didn't entertain those types of idiosyncrasies. My ego was huge during that time. I didn't think there was a player out there whose game was strong enough to knock me off. I had to valet park. There were no open parking spaces on the street or in the parking lot. There was the usual array of slick mobiles. Just before we pulled up to the valet, Penny, came out with a snort of girl, and we had a quick one and one. After I turned my keys over to the valet, he spouted. "This bad mother is going right up front." And that's where he parked that bad mother...up front and personal.

From the moment we stepped into Chick Springer's Lounge, we were met with a festive atmosphere. It was apparent that players came to party. There were so many sharp good-looking people on board, that one could liken it to a Hollywood soiree. George Clinton's hit flashlight was pulsating and there was some Mackin' going on up in Chick's that night. The next thing to strike my fancy was the large colorful poster highlighting the affair, proclaiming. "Mack-of-the year Gala, 1981. The mighty Macks representing." It then went on to list the pimps and pros being recognized that night. The list included Aubrey, whom, I knew from my wig-selling days downtown. He ran his pros out of the Columbia Bar. Aubrey was a handsome, high-yellow, smooth-talking Macaroni. He represented the game well. Then Andre's name was at the top of the list, because his name started with an "A," and he designed the poster. Drey was a walk 'em down, ride 'em down, take 'em out of town playa.' Then, you had Jimmy Blue, Baby Ray, and Citris, a gold tooth playa.' That was 1981, Citris was ahead of his time in that regard. Then, you had Joe Cash, who, in my estimation had one of the all-time great pimp names. Navaro, was up next. Navero drove a beauty of an automobile: a vintage, white Rolls. I picked Navaro to win tonight's award. Black Rita's name was nestled between Danny Moore's and Chico's. J M's name was in place: he was Andre's road dog. They Macked pros cross-country together. Then I saw "Fass Cass," that gave me a blast to be recognized. Also gracing the Mack roster were Florida Bobby, pimpin' Dee, Westside, and Scooter, an up-and-coming super Mack. He was a quintessence pretty boy, pimpin' phenom, a cross between Sugar Ray Leonard, and El Debarge. I looked through the sea of game and spotted Scooter, the savvy pimp, with his back leaning against the bar, with his elbows resting on the edge of the bar. He was leaned back, like a big Mack, getting much action, sucking it all in with drink in hand, entertaining a slew of movie-star fine white pros. The movie star pros attracted other players and lames who wandered into Scooters circle. One lame cracked on one of Scooter's pros for her name. Scooter, quickly intervened with his quick-witted delivery. "They're the first ladies, and I'm the President." The tongue-tied intruder apologized and offered to buy the quick-witted pimp a drink. Scooter waved him off with. "I ain't no charity case." The befuddled intruder meandered his lame-ass on down the bar, out of sight...never to be heard from again. I found out later that Scooter wasn't lying. All three of those top-notch, white pros were his. I wanna' tell ya,' that was nowhere for a square. After giving Scooter his props for bringing some shine to the game, I gaffed down my drink and submerged myself into the sea of pro' stalkers and shit talkers strutting their wares like flamboyant peacocks, spreading their wings.

After taking a group picture with a dozen or so mighty Mack's. I looked toward the entrance and spotted J M, struttin' his white, mink-coat pimpin' peccadillo ass into the fray, Penny was standing near the entrance, postering like a vexed vixen, leaning against the cigerette vending machine. The bar was on jam. There was no place to sit. I watched as J M, ambled over to where Penny was standing. That's when I made a bee-line over to where he was now standing in front of Penny, giving her the third-degree with his fists planted firmly on his sides. He didn't see me standing behind him. He read Penny's eyes glancing over his shoulder. He turned his head around to find me standing behind him, checking the scene out. I don't think J M, knew the score regarding me and Penny. It was time to set the record straight for him. J M, whipped around facing me, then he extended his hand in recognition. I shook his hand and complimented him on his mink. That's when he started pimpin' on me. Give a pimp a compliment and an audience, he'll try to work the room on you. He made a sweeping motion with his hand across his mink coat, while weaving and bobbing his head. Then he spouted. "PFT, pimp for this," popping the collar on his mink coat. I thought, so that's what his license tag meant by the PFT. Cute, I thought. Well, I knew how to pimp a room too. I put my arm around Penny and squeezed one of her luscious titties, with my hand draped over her shoulder, and mimicked his line. PFT, pimp for this. He looked stunned as if I had made an mendacious statement, and snipped. "She with you now?" I said. "Thank you for turning her out for me player." I offered him a drink, grabbed Penny's hand, and pranced her through the crowded lounge, to meet and greet the heavy hitters on board that night.

Without fathers for young people to look up to and hold in high esteem, shady characters will always be lurking in the cut to take up papa's slack. I would like to pause for the cause, and expound a little bit on that pimp thing. There are all kinds of pimps in America. We're living in a nation of pimps. Some of the pioneers being the Englishmen, the Frenchmen, and the Dutch, who pimped and colonized whole nations of their natural resources and other precious materials. Some of the best pimps to come down the pike in the last five-hundred years were the slave merchants, who not only pimped the mother land of its natural resources; but, of its human resources as well. They pimped mothers, daughters, sons and fathers. Those who they couldn't pimp, they dealt with them much harsher than a little pimp slap upside the head. The slavers bull- whipped and murdered their game, if they got out of line. Then, there are the politicians, who pimp everybody. They lie to the mass's like a good pimp, to get elected. When elected, they pimp the system, their constituents, their slush funds, and their political pac's. Some even pimp the constitution, with their bias-slanted interpretations. And the list goes on and on, with cronyism and nepotism leading the way; or should I say pimpin' the way. Back rooms, shady deals... there's some real pimpin' going on in those smoke filled chambers. Like good pimps, politicians flaunt their stature for their own personal gains, like the pimpin' politician who got busted with his amateur pimpin' ass in Detroit, in the year 2008. He should have played it straight. Your average politician will make an ass out of your average street pimp, when it comes to getting paid. If they don't get played. So boys and girls, if you're thinking about doing some good pimpin' be a politician. Some of them are simply the slickest pimps out there, by far. Let's not forget the preachers, who've been pimpin' their congregations on American soil for centuries. That's why the so-called, ex-street pimps make the best preacher pimps. They know the terrain. I'm not advocating that every politician is a pimp; nor, that every preacher is a pimp; but, there is some pimpin' going on amongst their ranks. You have mothers and fathers, who pimp their children of their little child support payments, and their emotional support. Some mothers, but, not all mothers spend their child support funds on themselves to look good to men, so that in turn, they can have more babies, to pimp more child support dollars from multiple fathers. That is sort of like the "Welfare Queens" of yesteryear, who pimped the system for their own personal gains, while ignoring the needs of their children. Some mothers of today have revised the old "Welfare Queen" syndrome. I'm referring to those who are guilty of working the system for themselves, instead of for their children, as the new "Child Support Queens"...not all, but some. If the shoe fits, wear it. Fathers, that don't participate in their children's lives are leaving their children emotionally scared for life. When fathers shirk their financial responsibilities for their biological children, they are the new "Deadbeat Kings." When the poor kids become of age and begin to rationalize and reason, many find out that their pimps, (oops, I mean parents) have blown their child support on self indulgences. Many children are disconnected from their own fathers, both financially and spiritually. In many cases only mama knows the true identity of who dad is. There's also no emotional support or money for little Jill and little Johnny, when they're ready to go to college when they turn 18. I'm just keeping it real, as the youngsters say. My take on that is that the courts should put a certain percentage of child support payments into a trust fund for the recipients, until they're old enough to manage their own affairs. Leaving it in the hands of the crafty custodian pimps, sometimes just don't work out in the best interest of the child. I don't know how one would regulate the love and the dedicated caring of a biological father, but, funds can be managed. The poor child has to wait 18 years to sort out who the real deadbeat is. Many come to realize that they've been pimped by their own fuckin' parent, / or parents. You see, there are many types of pimps in America. Society just calls most of them something else. We're living in a "Nation of Pimps." Only a small segment of our society is brazen enough to call it what it is, pimpin.' And, tonight was our night, Baby.

As me and Penny made our way into the fray, there was an air of anticipation. Everyone was in good spirits, colorful words were being splashed about by fancy-attired and well coifed revelers. Jimmy Diamond, the-old pro' pimp, made his way to the stage and proceeded to rattle off the names of the finalists for the Mack-of-the year award in no particular order. As Diamond belted out the names of the nominees, each nominee stood up and took a bow. Pimpin' Dee was a nominee. He was a sharp dark-skinned pimp with a passion for mink seats in his custom Fleetwood. Thomas Patton, who was a recipient of the award in the 1960's, was still going strong. Westside, flaunted his pimp magic by motioning to his four, white pros to stand up and take his bow for him. When Danny Moore's name was called, he stood and saluted his fellow playa's and playette's, Chico, Navaro, Florida Bobby, Joe Cash. Then I heard Fass Cass. I stood and tipped my glass. When the list was complete, we all stood, saluted, and took a bow for the Macaroni's and pros in the house. The joint was on jam and the champagne was flowing. It was some celebrating going down that night. We kept it real, and there was no counterfeit in our game. Jimmy Diamond, went on to crown Florida Bobby, Mack of the year circa: 1981. When the bar closed, the good times rolled right on out onto the sidewalk before everybody hit their favorite after-hours joint.

There are overt and inward reasons why some of my brothers and sisters embraced the game. The main culprits were the usual bag of ills faced by our communities: racism, sexism, classism, and all the other 'ism's inflicted on people of the darker persuasion. At one juncture in our history in America, the game was the only game in town where black people had some semblance of self-reliance. Today's black youth have more options, to go on and do great things with their lives, to help guide our people out of the malaise of style over substance.

Penny, was so pumped up after the affair that she wanted me to drop her off on the stroll. She was ready to get paid. I dropped her off at Ted's restaurant, on Woodward. Then I went home and fell fast asleep.

It's 7a.m. the morning after the Mack's ball. Someone is ringing my buzzer off the wall. I rubbed the sleep out of my eyes, made my way to the intercom, and shouted. "Who is it?" Penny's voice shot back. "Open the door, Baby. It's me and Tyra." I buzzed them in. When they entered my apartment, they were chatty and bubbly. Penny, pulled a blow out of her purse and took a hit. Then she gave Tyra, a one and one. She turned and asked me if I wanted one? I turned to her and said. "The only thing I wanted was some dough." She responded with a peon's trap. I shook my head in shame, that she had bought me such a paltry trap. Then, she pulled out another knot. She looked at me, then she looked at Tyra, who pulled out her own knot. The girls threw their traps on the kitchen table. Penny, smiled and spouted. "You back in the box, Baby. Two for one. I told them that I was going back to bed. "Y'all wash up and get some sleep." One hour later, I had two freshly-scrubbed naked pros crawling in bed with me. I told them that they could entertain each other, "I'm going back to sleep. I have to be at the motel in a few hours." I fell fast asleep. What seemed like a few minutes was actually a few hours. I was awakened with Penny's tongue in one ear and Tyra's tongue in the other ear. Penny, purred in my ear. "Baby, I'm hungry," while stroking my shaft. Those two pros were testing me. I thought, maybe so, maybe no; but, it felt sooo good. Regardless, I brushed her aside. "It ain't time for that. Y'all get up and get ready to ride." Penny pouted. Get ready for what? I responded. "The first thing we're going to do is get something to eat. Then I'm gon' put y'all down at the motel. Y'all on probation for the next thirty days. Y'all past probation, we can make a home together." Everybody got fresh. I spied the traps on the dresser, and ordered Penny to go count it and bring it to me. Tyra grabbed the money and said. "I'll count it." She counted the money, then laid it in my hand. It was twelve-hundred smackaroni's. That was good money for a night's work in 1982. Penny called me Baby; but, Tyra didn't come at me like that. I knew there was some covert action going on between those two. Penny was my women. Tyra, was Penny's women. That was their little secret; but, it was no secret to me. I just made 'em think it was. Hell, all I had to do was manage Penny. Penny would handle Tyra. That was my little secret, and I was the only one who knew it. I also knew that all I had was two young pros looking for daddy. To me, I was pimpin' in the crudest psychological sense. I knew the girls were only trying to please daddy, in the deep confines of their subconscious mind. Hey, the girls chose that lifestyle a long time ago. At least I felt that they had me to look out for their best interest, and it wasn't about tripping on them. It was about the money, honey, the bottom line. They could have chosen a beast, who would have run their young ass's in the ground for his own ego gratification. I was firm, but fair, and nobody's square. No matter my concerns for them, they will have to throw down, and stay down, they wouldn't respect me no other way, and that's how it is. I ain't going to carry no young pros. It makes bad hustlers out of 'em. Besides, young pros take kindness for weakness, and we couldn't have that.

After we finished eating, I drove my car to the downtown lot. I still couldn't drive it to work. All I needed was to have one of the motel owners to get wind of me driving a new two-tone Caddy. We caught separate cabs to the motel. I wanted to keep things anonymous, as much as possible.

I arrived at the motel first. I relieved the day clerk. Shortly after that, Penny, and Tyra showed up. I put them in separate rooms, and told them to sit tight. There will to be no wandering the grounds bringing attention to themselves. I put emphasis on it. "All y'all got to do is stay put, and answer the fuckin' door when the Johns come knocking." I reminded the girls. "Just take care of your business, and your business will take care of you. The Johns will already be checked out, let's get paid." The girls played their parts well, and were getting the job done in grand style. I changed their rooms every day. I didn't want them to get bogged down in one spot. At night, when I got off work, we'd close shop. We usually walked the half-mile trek to the parking garage, east on Fort Street, for fifteen minutes. Then, we were sliding into the Caddy: out of sight, out of mind.

I was hanging out late one night in the 19th Hole on Chene Street. There were two 19th Holes. One was on Chene, and the other one was on Woodward, and Seven Mile. I was standing at the bar kickin' it with Lucky Chucky, and Peety Wheaty, when Perry Adams, a northend fellow much older than me came over. Perry, hung out in my old neighborhood on the northend, when I was growing up. Perry, pulled me to the side and said. "You know your boy died." I said who? Perry responded. "David Tate." I said. "You mean Little King David?" He said. "Yep." I asked Perry. "No shit. How did he die?" Perry exclaimed. "Kidney failure." I blurted. "When is the funeral?" Perry said. "Man, you late they buried him last month." I bought Perry a drink. Then we reminisced about David Tate, the wayward man-child, who introduced me to the night life as a teen. Rest in peace, "Little King David." Both the fellows, I was conversating with and Perry Adams, are no longer a part of this world. I feel blessed being the last man standing from that night in 1982. God, bless you all.

Back at the apartment Penny and Tyra were testing my last nerve. Something was gon' have to give. I had a rare day off and my trunk was on jam. The Caddy was gleaming, and I was looking and feeling mighty spiffy, while waiting on a traffic light on Woodward and Palmer, traveling north.

Then she walked past my idling mobile, waiting for the light to change. Before her feet hit the sidewalk, she turned and smiled at me. As she stared me down, our eyes were fixed on each other. She almost triped over the curb, as she stepped onto the sidewalk. I didn't know if it was me or the car getting all of that action. I thought that I'd better pull over. She was a keeper. I pulled over. She was heading toward the upscale "Park Shelton Apartments" on Woodward and Palmer, across the street from the Art Institute. She saw me pull over to the curb, and slowed down her pace. I jumped out of my car and asked. "Was it me or the car that you were smiling at?" She grinned and said. "It's you." Then I popped the trunk to have a reason for stopping her. I didn't want to come off as some kind of weirdo. She was no ordinary catch. She was a classy-looking sister, with an regal air of sophistication about her. I gave her my sales pitch. I told her that my store went out of business and I was making deals to sophisticated young gems such as herself. Come take a look? She looked the merchandise over and declined saying. "I don't do trunks." We both chuckled over the line. I quickly retorted. "That's ok I really stopped to say hello. Breakfast, lunch or dinner on me?" She peered at my car, then handed me her business card. She was a Principal at a school in Highland Park. The card had her phone number on it as well. I put the card in my pocket and I told her. "I'll be calling you real soon." She nodded in my direction. I jumped back in my shaught, (car) waved goodbye and finished my journey out Woodward. I thought about her all the way down Woodward. I was enamored with this new find. I forgot to get her name, luckily it was on her business card.

That was my hustle day and I had hit a good lick. I sold my trunk full of pieces wherever there were people: eastside, westside, northwest side, I was all over town pushing dry goods. By the time that I got back downtown, I had made seven or eight hundred dollars. Penny, was gone when I got back to the apartment. I stepped into a hurricane, I prided myself on being a pretty neat fellow. I wasn't used to that. Pros are slobs. I got to find them their own joint. I had an inkling that they were using drugs. I rationalized that they were two young for me anyway. I was really searching for a reason to distance myself from them. I felt a headache coming on dealing with those two knuckle heads.

A couple of months had passed and I had forgotten all about the young Principal, who had entrusted me with her business card. I met young women all the time and it was hard remembering them all. On a Sunday, before I was to start my evening shift at The Thunderbird Motel, on occasion you could find me perusing the fine art in the storied galleries of The

Detroit Institute Of Arts. That little ritual was inherited from my adolescence, when Mr. Hubbard, the German Social Studies teacher found time to introduce me and Malon Mckinny (Mack) to that glitzy art world. While attempting to decipher the delicate nuances of the lines and angles of a fine, Picasso, abstract. I heard a familiar voice behind me. "I wonder if Picasso, ever left a girl hanging without calling her?" When I turned around there she was, the woman from the business card in my wallet. The name on the business card was Tunie. I was surprised to see her and blurted. "I was just thinking about you." She glared at me with skepticism, stuck out her right hand and said. "Let's do this right this time. My name is Tunie." With a firm handshake I said. My name is "Arnold." No "Fass Cass," jazz, for that gem. Despite my shortcomings regarding my choice of women, I've always held to the notion that there was more to me than harboring pros. Maybe I've found someone to turn my player's card in for. Before I became conscious of self respect, anything superficial was good enough for me. I thought for a moment that this Tunie person was a breath of fresh air. She stood next to me... in her black and white hounds-tooth jacket, stylish black blouse and skirt, and rounding her attire out with a pair of black, patent-leather pumps, with a designer purse dangling from one hand, while her other hand rested on her chin with her thumb and forefinger spread across her jaw; delivering me an art history lesson. Slow down my beating heart. Could she be the catalyst to transform my life into a more positive sphere? I strolled the galleries with my new-found associate. She critiqued Gauguin, and Monet to me, and I critiqued, Picasso, and Van Gogh to her. It turned out to be a most pleasant afternoon, with a most delightful and charming young woman. We capped off our afternoon with lunch. Before parting company, I asked her for a dinner date. She replied. "As long as I'm picking the restaurant." I agreed and we set a date for the following Friday. The following Friday, I was looking forward to our date as I got dressed. I arrived at Tunie's apartment building, "The Park Shelton Apartments," located across the street from the Art Institute in mid-town. The Park Shelton, was a high-end, well- established hotel in its hayday...top-shelf all the way. Beginning in the mid-1970's, the Park Shelton, was converted into luxury condos for young professionals living and working at and around Wayne State University. I would find out through conversations with Tunie, that she was one of the first African- Americans, to purchase a condo in the Park Shelton. When I entered the foyer, the doorman called Tunie up to let her know that I was there to receive her. She ok'd him to let me up to her condo. I found the Park Shelton, to be an auspiciously, sturdy-ornate, grand building with plush carpeting to compliment the inlaid marble and bronze interior. Tunie lived in a 12th-floor corner apartment, that had a breath- taking view of Woodward, looking south to downtown. The windows were high and wide with no drapes. Every space on her walls were well-adorned with elegant art, landscapes, portraits, oils and charcoals, with an eclectic mix of prints and originals. It was a colorful array of art that I had never witnessed in someone's home...so elegant, so refined. After admiring her art for a minute, I knew right then and there that if I didn't steal her heart, I was surely going to steal her art arrangement ideas. Anyone who's been to my home and seen my art arrangement...well, Tunie's the culprit whose decorative ideas I stole a few decades ago. Tunie emerged from the back and we were ready to go to dinner. She would have to tell me the name of the restaurant she wanted to dine at. I just wanted to go someplace nice and quiet. Before I could ask, she asked. "Mind if I drive?" I said. "Who's car mine or your's?" She grabbed my hand and lead me to her building's attached parking garage. She lead me to a parking space, where we stopped in front of a 500 series (The big one.) Mercedes Benz. My first thought was, I done hit the jackpot in squareville. She steered the big, gold beauty onto Woodward Avenue. We drove north on Woodward, to an upscale restaurant in Royal Oak, called Dougs Body Shop. It had a unique theme: automobiles of the vintage type. There was the shale of a vintage Corvette, seemingly teetering on the edge of the restaurant's roof top. It was a great prop.

Once inside the restaurant, it was pure Americana, with an automobile motif. Photos of vintage automobiles plasterd the walls of the eatery. Patrons were served in booths designed from the shale of other vintage cars, completed with dining tables, it was cozy and different. After dining on steak and lobster, with a splash of champagne to wash it down, we were off to a good start. With an added dash of lively conversation, amid the quiet tinkling of crystal champagne glasses in the background. It made for a pleasant date. When the waiter brought the check, I reached for it. She put her hand over my hand, shook her head, no, then said. "Bacause I chose the restaurant, this one's on me." I blurted what I heard a pimp once say. "I'm not a charity case, I got this." Tunie told me to put my ego away and relax. "You can pay the tip, and its on you the next time, and you get to choice the restaurant, deal?" I smiled and said. "Deal." When we got back to her apartment building, she parked her car and walked me back to my car. She got in and I drove her back to her building. Before she got out, I asked her when would she like to do it again? She replied, with slyness in her voice. "We haven't done it the first time, yet." "Naughty girl." I replied.

She said. "Call me we'll set something up." I kissed her on her lips good-night. If Penny, and Tyra, knew I was entertaining a square, they would leave my ass.

On our second date a couple of weeks later, I chose the restaurant, a little jazz supper club located in the underground promenade in "Hart Plaza." (Dubbed down under.) I picked her up and drove my car this time. I had about seventy bucks on me and thought that should cover it. One must keep in mind that it was the early 1980's and seventy bucks was good bucks for dinner. Tunie, decided that we needed an expensive bottle of champagne to celebrate our second date. I scoffed, but, I didn't want to appear to be cheap. I was just counting the bucks in my pocket and didn't want to be caught short. I told her to order up. I had to go to my car. I left my date by herself, while I ventured out into the night in search of cash. The Thunderbird Motel, was less than a quarter mile away on Fort Street, where I kept an emergency stash of cash. It took twenty minutes tops, for me to make it down there and back in time to look into the eyes of a very nervous date, who smiled with relief, then asked what took me so long? I told her that, I had to remember where I had stashed my wallet in the car. We finished our date and everything went great.

Tunie, invited me to a baby shower. I declined, until she told me who the shower was for. Tunie and some of her girlfriends were throwing a baby shower for Black Patty, at Pattie's gorgeous home in an upscale neighborhood. I jumped all over the invite. Tunie, asked me to purchase a sterling silver baby creamer from Hudson's. I didn't mind. I knew Tunie was no cheap chick, and besides only the best for Black Pattie's baby. The shower was several weeks off, on a Sunday. I knew that the affair was gonna' be loaded with game. I asked Tunie, how long had she known Patty? She asked. "Why do you know her?" I replied. "She's only the classiest Dame, in Detroit, to grace the game in my time. Over the years, I'd run into her at various venues. " Tunie responded. "I've known her for awhile." I walked my date to her door and bid her goodnight. I told her that I was looking forward to seeing her again. She tip-toed and gave me a peck on the cheek. I liked her style.

After leaving my date I went home. To my pleasant surprise, Penny, and Tyra, were not there and what a relief I thought. I had a good night's sleep; but, I began to worry when I didn't hear from the girls all night. I went to work that evening. As soon as I got in the motel's office, I called my apartment looking for Penny and Tyra. There was no answer. I figured they were out getting busy. Boy, was I wrong. When I got off work, there still was no Penny, no, Tyra, and no messages. Now, I was beginning to worry. I thought all kinds of shit: were they in jail? Were they hurt? Had they run off? I knew one thing, they had to be somewhere. I hit the strolls along Wood-ward, all the way down to The Last Chance Bar, on Eight Mile and Wood-ward. I spotted two rollers from Penny's past. They were in the parking lot sitting on their car. One of the young thugs got off the car, and tried to block my entrance into the bar. I side-stepped him, and thought that was strange, as I slid into the bar. Once inside The Last Chance pro' bar, I was met by the usual low-life pros, John's, pimps, and one of my pimpin' bud-dies. My mellow man, James, from the northend, ran over to me and said. "Yo' woman just ran into the ladies room when you came in." I responded. "Oh yeah, the bitch tryin' to duck me." I had a delimma on my hands. Why was she duckin' me? Then it dawned on me that she was down here with those two fools frontin' in the parking lot. I pulled James, to the side and I asked him if he was sure that she was in the ladies room, before I acted ? James, assured me that indeed she was hiding in the bathroom. I pushed the ladies room door open with a little ump, and cold-cocked, Penny, dead in the chops with the door. She was cowering behind the door. When Penny, saw me standing there with my pimp face on, she looked like a fright-ened Gazelle, and I was the Lion. She blurted. "Baby, I'm down here gettin' yo' trap." I didn't jump on her, or anything like that. I just told her. "I told you that you were too young for me. You've got twenty-four hours to get yo' shit out of my apartment." I stormed out of the bar, jumped in my shaught and sped off.

During my ride, I thought about the situation at hand regarding the girls. I had gotten used to clocking dollars from, Penny, and Tyra; but, it was best to let 'em go. I understood that with drugs in the mix, I knew who would win that battle: the sack man. Penny, and Tyra, were now what was referred to as, "sack chasers." Women who got with rollers and exploited themselves for drugs, jewelry, outfits and a little cash, if they could find a roller sucker enough to pay them. There were plenty of them out there turning the game inside out, and turning prime money makers into skinny scalawags.

The landscape was changing, the game was changing. This, my friend, was the beginning of the end for Penny, and Tyra. The lure of the almighty narcotic was too strong for my pimpin' to compete.

After all I had finer and swifter pros leave me, and, or, I had kicked out than those two. I pity the po' fellow who came up with them. I had squeezed all the butter from those two ducks.

After not hearing from the girls for a couple of weeks, I thought about it, then I dumped their clothes on Penny's mother's front lawn. I rung the door bell; when no one answered. I threw their clothes on the lawn, I didn't want to do that, but, it came to that. My last thoughts were, farewell, so long, goodbye. I still had my clothing hustle and a few good recruits to fill the void. I was now managing the Thunderbird, and its sister motel, the Viking, over on Grand River, near the Lodge freeway. I was still chatting it up with my new hip square friend Tunie, with whom, I was enamored with. There was no heavy petting, just good clean fun.

The day of Pattie's baby shower was upon us and I took that Sunday off. The motel ran twenty-four seven; so I had to squeeze the shower in. I had already delivered the silver creamer for the shower to Tunie. The shower was to start around 6 p.m.. I got dressed-to-impress in my Sunday best. Tunie, had sent me an invitation with the address on it. Tunie would arrive early to help with the preparations.

When I arrived at that beautiful, tree-lined enclave... nestled in the heart of one of Detroit's swankiest neighborhoods...I knew I had arrived at the right address. There was a fine array of mobiles, hugging both sides of the street. Beautiful, well-groomed, well coifed guests came to pay homage to Miss Patty. Usually, when one thinks of a baby shower, it's a bunch of women getting together with gifts for their pregnant girlfriend. In Miss Pat's case men and women paid their respects. It was a more festive atmosphere than your average baby shower. When was the last time, you went to a baby shower dressed to the nines? That was my first baby shower, and I didn't know what to expect. I found it to be quite refreshing and civilized, with the usual top-shelf gamers on board. Everybody loved Miss Patty. Her home was something to behold, and she was a gracious host. I spotted, Jackie B, William L, Black W, Pimpin' Dee, Black Rita, they all were having a great time, along with, (May his soul rest in peace.) Florida Bobby, Thomas Patton, and a host of other mellow Detroiters. I was honored to be among their ranks, having a good time seeing and being seen. Everyone was on their "A" game on that beautiful, Sunday, summer's day, back in 1981. As I was leaving, Ronnie McNair, the one time Motown entertainer was arriving. I shook his hand as he entered the shower. He didn't know who I was; but, I recognized him as the entertainer at the dinner club in the promenade in Hart Plaza, where Tunie, and I were hanging out the night I had to duck out and replenish by bankroll. Later that night, I called Tunie, and we talked about the affair at Miss Pat's place. Shortly after our conversation my life started getting complicated.

Someone who worked for the motel, spotted me out and about in my new Caddy, and they couldn't wait to tell the motel owners what they had seen, to score some brownie points with the owners. Needless to say, a week after Miss Pat's party, Sam and Don, along with Don's son Bobby, summoned me out to their biggest motel, The Cranbrook, out on Eight Mile and Greenfield. I figured, it ain't no reason to punk out now. So I drove my two-tone Caddy out to the Cranbrook, and parked it right outside of their office, for all the motel owners to see. They were all leering out of the office windows; watching as I exited my vehicle, and strolled right up to the front door. I figured this is America, and I ain't hiding my car no mo.' When I stepped inside of their office, the first one to attack was Sam Braverman, one of the owners. The short, fat, cigar-chomping Jewish owner curtly snorted. "Arnold, I see we have a partner." Then Don Nuchios chimmed in. "I don't even drive a Cadillac. How can you afford that beauty?" I made up some dribble about an uncle dying and leaving me a taste. I don't think they bought the story; nonetheless, they said ok, go back to work. After I left our little meeting, I felt that I was working on borrowed time. I was determined to make the most of it. A week later before I could come up with an exit strategy or hit a good lick, all three owners came down to the Thunderbird, and blitzed the motel, just before my shift was up. Don, blitzed the office area, where I was stationed. He grabbed the registration roster and matched the rooms with the keys in the key slots, trying to catch me slippin.' Little did they know, I didn't make my money stealing room rent, so the registration roster was in order. Sam and Bobby, physically checked the rooms. They hit so fast that I didn't have time to warn the girls. I was cold-busted. Sam, had entered two of the supposedly vacant rooms, and found a pro' in each room. One of the girls was handlin' her business. Sam, gave the girls five minutes to vacate the premises, or he was calling the cops. When I saw half-dressed pros running out of the rooms, I knew the gig was up. Don, standing in the business office, said. "I think it's time we parted company, Arnold." Before I departed, I asked Don, how did they know? Don simply replied. "We got a phone call from a little birdie." I'm not exactly sure; but, I think that little birdie's name was, Penny. I packed up my gear and headed out into the hot, steamy night. I had two things still going for me: I was young and I had a bankroll. For a little encouragement, I rationalized that I've been kicked out of better joints than that and survived.

As the sun came up the next morning, I was unemployed and had lost my base of operations. The system got me two-for-one: lost job, lost hustle. I still had My Caddy, and my name. I still had my merchandise and my game. On the other side of that coin, I still had my car note, my rent, and my up-keep to maintain. The first thing on my agenda was to shore up my stock. I was caught between a rock and a hard place. I had to make it happen, my life style was at stake. I hooked up with a young square, named April, whose brothers were local thugs, growing up on the northend. For as long as I can remember, her family lived on Bethune and Oakland. The shop where I purchased my raffle tickets was located right next door to April's house. April, saw me in my two-tone Caddy, while I was placing an emergency order of raffle tickets at the printing shop.

After losing the gig at the Thunderbird, that little fling with, Tunie, had dissipated. I just didn't have the time or means to pursue her. Tunie was not an easy women to come up with. She had a brain and morals; none of that pimp, pro' shit for her. She was much better than that...another time and place I thought. For once in a good while, I was on my own...no woman, no job, no real destination for the future. I figured, I'll just have to put my clothing hustle on a higher priority. I had no choice, that's all I had for the moment.

I invested the bulk of my bankroll into replenishing my stock. Selling clothes from the hip was a tough nut to crack. Everything I made had to be spent paying bills. As my source of income melted, I found myself eating at Beanie's house more and more often. On occasion, I would take a nap on her couch.

On one such occasion I was napping on her couch one night, when suddenly, I heard a familiar sound pierce the calm: a burst of gun fire. Gun fire had become a normal occurrence in my mother's northwest side neighborhood, so I paid little attention to it and kept right on napping. Shortly thereafter, there was a tap at my mother's front window near where I was sleeping. My mother's neighbor, Jeff, a basketball player for the University of Detroit, was standing on the porch with a pained expression etched across his long face. Jeff belted. "You better come check out yo' ride man, they shot it up." My first reaction was: what the fuck, who's mad at me? When I stepped out into the night to check out my beloved, Caddy, I couldn't believe my eyes. The damage was pretty extensive.

There were bullet holes in the driver side-door, all the windows were shot out, bullets had ripped through the head rests and tore into the back seat. My first words to a stunned, Jeff, were. "Damn, I'm glad I wasn't in it." I felt lucky. I drove the bullet-riddled car down to my apartment building's garage, then settled into my apartment to contemplate my next move. The insurance had lapsed and I didn't have the will to drive it, so I decided to sell it.

I called around to some of the Cadillac dealers and got a positive response from a dealership on East Jefferson, near Chene Street. Its no longer at that location. The dealership's name escapes me. They made me an offer I could live with. After they paid off GMAC (General Motors Acceptance Corp.) the $8,000 balance I owed on the vehicle, the Manager gave me five $100.00 bills, shook my hand and then gave me the bum's rush out onto Jefferson Avenue, into a non-stop, monsoon rainstorm; where I was thoroughly drenched in the onslaught of rain. You know what, growing up in the ghetto prepared me for moments like that. I wasn't feeling as bad as I thought I would: I rationalized, as I rode the Jefferson bus, it was only glass, steel and rubber. I had one thing going for me as the bus dropped me off on Woodward, and Jefferson. I still had my youth. When I got back to my apartment, I took a nap. I'll deal with it tomorrow. I guess you can say that my beloved, Caddy, got played by the game of shoot- 'em-up, and that's the truth, Ruth.

I've been a witness to the antics of young Crack lords, as they strutted around our communities, pounding their mighty chests, as if they've conquered a mighty quest. The only thing you've succeeded at, is laying your own race to rest; whether that you layed them in their graves, never to be heard from again, or you catching hell in yo'stankin'cell, never to be heard from again. I'm aware that sometimes, in some places, there are meager options. It doesn't matter; the fall is always greater than the rise. If you chose the wrong options, you lose. Black people have to wake-up, before we incarcerate and murder ourselves into oblivion.

Crack genocide: circa 1980-?

Chapter 19

THE PLAGUE OF THE CRACK ATTACK

Looking through the prism of hindsight, little did I know at that time while reading an article (in 1983) about Richard Pryor, the raunchy comedian being set ablaze while smoking something called "Free Base," that, that little incendiary incident would be the spark that ignited the flame of self-annihilation throughout the African-American, communities across America. It was the beginning of the scourge, called Crack; and it was taking no prisoners. That little incident with Pryor, in California, piqued the curiosity of the whole nation. Evenually it flooded the world, with its tragic magic. That one incident picked up by all the minor and major media outlets proved to be more damaging to our communities than all the Klansmen, Nazi's and Skinheads put together.

From some clandestine labs secured deep in the jungles of the South American, cities of Columbia, Bolivia and Peru; they concocted the master of all addictive drugs, that will come to be hailed by many names: "Crack, Free Base, Rock, Boulder and Yayo." Regardless of what it's called, it had but one purpose: the ability to destroy those who partook of its toxic blend of cocaine, baking soda and cold water to coagulate it into solid form. It was then smoked in a glass pipe or some other make-ship apparatus, with a little 150 proof rum, or achohol, or a cigarette lighter for hard core Crack heads, to ignite Crack's costly fumes. Americans were getting hooked before they knew what hit them. The drug spared no one. It cut across all social and ecconomic groups... Doctors, Lawyers and Indian Chiefs. It had no respect for race or gender...black, white, yellow or brown...it didn't matter they all went down. Crack took its ugly toll on me, as well as some of my family members, friends and associates. The psychological dynamics are enormous when you smoke Crack, you won't have any friends. Once under

Crack's spell the only friends you'll have, is an eager Crack dealer and the almighty glass dick to suck on.

I would like to expound on the nefarious issue of drugs in the Black communities, and I'm coming at you as a brother. I have no idea what it is about most of our communities, that compels us to embrace any ill-conceived drug that is poured into our communities. It happened with "Achohol, Heroin, Weed, Barbiturates, Acid, Mescaline, Cocaine, Crack, Crank, Tee's and Blue's, Methadone," and a host of other mind-altering trickery. Hell, I would go so far as to state, that if some foreign entity dried out and ground up cow manure, sprinkled it with a little quinine and lactose, then packaged it as a new high; we probably would make the manure man rich. At times, I ponder if some of my fellow Black Americans, were (Myself included.) pre-disposed by some evil entities, to gravitate us toward self-destructive stimuli. You know! Black people have the power to put all dope slingers out of business; just like we empowered them. We have to unravel the mess that we've created. If all black illegal drug users were to stop using drugs (And I mean all illegal drugs.) for one month, it would dethrone, and chase the drug dealers out of our neighborhoods. If we went a whole year, we could chase them out of our lives. We must confront the beast where it lives, and it lives in our communities. We have to confront that poor mis-guided, grinning dope slinger, with his bag of tricks in hand, smiling wickedly at us, like he's the candy man. When confronted, we must look those merchants of bad tidings and death in the eye...long, hard and deep, then keep stepping around them or over them. Maybe one glorious day, we can wake up in a drug-free community. There would be no market in our communities for that crap, and it could cause a ripple effect; just think of all the murders, robberies and other crimes that could be squashed in our communities. I'm not naive enough to suggest that all crime would stop; but, it would sure put a significant dent in crime.

My brothers and sisters, do you realize how many white and black judges, cops, prosecutors, defense lawyers, turn keys, coroners, bondsmen, prison personnel, grave diggers and other support industries depend on your persecution and prosecution, your suffering and /or death; more than likely at the hands of another Black person?...two for one. Our indiscretions regarding drugs and black-on-black crimes have gone on to provide all of the above-mentioned, and other derivatives too numerous to mention, a prosperous life and deep pockets to help propel their children into college's and universities, to provide a better life for their families, and to keep their legacies alive. They don't want you to stop the bleeding, as long as you keep it in our neighborhoods. They'll be put out of business, if we stopped hating and victimizing ourselves. I say fuck 'em, let's put 'em out of business and uplift our own families and legacies. Maybe our children can grow up without that dark legacy of drugs and crime hanging over their heads; thus, stopping the vicious cycle of drugs and crime in our communities. Its not that far-fetched, it worked for me. Rollers don't come my way. They don't even know that I'm alive. Theres no money to be made by fucking with me. Our communities must get the logistics and the timing synchronized, then pull together collectively and effectively, and stop using drugs. Stranger things have happened on Planet Earth. Imagine just how much respect we would garner in our communities, if we get on the same page, as a unit, and say, "No to drugs." The police brass and politicians, along with other local officials, would begin to take notice and possibly start respecting our opinions concerning the quality of life in our neighborhoods. Our children can grow and earn true success. I'm proposing it. Is there some diabolical, charismatic, crafty leader out there up to the challenge? Just asking.

The year was, 1982, my beloved Caddy had been shot up. I had lost my job and hustle. I still didn't have a clue as to who my biological father was, and the new pimps in town were the hordes of new young Crack lords, who were spreading like fertile Jack rabbits across our cities. Looking back on that era, it was the beginning of the end; not only for most of those who called themselves pimps and hustlers; but, also for working people, squares, and many of those indivisuals who were holding our communities together. I saw it all unfolding like a deadly virus, knocking off thrill-seekers in its devastating wake. I must admit that I, like everyone else was curious about what could possibly be in that shit, that would cause ordinary people to do bizarre things to obtain it.

Money was getting tight and most of my mellow constituents had abandoned me. We went into our own separate Crack hells. What's that song by Frank Sinatra? "That's life. You're riding high in April, and shot down in May." Well, that's how my life was transpiring. "Riding high in April, shot down in May."

It was beginning to be a rough ride, with my funds almost down to nil. I had to alter my lifestyle to survive. My Aunt, Helen, had sold her portion of the house on Stoepel to Beanie. Beanie needed a tenant, and I needed a place to live. I couldn't afford the luxury apartment any longer. We agreed on rent and I moved into the upper flat at 16876 Stoepel, a stone's throw from the University of Detroit. It was time for a clarion call. A crisis was looming. Once again, I had to chase down the almighty dollar, and the dollar had wings. The city was being flooded with this new drug. Fresh, young dealers were cropping up everywhere. Most of them were dubbed roller's, as in "I'm rollin'" Before Crack, they used to call places where drugs were peddled, dope house's. With this new drug, they coined another term. They were now calling them Crack house's, and as the late, great actor, Paul Winfield, once spouted. "They were sprouting up like weed's on a lush lawn." I wanted nothing to do with them. So I took my last grand and headed to New York, to the "Fashion District" and Canal Street, to load up on knock-off merchandise, fake designer goods, watches, purses and clothes. I figured that I could grind my way up on a decent bankroll when I got back to Detroit, double my money, then I'll head back to New York, to replenish my stock and keep flipping my bankroll until I had some major dough. It didn't work out as planned. I found the going slow. The times were a changing, a paradigm shift, a different time and place and I couldn't keep pace. I didn't even have a car, at times, Beanie, would let me borrow her car. The problem with hustling with an off-brand ride, was that you don't get the same swift action. Potential customers were harder to coax over to the trunk. I could easily sell my merchandise with the Caddy, because people were more inclined to take a look. At the time it was difficult to deal with my usual customer base. I was competing with the Crack dealers. Even though it was a relatively new drug, Crack was sucking up all of the extra cash in the streets.

Pros were beginning to fall under the lure of Crack; so were most of the playa's and in some case's, the dealers themselves. There were more small -time dealers who came up missing in action for smoking up sacks they got on co-signment. At the time, the mass's didn't know about Crack's addictive powers. Once one tried it, unless they were strong-willed, individuals became hooked. There were no Crack-addicted role models. Those whose curiosity lead them to smoke Crack, were the pioneers who forged the trail for the Crack attack. I've read about, heard about, and in many cases seen with my own eyes, famous politicians, entertainers, and even members of the clergy who became addicted to Crack. Crack touched every facet of our country, from the mightiest to the weakest. I remember reading about a couple of young lawyer in Detroit's Mayor, Coleman Young's administration. The story was carried in the local media. The details of the tragedy stated that two young, Black lawyers, (A male, and a female.) whom, by the way were an item, they were arrested for a Crack house shooting. The two young lawyers were holed up in a Crack house, on a Crack-smoking binge for days, when the Crack house occupants, who happened to be young Crack selling thugs, accused the pair of stealing a Crack rock. High on Crack, that must have freaked the two legal eagles out. That was the sort of game that Crack dealers played on Crack heads, to induce sexual favors from female Crack heads, and/or, to extort extra money from male Crack heads. Sometimes it was just a game to amuse themselves, by jumping on vulnerable Crack heads. I'm here to tell you, some of those young rollers were beyond stupid. The story goes that the young thug wanted to rape the young female Crack head lawyer, and threatened bodily harm to her, if she didn't comply. The young thug left his pistol on a table for an instance to un-zip his pants, so that he could rape the young woman. That split second lapse gave the male Crack-head lawyer enough time to get the drop on the young thug. He caught the young thug slippin' and he snatched the loaded pistol off of the table. After he got the drop on the young thug. The lawyer shot the young thug, and was himself shot by someone else in the Crack house. Subsequently, the police came and carted the injured off to the hospital, and arrested those involved, including the young female lawyer, who was described in the newspaper as being distraught. The system snagged two, big, black fish in that little debacle.

Speaking of getting the drop on the young thug, there was a game Heroin dealers on the northend would play on some of their dope house clientele. That was long before Crack made it's debut. Well, anyway, some of the drug den dealers would place an unloaded gun on a table in full view of the drug den patrons, and wait for one of the junkies to grab the empty gun. They caught plenty of fish with the bait. When an unsuspecting junkie grabbed the empty gun and announced a holdup, the drug den dealers would look at each other wickedly and break out with a white tooth grin, before pulling their loaded weapons on the junkie, holding the empty planted weapon. When the junkie pulled the trigger, and it went click. The northend thugs would then beat the junkie half to death, just for kicks. I would advise any young person to run from the drug culture. There's some ugliness being played out, no matter what end of the equation you're on. I don't know what became of the young attorneys, they just got caught up in the malaise of the Crack epidemic, like most unsuspecting victims.

Detroit, even had a couple of newscasters and a sports caster lose their lucrative jobs on local news television stations, because of Crack's lure. One of the fallen newscasters, who got caught in a Crack raid, went on to say that he was doing it as a undercover news story. Yeah, and I got a bridge in Brooklyn for sale. Hell, even the mayor of Washington D.C., Marion Berry, was caught in a sting, on camera smoking Crack. When the law burst into his hotel room, they had to damn near pry the pipe out of the Mayor's mouth.

The early 1980's ushered in a whole new drug culture. With the advent of Crack, corner stores, party stores and record shops put Crack pipes, and other Crack paraphernalia up front, on display for all Crack heads and law -abiding citizens to see. That kind of crap was only tolerated in the black communities, until ordinances were passed to put a halt to that practice. Most decent folks didn't even know what the apparatus's were used for. Most squares figured it was something used to smoke weed out of; but, the Crack heads knew. The term "Crack head" was also born out of the Crack culture. This new culture was spawning a new generation of black criminals, who delighted in peddling the new money-maker and neighborhood-breaker. I caution my young brothers to be "carefull what you wish for, your wish may be granted." You could fill up Ford Field, (The home of the Detroit Lions.) many times over with all the young people who were victimized by Crack, in some form or another. Bus loads of young people have died, or were incarcerated with basketball scores for their prison sentences. The bulk of the victims were in their teens, early twenties, on up to their late thirty's; for example, I can recall a beautiful young medical student, her father was a famed physician. (Though her father, was dead at the time of my encounter with her.) Val, bless her heart, got caught up in the Crack epidemic. Val, was a beautiful, high-yellow, green-eyed beauty and so were her girlfriends. They were cut from the same privileged cloth. Val and her two girlfriends lived in the upscale neighborhood of Sherwood Forest, one of the swankiest enclaves in Detroit. I met Val, outside of a Crack house, in northwest Detroit. I was leaving a Crack house (in 1984), where Val, and her girlfriend were sitting in Val's Corvette, too intimidated to get out and cop their rocks. She waved me over, and when I stuck my head inside of her car window, I was pleasantly surprised to see these two, luscious buxom cuties seductively beckoning for my services to cop for them. I couldn't turn them down, not for their beauty; but, it afforded me "Fass Cass" an opportunity to make a Crack head move and work 'em for some of their drugs, split their rocks and keep half for myself. Even if they suspected something shady, there wasn't much they could do about it. I was bigger than them. Hell, if it had been, Pee-Wee, or Dogman, they would have gotten taken for their money, car and everything else they had of value. I considered them lucky, because, I only sneaked a pinch off each rock. The girls were satisfied with what I gave them. They offered me a ride home and I accepted. The young lady riding shotgun, scooted over and sat on the middle console in the two-seat vette, with her yellow legs gapped wide open. I could damn near see what she had for lunch. I enjoyed the ride and the view. I stroked the wet beaver a couple of times with my fingers before I departed. Crack heads are freaky like that. Less than a hour later, they were back ringing my bell for more. This time, when they dropped me off, they asked to smoke their goodies with me at my place. I guess that beaver stroke worked. I agreed. Now, I found myself with two hot, sexual-dripping, educated Crack heads. We had a Crack head ball. We made our trek back to the Crack house all night long, riding in the snow three-deep in a 'vette. I thought I was having fun; but, that was just a Crack head illusion.

At the best, the system will give young rollers a five-year run, before their lives come tumbling down like falling rain, that rain will be filled with pain for your community, for your families, and last, but not least, for yourself. If I were a young person today, I would run, not walk away from drugs. I would run away with the speed of light. I'm going to sound preachy now; but, I don't care, if one knuckle-head gets it, that's good enough for me. There are some forces out there designed to bring a nigga' down. They're called: snitches, envy, greed, treachery, stupidity, death, and ego. (Yeah, ego.) Just when you think you're on and poppin,' that's when the cops and robbers come a knockin.' I've seen first- hand, and heard through the grapevine, about my young brothers and sisters, muscling and murdering their way to the top. You better stop, before its yo' young ass in a funky cell they'll drop, or worse. I'm tired of my fellow Black men and women getting stuffed into stuffy cell blocks by the boat load like sardines, behind foreboding walls. Stop before you wind up in a box on somebody's hill, while your mother is left to beg God to forgive.

In 1983, that was the maze of madness I was faced with because of my choices: no car, no friends, and no ends. (money) I was done in for the moment. Whenever my back's against the wall, I think back to Martin Luther King Jr.'s speech at my high school in 1964. My life was in my hands and I'll have to find a way to save myself from myself. I, fell hard under the spell of the Crack attack. I stole, I lied, I went on week-long binges, fueled by Crack and achohol. I fell into all of the well-placed traps. I've been threatened by young rollers, and I've theatened young rollers. Hell, I was young myself, 25 years ago. I've been a witness to so much annihilation that it's impossible to chronicle it all in just one chapter. I've blown tons of money to young dealers. Back in the day, the rollers carried beepers. All one had to do was to beep 'em up, put in your special code, and viola, curbside service. I've witnessed Black people, White people and Brown people give away cars, furniture, jewelry, and even themselves for those small grains of tragic magic.

Some of the street dealers were so brazen that they advertised their wares on the front of their baseball caps. Their was this one little squirt, named Tony, who had. "No credit," embossed on his cap. Another sported the slogan, "Holder of a boulder," for all Crack-heads to see. There were so many cars, houses and Negro's shot up in the early 1980's, that it became an epidemic. Before Crack, a person's home was considered their sanctuary. Individuals were dealt with in the streets. With the new Crack culture, everything goes. There were no rules. You could have your house or car shot up for a myriad of petty reasons. That was the climate that I found myself in. In 1983 and 1984. Sometimes, I wonder how did we as a people, make it through that cloud of degradation. I suppose, if my people could survive the transatlantic journey, stuffed inside of slave ships like packed cattle, we can survive anything. Death for me at some points during those tumultuous times was a welcome quest. Yeah, it was that damn bad. I was in a hole and I couldn't get out, my idea at the time was to keep digging my way out, the hole only got deeper. Somehow through the grace of the "Almighty," I managed to claw my way out of that wretched hell hole, more dead than alive; but, I made it out.

The young women caught up in the Crack attack were once beautiful and bronze. Some were once intelligent and loving. When Crack got finished with them, they were left haggard and worn, devoid of self-respect and all desire. Many were left just a shell of their former selves. There was a lot of trading going on. Some selling themselves for as little as a five dollar rock. It would be absurd of me not to vilify the merchants of death and evil tidings; the young and old hooligans, who peddle that poison in the name of getting paid, to turn a hefty percentage of our people into ghosts. There's a long chain of command that stretches all the way into the jungles of South America, and there my friends, dwell the real culprits. They are the cause, and my once, beautiful people are the effect.

Looking back over two decades ago, I'm ashamed in the eyes of my maker that I allowed myself to be lured into and helped to perpetuate Crack's madness, by ingesting it. If there's anyone in heaven, or on earth willing to forgive me, for participating in my own genocide, I humbly accept.

I've been a witness to the antics of young Crack lords, as they strutted around our communities, pounding their mighty chests, as if they've conquered a mighty quest. The only thing you've succeeded at, is laying your own race to rest; whether it be that you laid them in their graves, never to be heard from again, or you catching hell in yo' stinkin' cell, never to be heard from again. I'm aware that at times in some places, there are meager options. it doesn't matter; the fall is always greater than the rise. If you chose the wrong options, you lose. Black people have got to wake up, before we incarcerate and murder ourselves into oblivion.

When I pulled myself up out of that gutter, I saw others who looked like me, scratching, clawing and pulling themselves out of there own separate Crack hells. Subsequently, most of them needed drug rehab' to keep them on the straight and narrow, and that's a good thing. I had my own rehab' strategy, just avoid drugs and those who partake of them. I wasn't going to find my salvation in a room full of addicts, trying to teach me how to stay clean. I personally needed to be around people who've always been clean, to show me how they did it..."different strokes, for different folks"... whatever works for you. My way worked for me. I just turned my back on that lifestyle and didn't look back. The split itself was euphoric. I liken it to walking into a dense, dark, jungle at one end, a jungle inhabited with beasts of all descriptions, clawing at my soul. I somehow managed to crawl out at the other end, more dead than alive. I had to learn how to walk tall again, and how to live again without Crack, that was in 1985, and I haven't looked back since. In the spring of 1985, I got wind of a job with the City of Detroit. It was for a Laborer and a Building Attendant. I looked them up and did the application thing. Several months later, I was called downtown to take exams for the positions. Within the same time frame, I sashayed over to Wayne County Community College, and applied for admission. Several months after filling out the applications for the city positions, I was informed to report for testing the following week, at Cobo Hall, in downtown Detroit. I now had a potential job.

I reflected on reading stories about the late, great, soul-crooner Marvin Gaye, going through his Crack-hell. "Wandering out of his house in California, with his shoes on the wrong foot, his clothes were dishelveled, Marvin, was strung out." I also read that family members had to chase Marvin, down, turn him around and lead him back to the house. Well, "I wanna testify." I could have been reading about my old self, with one exception: I had no family members to turn me around. Detroit, was full of mini-Marvin Gaye's at that time. Slumbering around with wide-eyed desperate gazes, stalking ghetto streets, searching and sniffing for pebbles of pain. Death, lurked, I had to get out or die. It wouldn't be easy, with Crack slingers belting, "Two for one," "Holder of a boulder," "Got them rocks" everywhere I turned. If you had a sliver of weakness, you were headed back to Crack hell. Most of the so-called real pimps pulled up stakes and skipped town, only to discover Mr. Cracky waiting on them, standing on street corners and in door ways, arms folded with a big, ole' shit-eating grin, waiting on a pimp to get weak. Wherever they migrated, the madness preceded them.

One such Detroit, pimp, was a Hollywood, good-looking, tall, handsome chap named Ronnie Love. He was a pretty, pimpin' nigga' to the bone. He went on over to Vegas, with his game and hit rock bottom. Ronnie didn't only lose his game; but, he also lost his life. I heard that fellow Detroiter, good pimpin' J M, got the po' boy a headstone. The word around town was that Ron, was an orphan; born up shit creek, without a paddle. I hail Ronnie Love, as one of the mighty Macks of Detroit, in his glory.

Many of those cross-country pimp's women also came up missing. They were swooped up by the Crack dealers. I'm not speaking about top-notch rollers. I'm talkin' bottom-feeding rollers. You know when they get through with 'em they ain't gon' be worth two dead fly's. God, only knows the psychological trauma inflicted on the children, observing and absorbing the Crack head rituals of their parents and other family members during Crack's hey day. Well, those kids are now adults. Some are blazing their own genocide trail for future generations to inherit. My wish is that most of those individuals found the strength and courage to fight the good fight. I hope that they were able to look inside of themselves for reasons to live a better and healthier existence. When I read the newspapers and watch the evening news on television in this 21st century, I'm not always encouraged. Yes indeed, the Crack babies have grown up and some of their peers are raining havoc and terror throughout America, like nothing we have ever experienced. I've been a witness to young children, so afflicted by their parent's drug addiction, that many had to be rescued by grandma' or the state. Some will indeed be scarred for life. At times, I feel that we as black humans, hate ourselves more than we love ourselves; crawling around on floors on all fours, searching for imaginary pebbles, crazed out of our fuckin' minds. You can always tell a Crack head's house. The window blinds will be bent in the middle, where they've been peeping out all night cracked out of their minds, looking for the Bogeyman, on the other side of the window. Crack heads will hurt you if Crack tells them to. For example, there was a gang of rollers who got high on their own supply. Two blood brothers were the leaders of a vicious street gang. They were so based out of their minds that when one of the brothers held the pipe too long, and didn't pass it fast enough. His brother waiting on the pipe, became agitated and shot his brother in the leg. ("Pass the pipe nigga' boom.") It was a crazy fuckin' time. One could easily get caught up in the conundrum, an inescapable paradox. That is only one illustration of the madness of that time. You can multiple that one incident a thousand-fold, with other incidences of Crack violence in most cities in America. There were just too many Americans caught up in the madness. It not only affected the abusers; but, also their families. It took a toll on the whole of society, and that's the truth, Ruth..

After taking a battery of entrance exams for "Wayne County Community College." I was accepted. Better news followed. I was informed that I had passed the written exam for Building Maintenance for the City of Detroit. All I had to do now was to pass the physical. That included a drug test. I cleaned my act up, and in two weeks I faced my last hurdle to gainful employment. The plan was to start at the bottom, get my credentials in order, while I gained some work experience. Then, when I earned my degree's, I would work my way up through the ranks. That's the epiphany that I envisioned anyway. I passed my physical, and in early August of 1985, I was working on the job. The going was tough from the start. I was assigned to Cobo Hall, as a Laborer.

The first day on the job, I had to unload a half-ton truck load of street barricades, non-stop. I guess they were trying to get the butter from the duck. They worked the dog shit out of me; but, it felt good. I was again using myself in a positive venue. For sixty days, I was on probation. I had to tow the line. After surviving my sixty-day probation period, I was permanently assigned to Frank Murphy's Hall of Justice, as a Maintenance Man, cleaning the municipal building. I worked the afternoon shift. Basically, I helped clean the judge's chambers in the municipal building where Recorder's Court is housed. Hey, it wasn't what I was used to. I figured I had to start somewhere. I was thirty-six years old, and time was of the essence. I had blown a major amount of time and money on non-sense. Some people called my new state of being, growing up. I was playing catch up to squares from my generation, who towed the line and stayed on point. Some were raising families and making a decent living in the square world.

Whistling Bob, once quipped. "There's nothing sadder than an old pimp, driving an old Cadillac, with an old whore at his side." That's why Bob, didn't let the community label him a pimp. He preferred being called a hustler. I had to get busy. When the game gets wind of me squaring up, and my new career path, I'll be black-balled by the game. I didn't give a damn, with images of me in that old Cadillac, with an old whore by my side, as Bob described it, kept me moving in the opposite direction. I wanted nothing more, to do with the game. I had come to realize that the only one being played is the playa,' he plays himself right out of a long, healthy, fruitful, and bountiful life, filled with children and joy. Without the madness and meaness that the game inspires. I got more good news. Wayne County Community College, accepted me as a student. I had to tweak my schedule to pull it off. Here's my itinerary: class's three nights a week, with a full load of twelve credit hours per semester; two class's on Monday, from 10 a.m. to 3 p.m. I had to be at work at 4 p.m.. I attended the Fort Street, downtown campus. I could walk to my job at Frank Murphy's Hall of Justice, with no time to spare on Mondays. I had a class on Wednsday and a class on Thursday. Those class's were also in the morning and afternoon, with the same scenario every day. Things were not all peaches and cream. There were some vexing problems. I was struggling with staying drug-free, during that stretch of my life's path. Regardless, I was determined to succeed. I never missed a day of school or work for two solid years and I'm proud of that.

Slim, had been recently paroled from prison and was living with Beanie, who had retired from Providence Hospital, due to diabetes difficulties. Again, that was a recipe for disaster. Slim, thought that because he had joined the N.A. ("Narcotic's Anonymous"), after being hooked on drugs for nearly two decades, that he was anointed some kind of drug guru. To make a long story short. We clashed big time. Beanie threw me out of the upper flat in the middle of the night: no notice, no court order, just get out. The only thing I took was my pride, school books (So I could study wherever I landed.) and the clothes on my back. I would pick up my other belongings later. To be honest, I really did bring that on myself. I had no one to blame for my predicament, but me. With books in hand, I hit the streets. I had to be in class early the next morning and at work in the evening. I walked once again in search of shelter; same as I did as a fifteen-year-old, several decades earlier. It wasn't winter that time, so there was no snow and ice to endure. Nearing the end of the block, I spotted an old beat up clunker rusting on blocks in the old geezer's yard, who lived in the corner house. The old guy who answered to the name Cabbage Head, often took in most stragglers; sort of like Lyle on the northend. I asked Cabbage Head, if I could sleep in the old car for the night. Cabbage Head, gave me his blessings and I was good for the night. I climbed into the old clunker and did my homework under the glow of the street light shining brightly over-head. I fell asleep with my head resting on two books for pillows; while one book rested on my chest. I was up at the crack of dawn. I wanted to be out of there before anyone I knew, saw me crawling out of the old clunker. I wiped the sleep out of my eyes, dusted myself off, gathered up my books and off I went in search of water to clean myself up. I caught the bus down-town to Wayne County Community College. Then I headed for the mens room where I proceeded to clean myself up a bit. I took what the game called, a "hoe bath," in the sink. Then I went and ate breakfast. It was a few hours before I had to be in class, so I headed to the library for a cat-nap before my class's began. After class I scooted on over to my job at Frank Murphy's Hall of Justice, ten minutes away. I was still in the dark. I didn't have a place to stay, and I hadn't connected with with a ride so that I could retrieve my belongings from Beanie's house. Hell, I surmised if I did pick them up, where was I going to put them? After slumming around for a few weeks I went to my credit union and applied for a loan. I was surprised that they loaned me a few thousand dollars. Once again, I ventured into famil-iar ground and rented a furnished apartment in the Town Apartments. This time, under a different set of circumstances. I managed to stay on track, re-gardless of my housing situation. I did what I had to do without breaking the law, or returning to my old ways. After I slumbered out of the fog, I felt confident about the direction my life was headed. Now, I was tucked away in my tidy furnished apartment. Shortly thereafter, I retrieved my TV and other personal belongings from Beanie's flat. I felt that I was starting a new life. With the money left over from my loan. I purchased a five-year-old Chevy Cavalier. I was on my way to squaresville, with real goals on the horizon.

The Town Apartment, had a huge roof-top-patio, complete with Bar-b-que grills, loungers and a magnificent view of Canada, and the Detroit River. On an occasional weekend, me and some of my friends would grill, con-versate and laugh the night away. One evening a friend of my cousin Micheal, was over. His name is TJ. TJ asked me to take him over to a motel in Highland Park, to rendezvous with a young cutie. I agreed to drive him to the motel. When we got to the motel, we were barely inside the foyer, when we were bum-rushed by about a half-dozen plain clothes, under-cover cops. They were there to bust a Crack dealer, in one of the rooms. Me and TJ, were there for other reasons. The cops grabbed us, and another unfortunate fellow standing in the foyer. The cops marched us down to a room, they had kicked the door open earlier during a drug raid. The problem was, there was no one in the room. That must have pissed the cops off real good. I guess when they saw us, they figured any black bodies would do. Three white cops, and two Negroe cops. I'm sorry; but, that's what they were. Because, Black men, and African-American men, don't help Caucasian men, jump on and assault other Black men, that's some Negro shit. That's just my take on that. The cops had us surrounded in a circle and began threatening us if we didn't fess' up to being the occupants of the raided room. The cops knew it wasn't our room. They just wanted to amuse themselves. We were surrounded by five, carnivorous, pissed-off cops, snorting rage and spewing venom. One of the cops, whom, I would come to understand was of Italian decent, he had on a long duster-type trench coat, and he had straggly, long, dirty-brown hair protruding wildly from under his baseball cap. He was up close and personal in TJ's face, while the other cops looked on in delight racking their weapons in our face. The short, stocky, tough-guy Italian cop began busting TJ, in the chops with his fist while screaming expletives at him. TJ doubled over and blurted. "You got the wrong person." TJ's nose started bleeding. That geeked up the Black cops. They couldn't let the White cop, get all of the glory. One of the Black cops, cupped his hand, Rotation Slim style, and pimp-slapped the cowboy shit out of the brother that they had dragged into the room with us. Then the other Black cop, started smackin' dude up-side his head. These were cops. There was no one there to save us. The other two White cops, turned their attentions to me. One elbowed me in the side. The White cop, eyeballed me intently, and blurted. "If this ain't your room, what do you do for a living?" If I was going to save my ass, that was my cue. I had to think fast on my feet. What came out of my mouth next could determine my fate, and theirs. I blurted. "I'm a student at U of D, and I'm a journalist major. Suddenly the mood changed. We were long-lost friends. The Black cops, started calling us "Cousin." They curtly admitted that they may have been wrong. They told us that we were free to go, no hard feelings. On the way out, TJ whispered to me. "Damn. How in the fuck did you come up with that?" "You've got to think fast on your feet, if you want to compete, that's all I can say T J." A couple of months later I got in touch with TJ, to show him an article in the Detroit Free Press newspaper. The article went on to state that an undercover narcotics officer named, Champanello, was killed after his crew raided a drug house on Mt. Vernon, and Beaubien on the northend. His crew had raided the drug house and arrested its occupants. A small group of undercover cops, stayed behind in the dark den to try and snag some of the drug house customers, who came by to purchase their drugs. A patrol unit with two uniformed cops, pulled up to the raided drug house, unaware that undercover cops, were hiding inside the dark drug den. When they stepped inside to check the raided premise, they were confronted by the undercover cops, hovering in the dark. One of the uniforms was confronted by Champanello. The uniform cop, told reporters and the police brass that, "he saw a shiny object in Champanello's hand, who was in plain clothes." The uniform thought that he was being confronted by bad guys. Both sides of the law, the uniforms and the plain clothes, opened fire on each other while shouting. "POLICE! POLICE!" at each other. The cops were shooting at the cops. When the smoke cleared they realized their mistake, and one of their own was left laying in a puddle of his own blood. Narcotics officer Champanello, was killed by friendly fire from one of his fellow police officers. They just didn't have their logistics and communications coordinated. There was no one else to blame. The bad guys had already been arrested earlier in the raid. The newspaper ran a photo of the slain cop. Officer Champanello, was the same cop who had assaulted TJ, a few months earlier in the motel room in Highland Park. Officer Champanello, was a tough guy; although, he wasn't tougher than a bullet. Isn't it ironic that he lost his 30 plus- year-old life at the hands of the good guys. Other cops. Rest in peace, Officer Champanello. I now realize that Officer Champanello, was only doing his job. I shouldn't have been in a place where drug deals were being made, and that's the truth, Ruth.

In the spring of 1987, I informed my family members that I was graduating from Wayne County Community College. I was getting my associate degree in Psychology, and a minor in Sociology. I also made the Deans list. That was a special day in my life. I've always held to the notion, at least in the back of my mind, that I would deliver my family into the 21st century through education. I was the first and only member of my family, and my mother's sister's family to earn a college degree, and I felt proud. I remember everyone was happy for me. The graduation ceremony was held at Ford Auditorium. The Reverend, Charles Adams, was the Commencement speaker. Reverend, Adams, delivered a rousing and inspirational message, laced with intelligence and insight. His message super-charged my thirst for knowledge. Although, I invited all of my family members, only my cousin, Louise, attended. Hey, I was good with that. I took it all in stride. I still felt in my heart of hearts that I was delivering my family onto the path of education and entitlement. I surmised that it only took us from the beginning of time to achieve that milestone in my family's history. Even though my son, Shannon, hadn't been born yet, I had established a precedence for future generations to follow. I figured at the time if I ever had kids, I'd look hypocritical trying to convince them to achieve a college degree when I didn't have one. Now, I can say I did it, so can you. Kids look to adults for guidance.

The best way to influence your child is to seek greater heights and establish a precedence for one's own legacies. Now, my son can never spurt. Dad you didn't go to college, why should I ? Some fifteen years later my cousin, Louise's daughter, Kim, became the second member of my extended family to graduate from college. At least the ball was rolling in the right direction. The University of Detroit, was recruiting, Wayne County Community College students. Making the Deans list put me on their radar screen. I applied and went through a battery of aptitude tests and entrance exams. I faired well enough to be accepted. Class's were scheduled to start in the fall of 1988. Even though U of D, was an expensive private school, with student loans and other financial incentives, I was on my way. U of D wasn't Wayne County Community College. If you couldn't cut the mustard, and if you couldn't maintain at least a 2.5 average, they couldn't use you. The curriculum was much tougher and the expectation bar was set much higher. I was 37-years-old. It was either shit, or get off the pot. I had my sights set on a degree in Psychology, with a minor in Education. I had about four months to prepare myself for the grueling fall schedule come September, of 1988.

I had three years seniority at my city job as a maintenance worker. With my associate degree tucked away, I embarked on a bachelors degree in Psychology, from U of D. All was not rosy, I was having personality conflicts with my pecan-colored supervisor. For some reason, she went out of her way to make my job harder than it had to be. Every time I turned around she was on my case. The last straw came when she asked me to scrub around the base of toilets with a tooth brush. That was not a part of my job description, and I was the only maintenance employee asked to do that. When she handed me a gleaming, white toothbrush, I thought. "This Lady done lost her mind." I grabbed the toothbrush from her hand; but, I'll be damned if I used it. My employment history with the city was pristine. I felt that she was trying to sabotage my career. I wondered if she knew that I once ran pros, if she did that would make her an ex-pro.' Is she trying to dog me because of my past? I thought all kinds of crazy shit about that situation. The second time she made the request, she put a little base in her voice, with that hand planted firmly on her hip. I was waiting for her

to wag her finger in my face, so that I could break it off. Thankfully, it did-
n't come down to that. I sensed a problem on the horizon and I had to act
on it. I'll be damn if I was going to scrub around anybody's toilet with a
toothbrush.

I went to my union and discussed the possibility of filing a grievance
against my supervisor for harassment. The union decided to have me transferred out of Frank Murphy's Hall of Justice. That was on a Tuesday. When
I reported to work the next day on Wednesday, she was more determined
than ever to make me scrub toilets. I was determined not to scrub toilets.
She was standing at the time clock waiting for me with a fresh toothbrush
dangling from her hand, with that other hand planted on her hip. Again, she
gave me a stern warning. "If you don't comply, I'm going to write you up. If
you don't like it, file a grievance with your union." I thought. "You're a day
late, and a dollar short." It's already filed. In my mind, that wasn't about me
scrubbing. It was about a power play. She was flexing her supervisory muscle against a man. I wasn't the one. In my mind I thought I'll hurt her, then
quit that fuckin' job. The next day she was again waiting by the time clock.
She rolled her eyes at me and kept stepping. I figured, roll your eyes all
you want. But, she ain't kicking no ass. She didn't know that I could have
choked her to death with one hand. That's how mad I was. Just in the nick
of time my union steward came on the floor that I was assigned to, and
handed me my marching orders. I had been transferred to The Water Department, a few blocks away. If I could have, I would have turned a back-
over flip. That was on a Thursday, and my last day to work at Frank Murphy's
was tomorrow, Friday. I was to report to my new position Monday afternoon. I asked my steward not to let my supervisor know. "I'll give her the
paper work myself." He agreed. Needless to say, there was no scrubbing
toilets that night either. Again she was waiting by the time clock at the end
of the shift, just glaring at me. She checked to see if I had complied with
her directive every night at the end of the shift. I thought she must have
discovered that I hadn't scrubbed the toilets. The next day, Friday, would be
my last day of work at the courthouse, I could have taken the day off; but,
I wouldn't have miss that day for nothing. It was my turn to humiliate. I
thought. I've been dealing with pros way tougher than her.

When I reported to work the next day, my last day, I wouldn't have to
risk losing my job over ego shit anymore after tonight. I was feeling brazen
as hell. When I punched in, my supervisor advised me to have that job done
by the end of the shift or she was going to give me three days off. I looked
at her with a friendly "Cat-ate-the Canary grin" and spouted. "I'm so sorry

that I gave you a hard time, please forgive me. I'm going to do a really good job." She looked at me with skepticism and said. "O k, you've been warned." With my transfer papers stuffed in my pocket, I made my way to the time clock at the end of the shift. As usual, my supervisor was standing in front of the time clock, this time with her arms folded, looking grimmer than grim, waiting on me to make my way to the front of the line to punch out. When, I got to the front of the line she started berating me in front of the other employees, trying to make an example out of me. I stared at her intently and let her finish her spill. She finished with. "Be prepared Monday, to get three days off." "I don't think so. I won't be here Monday." She retorted. "Well, I'll see you Tuesday." I replied, with a tinge of sarcasm inflicted in my remarks. "I don't think so, I'm out the dooh, you won't be seeing me no mo." I pulled my transfer papers out of my pocket, flicked them at her, and bellowed. "You've been played, Baby. I've been transferred to higher ground." Then, I got up close and personal and whispered. "You know what you can do with that toothbrush." Then I waltzed down the corridors of "Justus" (Justice), amid cheers and laughter, with my ex-supervisor standing by the time clock with her cheeks turning cherry red. She was so mad that she was shaking in her shoes, as she crumbled my transfer papers in her hand. I thought, one for the good guys, goodbye, Frank Murphy, hello Water Department.

I had another surprise. I was being garnisheed by the Federal Goverment, for back taxe's. Thus, making it impossible for me to maintain any semblance of a flourishing lifestyle. I came up with an alternative lifestyle. I was going to be attending U of D, full time in the fall. I decided to apply for lodging in one of the dormitories at U of D. I figured that I was going to be the oldest student (At forty-years-old.) residing in the dorms. I rationalized that it would only be until I paid the I R S off. Desperate times called for desperate measures. I was a square now and had to play by squares rules. I was accepted in the dorms; but, there was one catch, I would have to have a room mate. My first thought was that I would have to share space with some pimple-faced kid. As fate would have it, I had a class with a young basketball phenom, who was dubbed the best high school basketball player in Texas. His name was Jerry Davis. Jerry was highly recruited by many schools. He chose U of D. Jerry needed a room mate and so did I. Jerry didn't know anyone in Detroit, except the coaches who recruited him, and he needed a friend. Jerry was a long way from home. I showed him and another basketball recruit from Texas, named General Lee, the city, some cultural institutions and the club scene. Jerry was young, black and country, and he was built like a brick shit-house at 6' 5" and 230 pounds, all muscle. His home town was in Waco, Texas. It was a slow city compared to Detroit. Jerry, had his space and I had mine. I knocked off a young cook. She worked in the school's cafeteria, her name was Nicki, and she served me swell. I didn't have to worry about eating. Being the star player's on the basketball team, Jerry and his mellow, big General Lee, from Tyler Texas (Who himself was 6'10"), had all the female students lusting after them. Black, white, and Latino girls wanted some of that Texas beef. They beat Jerry, and Lee, for their beef every chance they got. I thought the two Texans, were running a meat market, without getting paid. The girls used them like they were sex machines. Jerry had three cuties who stood out. One was a well-off, blue-eyed white chick, whose father was a dentist. Her name was Kathy. Then there was the Latino chick, who was dripping with sex appeal, and a black chick whose body was all that and a loli-pop. There was one problem: Jerry, was always broke and borrowing money from me, and most of the time I was broker than him. Between working for the city and paying for my books and class's. I didn't have money to loan him all the time. Plus, I was trying to keep up my payments to the IRS. Jerry, was running girls out of the dorm like it was Grand Central Station, in New York city; but, he wasn't getting a dime for his effort. On top of that he could never finish his homework.

One night, after a long day of class's in the morning and afternoon, then eight hours on my job. I was approaching our dorm room, when one of Jerrys beauties was leaving. As, I was settling into my space, Jerry cracked. "Hey man, can I borrow five dollars?" It was time to have the talk with Jerry. I was hoping that I could leave the game behind me; but, I had to pull little brother's coat. I said. Look Jerry, you got at least six movie stars that love yo' bad ass. Jerry, mumbled. "Movie stars?" I replied. "Yeah, movie stars. Y'all just don't know it. They love yo' bad ass and they want to do for you in the worst way. "If you don't ask, you won't receive." I went further. "When you lay down by yourself, seven women lay down by themselves, you're a precious commodity. Just like all those schools wanted your serv- ices and you chose U of D. They gave you a free scholarship worth thou- sands of dollars. It's the same with women, they like doing things for their man. A lot of square men don't know that. The ones that do get all the gravy, while the square fellows get only the drippings, and most of them have to pay for that in some covert way or another. I love me some sex; but, you can get mo' sex, with mo' dough." Jerry, to say the least was per- plexed. I broke it down for the kid. "You need one of the girls washing your dirty draws, one doing your homewok and one ironing your clothes. That rich blue-eyed angel who's enamored with your black Angus beef, should keep yo' pockets on jam. Just call it a gratuity for sex." That brought a smile to Jerry's face. I said. "Damn, Jerry, I should be asking you for dough." For a hot minute, my mind was transfixed back to the streets. I said. Man, look hear. "All I have is a cook Jerry, you ever see me hungry? Hell, naw." I echoed. Then Jerry said something that made me chuckle, "You think that I could do something like that?" I said. "You big cock-strong baby Bull, if you can talk, you can walk, Baby!" I then said. Matter-of-fact, call Kathy, up right now and tell her to bring you a hot breakfast. Don't ask her, tell her to bring you a hot breakfast and a few dollars in the morning before she goes to class. Kathy, as well as the other girls, lived on campus also. Jerry called her up and sheepishly made his request. I wasn't worried. If it worked, he'll get better... greasing of the palm will do wonders for his confidence.

When morning came, I was up and raring to go to morning class's. As I was leaving, blue eyes was strutting her stuff down the hall toward the room. She had a restaurant-bought breakfast dangling in her hand. She was chewing gum and smiling like a "happy hooker." I knew the look, and I knew who the breakfast was for. That brought a smile to my face as I made my way to class.

When I got off work that night and was heading toward our room, "Black Beauty" was sashaying out of our room; humming and switching her ass with a laundry basket load of Jerry's dirty clothes, draws and all in tow to wash for him. When I stepped into the room. Jerry, gave me a big bear hug and blurted. "Man that shit worked." Then he reached into his pocket and handed me a ten dollar billl. I said. "You only owe me five." He said. "The other five is for giving me what you call the game, man. I can't believe it worked." Jerry, beamingly spouted. "Kathy gave me fifty dollars and I ain't got to pay her back." Then I said. "If she gave you fifty, she'll give you five hundred, try that next time. You done broke luck young blood." He didn't know what that meant. I said. "You'll figure it out." I didn't feel right dumping that sordid madness on the young man. If I told him that breaking luck to a pro' meant turning her first trick of the day is the hardest. Thus, when they turned their first trick, they broke luck. Then, I would have to explain that he broke luck with his first trap, and the rest of the traps would be a piece of cake. Then, I would have to explain what trap meant. Besides, I didn't want to clutter his mind with that distorted lexicon called the game. That's as much game as he was going to get out of me. Jerry asked me, where did I learn that from. I said. "Look Jerry, I'm a little older than you. I've forgotten more than you'll ever know about the game."

I felt in a kind of awful way that I was poisoning a young man's mind and I didn't come to U of D, for that. It just slipped out. I didn't want to spoil the young man's natural progression. I hope, I didn't ignite a fire that leads that young man down the road to damnation. Getting paid by a pro' or square does funny things to a young man's ego, and that's the truth, Ruth.

After two years of gains and set backs in my academic and personal life, I found myself on the verge of obtaining a bachelors degree in Communications. I had to change my major from Psychology, to Communications, due to a scheduling conflict. I would have had to go to night school to obtain the class's I needed to earn a degree in Psychology. I tried to get a shift change from my employer; but, to no avail. Thus, I took what was offered, a bachelor of arts in Communications, with a minor in Psychology. I had one more hurdle before I could graduate. Math was a requirement and Liberal Arts students, had to pass three credit hours in an advanced Math class. I put it off as long as I could. I elected Math as one of my class's at the I Ith hour. The class was Linear Algebra. Math was always my weakest link, that's why I avoided it. Now, I had to pay the piper. Linear Algebra, sounded like a foreign language to me. As the semester waned toward the spring of 1990, the finals came and went. Now, I had too wait to see if I had indeed passed my Math exam. In other words, I had to sweat it out. I needed at least a "D" to pass. I was passing in my other class's, so a "D" wouldn't put me below a 2.5; but, an "F" would. Everything hinged on my Math exam. On the day of reckoning, as I checked the bulletin board for exam results I was stunned, as I stared in disbelief. I passed all my class's, except Math. I was looking into the jaws of a big fat juicy "F" and I panicked. All of the shit that I've been through, and came through with nerves of steel. I got an "F" in my Math class and I almost keeled over. I thought long and hard on it. The painstaking studying over the years, the deadlines I raced to meet, all the essays and term papers I submitted. I've staved off sleep, forging ahead to meet yet another deadline, the research, the endless hours spend in the stacks of libraries, and it came down to a fuckin' "F" in Math, and it was almost more than I could stand. After agonizing over my dilemma. I stood up, dusted myself off, and marched down to my Math professor's office. My Math professor, who happened to be of Arab decent, was a pretty fair and understanding man. After asking him if I could take a make-up exam, he agreed; but, he cautioned that if I didn't do better on the make-up, that was it. I would have to live with whatever, I agreed.

He had to submit final grades at the beginning of the following week, so I had to take the exam at the end of the present week. I felt relief. I was determined not to let that stop me. Well, ladies and gentlemen, I got more than enough. I got a big ole' "C" on the make-up exam, and I owe it all to Jerry's white girl, Kathy. She tutored me in Linear Algebra, and helped make it possible for me to earn a college degree from The University of Detroit, class of 1990. I was 42-years old. I felt like crying; but, I couldn't, I'm not the crying type. It's always been hard for me to cry. In some innate place buried deep in the sub-regions of my mind, to me crying is a sign of weakness, and I would be willing to bet it has much to do with my childhood. When my grandfather died in my mothers arms, the tears flowed easily and heavily.

I informed all of my family members. Again, that was a special day toward my family's plunge into the 21st century. We can now be counted amongst the educated. I had a full-blown college degree. It wasn't all that to some folks; but, to me it was everything. I thought about all the strife and bullshit my ancestors had to endure, scratching out a living in these "United States," so that maybe one of their own could break through and deliver our family into the arenas of education, and I did it! Precedence has been established, we broke luck. My family's history until the end of time, will state that, Arnold Hannon, was the first in his family to graduate from college. With God's love, I won't be the last. There are far greater heights to be achieved. I say go for it. The ideal is to make this a smarter, broader thinking, more caring family.

Everyone showed up for my graduation: Sybil, Evie, Louise, Beanie, Runt, and my girlfriend at the time, Nicki, and her family: her mother, step-father, sister and brother. I appreciated them all. They were very supportive of me. Unfortunately, Slim didn't attend; but, I expected that. When I talked to him about my graduation, he seemed agitated that I would bring it up to him. He didn't value education, so he cared less then a fuck about me graduating from college. His reply was. "Anybody can be an educated fool." I said. "Why don't you try it?" He was staying with Beanie, at the time. He was working, trying to clean up his act. That was good. I thought going to school would only strengthen him in that resolve. He took it personal, then he started attacking my character. "One of the last refuge's of a scoundrel, is patriotism." I would like to amendment that proclamation... and to assault a persons character.

A few months thereafter, Beanie told me that Slim, had enrolled in Wayne County Community College, to prove that any fool could do it.

Well, he didn't last six months in a Community College. So much for "what any fool can do." He found that higher education was no joke, it's work. Graduation day was the proudest day of my life. It all went down at Callahan Hall. The home of the U of D Titans Basketball Team. That was my day and I proudly strutted around my mother's northwest side neighborhood, located across the Avenue, from U of D, in my cap and gown. I strutted for all Crack heads, doubting Thomas's, and those contemplating higher education to see. After walking across the stage and accepting my degree. I found a tear in the corner of my eye. After graduation, Nicki, and I moved into the Town Apartments, in June of 1990, eager to plot my next move in life. It was time to get back to Beanie, who was now a diabetic, about that father thing. At U of D, I had a science class that featured DNA in it's curriculum. I discovered that humans inherit 46 chromosomes, 23 from their mother and 23 from their father. I was in search of the link to my missing 23 chromosomes.

I applied for my Social Security Card when I was thirteen, I had to get my birth certificate. I went down to Herman Kiefer Hospital, where birth records are obtained for the citizens of Detroit. When I got my birth certificate, under "Father," it simply stated "Unknown." I didn't know it then; but, that was the beginning of my half-century quest for the never ending search for self.

Arnold Hannon: Birth Certificate incomplete

Chapter 20

NO SWEET LULLABY'S FOR ME

My quest for a new beginning was stalled. I was now $50,000 in debt, with student loan payments on the horizon. The plan was to go on to law school. I took the LSAT exam ("Law School Aptitude Test.") and passed. Unfortunately, I couldn't afford the high cost associated with becoming a lawyer, and I wasn't getting any younger. I put law school on the back burner, and concentrated on building a career with the City of Detroit, which would prove to be harder than Chinese Math. I didn't realize that there were so many insecure haters in lofty positions, and those were black haters, discriminating against other people who looked like them. Forget about merit and hard work, it was about suckin' up to an ass-hole. It was as if some of our home boys and girls took a page out of the White man's manual on how to discriminate. Some middle managers would promote the guy with the least education and potential, thus eliminating his competition. I suppose you had to work there to understand all of the shenanigans going down. Cronyism and the good, old, Black boy click ruled. One had to eat much humble pie to even play the game. I couldn't go out like that, playing the suck-up game. I didn't bust my ass earning my credentials so that I could kiss somebody's ass with a 9th grade education and a 19th Century mentality. I didn't play the game and my career potential suffered. So be it. I came through it all, with my manhood half-way in tack.

I was also having a tough time with my new mate, Nicki. It just wasn't working. She was much too young and broke for the kid, and our heads were in different places. I had rented the apartment, and everything that didn't belong to the Town Apartments, belonged to me, with the exception of her clothes. I put it to her like this, I said. "Nicki, I think it's time for you to catch up with your crowd." She had all of the symptoms of a Crack

head. She tried to play it off, not realizing that I had been where she was headed. One month after moving in with me, she moved out. Along with her went her contributions. They were a small, light bill here, and a gas bill there. Nothing major; but, still I was going to miss it. I was scrambling to stay afloat. It was going to be tight, until I could turn the corner financially.

Then, the unthinkable happened. A transfer employee from the Waste Water Sewage Plant, whom, was a real nut case, tried to dress me down in the men's locker room in front of other employees. He started flexing on me, trying to garner a reputation off of me. I wasn't buying it. I got the last word in and it was a stinger. Like Smokey Robinson, sang. "The hunter got captured by the game." In our case, the hunter got stung by the game. I can't recall exactly what I stung him with; but, boy did it piss him off, he stormed out of the locker room amid laughter and ridicule from those present. Somebody warned me to watch my back. I replied. "For what? This ain't prison." Black men, have been so firmly indoctrinated into that prison culture that at times, some of my brothers can't distinguish between whether they're locked up or free men. I paid little attention to the warning. I was on my job trying to make a honest living.

I was assigned to the third floor. One must keep in mind that we worked the afternoon shift from 4 p.m. to midnight. The bulk of the department's personnel worked the day shift, so that rendered the building virtually devoid of employees from the day shift. At about 9 p.m. or, so that same evening, that fool from the locker room came storming off the elevator headed straight for me with his fist balled up tight, biting his lower lip looking for a fight. I heard the ding of the elevator. I looked up just in time to prepare myself for his onslaught. Shug, was his name. He came charging at me, throwing hay makers at my head. The fight was on. Me and dude were the only two on the third floor, and we damn near wrecked it, fighting and tussling over desks and chairs. I felt a flash of pain in my right hand. I looked down at his hand. That goon had a knife in his hand. I'm no fool. Fist versus knife was a no-win situation for me. That was my cue to exit stage left, through the stairwell door, then down the stairs. I didn't stop until I reached the first floor exit, where I bolted out of the door and made my way out onto the sidewalk, where I scurried around to the front of the building and entered through the front main entrance door, where I alerted the security guard on duty about what had transpired. The security guard alerted other security personnel while she administered first-aid-to my wound. The security team detained Shug, then sent me and him home pending an investigation. The next day when we reported to work, security was waiting by the time clock. Security informed us that we were given 29-days-off, pending termination. That meant that we were fired until we went before an arbitrator, which on average takes about a year. That also meant that I would have to go without a pay check for up to a year. There were no witnesses, so it will be his word, against my word as to who was guilty. The year was 1990. I had reached the pinnacle of heights, by graduating from college, and the depths of the deep, by getting fired from my city job, all within months of each occurrence. The rent and other bills had to be paid. With no income coming in, I had to get busy with the quickness. With my last pay check, I paid my rent up for a couple of months. I decided to shore up my resume and test the job market, and the power of my degree.

My first inquiry was the Detroit Public Schools, as a substitute teacher. Everything went smoothly. I had the credentials to become a substiute teacher. I passed a battery of tests. That all took several weeks to run its course. I just knew that I was "In like Flynn." I had one last hurdle, an FBI fingerprint check. Well, that little incident in Grand Rapids, with Sonny and Mack, would prove to be my Achilles heel. Even through I beat the rap, it was still on my record. I received the rejection letter from the Detroit Public Schools Personnel Department. The letter went on to state that they were sorry to inform me that my services will not be needed because of a failed FBI screen. I was devastated. I was not expecting that. With a college degree from one of the best, academically-respected schools in Michigan, something that I was involved with two decades earlier and exonerated on, was now rendering my degree toothless; but, I didn't give up. With time running out as fast as my bankroll, I had to come up with something. I came across a job posting from the Wayne County Juvenile Detention, as a Counselor. Once again, I tested for the position. Again I passed another test and I had all my credentials in order. Again, the same results. That thing in Grand Rapids, blocked my career path. Now, I was perplexed and didn't know where to turn. I know, I didn't want to return to the streets. I had several options to keep me afloat for a few more months. I didn't know how much longer things would play out. When you're out there living on the dole, it feels like forever, time just creeps by. Whatever, I was in it for the long haul. I was determined to have my day in court. I cashed in an insurance policy that had a cash value of about $1200. Then I cashed in my annuity with the city. I was technically terminated, so I had that option. I had been on the job about three years and had built up about four grand and some change. It would prove to come in handy. I discovered that my arbitration hearing was a year into the future.

I spotted an ad in one of the local trade papers. "Grants for Public Access Television Programs." I thought about it. My degree was in Communications. I had taken class's in Radio and Television Production, and I had helped produce radio and television programs for classroom projects. I was the perfect candidate. My talents included on-air host, and news anchor for classroom productions. I cut the ad out, then scurried downtown to Public Access Television, and inquired about their ad. I was informed that I needed a resume and a tape of programs that I was involved in, and /or, had helped produce. I had to have been on camera, or was listed in the credits. My credentials were in order. All that was left for me to do now, was to head over to U of D, and pick-up copies of the classroom productions that involved me. At U of D, I had my pick of the litter of programs involving me. I had to fill out some forms and get copies made off of the master tapes, and that's exactly what I did. After gathering and presenting all the necessary materials to the Public Access Television Board. I was approved for ten grand to produce a television program for Public Access Television. I had to produce it from scratch, from the rooter to the tooter. Before I got a dime of the grant money, I began writing and plotting my course as to which direction, I was taking my program. I wanted the program to be entertaining, interactive, and intelligent. That was asking a lot for ten grand; but, that was the premise for my target audience. I came up with a dilly entitled, "What's Bugging You?" A quirky spontaneous, man-on-the street piece.

The premise of the program was to take the camera to the people. I was the on air talent. I needed a camera, and a sound man. Why pay someone else, when I was available for the on-air-talent. Hell, I'll pay myself. I could come in under budget and keep the change, or I could go over budget and pay the difference. Which one do you think I chose? As long as the show was thirty- minutes long. I was good to go. Now, I had to find a camera, and a sound man, with editing skills.

Then, I remembered Hassan, who along with me and a group of other Barden Cablevision interns, trained for "Barden Public Access Station." Barden's produced shows in conjunction with Public Access. Thus, Hassan, would be the perfect candidate. Hassan was a young Black man, of humble means; regardless, he was smart as a whip when it came to the technical side of TV production. I was at least ten years older than Hassan. We worked on several productions together at Barden's Cablevision. That's how we met. Hassan, was the go to guy in the group. When there were production problems, whether it was camera, sound, lighting or editing problems, Hassan was the man. The boy had skills when it came to TV production. I called him up and filled him in on what I had going and emphasized emphatically, how much I needed his help. Hassan eagerly accepted my offer and we were on our way. I lived downtown, so I decided that was our location. We set up our camera and sound equipment on various busy downtown streets, where the foot action was the heaviest. I, with my microphone in hand, and Hassan dutifully manning the camera and sound equipment; we went to work. We had already shot the exteriors of downtown Detroit, from my apartment balcony in The Town Apartment Building. We shot our introduction to the show in Barden's studio. All that was left for us to do now, was to get some interviews in the can. That's what we were doing out on the street. Our premise was to pose the question, "What's Bugging You?" Then wait for a response. Anything that was bugging an indivisual, my show provided a venue where one could air their gripes. Their pet peeves ranged from child support, to divorce court, city goverment, politics and taxes. I even had a few politicians stop to offer their commentary. Homelessness was a major concern. I also had comments from children, whose parents bugged them, and from parents whose children bugged them. It all made for good local television. My theme was giving a voice to the voiceless in our city. We shot a few hours of interviews, then edited it at Barden's Cablevisions editing studio. All of our equipment was on loan from Barden. Thus, leaving the Lions share of the ten grand for me and Hassan. The finished product was a success, and we came in on time with the production.

A month or so after delivering the finished product to Public Access, a friend of mine called me up and told me that I was on television. I turned on the TV, and I'll be damned, there I was, live and in living color. It was my show. The progam ran every night for a month straight on the Public Access Channel. I called Beanie, and everybody else I knew, and told them to turn on channel ten. Beanie, treated it like it was a major event. That made me feel good. I was feeling good, because I finally got some miles out of my degree. It wasn't a total waste. I was 41 and there wasn't much wiggle room for career planning.

I had another vexing problem facing me. Most places weren't hiring 41-year-old ex-pimps, with only a bachelors degree. I had too many young heads to compete with. Even though I was a college-educated man my problems were far from over. After completing, "What's Bugging You?" I still had months to go before my case came up for arbitration. After being rejected for employment for various reasons: not enough experience, too old, that Grand Rapids thing, and other underlying circumstances out of my control. I then turned to something I was familiar with, sales. I applied and was hired by Art Van's Furniture Store, in Livonia, Michigan. Art Van, is a furniture icon in Michican. Mr. Van started his business in the fifties, selling furniture out of his garage. I appreciated the opportunity to make an honest buck during that stretch of my life's journey. I could have easily waned and pressed myself back into the game, that would have changed everything. I might not be here today, writing my memoirs.

With the grant money from Public Access, coupled with the cash from my insurance policy and annuity, plus the wages I made from selling furniture, I had more than enough money to stay afloat. I guess the powers that be thought that I was a quitter and would roll over and starve to death. I had the audacity to thrive.

Eight or nine months later, my day in court was upon me. Me and the other party invovled in the fight, appeared before a Labor Arbitrator regarding the assault that they were calling a fight. I suppose that the city was trying to get two-for-one. They didn't care who was guilty or innocent. During the arbitration proceedings, me and dumb ass were grilled about the particulars of the incident. He gave his version, and I gave mine. What saved my job was the arbitrator himself. During the middle of the proceedings, the arbitrator looked up, took off his glass's, then pointed at Shug, and said. "Don't I know you?" Shug said. "Yes sir. I appeared before you a couple of years ago." Then the arbitrator retorted. "Yeah, you did. I remember now. You came before me for assaulting your supervisor at the Waste Water Treatment Plant. You threw hot coffee in your supervisor's face and I suspended you for a year. You must have just gotten back to work and you're already involved in another altercation." Shug, shrugged his shoulders, then answered. "Yes, sir." The arbitrator went on. "Its no coincidence. I believe that you assaulted Mr. Hannon. Therefore, I'm going to uphold your termination without prejudice from the City of Detroit. Mr. Hannon, I'm going to send you back to work ASAP. Mr. Hannon, you can file for back pay through the unemployment commission." And that's what I did. I received my back pay for the entire 11 or 12 months that I was off. I was exonerated and the city attorneys were pissed. They bulked and protested to no avail.

During the time that I was off, I had a couple of pros approach me about revitalizing my Mack hand. I told them. "No deal and that's for real." One of them couldn't leave well-enough alone. She wanted to know why, didn't I still like money? I told the young, misguided stepper that I still liked money; but, not like that. "Y'all growing up, and I'm slowin' up. Its time for y'all to catch up with y'all's crowd and have a nice life." Fast-lane money was easy come, easy blow. I was ready for my dough to stick and grow. I had to tweak my schedule a bit to keep my job at Art Van's. I was a pretty reliable sales person in terms of closing the deal on my sales. I showed up early and left late as a full-timer. I informed the store manager at Art Van's that I had gotten my old job back with the City of Detroit, and that I may have to leave the furniture business. At the time, I felt that my chances for advancement and the benefits were more favorable with the city job. I worked at the suburban store in Livonia, just outside of Detroit. The store manager asked me to consider part-time employment with reduced hours: four hours on Sunday, and weekdays, and eight hours on Saturday. I needed the loot and I agreed. Working eight hours at my city job and the hours that I agreed to at Art Van's made for a pretty full day. There was no time to socialize.

My love life suffered, until I met a young lady, (We'll just call her Queeny.) at a career-day event at Wayne County Community College, my first alma mater. The young lady, was selling what she called a Medigram. That was in the spring of 1990. Medigrams were the 1990's version of today's Blackberrys. The medigram was a bigger and cruder instrument than today's Blackberry. When Queeny, approached me with her sales pitch, she introduced herself. She was at least ten years younger than me. I liked her spunk and enthusiasm, plus she wasn't bad looking. I didn't buy a Medigram. My reasons were simple: who would I Medigram? No one I knew had one, so I passed. I did ask for her phone number. She declined; but, took mine. She called. We had our little fling, did our little thing and hopefully we produced a little king. I trusted her, their was no DNA test. She named my son after her brother and father. The funny thing about all of that, is that, I had asked her for her hand in marriage to make an honest woman out of her, and to leave my son a legacy. She declined my offer of marriage, and that struck me as strange. I kept my suspicions to myself. She said, that she needed to focus on her career. Yeah, right; I thought, the young woman appears to have ulterior motives regarding our relationship: you can read whatever you want into that refrain. I think I got played. With some squares if you ain't a complete idiot for them, you're flawed. I had to abide by her wishes, she and the courts had me by the balls, what else could I do? I eagerly wanted my son to inherit my surname. Son, if you're reading this, I would have named you, Shannon Hannon. Your mother chose something else. It wasn't much that I could do about that either. She sure didn't mind cashing a check every month with my name and sweat imbrued in it. She used to remark that she was an independent person. Yeah, right, you can't be independent with your hand all the way up to your elbow in somebody else's pocket, based on a premeditated lie. I questioned how much financial support and love had Shannon, received from his grandfather and brother. I dare to say zilch.

As of this writing son, you're 16-years-old and I am faithfully fulfilling my fatherly duties as I was ordered to do by the court. I evenually petitioned for a DNA test. The Friends of the Court and your mother declined my request. Her stone cold silence on the subject spoke volumes. The only thing they allotted me was two-and-a half-days a month of visitations. My protest fell on deaf ears, the court abided to her every demand. What is she trying to hide? "No lie lives forever." It will eventually find its way to the surface. Then, one has to invent another lie to facilitate the first lie. I just hope you don't wake up one day, long after "I am no more" and find out that we had been living a lie. That would be so unfortunate and devious on so many levels. Some women, while plotting to cut a man's throat, at times end up cutting their own child's throat as well, two-for-one. I feel that you are a part of me son; but, I realize that strange things can happen to people with honorable intentions. I haven't missed a day of court-arranged visitations in 16 years. I also volunteered to pay the maximun child support from day one of your birth. I provided gifts and love on your birthdays and holidays; beyond that, it was out of my hands. The courts, didn't even consider my motions for joint custody. They rendered me powerless in the day-to-day interacting with you. Let's not forget, that It was I who initiated child support proceedings, from day one of your birth. You know it was nice for your mother to recognize your grandfather and her brother, by giving you their name. Hell, I helped bring you into this world, where do I fit into the equation? I don't think your grandfather and uncle did without, so that you could have a decent life. Your uncle don't even live in this town, and your grandfather died when you were an infant. I stuck with you until you were able to take the reins of your own life. I love you son. If you should happen to have children of your own, under similar circumstances, perhaps you will understand how difficult the system can make it for fathers of children born out of wedlock. Your uncle, nor did your grandfather give you life. I did, unless there's something I'm not privy to. My fifty-two-year odyssey is over in search of my own biological father, and I came up short. I'm man enough to live with that. I hope you don't have to suffer the same fate. Your mother is the only one who knows for sure. I'm a firm believer that if one sells their soul to the devil for a few pieces of gold, they're capable of anything. At the end of our relationship, I let her think she was fooling me. The only person she was fooling was you son and herself. I believe that sometimes, it's more about hurting someone and greed than doing what's right. Her reasons are exclusively hers. It will always be a mystery to me, as to the why. Regardless, I have accepted it, so long as you can grow up to be a well adjusted human being. There's already too many nut cases running wild in America's streets.

No need of your mother trying to hurt me, I've been numb to hurt feeling since my introduction to this world. Not knowing one's father's name can make one oblivious to emotional trauma. I refuse to let anyone, or anything hurt me again in this life, and that's the cold blooded truth, Ruth.

After me and Queeny, went our separate ways, I met a young, two-fisted tall, drink of water. She was a neighbor in my apartment building named, Ruby McGhee. The Town Apartments had a cozy little bar right off the lobby. I met Ruby, in that little bar. She was sitting off to the side at a table with her girlfriend, sipping on a drink. I noticed her noticing me, sipping on my drink sitting at the bar. I leaned into the bartender, an old-school, Mafia-type, white-haired Italian gentleman, named Dominick. I asked Dominick, to give the ladies whatever they were drinking on me. Dominick obliged my request and delivered the ladies their drink. Dominick came back to the bar and said that the ladies said. "Thank you, and would you like to join them?" I shook my head up and down, yeah. Then, I carted my drink over to their table and introduced myself to them. The ladies introduced themselves to me. The young lady, who lived in my building was the one I had my eye on. She was a tall, long-legged drink of hot chocolate. Her name was Ruby Mcghee, and her friends name was Pauline. After kicking it for a minute, I got Ruby's phone number, then bid the two ladies good night. I had intentions on seeing Miss Mcghee, again. It wasn't long before I saw her on the roof- top patio in our building. She was kicked back enjoying the view of Canada, while sipping on a cool drink, with nary a man in sight. She looked up and smiled at me grilling my dinner on the outdoor grill. I struck up a little conversation. One thing lead to another and before we knew it, we were like old chums in a couple of weeks. We dated often, sometimes on me, sometimes on her. Dating quickly blossomed into romance, which led us to Toledo, Ohio, with her girlfriend Pauline and her husband, Tyrone, in tow to witness our marriage. Ruby worked and had a pretty good janitorial business to boot on the side. Ruby also helped me with my clothing hustle, she was a good catch. I figured that I had a wife with skills, who used her mind, instead of her behind to make a buck. For a few years we were content. Beanie, liked Ruby, and Ruby, liked Beanie. Ruby was a laid-back mild-mannered indivisual, who came into my life when I needed a friend.

Eventually the good times stopped. We liked living downtown. We upgraded our lifestyle by moving into the Trolly Plaza Apartments. Ruby was used to living on the cheap. I rationalized. "Who wants to live cheap?" I convinced her that together we could do great things. (An old pimp line.) The Trolly was nice. I spied the young tenders frolicking in the swimming pool from my seventeenth floor balcony. Ultimately, we fell out. The culprits were the usual set of ills: sex, money, and drugs. I came home from work one day and Ruby was gone. So were our furnishings. The only thing that she left me was a key and a key hole. Once again, I had to scramble to stay afloat. The lease was in both of our names, so I had thirty days to move, and that's what I did. I moved across the street to one of Detroit's ritziest addresses downtown, on Washington Boulevard. The Carlton Apartment Building, had a distinctive, checkerboard, yellow and white facade. It was a taste of Paris, in downtown Detroit. Ruby was gone and I was all alone. I purchased a new sporty, Cadillac Cimmaron, it was a new brand in the Cadillac family at that time. I needed a car, and thought, why not? Then I purchased one.

Fast foward to 1994. Beanie's health was beginning to wane. Diabetes had slowed her down. She asked me to move in with her, to help her with her day-to-day needs, like shopping for groceries and household chores. I told her that I would come over on an, as needed basis, and if the situation got worst I would move in. Within a year, her health took a dip. Her kidneys failed, and she had to be taken to dialysis three days a week for four hours. Then, she had to be picked up, so I moved in with her. I thought maybe I could gently coax her out of information about my dear old dad. Again, I knew it would have to be a delicate dance. I still had visitation privileges with my son every two weeks, though at times, I struggled mightily with his mother, having to haul her ass into court on more than a few occasions to maintain that privilege. I think that my son's mother's only concern was his pimp support check. She put on an act worthy of an Academy

Award. I fell for it, hook, line and sinker. I wanted to believe, bloodlines are important to me. She acted convincingly concerned about me and the kid bonding; but, her actions spoke volumes in that regard. She blocked my attempts for joint custody. I've done my share of pimpin,' but, I never pimped my child. I hope she salted away some of the tens of thousands of dollars I paid in child support away for him when he steps out on his own. I wouldn't bet on it, and that my friends, he can look to the Friends of the Court for blame. Once the money was deducted from my pay check it was out of my hands. Time will tell who the real dead-beat is. This is coming from a guy who not only didn't receive a dime from his own father; but, also has never even seen his picture and I don't know his name. I earned the right to gripe about those court-ordered shakedowns. I would rather have raised the kid myself. If I had received any support help from his mother, I would have had it put in a trust fund. I've been there. I started out in life broke. I would have loved having a nest egg when I turned eighteen; but, what do I know, the courts and the mothers have all the answers on how to rear children. That's why the jails and cemeteries are rife with young bodies. Spending support funds on fake finger nails and shoddy hair weaves, don't equate to child support. This is one man's opinion, and it doesn't apply to all mother's. On a more positive note, the times me and my mother spent with my son are priceless. It allowed Beanie, an opportunity to bond with her grandson when he was over for visitations, that made my mother very happy. In 1995, my mother's son, Slim, moved into the upper flat and it was just a matter of time before I had to go. Some things you just don't have to wait around for the results, you already know what's coming. He came in and shanghaied Beanie's life and tried to do the same with me. No way, Jose. I wasn't buying it.

I was standing in the first floor lobby, hovering around the security guards desk, shooting the breeze with Jeremy, one of the security guards in the main office of the Water Department, where I worked. When out of the corner of my eye, I spied her getting off the elevator. My eyes followed her out to the front entrance, where she scooted into the front seat of the waiting Cadillac. It was lunch time and I figured that some lucky so-and-so had her covered. Regardless, I sure liked what I was seeing. She was a high-yellow-long legged piece of work and I was curious. I knew she was a long-time employee and I found out from my fellow basement dweller, Jay Crocket, another long-time employee, that she worked on the 4th floor. Even though I had ten years seniority, and she appeared younger than me, she had much more seniority than me. I also found that out from

Jay. Every time I saw her, I wanted to do something to try and get her attention. She hardly even noticed me. I figured with me being on the low end of the department's spectrum, that maybe she was out of my range. From time to time, I would see her moving about the building. She even spoke to me on occasion. I thought she was a genuine, nice, friendly young woman who was always smiling, and she walked with a confident heads-up stride. I was apprehensive and to embarrassed by my lowly blue collar job to hit on her. I was now what was titled a Building Operator, responsible for mechanical maintenance on machinery and other skilled maintenance duties. I tested twice for the job before I passed the Civil Service Exam.

I participated in a departmental program dubbed "Cultural Change." It allowed me the opportunity to work in the Comunications Department. With my degree in Comunications and experience in studio production, that was a perfect fit for me. Even though it was a strictly volunteer service and there was no monetary compensation, it gave me an opportunity to show my stuff. I was allowed to take time off of my regular job and get paid, so long as I was working on a production. In my mind, it improved my image by deflecting some of the negative connotations associated with maintenance workers.

No one knew that I had a plan. I was looking at the big picture. I had employees from the department, from the director to maintenance workers, complimenting me on my on-air performances. That made me feel worthy and it boosted my self-esteem. The permanent staff in the Comunications Department, were the supervisors of our projects. Someone in the department recognized my talent and put me out front, as the on-air talent. The Water Department, had its own television production studio, geared toward public relations for the department. That brought the Water Departments, productions into the homes of Detroiters through the Water Department's Public Access Channel, provided by the customer's cable service. I was now working the day shift and interacting with regular hourly employees. There were a lot of good-looking women working at the Water Department. I was determined to get me one, so I had to get busy. Not just anyone; but, someone I could give my all to. As luck would have it, my mechanical maintenance services were needed on the 4th floor.

When I arrived on the scene, the problem was right over the long-legged beauty's desk, a light fixture in need of service. I greeted her with a modest smile. She smiled back. With that, the flirt was on. When I took care of that small problem, I noticed the coffee mug on her desk. It was one of those commemorative, souvenir ceramic cups. It was a Van Gogh. On one side of the cup was Van Gogh's famous painting, Starry Night. On the other side it had one of Van Gogh's self portraits, the one featuring Van Gogh's bandaged ear. That was the perfect ice breaker to get her attention. I always figured that I was half- way home with a woman, if I could get their attention. This was different. This was a shot in the dark. After exiting my ladder, I replied to long legs."All set, you're back in business." Then I remarked. "Nice Van Gogh you got there." She seemed perplexed. Then I pointed at the coffee mug on her desk. She looked at it puzzled, and said. "Oh, is that what it is?" I went on to explain that I was a fan of Van Gogh, one of Europe's greatest artists. She said. "Tell me more." I proceeded to give her an art history lesson on Van Gogh. I took her to school. I told her that he was famous for his raised-brush strokes and vivid colors. Then, I went on to explain that he had cut his ear off in a fit of madness. I pointed to the self-portrait of Van Gogh's image, with his bandaged ear on one side of her cup. I picked the cup up and pointed to the Starry Night, image embossed on the other side of the cup. I went on to explain that the original paintings of those images were auctioned off at Sotheby's in London, for about sixty million dollars. She asked. "What is this Sothebys?" I had her ear and her interest. All I had to do now was to close the deal. I went on to further explain to her that Sotheby's was a world-class auction house in London, recently purchased by the American billionaire, Al Tubman, who happened to be a Michigander. She said. "You know a lot about art don't you?" I said. "Indeed I do." Then, I grabbed my ladder and headed to the elevator to go back to my work area. When I looked back over my shoulder, I saw her holding the cup up to the light examining it with fresh vision. She was smiling. Ding, the elevator had arrived. I got on the elevator and swooned all the way down to the basement. If I'd known squarevile was that nice, I would have visited their sooner.

When I got back down to the basement, I ran into Jay Crockett, who noticed the pep in my step and commented. "Somebody been smiling at you upstairs." Then I broke out in a big, ole,' yeah, grin. I guess it was written all over my face. I told Jay."I just met the woman, I'm going to marry." Jay broke out laughing and said."Who's the lucky lady?" I noticed her name plate on her desk. It said. "Terry Coleman." Jay's eyes bulged as big as Buck Wheat's, leading me to believe that I was on to something.

A couple of weeks went by. I couldn't conjure up the nerve to ask her for a date. One slow work day, me and Jay, were kicking it in the locker room. I spoke to him about my reluctance to ask Terry, for a date. He replied. "Look man, go for it." And that's what I did. I owned a year-old, gold, 1995 Cadillac Eldorado. That time around it was a square's ride. I had nice wheels to pick her up in. I purchased two tickets for the main floor of the Fox Theater, to go see the Whispers, in concert. It was around Christmas time in 1996. All I had to do, was to get her to accept, or I would be sitting next to an empty seat. The concert was in two weeks. I ventured up to her floor, and headed over near her desk. She didn't look up. I whispered so meekly. "Would you like to go see the Whispers?" That she didn't hear me. She looked up and said. "Did you say something?"

Now I was embarrassed. I sheepishly spouted. "Can I have your phone number?" She looked at me, wrote down her number on a slip of paper and handed it to me. The prefix revealed to me that it was an inter-department number. After I called her up, I froze like a popsicle when she answered the phone. I had to let it go, I was at the point of no return. I closed my eyes and said. "I've got two tickets to see the Whispers. It would be my privilege to have you as my guest." She responded. "Can I call you later? Let me have your home phone number." I was staying with Beanie, helping her out. I didn't want the new find to think that I was a mama's boy. I gave her the number anyway. She didn't call that evening.

The next day when I saw her entering the building, I held up two fingers to remind her that I had two tickets. She came over to me and said. "I'm sorry. I don't date where I work." I said dejectedly. "I understand." I skulked all the way down to my work area. It was a major let down. I had a phone call at home that same evening. It was Terry. I said. "So you called to break my heart again." She began by saying. "I'm not into breaking hearts. I just thought it wasn't a good idea to date where I worked. I just wanted to call and personally tell you that." I tried one of Tunie's lines. "Let's start over. I'm Arnold Hannon." She said. "I'm Terry Coleman." Then I said. "I'm single." She said. "I'm single too." I said. "I like poetry." She said. "I like to hear poetry." Then I said. "I still got two tickets and I'll throw in a caveat. If you don't like the show, and /or the company; then dinner's on me. Its a win-win situation for us." She said. "So when is it, and what time are you picking me up?" With a little slickness inflicted in my tone. I said. "I won't be late. I'll see you at eight, Friday night. I hope that's great." Terry laughed and remarked. "Do you speak in rhyme all of the time?" I said. "Sometimes; but, apparently, not as well as you." We laughed some more. I said. "I'll see you Friday." She said. "Yeah, Friday."

I had been pretty celibate during that run in my history. Hopefully,

Terry, will take a liken to me. Friday, she called and said that she would be running late, and that she'll meet me inside of the Fox Theater's Box Office. It was winter and I didn't want my date hovering in the lobby waiting on me too long. Terry brought the gentleman out in me like that. I doubled parked in front of the ticket office, jumped out of my car, then darted into the ticket office and swooped Terry, up right quick. We darted back to my illegally-parked vehicle, and off we went in search of a parking lot. I found a lot, parked my vehicle, grabbed my date's hand and then we scampered across the street, into the warm confines of the Fox Theater.

After buying a round of drinks, we were ushered to our seats, where we fell in love over a love song coming from the Whisper's, decked out on stage. It turned out to be a festive evening, with theater patrons in a mellow mood. Terry and I had a good time and she liked the company.

Back at work it was kind of awkward. I had to find a way to keep the moment fresh, mostly for her. I was already smitten by her regal charm. I thought about how could I get her to respond to me on a more personal level. I wasn't about to hang out in her work area, How can I communicate with her without disturbing her peace? I decided on poetry. I called a couple of days after our concert date and asked her again if she liked poetry? She responded by saying. "If it's good poetry." I responded."Then its good you'll gonna get. I've got some real good poetry just for you." "Let's hear it," she replied. I told her that I had to give it to her so she can read it for herself. I explained further. "If I recited it over the phone you might forget it. If I give it to you in written form, you can read it at your leisure, and if you like it, you can read it over and over again." Terry, said. "if I read it over and over, then it must be good." I said. "I'll run up and lay it on your desk." She ok'd my request and that's what I did. I placed the poem on her desk, it was a beauty I was fond of, written by the well-versed poet, Edwin Markham. The poem stated. "You drew a circle that left me out, heretic rebel a thing to flout, but love and I had the wit to win: we drew a circle that let you in." I was anxious to get her response.

The next night Terry, called me at home and said. "You were right. I read it over and over. Just like you said." Then she said. "It was really nice, was it something you composed?" I told her. "I can't tell a lie. Its from the pen of a gentleman poet named, Edwin Markham, who was dead long before I was born." With a gentle laugh she remarked. "That's ok. I still couldn't resist it." I told her. "Thanks for accepting my gift of words, that express my sentiments for you." I felt in my heart of hearts that me and Terry, were making a connection. It was like we were plugged into the same energy source. I've been in love before, mainly with myself, or when some material gains were invovled: automobiles, jewelry, clothes, and an occasional girlfriend; but, never with a woman, like Terry. Whatever good comes of this will be the icing on the cake, with a cherry on top. Before we hung up, I asked, Terry, would she like to play a game with me? Curiously she asked. "What kind of game?" I said. "The poetry game. You present a poem a day to me, and I present one to you each day. See if you can out-verse me, the winner gets a sweetheart kiss." Terry spouted. "You're a slick one aren't you, Mr. man." Then we laughed. Yeah, laughter is contagious. She agreed and I gleefully stated. "I want my poem Monday." That was on a Friday. I had all weekend to hook up a poem. We bid each other good night. Boy, it's nice being in love. I felt like chewing some gum and strutting like a "happy hooker."

Beanie's health was beginning to deteriorate and she became more and more dependent on me and Slim, who was still living in her upper flat. In a pensive moment of privacy on a Sunday, evening, me and Beanie, were having dinner and casually conversating about nothing in particular. Then I changed the subject. I said. "I've been thinking about that father thing," as gently as I could. I didn't want to rattle her cage. I just wanted to shake the family tree and see what falls out. Beanie, spoke politely. "Arnold, now's not the time." I finished my meal and quietly said. "Maybe tomorrow?" Beanie nodded her head and continued eating her meal in icy silence. I sat there in thought. Was it really that bad, my being born? At times, I would catch my mother staring at me, searching for something much deeper than my face.

After a good night's sleep I grabbed my "Great American Poetry Book" and searched for the perfect poem. It became a challenge trying to communicate with Terry, at work without disturbing the natural order of her department, and without bringing attention to our little fling. I've always believed that the best way to handle my business, is to keep others out of my business. The Water Department, was like a small town. News traveled fast in that huge municipality called the Water Department. After perusing my poetry book, I picked out a little verse. At the last minute I changed my mind. I wanted to give her something simple and from my heart. I didn't want it to be too heavy, but, rather something smooth and fun, so I came up with this little original diddy from my pen. "My feet are fleet, as I run through the street. It's you my love I'm running to greet."

Monday afternoon we exchanged poems, she handed me a poem by Robert Frost, "The Road Less Traveled," and I handed her my little original, "My Feet are Fleet." We were off to a good start. I had her thinking about me and that was good. I'm three-quarters of the way up the mountain of love and friendship. Those were shared, invaluble moments, and my friends, in my mind that's what happiness is: fleeting moments of glory; like a scorched blistered hand with cool water pouring through it's fingers. When the flow of the cool water stops, the happiness ends.

Our little fling started with the simple and sublime. Then we ventured into the heavy rhyme. I had the advantage over Terry. I had the telephone-thick book of "The Great American Poems," with over two thousand poems, covering all facets of poetry on loving, living, giving and forgiving; just to name a few of the book's topics. Sorry, Terry. I was out to capture your heart, and I did. You had captured mine from the start. The nights I spent with you in my arms are so sacred that I dare not share. Terry, and I became engaged. It was time for me to bid Beanie's house goodbye.

I promised her that I would call her every day, and that I would do her grocery shopping for her every Sunday. That made Beanie, sad and my brother happy. She was now under his control. I told her this is 1996 and I wasn't getting any younger. So I had to follow my heart. I moved my belongings, including my big screen TV and art collection into Terry's downtown apartment, on East Lafayette. I presented her with a wedding ring on New Year's Day of 1997.

We went on to get married in June, of the same year in sunny Las Vegas, Nevada. We chose Vegas, because we needed a vacation, and we could have our honeymoon, all neatly wrapped in one package...three for one, marriage, vacation, honeymoon. Our wedding party consisted of a small contingent of friends; three couples. The date was June 28th 1997. Mike Tyson, and Evander Holyfield, duked it out that same night at Ceasar's Palace. At Metro Airport, there were a lot of fight fans flying to Vegas, for the big heavyweight bout between the two champions. I didn't like flying. If it wasn't a special occasion, no way was I flying. I had to ride in some pretty creeky aircrafts in the millitary, including helicopters. Flying always made me nervous and I vowed to stay land-locked. Now I had no choice. Terry, was looking forward to us flying and making the trip together.

Thirty thousand feet in the air with a plane load of revelers headed to Vegas, there was a festive air of anticipation on the Northwest Airlines flight; until we heard a loud pop coming from one of the wing's engines.

Suddenly, the festive air of anticipation turned graveyard silent; not a word was uttered. The pilot's voice came over the intercom with news that left many on the plane praying out loud. The pilot's calm voice replied. "We are experiencing engine problems with one of our engines. Everything is under control. We're going to land at the nearby Minneapolis Airport." The pilot sounded quite reassuring but, it didn't do my nerves much good. I sat in stone cold silence, contemplating my descent into eternity, as I absorbed the nervous chatter going on around me. I looked over at Terry, sitting next to me and she was cool as a cucumber, which made me relax, as I gulped down my vodka and tonic on the rocks. If I'm going to die, I'm going to die high, with the woman I professed to love sitting beside me, ready to take on eternity together. It was not to be. We landed in Minnesota without another hitch. We had to wait on a replacement flight. That ended up being a ten hour ordeal. In Minnesota, it weighted heavily on my mind to hop on a train or bus as some of the other passengers did to finish their jaunt to Vegas. Terry convinced me otherwise.

Some sixteen hours after leaving Metro Airport, located on the outskirts of Detroit, we landed in Las Vegas. Because of the plane's delay, there was another five-hour wait to get our reserved rooms at the Rio Suedes Hotel. That was my first visit to that glitzy desert oasis, carved out in the middle of nowhere. It was a hot, humid night when we landed. It will be a week of fun, loving, and connecting. To get married in Las Vegas, all one had to do was apply for a marriage license at the Clark County Court House, then find a wedding chapel, and that's what we did. We settled on The Little Wedding Chapel, In The Desert, the same wedding chapel where Elvis Pressly, got married. That was a big deal to me. I am a big Pressly fan. On our wedding day, my bride looked beautiful in an ivory chiffon and lace wedding dress, adorned with pearls. I sported a lavender gabardine suit, accessorized with a white, french-cuffed shirt, and white tie. We looked good enough, well, to get married, and that's what we did. We rented a limo' to deliver us to the church on time. At The Little Wedding Chapel, we exchanged our wedding vows, amid the nervous stares of other couples waiting to get married. When we came to the final statement. "You may kiss the bride." We embraced with the passion and closeness of Siamese twins. We were firmly embraced...spiritually and physically. After the ceremony we rushed out into the warm glow of the evening sun smiling down brightly on us. Then, we collapsed our bodies into the cozy confines of the back seat of the waiting white limo,' lovingly embracing each other, to enjoy the spoils of Las Vegas, for three more days. Our flight home was unevenful. I now had a loving wife and a new lease on life. Once home we settled into our marriage, plotting our course for the future along the way.

Terry was making more money than me. Neither one of us had a problem with that, like some insecure men. To help keep our budget balanced, I revisited my clothing hustle; but, with a different spend on it. I sold to my fellow Water Department employees. I would take their orders for designer garments, jewelry and purses, and on occasion designer shoes. I filled the orders as I went; thus, cutting down on excess inventory. I mainly sold on credit, collecting my ends on pay day. Every pay day, I was knockin' off seven, or eight-hundred bucks a week, coupled with my paycheck: Terry, didn't make more than me for long. I was surprised how smoothly my little sideline hustle went. I didn't have to worry about my easy-to-corrupt supervisors. I threw them a bone every now and then, and they were good to go, on the cheap. My main supervisor was a short, ("He was so short he had to tip-toe to put his hat on.") Nepolionic complexed God, fearing (According to him.) insecure S.O.B.. Every now and then I would take J.L. my supervisor to lunch, throw him a shirt or a pair of pants to look the other way. I don't think he considered God, in that equation. He needed a friend and I needed an accomplice, so it worked out well for both of us.

Terry, had started going back to college at night at U of D, in 1999, to earn her a degree in business. I purchased a new Jaguar. That's when the haters started sharpening their fangs, grappling over how I could afford a Jag. I let them grapple, while I kept on riding. I had been down that road before, so I could handle the haters.

Over the years, there were more vacations, more art purchased, and more nights on the town in fine restaurants. We were living a good life. My wife, Terry, never had children, and I questioned her about that. She stated that it was never quite the right time and she didn't want to bring children into the world with the partners that she had in her younger years. She said, something that made me feel appreciated. She said. "If I had met you twenty years earlier, I would have had a boat load of kids." I thought to myself, I don't think so. Twenty years ago I would have made a lousy father. I kept that little tidbit to myself.

In the year 2000, every Sunday, like clockwork, I arrived at Beanie's to do her grocery shopping. Her health had begun to deteriorate more and more, and she needed our help more than ever. With Slim, living in her upper flat, he handled the day-to-day running of her house, and paid all of her bills for her with her income from Social Security, and equalty loans on her house. That was ok by me. I was nobody's charity case, I knew what was going down and there wasn't much that I could do about it. When your sick mother cuts you out of her affairs, ain't much you can do; but, accept it.

I remember Ruben Hurricane Carter, the ex-boxing champ commenting on spending twenty-years in prison for a crime he was later exonerated on. A reporter asked Carter, if he was bitter? Carter, stated in a gentlemanly manner. "Bitterness only corrupts the vessel that carries it." I took my cue from Carter. I was not going to let that foolishness corrupt my vessel. I remember a song Beanie used to sing around our house. "Mama may have, papa may have. God, bless the child that has his own." I can thank God, that I always had my own, no matter how large or small, it was mind.

The only people who can break a man's heart (From my perspective.) are his parents, his children and his wife. I wasn't going to allow any more of that, no matter who the antagonists are. My goal in my life is to exit this great planet with as less added strife as possible, and to inflict as less strife on others as possible. That's the truth, Ruth.

My brother, Runt, went on a gallivant, following his ex-girlfriend, Gloria, and their three children to Florida, when they were evicted from their northwest side flat. Gloria and the kids were gone a couple of weeks, before Runt decided to hop on a plane with a one-way ticket to Florida, in search of his children. Word filtered back to Beanie, that Runt had finally caught up with his family. That was in 1992.

Soon after he reunited with Gloria and the kids; he quickly fell out of favor with Gloria again. She left him again. This time, she settled in Ohio, and left Runt in Florida, strung out on Crack. Runt reminded me of Wig, in a way. Life seems determined to beat some folks down, and they just can't get up. Runt, had bitten off more of the substance abuse pie than he could chew. He knows his family members phone numbers in Detroit. Runt was a transient in Florida, and hard to get in touch with. Beanie had an old phone number of his, and that was it. A few years later word filtered back to Beanie, that he was living on the streets of Florida, as a cold-blooded, Crack head. I prayed that was not the case.

In Febuary of 2000, Beanie was a very sick woman. She called me one bitter cold night with some bad news. She was crying...right away I thought about Runt. She called Runt by his real name, Eugene. She said. "I just got a phone call from a woman in Florida, who said that Eugene was found dead in an abandoned building." He had Beanie's phone number in his pocket. That hurled Beanie into melt-down: the fears, the tears. Now, we had to plan a course of action on how to get Runt's body back to Detroit, and then, plan his funeral. That was a bad time for my mother and her family. Slim, was out of town and Beanie, was at home alone.

I went over to Beanie's house and spent the night. I fell asleep in the small spare bedroom; thinking about my brother, laying dead in some dive far away from home. I couldn't hold back the tears; as I laid alone in the dark room. I was up early the next morning. I had to be at work at 8 a.m., Beanie was awake. She had been laying in bed all night wide awake, unable to sleep. I fixed her breakfast, then headed out into the morning darkness. There was a heavy snow storm, and I wasn't in the mood to work that day, so I went home and called in sick. I decided to call the one number in my phone book where Runt, at times laid his head. I was trying to snag some definitive information about him. Beanie, had called that same number earlier with no luck when she got the bad news. We also called, The Dade County Coroner, The Dade County Police Department, and a homeless shelter that he frequented between jaunts at his girlfriend's house. I called the number in my phone book, and behold to my surprise she answered the phone. I told her of our concerns back in Detroit, about the news of Runt, being found dead in an abandoned building. Before I could say another word, she said. "Wait a minute." Then I heard her say. "Gene wake up it's your brother in Detroit." A sleepy, Runt, got on the phone and said. "What's up?" I said, with much emotion inflected in my voice. "Man, why don't you call sometimes, or something? I explained. Some broad called Beanie, and told her that you were found dead in an abandoned building." He was woke now. The news jolted him out of his sleep. He said. "I ain't dead. I know who did that. It was my girlfriend's daugther. I know it was her. She don't like me, and I don't like her. She don't want me with her mother. Wait until I see that bitch." I informed him that Beanie, was a very sick woman and didn't need that kind of drama. I demanded him to call his mother, I told him, regardless of his problems, he should stay in touch with his family. He apologized and said. "I'll call Beanie." Before I hung up, I barked. "Do it now." I quickly called Beanie, and told her that, Runt, wasn't dead, and that I had just finished talking to him. Before I could finish explaining to her, the phone's "Call-waiting" beeped. I said. "That's Runt calling you. I'll talk to you later." With that settled, I went about my day feeling relieved that my brother was still amongst the living.

A month or so later, me and my wife ventured over to Beanie's house on a Sunday, evening. I had called her earlier to remind her to get her grocery list ready, because I was on my way. She didn't answer the phone. I knew that she was at home. When we arrived at her house, I let us in with my key. When we entered Beanie's bedroom, she was sitting on her bed half-naked, disoriented and babbling out of her mind. On the dresser next to her bed sat a large strawberry milkshake, almost empty of its contents. Beanie, was a diabetic, I wondered why a milkshake on her night stand, nearly devoid of its contents? Someone had to have given it to her. She couldn't walk, so she definitely couldn't go out and buy it herself. There was no one in the house upstairs or downstairs but her, it was eerily quiet, and it had been that way for hours. I immediately called 911 and ordered an Emergency Medical Service vehicle. When EMS arrived they checked her vitals and took her blood sugar count. Her blood sugar count was off the charts. One EMS technician commented. "Who had the milkshake?" I replied. "Apparently my mother did." Then the female technician said. "If she's diabetic and drank all of that, then she's playing with her life." One of the technicians handed me Beanie's purse laying on her bed, then she asked me to pull her medical card out. They were taking her to the hospital. I decided to take her purse. They dressed her, then rushed her to Sinai Hospital. I followed them in my car.

At the hospital, I sat in the waiting room for at least eight hours; while they tried to stabilize her. Seven hours after Beanie, entered the hospital, her youngest son, Slim, came barging in the waiting room like an uncivilizied maniac. He didn't ask how she was doing. He started demanding her purse. That was the only thing that he was concerned about. I told him to go fuck himself, and that I wasn't giving him shit. Then it got real ugly. He was like a maniac, screaming and cursing like the idiot that he is. "Uncivilized" wouldn't begin to describe that oaf's behavior; while Beanie, lay in the back fighting for her life. I told that degenerate mother scratchier about the milkshake and left it alone. Like always, the last refuge of that scondrel, and bully is to attack my character, then he threatened to shoot me. That only intensified my rage. If the security guard hadn't intervened, one of us would have needed the emergency room service. The security guard ushered both of us out into the night. He was spewing hatred and bodily harm to-ward me, and me, the same toward him. The only tangible connection I had toward him was that we shared the same mother. Of all the bastards I could have had for kin folk, I got him.

After a couple of days in the hospital, Beanie, came around and her youngest son Slim, worked his evil magic on her, poisoning her mind toward me. It was ok by me. I didn't expect anything less from him. A day or so later, Beanie, called me up and asked me why did I take her purse? She did-n't even remember what had happened to her; just some bullshit her loath-some son filled her weakening mind with. I told Beanie, that I had her purse with all of her contents intact. "You can get it anytime you want it. I was holding it for safe-keeping. Hell, I am your son." I didn't blame my mother. I knew who was behind all of that. She said. "I'll send Slim, over to pick it up." I told her that she can send somebody else to pick it up, because he wasn't welcome in my house. I figured that if I didn't see that "Rascal" again in my life, it would be a blessing. Beanie, sent my cousin Evie. When Evie ar-rived. I told her to tell Beanie, that if she needed my help again, I hope I'm allowed to help her, and I'll talk to her later. I saved my mother's life on that Sunday, evening. If I had stayed home that day, my mother would have died. I didn't want her purse. I was not a charity case. I was trying to be a good son. I vowed, then and there that I loved my mother; but, if I didn't see her son's face again, it would be a wonderful blessing for me. If I should perish from this good earth before him. May God, bless his soul. That's the truth, Ruth. I still called Beanie, everyday and continued to do her grocery shop-ping for her. I tried to avoid her son at all cost.

My mother's health began to wane in the following months. In April, of 2001, with her sixty-eighth birthday approaching, she called me up, with a weak voice she said. "Arnold, come on over son. We got to talk." Beanie never called me son like that before. Finally, I thought, fifty-two years after my birth, I may be on the verge of learning the identity of my biological fa-ther. I couldn't get there fast enough as I hurriedly dressed. When I ar-rived, I let myself in with my key; then, I headed to my mother's bedroom, where she lay motionless. I stood over her, looking down at her. She said. "Pull a chair up, Arnold." I pulled up a chair next to her bed. There was a long pause, then she placed her closed hand in mine. I opened her hand and held her fingers. I leaned in as close as I could. I intended to savor every utterance that passed through her trimbling lips. Her first words, were words that she'd never used on me. She said. "Son, I love you." It didn't reg-ister at that moment. It took a minute for that realization to come to me. When it came to me, I felt a flush of gratitude come over me. With tear-stained cheeks, I too said, two things to my mother that she had never heard me utter before. I said. "Mama, I love you too and I want you to get better." I had never called her "mama" and I had never told her "I love you." I guess it was learned behavior on my part. After all, I had never heard her use those "I love you" words on me. You know what, it felt good. It released a lot of bad air from my heart. Then the mood turned seriously, serious. With buckets of tears streaming down her face, with her eyes tightly shut, she said. "Arnold, I didn't know this father thing would haunt you this long. You're smarter than I thought you would be. I prayed that you would just forget about it." Then she went on to explain that when she was fourteen years old, a couple of weeks shy of her fifteenth birthday, on a warm spring morning, she was taking a short cut to Garfield Jr. High School, to her eighth grade class. She went on to say that she didn't make it to school that day in 1948, because she was approached by five young thugs. She called them men. I called them thugs. Anyway, they accosted my future mother, dragged her into an abandoned building, and brutally rapped her...all five of those cold-blooded urchins. They left my future mother, to stew in their body fluids. They scampered away like crazed Jackals. They scarred her for life. Amid, the grime and debris, she picked herself up and cried all the way home to her angry father. Beanie's mother died when Beanie, was thirteen. She had only her father, James, to turn to for comfort. James, I was told was beyond angry. The Hannon, family was shamed by that act. They dared not reveal the particulars of the act. They just kept quiet about it, hoping it would just go away with time. They didn't want negative aspersions cast upon our family, by judgmental neighbors.

It wasn't long before Beanie, dropped out of school. She was pregnant with me, her first child, father unknown. There were no DNA tests back in 1948. I applied for my Social Security Card, when I was thirteen years-old. I had to get my birth certificate. I went down to Herman Kiefer Hospital, where birth records are obtained for the citizens of Detroit. When I got my birth certificate, under "Father," it simply stated "Unknown." I didn't know it then; but, that was the beginning of my half-century quest for the never-ending search for self. I remember back in elementry school, Jr. high, even high school and college, and on millitary forms as well; I would always come to the space reserved for "Father." I would always just write "none." It was no secret, I was a bastard. As I see it, all living things are re-cycled sperm. Passed down from one generation to the next generation. I will be until the day that I die, curious about my sperm donor, Its my DNA makeup. I can't change that, regardless of how it came to be.

My mother's only hope was an education. She was pregnant with me and couldn't complete her education. Is God, punishing me to punish the rapists? Now that it has been dropped in my lap, its difficult for me to fathom, because I wasn't around. I'm just the effect of the cause, a chain of actions set into motion long before I came to be. If I had, had an inkling that my conception would scar Beanie for life, I wouldn't have swimmed so fast to fertilize her egg. Out of the millions of sperm cells competing for my mother's egg. I rung the bell. I have many regrets in life; but, being alive isn't one of them. If God, didn't want me to make it, he would have slowed me down and I would have lost the sperm race.

My mother was laying there now sobbing uncontrollably. It was like she was reliving that nightmare. It was as if she was washing away decades of pent up pain. She was truly the victim in this real life tragedy. At that moment all I could do was hang my head in shame, for questioning her and for being born. I felt so hapless. I didn't know what to say or do. I put my head on my mother's bosom, and cried like a baby in my mother's arms. She assured me that everything would be all right, and that it wasn't my fault. I finally understood my mother's bias toward me. Every time she cast her gazes upon my face, it must have been a harsh reminder of a time that was unkind to her. I thought about how hard it must have been for her to come to grips with what had happened to her, with me there as a steady reminder. As my head rested near hers, I thought that she could have adopted me out; but, she didn't. That showed me the character of my mother.

The Subconscious mind knows all. It keeps a detailed ledger of all events in our lives. It took me back to my first day of school. I saw my mother dressing me in my kindergarten finery, clutching my hand as she lead me into my first day of school. Some moments in an individual's life are so private and personal that there's no room for others, just mother and child. That was one of those moments for me and Beanie. No mortal in this freaking world can undue it. Then, I thought about how much she must have cared for me, by never uttering a hateful thing regarding that cruel act; not a hint of the tragedy bestowed upon her as a very young girl. As day turned to night, the tears continued. I had a half-century of questions. "Why didn't you have the bastards arrested? Why didn't you have an abortion?"

As I rattled off my list of whys, I looked up and noticed my mother had cried herself to sleep. I kissed her on her cheek, then checked her house to make sure everything was locked and secure, then I went out, got into my car and cried all the way home. I muttered to myself. "Damn, five nigga's raped my mother and one of those bastards is my sperm donor." I'm so thankful that my mother spared me from years of agonizing grief. At that moment I wanted to kill all five of those sons of bitches. Reality seeped in, they were old and feeble, or probably dead now. Then, I realized that act was my only ticket into this world and I cried some more. The irony of it all, the perplexities of trying to figure it all out left me numb. I was plunging into meltdown, grinning like a maniac. So boys and girls, ladies and gents. "Be careful about what you wish for, because your wish may be granted." There were. "No Sweet Lullaby's For Me." And that's the truth, Ruth.

A month later without my input or knowledge, or any other family member's consent, my mother's son took over her affairs, then stuck her in a stinking run-down nursing home on Fenkell Avenue, in northwest Detroit. When I visited her there she was babbling out of her mind. I was powerless to step in. I had checked out a few Hospices, in the Metro Detroit, area and if consulted, I would have done all that I could to get her in a Hospice; but, it was out of my hands. I was a "day late and a dollar short." I tried not to run into her son. I did my best to avoid him; but, to no avail. I ran into him a couple of times. He was leaving when I was coming, or coming when I was leaving. Beanie didn't recognize anyone. She babbled out of her head, and it broke my heart to see my mother like that. She had always been a strong, vibrant person. My mother suffered with a multitude of medical problems, including Alzheimer's disease.

On June 6th 2001, at 4 a.m. it was raining cats and dogs outside. The ringing telephone jarred me out of my sleep. I knew from experience that a phone call at that time of morning can never be good news. I braced myself as I timidly answered the phone. It was a doctor at Sinai Hospital. He told me that my mother was gravely ill and that I better get down to the hospital ASAP. I hurriedly dressed, then, I rushed out into the pouring rain, jumped into my car, then hit the freeway; sloughing all the way in the most wicked rainstorm. When I entered the empty waiting room, I was greeted by a doctor and a nurse. The White doctor said that he was sorry. Then he delivered the knockout punch. "Your mother has passed. We did all that we could do to save her." The doctor then pointed to a set of big double doors and stated. "You can go through there to be with your mother." I walked to the doors and broke down. I couldn't go in. I didn't want to see my mother's lifeless body. I wanted to remember her alive and vibrant. I turned from the doors, then I headed to the nearest pay phone and called my cousin, Sybil, who was close to Beanie, and whimpered, "Beanie's gone." Sybil said. "Don't worry. I'll let everybody know." I said. "Thank you." Than, I hung up the phone. I turned to the doctor and nurse and thanked them. I walked out into the subsiding rainstorm, entered my car, then I took the long route home. For the first time in my life, I was living in a world where my mother no longer resided. The ride home was surreal. It was almost like driving in a dream.

The confluence of events leading up to her funeral were another whole story. It was nasty and bizarre, how my mother's son, Shanghaied, her funeral and the probate proceedings. First, he gave her the cheapest funeral imaginable. Again, without any consultation from anyone related to my mother, with more than enough of her own funds to give her a decent funeral, he chose the Pope Funeral Home, which went on to make the evening news shortly after Beanie's funeral, for leaving a dead body and cremated ashes in their vacant, abandoned funeral home. To this day, I don't know where my mother's cremated remains are. As far as I'm concerned, they could have been scattered amongst the debris, left behind in the abandoned funeral home. There are a hell of a lot of things to write about all of that: but, I think it's best to leave it alone. "Goodbye, Beanie Mae. I know I have a friend in heaven." I settled my rights away to most of my mother's possessions and assets in probate court. Hell, most of the community assets had been pilfered and plundered anyway. At that point, I would have done anything not to see her son's face again in this life time.

I ran into an old friend, who relayed to me that, Penny, had died of an overdose in her grandmother's basement. She wasn't even forty yet. Even though I hadn't seen Penny in many years, I still felt bad about her demise. "God, bless you Penny." I also heard that, Sonny Jackson, Mack, Mckinny's main man, was doing life in prison for murder, that was in the late 1990's. Even when he wasn't locked up, the world lost Sonny, eons ago.

When I look back on some of the events in my own life. I have much to ask God, to forgive me for, and to forgive me (at times), for feeling sorry for being born. When that happens, I think about an ex-judge in Detroit's Recorders Court, who I found myself standing before in my late teens, for sentencing on a minor charge. He had mercy on me and sentenced me to probation. His name was James Del Rio. He was also a State Representative, during his illustrious career, before becoming a judge. Soon after sentencing me, I read an article about Judge Del Rio. The article stated, that Judge Del Rio, entered this world in a bind himself. He was found abandoned as an infant and put up for adoption. He managed to succeed regardless of the curcumstances surrounding his introduction into the world. Judge Del Rio, will always be an inspiration to me. When I'm having one of my, why me moments, I think about Judge Del Rio. Like I stated early on, no matter how deep the hole one finds his or herself in, there's always someone in a deeper hole.

In 2004, me and my loving wife, Terry, purchased our first home together. After searching for a solid year, the last condo our agent showed us was a keeper. When we stepped inside, we immediately knew the search was over. It is a beautiful condo that was once owned by the first, Black Judge, in Michigan. Judge Alvin Davenport, who died in the 1980's. I also inherited portions of Judge Davenport's world class rose garden, that has been blooming every year since the 1960's. I am now an avid gardener. I am no longer just a writer. After my memoirs were published. I'm now officially a writer/author. Writing my memoirs has truly been a labor of love. Finishing my memoirs, feels as though I have lifted a mighty burden off of my heart. I can go on with the rest of my life, with peace in my heart. I may not ever know my father's face or his name; but, I'm not in prison or dead; nor am I a bum, like many had predicted. I'm not as accomplished as, Judge Del Rio, and Judge Davenport; but, I do have a lovely home and flower garden, a beautiful and loyal wife, and an art collection that I'm proud of, and I must say. I do enjoy my new black cherry, Cadillac. I've written my memoirs, and I am now embarking on writing a novel. My sanity remains intact and I've discovered humanity, forgiveness, peace and closure; along with a dash of humility. Yes, I'm also stuck in my persnickety ways, absorbing life one breath at a time, moving placidly, taking my time to enjoy every wakening moment. The greatest gift that God, has allotted me, other than life itself. Is that God, has allowed me, Arnold, to live long enough, as a free Black man, in these United States of America, to unravel and understand some of the mysteries surrounding my existence. That's good enough for this po' boy, conceived from the loins of a rapist. In the overall scheme of things regarding my anonymous 23 chromesomes. I guess that one can say that, the ex-player, got played, by the game of life. Straight up! That's the cold, blooded, naked truth, Ruth.

The Cold Blooded Bitter End.

7-22-2007

Poems from the pen of Arnold Hannon The 1st

Bloodless   July 15, 1999

There seems to be a need for others to see me bleed would it make their own life a better read, might this be the catalyst that helps them succeed dance on ladies and gents and have one on me. A life that is bloodless and fancy free.

My Love   July 15, 1999

My feet are fleet as I run through the street, it is only because it's you my love I'm running to meet.

Today   July 15, 1999

Today, Today, today rushes in another day and all my tomorrow's are made this way. One sunrise at a time, ready or not I must rise and shine, if I stay this course tomorrow is mine.

Be OK   July 17, 1999

The plane went down with a deafening roar silencing a righteous voice forever more. Family and friends, and the nation pray that Americas son and companions will be ok.

Where's Papa   July 21, 1999

Where's Papa these words ring hollow where there's no answer or trail to follow. Where's Papa as if I had to know. Where's Papa, take this money go to the show. This is something no one wants to hear, Where's Papa can I say it any clearer. From a child's perspective you need not know. Many years later these words still dance in my head, Where's Papa, maybe he's dead?

Poems from the pen of Arnold Hannon The 1st

Pearls of Wisdom   August 15, 1999

Pearls of wisdom are so unique. Pearls of wisdom is what I seek. Speak to me of lines that rhyme, of mines whom finds the time to define these rhymes. Pearls of wisdom are gems so sweet makes it more palatable for me to compete.

Wings of Love   August 12, 2001

Tonight the wings of love grabbed me and flew me away past the mountains, thru the stars and along the milkyway. as I clung to love's wings it was if I were a child at play zooming along the milkyway.

Ode to Larry   September 14, 2001

I picks my nose, I picks my toes, then I goes and picks you a rose.

Oblivion   April 11, 2004

I find myself in this sullen place surrounded by strangers without a face. As I look out my window through weakening eyes, I can faintly see the setting Sun. I can feel my life slipping into Oblivion.

About the Author

Arnold Hannon, was born in Detroit, Michigan, to fifteen-year-old, unmarried, Bennie Mae Hannon, on December 15th, 1948. Arnold, is the eldest of three sons, born to Bennie Mae. Arnold, attended Detroit Pubic Schools, and received a G.E.D. soon after dropping out of Northern High School. He went on to earn his associate degree in psychology, from Wayne County Community College, in 1988. He earned his bachelors of arts degree in Communications, from the University of Detroit, in 1990.

Before, Arnold's, under graduate education began, he earned his masters degree, in streetology, from the school of hard knocks. Same school, that Iceberg Slim, and Donald Goines attended. The American Scheme, is Mr. Hannon's literary debut. It took him a half century to live it, and three years to write his remarkable journey, through life in a very tough-city called, Detroit, Michigan.

The American Scheme is steeped in, Detroit, culture and legend. I attempted again to capture a golden era in Detroit's history, before it fades into oblivion. To all the Gamers out there, this one's for the Game to.

I hope that my story will inspire others born into hapless situations out their control, to examine the psychological, barriers, that may be impeding their growth, and an opportunity to live a long and bountiful life. God, bless all who are chasing "The American Dream." "You must tread cautiously. You don't wanna' get played by the "The American Scheme."